Realizing the ASEAN Economic Community

The **Institute of Southeast Asian Studies (ISEAS)** was established as an autonomous organization in 1968. It is a regional centre dedicated to the study of socio-political, security and economic trends and developments in Southeast Asia and its wider geostrategic and economic environment. The Institute's research programmes are the Regional Economic Studies (RES, including ASEAN and APEC), Regional Strategic and Political Studies (RSPS), and Regional Social and Cultural Studies (RSCS).

ISEAS Publishing, an established academic press, has issued almost 2,000 books and journals. It is the largest scholarly publisher of research about Southeast Asia from within the region. ISEAS Publishing works with many other academic and trade publishers and distributors to disseminate important research and analyses from and about Southeast Asia to the rest of the world.

Realizing the ASEAN Economic Community

A Comprehensive Assessment

Edited by
Michael G. Plummer and **Chia Siow Yue**

ISEAS

INSTITUTE OF SOUTHEAST ASIAN STUDIES
Singapore

First published in Singapore in 2009 by ISEAS Publishing
Institute of Southeast Asian Studies
30 Heng Mui Keng Terrace
Pasir Panjang
Singapore 119614
E-mail: publish@iseas.edu.sg
Website: http://bookshop.iseas.edu.sg

This work was prepared in the course of USAID Regional Development Mission Asia Contract No. 486-I-00-07-00008-00, Task Order 01, ASEAN-US Technical Assistance and Training Facility, Phase II under the ADVANCE Program.

Disclaimer: This document is made possible by the support of the American people through the United States Agency for International Development (USAID). Its contents are the sole responsibility of the authors and do not necessarily reflect the views of USAID, the ASEAN Secretariat, the ASEAN Member States, the United States government, or the publisher and its supporters.

ISEAS Library Cataloguing-in-Publication Data

Realizing the ASEAN Economic Community : a comprehensive assessment / edited by Michael G. Plummer and Chia Siow Yue.
1. ASEAN.
2. Free trade—Southeast Asia.
3. Southeast Asia—Economic integration.
4. Southeast Asia—Foreign economic relations.
5. Southeast Asia—Commercial policy.
I. Plummer, Michael G., 1959–
II. Chia, Siow Yue.
HC411 R28   2009

ISBN 978-981-4279-34-5 (soft cover)
ISBN 978-981-4279-39-0 (E-book PDF)

Copy-edited by Nathan Associates, Inc.
Typeset by Superskill Graphics Pte Ltd
Printed in Singapore by Utopia Press Pte Ltd

Contents

Illustrations

Tables

Table 5-9   ASEAN Human Development Indicators   125
Table 5-10   ASEAN Gini Coefficients   131
Table 5-11   Relative Size and Employment in Nonagricultural SMEs, 2000 (est.)   131

Table 6-1   Who Competes with Whom? Rank Correlations of Exports to
              OECD Countries, 2005   145
Table 6-2   Export Intensities, 2006   147
Table 6-3   Gains from ASEAN's Regional FTA Network   155
Table 6-4   ASEAN's Wider FTA Possibilities   157

Table 7-1   Summary of AEC Benefits for Stakeholders   172

Table A-1   Comparative Trade Regimes (2007/2008)   191
Table C-1   Sensitivity Analysis Results for All Countries (Dependent variable:
              in GDP per capita)   199
Table C-2   Sensitivity Analysis Results for Developing Countries (Dependent variable:
              in GDP per capita)   201
Table C-3   Sensitivity Analysis Results for All Countries (Dependent variable:
              share of FDI in GDP)   203
Table C-4   Sensitivity Analysis Results for Developing Countries (Dependent variable:
              share of FDI in GDP)   205

Exhibits
Exhibit 4-1   Four Pillars of the ASEAN Comprehensive Investment Agreement   85
Exhibit 4-2   Excerpts from Joint Ministerial Statement of 12th ASEAN Finance Ministers
              Meeting Regarding ASEAN Roadmap for Monetary and Financial Integration   87
Exhibit 4-3   Toyota's Innovative Multipurpose Vehicle Project   93
Exhibit 4-4   Regional Integration and the Deepening of Production Networks:
              The Automotive Industry in the EU and ASEAN   103
Exhibit 4-5   Capacity-building Spillovers from FDI   109

Exhibit 5-1   Case Study of the Thai Automotive Industry   135
Exhibit 5-2   Malaysian Electronics Industry   136

Foreword

It has always been my cherished belief that if ASEAN succeeds, it will bring about positive consequences for ASEAN and the entire global community.

The ASEAN Economic Community is one of the three pillars of the envisaged ASEAN Community by 2015, which also comprises the ASEAN Political-Security Community and the ASEAN Socio-Cultural Community. Using the analogy of interlocking threads which hold a piece of fabric together, building an ASEAN Economic Community that provides economic stability and ensures continued economic growth will contribute towards peace, security and social progress, and thereby connect the region together.

ASEAN is weaving this piece of fabric based on the design of the ASEAN Charter and the Roadmap for an ASEAN Community (2009–2015). This book *Realizing the ASEAN Economic Community: A Comprehensive Assessment* attempts to communicate potentials, opportunities and challenges of community building to our people. It brings the vision of an ASEAN Economic Community to life by expressing it in concrete terms so that stakeholders such as the private sector and the consumers can identify with it and see the impacts that it can potentially make. More importantly, I hope that each stakeholder will assist in weaving this tapestry of the ASEAN Economic Community together.

For this, I am grateful to the US Agency for International Development and the US Department of State sponsored ASEAN-US Technical Assistance and Training Facility, and the various contributors who responded to the ASEAN Secretariat's request and made this book possible. This book reveals that the ASEAN Economic Community, if realized, will bring about an increase in economic welfare and real income in ASEAN and all member states will stand to benefit. While regional economic integration can create short-term adjustment costs, these costs should be more than offset by the benefits generated by well-targeted reforms in the longer term.

I hope that this book will strengthen our conviction that the ASEAN Economic Community will bring about a more prosperous, stable, competitive and equitable ASEAN. If ASEAN succeeds, it will be good for the region and the world. It is now the time to act expeditiously and credibly!

Surin Pitsuwan
Secretary-General of ASEAN

Executive Summary

The global economy and Asia in particular constantly produce challenges and opportunities for ASEAN and its member states. ASEAN economies must respond to the exigencies of the international marketplace; compete intensively for markets, investments and resources; adapt to the economic rise of China and India; and develop competitiveness and economic vigor sufficient to weather global economic shocks — a need underscored by the current global economic crisis. Greater economic cooperation and integration can help ASEAN Member States meet these challenges and seize opportunities as they emerge. In this regard, the ASEAN Economic Community (AEC) is a bold step in economic reform. As envisaged it is comprised of four parts:

1. A *single market and production base*, characterized by a free flow of goods, services, investment, and skilled labor, as well as a freer flow of capital.
2. A *competitive economic region*, characterized by sound competition policy, consumer protection, intellectual property rights protection, infrastructure development, sectoral competition in energy and mining, rationalized taxation, and e-commerce.
3. *Equitable economic development*, characterized by SME development and enhancement of the Initiative for ASEAN Integration.
4. *Integration into the global economy*, with ASEAN centrality and participation in global supply networks.

The creation of a single market and production base should allow ASEAN to benefit from efficiency and economies of scale in value-chain processes, while other aspects of the AEC will boost competitiveness, strengthen ASEAN's institutions, and improve the region's socioeconomic environment. ASEAN Member States intend to complete the AEC by 2015; meeting that deadline will require support at all levels and recognition that implementation will face opposition in some quarters. Securing support, assuaging stakeholders' concerns, and countering opposition, in turn, requires understanding the full implications of the AEC for ASEAN and ASEAN Member States.

ECONOMIC BENEFITS

Applying a computational general equilibrium (CGE) model under several scenarios, we estimate that ASEAN economic welfare should rise by 5.3 percent, or $69 billion, relative to the baseline — more than six times the effect estimated for AFTA, even under conservative assumptions. We also estimate that the AEC will increase ASEAN real income significantly and that all member states will benefit from the AEC. Other estimated benefits include the following:

Expanded trade in goods. Our model shows that the AEC will expand ASEAN trade in goods, with exports outpacing imports in all but three manufacturing sectors. Many of these areas offer important opportunities for the region to join global production chains. Our estimates also confirm the value of keeping the AEC open, a position advocated in the AEC Blueprint: extending the AEC to include "+1" agreements with its East Asian neighbors increases the aggregate welfare benefits to ASEAN by two-thirds, and by an additional one-third if the United States and the EU are added.

Greater inflows of FDI. FDI will likely increase as barriers to production networks are removed and as policies in the ASEAN Comprehensive Investment Area (ACIA) are implemented. Production networks, in turn, should be particularly advantageous to SMEs throughout ASEAN and in the CLMV countries in particular. The AEC could increase FDI stocks 28 percent to 63 percent ($117–$264 billion relative to 2006 inward FDI stocks). Contribution to annual income growth could be (conservatively) on the order of 0.5–1.0 percent of GDP per annum. Over time, this effect could be considerable, given the potential of ASEAN Member States to expand in existing production value chains and enter new ones.

Rise in per capita GDP. To estimate the direct effects of behind-the-border measures and best practices spread by means of the AEC, we use "extreme bound analysis". Our projections suggest that competition policy alone could raise per capita GDP by 26 percent to 38 percent in the resource-rich original group of ASEAN countries; this includes an increase of 8 percent to 14 percent due to foreign investment attracted by policy reform. These figures are on par with estimates of the economic impact of joining the EU.

Narrower development gaps. By creating opportunities for production networks and spreading best practices that boost productivity, the AEC should help the CLMV countries converge with the rest of ASEAN, a process that has already started. Productivity improvements will be greatest in the least-developed economies.

Flexible labor management that attracts investors. Allowing skilled workers to move about freely will make ASEAN attractive to foreign investors, encourage mutual recognition of professional qualifications, and engender regional cooperation among training institutes, universities, research institutions, and the like. Countries with shortages of skilled labor may benefit the most, and professionals and skilled workers will be able to seek better jobs and higher earnings.

Competitive consumer markets. Consumer markets will feature a cheaper and wider range of imported goods and services, greater domestic competition, and more extensive consumer protection. Institutional improvements under the AEC (e.g., in financial markets, infrastructure, and harmonization-related structures) should encourage growth in the private sector and make the public sector more efficient.

In sum, the net economic benefits of the AEC should be large, perhaps well beyond the 5.3 percent increase in welfare due to "AEC value added" derived through our conservative CGE model. Other likely gains not modeled include

- Lower cost of capital due to freer movements of capital and improved financial systems;
- Greater efficiency and boosts to GDP due to freer movement of skilled labor;
- Benefits from "ASEAN One Voice", that is, ASEAN centrality in external relations and a stronger voice in regional and global affairs; and
- Greater macroeconomic stability due to implementation of conservative policies necessary to support the AEC.

STAKEHOLDER BENEFITS

ASEAN Member States. Member states are expected to experience employment growth, faster economic growth, larger inflows of FDI, better resource allocation with consequent improvement in productivity and competitiveness, scale economies and fragmented production. They will be able to extend their participation in production networks and global value chains, enjoy a larger regional market and more technological and human resources, and benefit from greater intraregional trade and investment, adoption of efficient international standards and best practices, and protection of intellectual property rights, which will attract technology-intensive FDI and R&D. Member states will be able to leverage the AEC to undertake sensitive domestic reforms, while faster growth and related efficiencies will raise tax revenue, offsetting any loss in tariff revenue. Through "one ASEAN voice," member states will be more effective in international and regional forums; economic gains through ASEAN hub FTAs are estimated to be large.

CLMV countries. The CLMV countries stand to gain the most from the AEC through liberalization and reform that boosts efficiency and competitiveness. They will also benefit from greater access to capital, investment, technology, technical assistance, development experience, and best practices; greater participation in global production networks and value chains; and the influence of joint positions taken by ASEAN in regional and international negotiations.

Businesses, including SMEs. Businesses of all sizes will benefit from greater market access, lower input and transaction costs due to tariff and NTB elimination and improved services regulations, and better trade facilitation processes for customs, logistics, transportation, ICT, as well as rationalized rules of origin and product and technical standards.

Investors. Benefits will accrue from the right to invest, national treatment, improved investment protection and dispute settlement, and from more liberalized capital markets and financial services. Local investors will be able to form joint ventures with foreign investors and the smooth flow of skilled labor will create more management choices.

Professionals and labor. Unimpeded by artificial barriers, professionals and skilled workers will be able to seek better jobs and earnings. In expanding industries, services and firms will benefit from increased employment and higher wages.

Consumers. Consumers — stakeholders who tend to get little attention in ASEAN integration processes — will benefit from access to cheaper and wider range of imported goods and services, a more competitive domestic market environment, and consumer protection.

Global partners. The AEC's emphasis on open regionalism, with low trade and investment diversion, will engender a dynamic and economically resilient ASEAN able to contribute positively in international fora such as WTO, IMF, World Bank, and in regional forums such as APEC and ASEM.

In sum, the AEC has the potential to generate significant economic benefits for nearly all stakeholders in the region. The region will also gain political and macroeconomic stability and ASEAN can become a potent force in international fora. Nevertheless, as in the case of any policy change that leads to greater efficiency, there will be costs as well as benefits. For example, as less efficient sectors contract in favor of more efficient ones, jobs will be lost and workers may experience short-run unemployment. Clearly there is a need for appropriate policy responses at the national level to facilitate this structural change, hasten the restructuring process, and assist displaced workers through adjustment assistance, job-search help, and re-tooling programs.

Still, our results show that the gains of the AEC will be far greater than the losses, and the net benefits to all member states should be high. Realizing the potential of the AEC will require mustering the political support for effective implementation of the AEC Blueprint and beyond.

Acknowledgements

Undertaken at the request of the ASEAN Secretariat, this study was prepared under the US Agency for International Development and US State Department funded ASEAN-US Technical Assistance and Training Facility, and executed in cooperation with the East-West Center. It would not have been possible without the indefatigable work of a number of scholars, administrative and research providers, and institutions that are identified below.

The editors and managing authors of this report are Michael G. Plummer of the Johns Hopkins University, SAIS-Bologna, and the East-West Center, and Chia Siow Yue of the Singapore Institute of International Affairs. They would like to thank the institutions contributing to this study: the Thailand Development Research Institute (TDRI), the Asian Development Bank Institute (ADBI), the Centre for Strategic and International Studies (CSIS), the Philippine Institute for Development Studies (PIDS), and the Malaysian Institute for Economic Research (MIER). Specifically, ADBI and MIER contributed to Chapter 2; TDRI, Chapter 3; PIDS, Chapter 4; CSIS, Chapter 5. As authors of Chapter 1 and Chapter 7, they acknowledge the excellent research assistance provided by Hazel C. Parcon, Dae Woo Lee and Astrid Haas for those chapters.

The team that co-authored Chapter 2 was led by Dr Zakariah Rashid of MIER. Dr Fan Zhai of the ADBI conducted the CGE simulations for that section, and Peter Petri, Michael Plummer, and Chia Siow Yue contributed as well. Chapter 3 was authored by Wisarn Pupphavesa and Sumet Ongkittikul of TDRI, and Santi Chaisrisawatsuk and Sasatra Sudsawasd of the National Institute of Development Administration (NIDA). They would like to acknowledge the stellar research assistance of Kraivin Paripont Chintakananda.

The authors of Chapter 4, Rafaelita M. Aldaba a Senior Research Fellow at PIDS and Josef T. Yap, President of PIDS, were supported by Peter Petri of Brandeis University and the East-West Center, who wrote the sections on FDI stocks and the empirical effects of the AEC on FDI flows. Mssrs. Aldaba and Yap are grateful for the excellent research assistance of Fatima Lourdes E. del Prado and Donald B. Yasay.

The authors of Chapter 5, Dionisius Narjoko, Pratiwi Kartika, and Teguh Wicaksono of CSIS, thank Hadi Soesastro, Haryo Aswicahyono, and Raymond Atje for their substantial contribution in conducting research and drafting the chapter. They are also grateful for comments from those who participated in the project's July 2008 workshop.

The author of Chapter 6, Peter Petri, is grateful to members of the ASEAN Secretariat and Professors Michael Plummer and Chia Siow Yue for their advice and to Yuki Masujima, a doctoral student at Brandeis University, for excellent research assistance.

Study authors benefited from the direction, input, and ideas of the ASEAN-US Technical Assistance and Training Facility and the ASEAN Secretariat itself. They are very grateful for the contributions of Timothy Buehrer, Noordin Azhari, and Lim Chze Cheen during all phases of the study. In addition, James Wallar offered excellent advice during the conceptual phase. They also received help from the ASEAN Secretariat, particularly in updating information on intellectual property regimes in Chapter 3. From the East-West Center, Charles Morrison, Nancy Lewis, and Phil Estermann provided comments, ideas and encouragement; Ralph Carvalho, Tina Tom, Kimberly Fujiuchi, and Laura Moriyama provided excellent administrative support; and Hazel Parcon, Shawn Arita, and Astrid Haas provided solid and timely research assistance. This project builds on past and on-going East-West Center research on ASEAN economic cooperation and integration led by Seiji Naya, Michael Plummer, Peter Petri and others.

Finally, the usual disclaimer applies: the contents of this book are the sole responsibility of the authors and do not necessarily reflect the views of the participating institutions, the ASEAN Secretariat, USAID or the United States government.

About the Contributors

Michael G. Plummer is Eni Professor of International Economics at The Johns Hopkins University, SAIS-Bologna, and (non-resident) Senior Fellow of the East-West Center. He is Editor-in-Chief of the *Journal of Asian Economics* and Director, American Committee for Asian Economic Studies (ACAES). Previously, he has held teaching, research and management positions at Brandeis University and the East-West Center. He has also been a Fulbright Chair in Economics (Viterbo) and Pew Fellow in International Affairs (Harvard University). His main academic interests relate to international trade, international finance, and economic integration, especially in the Asian context. He has published extensively in these areas. Professor Plummer serves on the editorial boards of the *Asian Economic Journal*, *World Development* and the *ASEAN Economic Bulletin*. His Ph.D. is from Michigan State University.

Chia Siow Yue has been Senior Research Fellow, Singapore Institute of International Affairs (SIIA), since November 2002. Previously, she was Regional Coordinator, East Asian Development Network (1997–2004), Director, Institute of Southeast Asian Studies (1996–2002), and Professor, Department of Economics and Statistics, National University of Singapore (1967–1996). Her main areas of research are development economics and international economics, with a focus on Southeast Asian economics and Singapore. She has published many articles, books chapters, and books in these areas. She also has extensive advisory and consultancy experience, including research consultancies for the World Bank, World Bank Institute, ILO, International Trade Centre (ITC), UNCTAD, OECD, UN ESCAP, Asian Development Bank, and the ASEAN Secretariat. She is on the editorial committees of several academic journals and, at various times, has been a member of committees related to the Pacific Economic Cooperation Conference Trade Forum; Pacific Economic Cooperation Conference in Singapore (SINCPEC) and the Pacific Trade and Development Conference (PAFTAD). Her Ph.D. in economics is from McGill University.

Rafaelita M. Aldaba is currently Senior Research Fellow at the Philippine Institute for Development Studies. She was Team Leader of the Asian Development Bank's Asia Regional Integration Center in 2008–2009. Her research work covers trade and industrial policy and regional integration along with competition policy, small and medium enterprises, and foreign direct investment. She has written various papers on these topics for the World Bank, Asian Development Bank, Economic Research Institute for ASEAN and East Asia, and the East Asia Development Network. She finished her Ph.D. in Economics at the University of the Philippines and completed advanced studies in International Economic Policy Research at the Kiel Institute of World Economics in Germany.

Santi Chaisrisawatsuk is Assistant Professor, Associate Dean for Academic Affairs, and Director of the Center for International Economics and Development Studies (CIEDS), School of Development Economics, National Institute of Development Administration (NIDA), Bangkok, Thailand. His main interests are in the areas of International Economics, Econometrics, Economic Development, and Monetary and Financial Economics. He has published a number of articles in these areas, including in *Applied Financial Economics*, the *Journal of Asian Economics*, the *Indian Journal of Economics*, and the *Asia-Pacific Trade and Investment Review*. His Ph.D. in economics is from Southern Illinois University. He also holds degrees from Indiana State University and Thammasat University.

Pratiwi Kartika is an economist at the Centre for Strategic and International Studies (CSIS). Her research focuses on the issues of trade, industrialization, and macroeconomics. She received her BA in Economics from the University of Indonesia (2005) and a Master of International and Development Economics from the Australian National University (2007).

Dionisius Narjoko is a researcher at the Economic Research Institute for ASEAN and East Asia (ERIA). The research of Dionisius Narjoko concentrates on topics related to industrial organization and international trade. Dionisius Narjoko also works on a wide-range of research areas related to ASEAN economic development, such as developmental gaps between member countries, prospects for an ASEAN Economic Community (AEC), and service sector liberalization in the region. He graduated from the Australian National University.

Sumet Ongkittikul is a research specialist at the Thailand Development Research Institute (TDRI). He holds a Ph.D. in Social Sciences (Transport Studies) from Erasmus University, Rotterdam, the Netherlands. His main research interests are in the fields of transport policy, transport regulation, and logistics.

Peter A. Petri is the Carl J. Shapiro Professor of International Finance at the Brandeis International Business School (IBS) and a Senior Fellow of the East-West Center in Honolulu, Hawaii. He served as Dean of IBS from its founding in 1994 until 2006. He has held appointments as a Fulbright Research Scholar and Visiting Scholar at the OECD, the Brookings Institution, Keio University (Tokyo) and Fudan University (Shanghai). He has consulted for the World Bank, the OECD, the Asian Development Bank, APEC, and agencies of the United Nations, the United States and other countries. He serves on the editorial boards of journals dedicated to Asia-Pacific research and is the Convener of the East-West Center's East-West Dialogue. He is a member of the Board of the US Asia Pacific Council and the PAFTAD International Steering Committee, and a former Chair of the US APEC Study Center Consortium. He received A.B. and Ph.D. degrees in economics from Harvard University.

Professor **Wisarn Pupphavesa** is currently Advisor on International Economic Relations at the Thailand Development Research Institute Foundation (TDRI) and also a Member, Sub-Committee on Research, the National Anti-Corruption Commission (NACC). He was a Director of Export-Import Bank of Thailand (2007–2008), Dean of the School of Development Economics (1995–2001) and the founding and first Director of Center for International Economics and Development Studies (2001–2005) at the National Institute of Development Administration (NIDA). He was appointed as Honorary Advisor to the Minister of Commerce (2006–2007), Member of the Council of Economic Advisors to the Prime Minister (2001–2005), Member of the International Economic Policy Committee (1977–2003) and Member (Thailand's Representative) of the High Level Task Force on AFTA-CER FTA (November 1999–November 2000). He received the Outstanding Research Work Awards of 1990 from the National Research Council of Thailand. He won the John F. Kennedy Scholarship for graduate studies in the United States. His Ph.D. (Economics) is from the University of Hawaii at Manoa.

Zakariah Abdul Rashid is the Deputy Director of Malaysian Institute of Economic Research (MIER) and professor of economics at the Universiti Putra Malaysia (UPM), where he was formerly the deputy dean in the School of Postgraduate Studies. He was Head of the Economics Department of UPM before being promoted to the position as deputy dean. In addition to teaching at both undergraduate and graduate levels, publishing many articles, editing academic journals and speaking at seminars and conferences, he has been principle investigator to many research projects. He has been awarded as an Outstanding Consultant by the UPM. His areas of specialisation cover a wide-range of topics, including Development Economics, International Economics, Islamic Economics, and sectoral studies, including in the textile, pharmaceutical, and chemical industries.

Sasatra Sudsawasd is an Assistant Professor and Associate Dean at the School of Development Economics, National Institute of Development Administration (NIDA), Bangkok, Thailand. Dr Sudsawasd earned a Ph.D. in Economics from Georgia State University. His areas of interest are international economics and public economics. He has published articles in the Review of International Economics, ASEAN Economic Bulletin, and the Asia-Pacific Trade and Investment Review.

Teguh Wicaksono is an economist in the Department of Economics, Centre for Strategic and International Studies (CSIS), which he joined CSIS in 2004. Currently, he is also a lecturer at the Faculty of Economics, University of Indonesia. His research focuses on a wide range of topics, including labour economics, poverty, trade in services, and regional economic integration. He received his B.A. in Economics from the University of Indonesia and his Master's degree in economics from the University of Sydney.

Josef T. Yap is President of the Philippine Institute for Development Studies where he specializes in macroeconomic policy and applied econometrics. He finished his doctoral studies at the University of the Philippines and went to the University of Pennsylvania on a post-graduate program. His current research interest centers on regional economic integration in East Asia. Dr Yap was team leader of a study on integration strategies for the CLMV countries under the auspices of the ASEAN-UNDP Project Facility and was actively involved in the establishment of the Economic Research Institute for

ASEAN and East Asia (ERIA). Dr Yap is co-author of the book *The Philippine Economy: East Asia's Stray Cat? Structure, Finance and Adjustment* and is an Associate Editor of the Asian Economic Journal.

Fan Zhai is a Research Fellow of the Asian Development Bank Institute. Previously, he was an Economist in ADB's Economics and Research Department, and had worked in the Ministry of Finance and the Development Research Center of the State Council in the People's Republic of China (PRC). He holds a Ph.D. in system engineering from the Huazhong University of Science and Technology, PRC.

His research focuses on the development of applied general equilibrium models and their applications in trade, social security and environment issues in developing countries. He has published articles in several professional economics journals. He and his co-authors were awarded the Sun Yefang Prize in 2003, which is the highest biannual award for economists in the PRC.

1
Introduction

Michael G. Plummer and Chia Siow Yue

At the Twelfth ASEAN Summit in Cebu in January 2007, ASEAN decided to create an ASEAN Economic Community (AEC) by 2015. This milestone reflects growing awareness that ASEAN must deepen and hasten its economic integration in order to cope with serious challenges. The end of the Cold War, thawing relations among countries in Northeast Asia, and the economic rise of China and India are testing ASEAN's traditional role in regional cooperation and its economic competitiveness even as member state governments struggle to ensure political and social stability as well as inclusive and sustainable growth. In addition, the financial crisis of 2008 — itself partly the result of insufficient cooperation in addressing global imbalances — revealed ASEAN's stark vulnerability to shocks it did little to create.

How can deeper economic integration help ASEAN and member states weather these challenges? Integration is expected to promote regional economic resilience and the delivery of regional public goods; raise the international competitiveness of individual Southeast Asian countries that must be able to compete, particularly against China and India in the global marketplace; and give the region "one voice" in shaping the mechanisms necessary to contain and manage economic crises whatever their origin. In short, to maintain its traditional role and the competitiveness of member states ASEAN must keep the "economic center of gravity" from shifting rapidly to the north by proceeding with its ambitious plans for an AEC.

The *process* for achieving the AEC by 2015 is critical. ASEAN Member States have fewer than seven years to execute a complicated reform agenda (see Appendix A for a summary of AEC components). That short time span has led to cynicism among detractors, but ASEAN did well to establish a timeframe for erecting various aspects of a single market and production base — and in getting member states to gauge progress on compliance "scorecards." From an economic viewpoint, however, the top priority should be putting in place the correct *policies* for a unified market. The single market program in the European Union (EU), for example, was supposed to be completed between 1986 and 1992.

Though not all directives were in place even by 1994, most were and the program was extremely successful in setting the EU on the path to deeper integration and eventually a monetary union.[1]

The AEC constitutes a propitious opportunity for the region to enhance its competitiveness through concerted economic liberalization, reform, and cooperation. It will no doubt face political opposition, so one must understand what is at stake — the benefits as well as the already well understood costs. Thus, in rest of this report we discuss the implications of the AEC for regional markets in goods, services, and skilled labor (Chapter 2); for competition policy, infrastructure, and intellectual property rights (Chapter 3); for investment and capital flows (Chapter 4); development gaps (Chapter 5); and regional competitiveness (Chapter 6). In Chapter 7 we summarize the economic benefits of the AEC for stakeholders and present an empirical assessment of the economics of the AEC.

In the rest of this chapter, we present an overview of trends in ASEAN economic integration: overall economic performance, the direction and structure of trade in goods and services, changes in commercial policy, and trends in foreign direct investment (FDI). We conclude from this baseline assessment that reform in ASEAN has been impressive but the region still has a long way to go, as demonstrated by the World Bank's rankings of ASEAN countries in its annual *Doing Business* survey.

ASEAN ECONOMIC GROWTH AND PERFORMANCE

Economic growth in ASEAN has been impressive by any standard and growth rates in some member states — Singapore, Malaysia, Thailand, and Vietnam — have been among the fastest in the world (Figure 1-1). This experience has not been monotonic; the Asian Crisis of 1997–1998 severely affected several ASEAN economies. While several remain on a lower-growth trajectory most have rebounded well.

On matters of economic performance, several points should be noted. First, while the economic performance of ASEAN Member States varies greatly, growth rates are increasingly correlated since the Asian Crisis.[2] Important factors include economic reforms in the region and "fragmented trade" in Asia, which is underscored by the rise of intra-industry trade.[3] For Singapore, Thailand, and Malaysia intra-industry trade constitutes over half of trade with Asia, and for Indonesia and the Philippines between one-third and two-fifths.[4] These figures are up significantly from just a decade ago, when no country's share was more than about one-third.

Second, rapid structural change in the region is due in part to ASEAN's outward-oriented development strategy, which views globalization as an *opportunity* to be seized. Economic reform has facilitated the flow of factors of production across sectors in such a way as to reduce the costs of economic transition and permit efficient reallocation of resources.

Third, international trade has been driving structural adjustment. Exports as a percentage of GDP have been rising in all countries; for ASEAN as a whole, exports/GDP came to 70 percent in 2007, up from just 28 percent in 1984.[5] This is a phenomenal increase in the internationalization of the ASEAN economies in absolute terms and relative to the rest of the world. China and India, with respective export/GDP shares of 38 percent 29 percent, were relatively closed compared to ASEAN.

Fourth, the current economic crisis will likely cause a decrease in intraregional trade in absolute and relative terms. This is because of the real shock to trade flows characteristic of all crises and the effect of the crisis on international production networks, which will disproportionately affect intra-Asian trade.

Figure 1-1
GDP Growth in ASEAN Countries, 1987–2007

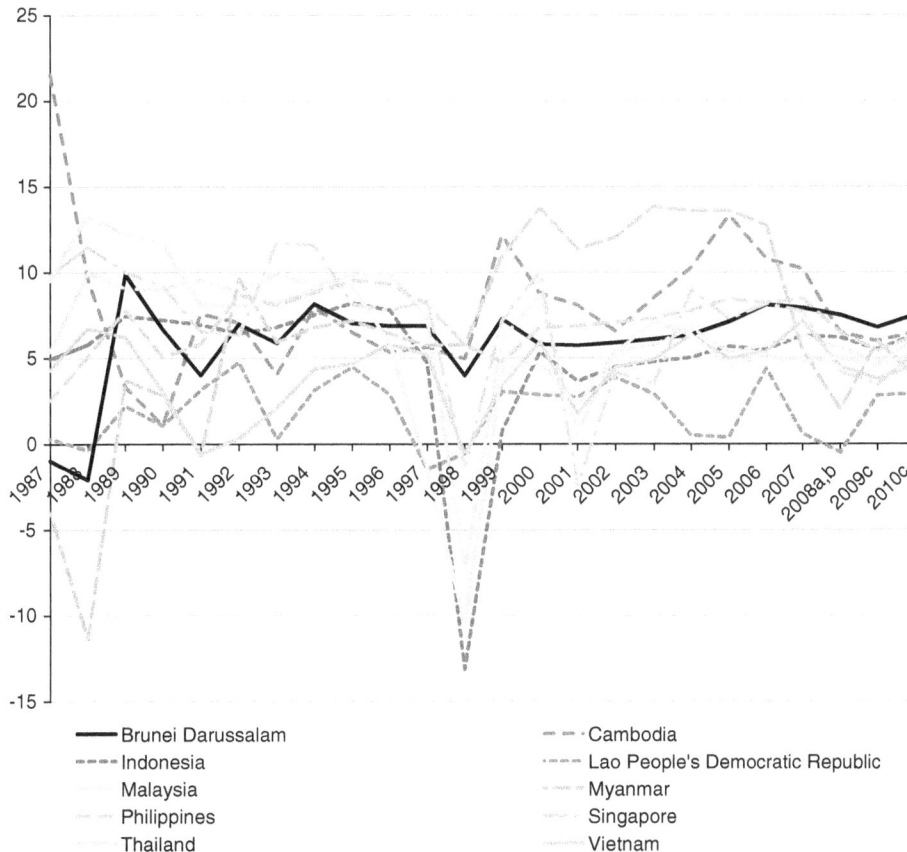

—— Brunei Darussalam	— — Cambodia
- - - Indonesia	- - - Lao People's Democratic Republic
Malaysia	Myanmar
Philippines	Singapore
Thailand	Vietnam

Notes: 1) Data for Cambodia, Indonesia, Lao PDR, Malaysia, Philippines, Singapore, Thailand, and Vietnam are from the Asian Development Outlook 2008 (http://www.adb.org/media/Articles/2008/12621-asian-gdp-comparisons/).
2) 2008 data for Brunei Darussalam and Myanmar are forecasts from the World Economic Outlook.
3) 2009 and 2010 Estimates are from the IMF World Economic Outlook.
Source: International Monetary Fund, World Economic Outlook Database, October 2008.

STRUCTURAL CHANGE AND TRADE PATTERNS

A changing export mix implies dynamic structural change. To examine such changes over time, we correlate the ranking of exports of ASEAN economies — including Japan, China, and India for comparison — to the region's largest export markets (i.e., the OECD aggregate, the EU, the United States) over the past ten years, separating them into three periods: 1996–2000, 2000–2005, and 1996–2005 (full sample).[6] This allows us to rank the exports in each year (1996 with 2000, 2000 with 2005, 1996 with 2005) to see how the export structure of each country has changed. If the structure of a country's exports over the 1996–2005 period does not change, rankings will be identical and the correlation perfect (i.e., +1). If the export structure of 2005 is much different than that of 1996, the correlation will be low. Near perfect correlation suggests a mature economy specializing in sophisticated manufactures or a developing country that is not diversifying. Low correlation suggests a dynamic economy undergoing considerable structural change. Therefore, low estimated correlation coefficients suggest dynamic structural change and high ones the opposite.

To shed light changes in export structure, we use a disaggregated export database (5-digit SITC, yielding up to 3,000 observations per series) and apply the Spearman Rank Correlation Coefficient (SRCC), a nonparametric statistic that correlates two series. It varies from +1 (perfect correlation) to −1 (perfect negative correlation), with 0 suggesting no correlation. Using the general OECD market as the unit of analysis, we see in Table 1-1 that Japan's export structure has stayed the same since 1996, with an estimated correlation coefficient of 0.87 for all commodities. This is expected for an advanced industrial economy with a strong and stable comparative advantage in electronics and automobiles. Japan, therefore, may be used as a benchmark. The SRCCs for the ASEAN countries range from 0.59 to 0.68, suggesting far more dynamism than Chinese exports and on par with those of India.[7]

Product Mix

Indeed, the product mix in ASEAN trade has changed significantly, from a bias toward natural-resource-intensive goods to a far greater dependence on electronics and other relatively sophisticated manufactures. This is true for imports and exports. Machinery and transport equipment constitute almost half of ASEAN's exports and imports, with the export share having risen significantly since 1990 (Table 1-2). Manufacturing exports now account for almost three-fourths of ASEAN's exports, up from less than two-thirds in 1990.

The change in ASEAN's top ten exports and imports at the sector level also reflects the growing significance of machinery and transport equipment (SITC 7) (Table 1-3). The biggest change is seen for thermionic valves (SITC 776), whose export value rose from $12 billion in 1990 to $120 billion in 2006, accounting for 16 percent of ASEAN's total exports of $759 billion. ASEAN exports nearly

Table 1-1
Structural Change in ASEAN Exports to Major Markets (Selected Years, SRCCs)

	OECD			EU			US		
	96–00	*00–05*	*96–05*	*96–00*	*00–05*	*96–05*	*96–00*	*00–05*	*96–05*
Brunei	−0.11	0.11	0.33	0.02	0.12	−0.04	−0.12	0.07	0.28
Cambodia		0.65			0.06			0.78	
Indonesia	0.76	0.73	0.59	0.6	0.56	0.53	0.69	0.67	0.46
Malaysia	0.75	0.73	0.66	0.62	0.65	0.54	0.74	0.65	0.54
Philippines	0.79	0.78	0.67	0.57	0.56	0.5	0.8	0.74	0.66
Singapore	0.73	0.71	0.61	0.65	0.63	0.54	0.66	0.68	0.58
Thailand	0.79	0.77	0.68	0.7	0.7	0.65	0.76	0.72	0.62
Vietnam		0.59			0.42			0.38	
Japan	0.93	0.91	0.87	0.9	0.87	0.84	0.9	0.88	0.82
China	0.85	0.84	0.72	0.82	0.85	0.73	0.79	0.79	0.65
India	0.74	0.66	0.57	0.75	0.72	0.66	0.65	0.61	0.48

Notes: Brunei values are from 1994, 2001, 2003, due to missing values; Cambodia correlations performed with 2004 instead with 2005 data; Vietnam correlations performed with 2004 instead of 2005 data; + Correlation includes only commodities with value >=$250,000.
Source: UN-COMTRADE (5-digit SITC).

Table 1-2
Sectoral Distribution of ASEAN Trade, 1990 and 2006 (1-digit SITC as a percentage of ASEAN trade)

Trade Flow	Commodity Description	1990	2006
Exports	0 Food and live animals chiefly for food	8.96	4.51
	1 Beverages and tobacco	0.77	0.38
	2 Crude materials, inedible, except fuels	6.83	3.95
	3 Mineral fuels, lubricants and related materials	20.32	14.51
	4 Animal and vegetable oils, fats and waxes	2.35	1.95
	5 Chemicals and relates products, nes	3.62	7.41
	6 Manufactured goods classified chiefly by materials	11.06	8.54
	7 Machinery and transport equipment	30.73	46.30
	8 Miscellaneous manufactured articles	12.62	9.84
	9 Commodities and transactions not classified elsewhere in the SITC	2.72	2.60
Imports	0 Food and live animals chiefly for food	4.84	3.67
	1 Beverages and tobacco	0.81	0.43
	2 Crude materials, inedible, except fuels	4.27	2.39
	3 Mineral fuels, lubricants and related materials	11.41	17.66
	4 Animal and vegetable oils, fats and waxes	0.37	0.26
	5 Chemicals and related products, nes	9.67	8.45
	6 Manufactured goods classified chiefly by materials	15.68	12.25
	7 Machinery and transport equipment	43.23	46.54
	8 Miscellaneous manufactured articles	6.29	5.93
	9 Commodities and transactions not classified elsewhere in the SITC	3.00	2.42

Source: UN-COMTRADE.

one-third of the world's thermionic valves ($379 billion), which include television picture tubes; other electrical valves and tubes; diodes, transistors, and similar semiconductors; electronic microcircuits; and Piezo-electric crystals. In other words, these exports are part of an electronics value-chain in which ASEAN is the key link. The fact that imports of SITC 776 came to $100 billion testifies to this. One hopes that this success can be duplicated as the AEC is implemented.

Intra-ASEAN Trade

The pattern of intra-ASEAN trade has also been changing. Though intra-ASEAN trade still accounts for only 26 percent of member states' trade, it rose by more than 50 percent from 1990 to 2006 (Figure 1-2). It is no surprise that the shares are relatively low, as ASEAN members are small and medium-sized developing countries whose inflows of FDI — and links to production chains — come mainly from outside the region. But if one controls for the size of the ASEAN economies in global trade, intra-ASEAN trade is actually four times higher than would be the case if these were randomly distributed countries.[8] Moreover, ASEAN has become considerably more significant in the total trade of some individual member states (e.g., transitional countries, such as Vietnam and Lao PDR, but also the Philippines and Brunei Darussalam) (Figure 1-3). We note also that no ASEAN Member State does less

Table 1-3
Top Ten Exports and Imports of ASEAN, 1990 and 2006

EXPORTS (US$ billion)			
1990		2006	
333-Petrol oils & crude oils obtained from bitumen	12.1	776-Thermionic, cold & photo-cathode valves, tubes	119.6
334-Petroleum products refined	11.5	334-Petroleum products, refined	47.4
776-Thermionic, cold & photo-cathode valves, tubes	9.5	752-Automatic data processing machines & units	47.3
752-Automatic data processing machines & units	7.5	759-Parts of and accessories suitable for 751-752	38.7
764-Telecommunications equipment & parts	6.2	333-Petrol oils & crude oils obtained from bitumen	32.3
341-Gas, natural & manufactured	6.0	764-Telecommunication equipment & parts	29.9
751-Office machines	4.2	341-Gas, natural & manufactured	20.9
232-Natural rubber latex; nat. rubber & sim. natural	3.8	931-Special transactions & commod. not classified	16.0
931-Special transactions & commod. not classified	3.7	772-Elect. app. such as switches, relays, fuses	14.7
634-Veneers, plywood, improved or reconstituted	3.6	232-Natural rubber latex: nat. rubber & sim. natural	13.6

IMPORTS (US$ billion)			
1990		2006	
333-Petrol oils & crude oils obtained from bitumen	11.8	776-Thermionic, cold & photo-cathode valves, tubes	109.9
776-Thermionic, cold & photo-cathode valves, tubes	10.8	333-Petrol, oils & crude oils obtained from bitumen	61.7
334-Petroleum products, refined	6.3	334-Petroleum products, refined	41.3
764-Telecommunications equipment & parts	6.2	759-Parts of and accessories suitable for 751-752	28.2
792-Aircraft & associated equipment & parts	4.3	764-Telecommunications equipment & parts	25.0
728-Mach. & equipment specialized for partic. uses	4.0	772-Elect. app. such as switches, relays, fuses	15.0
751-Office machines	3.9	752-Automatic data processing machines & units	12.7
674-Universals, plates, & sheets of iron or steel	3.7	778-Electrical machinery & apparatus, n.e.s.	12.4
931-Special transactions & commod. not classified	3.2	792-Aircraft & associated equipment & parts	10.0
772-Elect. app. such as switches, relays, fuses	2.9	728-Mach. & equipment specialized for partic. uses	9.3

Source: UN-COMTRADE.

Figure 1-2
Distribution of ASEAN Trade (Exports and Imports)

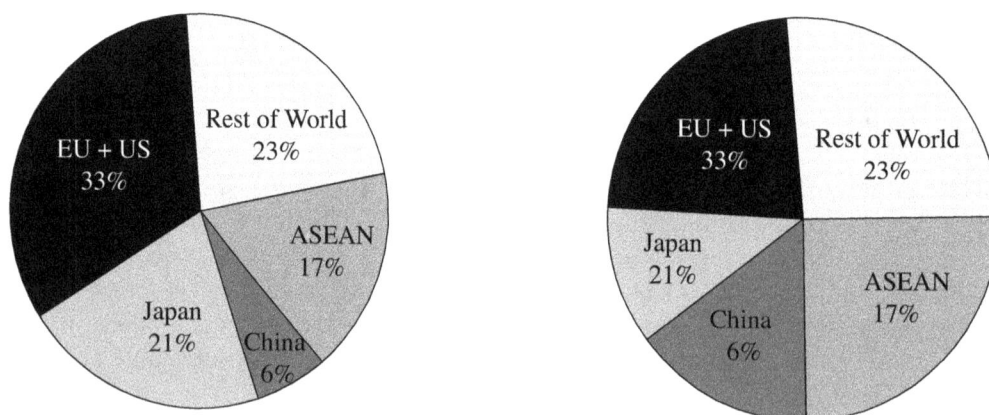

Source: UN-COMTRADE.

Figure 1-3
Intra-ASEAN Trade as a Percentage of Total, 1987–2007

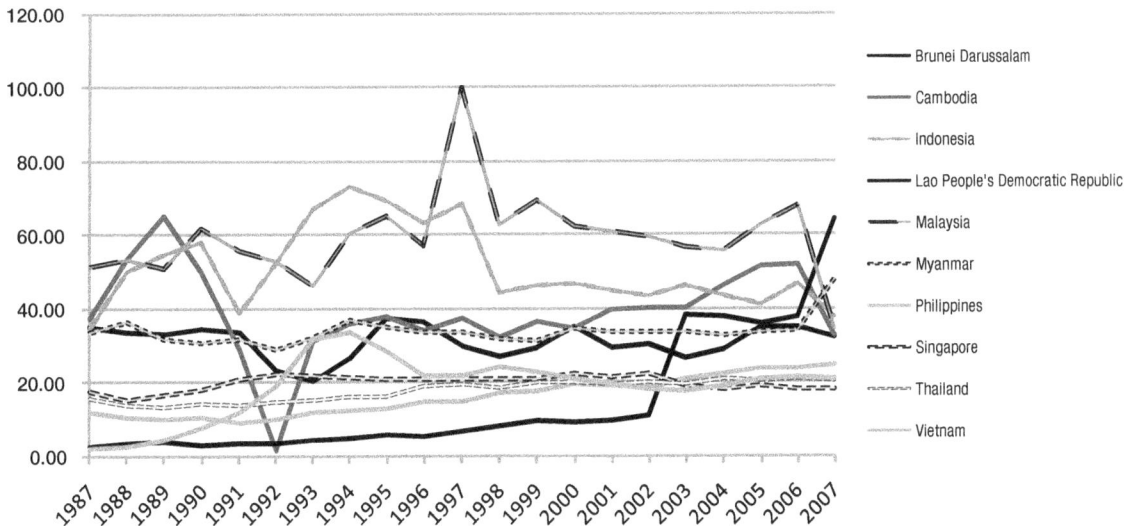

Source: IMF Direction of Trade Statistics.

than one-fifth of its trade with the region, save, perhaps, Singapore, whose share is about one-fifth. A quarter of a century ago, only a few did more than that.

Extra-ASEAN Trade

Almost three-fourths of ASEAN's trade is with the rest of the world, an indicator of the importance of outward-oriented policy. An ASEAN "fortress" of closed regionalism would have highly detrimental efficiency effects and alienate ASEAN's most important markets. As shown in Figure 1-2, the region's direction of trade has changed significantly since 1990 and has become more symmetric: the shares of the United States and EU in ASEAN exports were 26 percent in 2006, down from 30 percent in 1990 and currently of the same magnitude as intra-ASEAN trade. Meanwhile, China's share skyrocketed from 2 percent to 10 percent and Japan's plummeted from 21 percent to 11 percent. This means that China and Japan together in 2006 took on a 21 percent share. Thus, the shares of ASEAN itself, US+EU, China+Japan, and the rest of the world in ASEAN total trade are actually quite similar.

CHANGES IN COMMERCIAL POLICY

Myriad economic studies on Asian growth and development stress that ASEAN's success is based largely on an outward-orientation in trade and investment.[9] Succeeding in international markets requires macroeconomic stability, correct microeconomic signals, solid infrastructure, forward-looking policy (e.g., for developing human capital, building capacity, disseminating information on international markets, overcoming market failures), and a well-prepared private sector. Securing these conditions and seeing outward orientation bear fruit often takes a great deal of time, trial and error, and patience.

ASEAN's commercial policy has become increasingly liberal but most member economies still have much to do in commercial policy reform. Later in this chapter and elsewhere in this study, we stress that the AEC should be a catalyst of policy reform at the national and *regional* levels, and make it easier to advocate the region's interests at the global level (e.g., in the WTO). Hence, it is useful to take stock of how commercial policies have changed in ASEAN and where we stand today.

Tariffs

One way to capture the reform process is to focus on trade liberalization, for which data on tariff- and tariff-equivalent barriers to trade are fairly good. We do this in Figure 1-4 for the most recent tariff data available.[10] Figure 1-4 includes trade-weighted average applied tariffs for various manufactured products and agricultural products in a comparative context. A more detailed picture of the comparative trade regimes, including percentage of commodities that are tariff-free and maximum tariffs, is presented in Appendix A. We note four points.

- First, protection tends to be much higher in agriculture than in manufactures, with the exception of chemicals and transport equipment for some member states. Note the symmetry in tariff structure: where tariffs are very low, they are low across all countries; where they are high, they tend to be high in most countries.
- Second, Singapore is essentially a free-trade economy and has been so for a long time. Brunei has cut tariffs to essentially zero for all but a few manufactures.
- Third, in Indonesia, Malaysia, Philippines, and Thailand tariffs on manufactures have come down and sometimes significantly, with average tariffs being less than 10 percent in all sectors except a small increase in some manufactures in Malaysia and in miscellaneous manufactures in Thailand.
- Fourth, the percentage of tariff-free commodity lines in the electrical machinery sector in ASEAN (Appendix A, Table A-1) is fairly high for the original ASEAN countries (Indonesia, Malaysia, the Philippines, Thailand and Singapore), ranging from 21 percent (Philippines) to 100 percent (Singapore) of product lines.

Nontariff Barriers

While nontariff barriers (NTBs) are also important barriers to international trade, data on NTBs are notoriously difficult to obtain. Their evaluation is also fraught with difficulty since they vary greatly in substance. We may know exactly what the (static) economic effects of an import quota would be, for example, by calculating a tariff equivalent. But what about a required licensing arrangement? The effects of the latter would certainly be less restrictive if the licensing arrangement were more-or-less automatic as opposed to discretionary, but how does one distinguish this difference in the data on the presence of this type of NTB? Moreover, should antidumping duties be included in NTBs? Most economists would agree that antidumping duties tend to be protectionist rather than compensating for

Figure 1-4
Comparative Tariff Structures of ASEAN Countries (ad valorem 2007/2008)

A. Manufactures

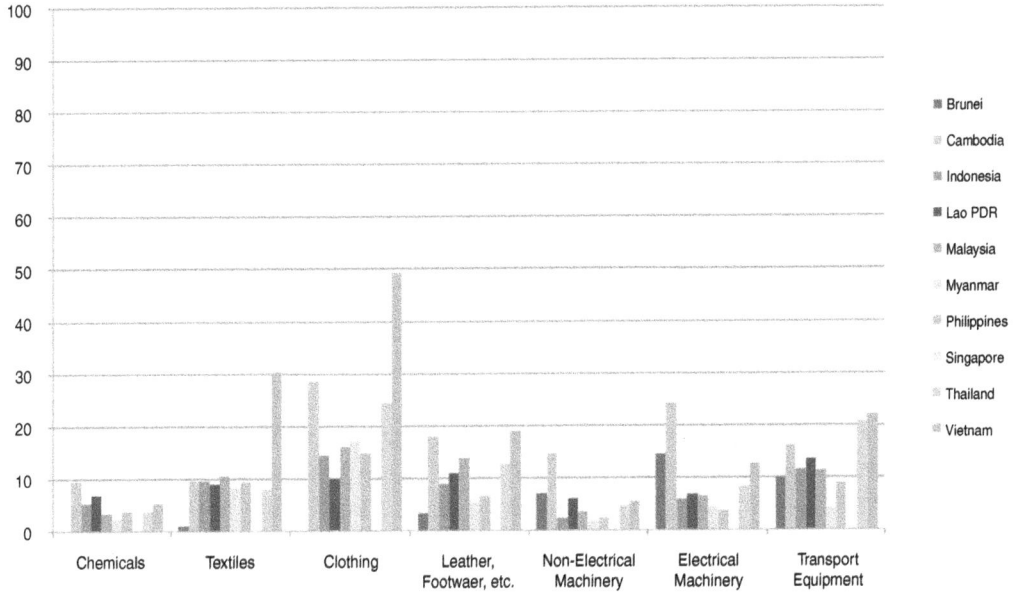

B. Agriculture

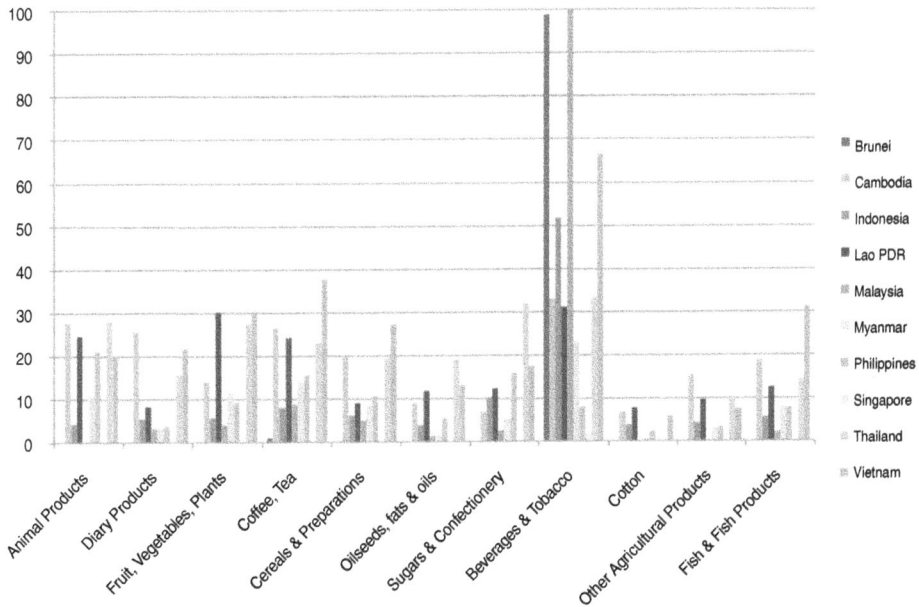

Note: Tariffs are average applied MFN rates, 2007.
Source: WTO Tariff Profiles 2008.

some nefarious pricing strategy of foreign firms. But one cannot deny that dumping sometimes occurs, and antidumping duties are permitted by the WTO (under certain general guidelines). In any event, classifying antidumping in some aggregate measure of NTBs might be theoretically correct but extremely complicated.

The Uruguay Round addressed NTBs, particularly by "tarifficating" existing quotas in many sensitive agricultural products and doing away with "orderly-marketing arrangements" such as the Multifibre arrangement (MFA), which was phased out under the Uruguay Round Agreement on Textiles and Clothing (ATC). In fact, some of the changes in tariffs — particularly in agriculture — were less impressive or even resulted from turning NTBs into transparent tariffs that were then normalized and easier to liberalize. Agriculture arrangements are still complicated but were greatly improved through the Uruguay Round. And quotas are supposed to be a thing of the past.

Feridhanusetyawan's (2005) trade restrictiveness indices for Asia classify NTBs as restrictive, intermediate, or open. The only economy with a clean bill of health for NTBs in ASEAN is Singapore. NTBs in Indonesia, Malaysia, the Philippines, and Thailand are intermediate, and in Vietnam (which joined the WTO after the numbers were compiled), Lao PDR, and Myanmar they are restrictive. An earlier study provides more disaggregated NTB tabulations for seven ASEAN countries (Table 1-4).[11] In the aggregate, NTBs affected a small percentage of product lines in ASEAN countries in 2001, with Thailand and Brunei having the highest NTB coverage at over three percent and the rest at about 2.5 percent or less. Moreover, the NTBs tend to be concentrated in agricultural products, with the exceptions of iron and steel in Vietnam and Malaysia and textiles and clothing in Malaysia. As NTBs have continued to fall throughout the 2000s, the situation has continued to improve, though there continue to be significant "spikes."[12]

Commercial policy reform in the ASEAN region has been extensive. Rather than retrenching workers and raising tariffs in the wake of the Asian Crisis, the affected economies liberalized. And

Table 1-4
Nontariff Barrier Coverage Ratio, 2001

Product Category (SITC)	ASEAN						
	Brunei	Indo	Malay	Phil	Sing	Thai	Viet
Primary Products (0-4,68)	6.49	4.43	3.02	0.74	0.61	6.32	0.43
Agriculture (0-2,4)	7.61	3.35	3.53	0.76	0.72	6.67	0.41
Mining (3,68)	0.00	10.84	0.00	0.61	0.00	4.22	0.54
Manufactures (5-8,less 68)	2.43	1.07	2.41	1.92	0.13	3.30	1.23
Iron and steel (67)	0.00	1.87	7.97	0.00	0.00	0.00	21.74
Chemicals (5)	3.41	1.56	0.75	4.67	0.00	0.24	0.12
Other Semi-manufis (61-64,66,69)	6.72	1.22	0.90	0.60	0.00	1.47	0.41
Machinery & transport equip (7)	2.90	1.92	4.29	1.92	0.56	1.39	0.00
Textiles and clothing (65,84)	0.00	0.00	0.30	0.00	0.00	13.50	0.00
Other cons goods (81-83,85,87-89)	0.00	0.00	4.31	2.65	0.00	0.00	0.00
Other products (9)	0.00	0.00	0.00	8.33	0.00	0.00	0.00
All products (0-9)	3.35	1.82	2.54	1.68	0.24	3.97	1.03

Note: Calculations based on incidence of nontariff barriers using UNCTAD database.
Source: Bijit Bora, Aki Kuwahara and Sam Laird, Quantification on Non-Tariff Measures, UNCTAD Policy Issues in International Trade and Commodities Study Issue, No. 18, 2002, Table 2.

reform often goes further than what tariff indicators suggest, particularly for transitional economies that have established new commercial policy regimes. Certain sectors have high tariffs, sectors with seemingly low averages have tariff spikes, and NTBs continue to be a problem in many countries. In sum, commercial policy liberalization has been impressive and in some ways spectacular, but much more needs to be done.

To summarize this subsection, we note that:

- Structural change in ASEAN has been dynamic and in favor of sophisticated manufactures, particularly electronics. ASEAN's trade with the world has also been changing considerably, with intraregional trade rising, and trade spreading symmetrically across the US+EU, Japan+China, ASEAN itself, and the rest of the world. Nevertheless, ASEAN does almost three-fourths of its trade with non-regional partners.
- Domestic policies vary widely across the region but ASEAN's policies have been liberalized as part of a unilateral commitment to economic reform, concerted liberalization through AFTA and other ASEAN initiatives, and in the context of the WTO. The result has been dynamic trade performance and an increasingly interdependent region.
- Nevertheless, many ASEAN Member States have significant border-related barriers in many sectors. To integrate effectively into international value-chains and attract tasks associated with fragmented trade, exploit economies of scale, and enhance efficiency, concerted action needs to take place in numerous non-border, as well as border, areas. The ASEAN leaders understood this when they developed the AEC and the AEC Blueprint: the focus is on border-measures as well as on beyond-the-borders opportunities for cooperation.

TRADE IN SERVICES

Trade in services constitutes over one-fourth of global trade and 20–30 percent of value-added in GDP in the ASEAN Member States.[13] This sector is now essential to ASEAN Member States' global economic interaction in and of itself and as a facilitator of trade in goods and FDI. One study shows that the services sector was the dominant contributor to GDP growth in the late 1990s in the largest ASEAN Member States, save Indonesia, where it was somewhat below that of manufacturing.[14] Even though services matter a great deal, economic cooperation in services has progressed little in ASEAN.[15]

Travel, transport, and other business services together constitute 84 percent of ASEAN's services exports and 75 percent of its services imports (Table 1-5). From 1990 to 2007, total ASEAN exports of services grew 350 percent, going from $29 billion to $130 billion. Imports grew even faster, going from $28 billion to $154 billion over the same period. Hence, the trade balance in services has gone from a slight surplus in 1990 to a $24 billion deficit in 2006.

As Figure 1-5 shows, services exports of ASEAN Member States, especially the CLMV countries and Indonesia, have experienced a great deal of volatility over time, far more than trade in goods. This is only natural, given the diverse nature of services. Export growth took a strong hit during the Asian Crisis, but the recovery since 1998 appears to be on a trajectory that will approach pre-Crisis growth rates, which were about 20 percent per annum.

ADB (2007) affirms that the ASEAN development process more or less conforms with what has been known as a "Kuznets process:" as development proceeds the contribution of agriculture to GDP falls over time; manufactures rise, peak, and then begin to fall; and services rise in importance

Table 1-5
Distribution of ASEAN Trade in Services, 1990 and 2006
(by service category as a percentage of ASEAN trade in services)

Trade Flow	Service category	1990	2008
Exports	Transport	17.33	26.55
	Travel	45.33	30.09
	Communications	0.00	2.48
	Construction	0.01	1.98
	Insurance	0.39	1.60
	Financial Services	0.00	3.41
	Computer and information services	0.00	1.09
	Royalties and license fees	0.00	0.63
	Other business services	33.29	26.98
	Personal, cultural and recreational services	0.00	0.89
	Government services n.i.e.	2.28	0.71
	Total services (US$ million)	29,336.89	129,995.66
Imports	Transport	46.84	39.75
	Travel	19.68	15.83
	Communications	0.00	1.62
	Construction	0.02	2.07
	Insurance	4.92	3.91
	Financial Services	0.00	1.04
	Computer and information services	0.00	1.04
	Royalties and license fees	0.73	9.58
	Other business services	24.87	19.30
	Personal, cultural and recreational services	0.00	1.21
	Government services n.i.e.	1.76	0.74
	Total services (US$ million)	28,694.75	154,406.89

Source: UNCTAD Handbook of Statistics.

throughout the development process. The contribution of services trade to GDP is also rising and will likely continue to do so. Moreover, given the importance of certain services as a facilitator of trade and as an input to value chains, economic cooperation in services is a key aspect of the AEC program.

If trade in services data are difficult to come by, related information on protection is even scarcer. As noted, tariffs are straightforward; they are applied at the border. Tariff-equivalent estimates of NTBs in goods are much more complicated but can be inferred through differences in national market prices and global prices. But protection in services trade poses even greater difficulties, not in the least because some types of services ("Mode 3") require FDI.

Ochiai (2006) rates restrictiveness of trade in services in the ASEAN priority sectors with a score of 0.5 (where 0 is completely restrictive and 1 is completely open). In contrast, in the priority goods sectors, tariff protection averages at 3.7 percent in the CEPT and 10.4 percent in the MFN tariffs.[16]

Some economic modelers have endeavored to estimate tariff-equivalent barriers to trade in services by country and sector in order to show the effects of liberalization of trade in services. Table 1-6

Figure 1-5
Growth of Services Exports of ASEAN Member States

ASEAN Total and Selected ASEAN Member States

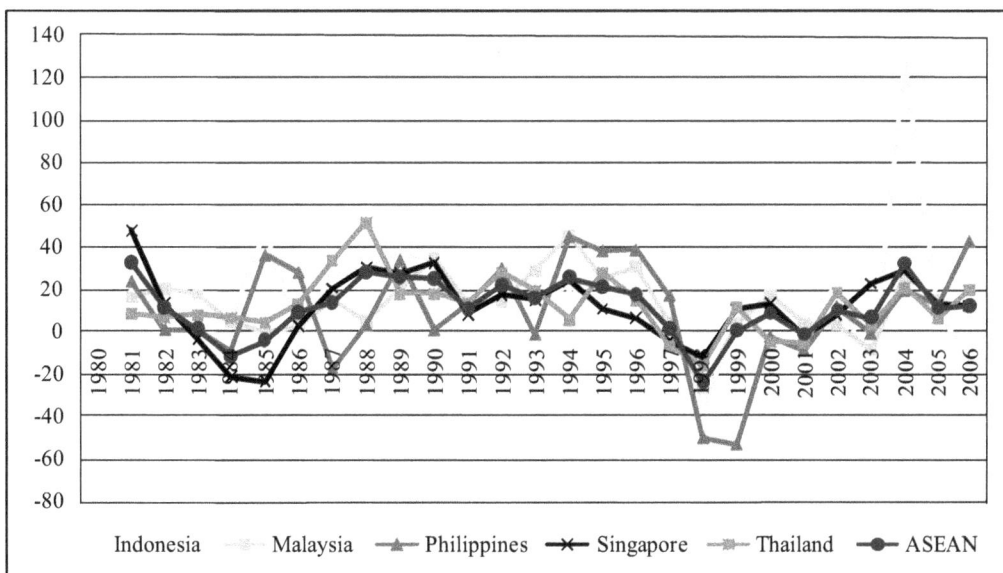

Indonesia — Malaysia — Philippines — Singapore — Thailand — ASEAN

Cambodia, Lao PDR, Myanmar, Vietnam

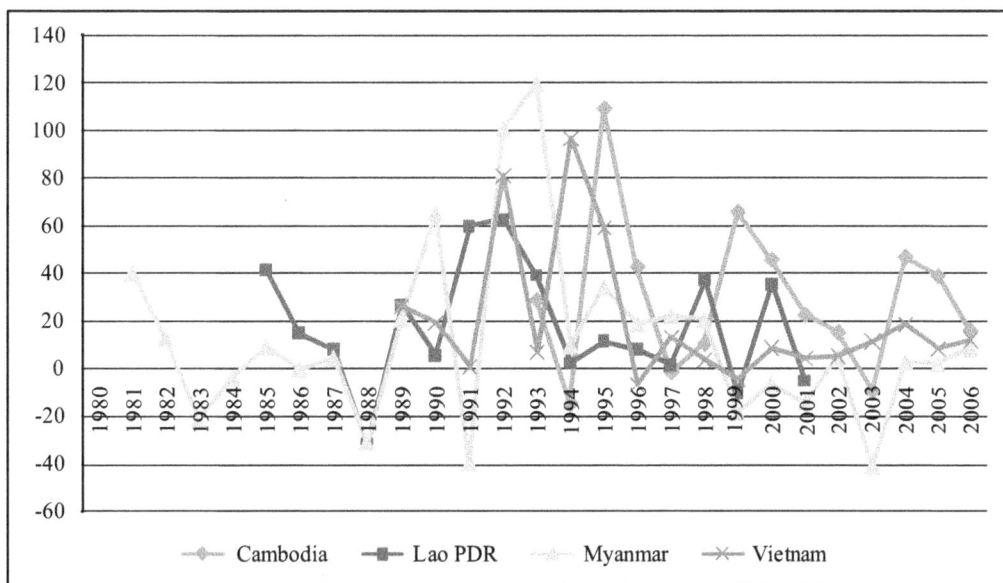

Cambodia — Lao PDR — Myanmar — Vietnam

Notes: ASEAN Total excludes Brunei, Cambodia, and Lao PDR. Data for Vietnam is from 1989 onwards.
Source: UNCTAD Handbook of Statistics.

Table 1-6
Ad Valorem Equivalents of Barriers to Trade in Services

	Indonesia	Malaysia	Philippines	Singapore	Thailand	Vietnam
Electricity, gas and water	0	0	0	0	0	0
Construction	6	4	15	0	13.5	6
Trade and transport	12	4.5	17	2.5	17	7.5
Other private services	21.5	3.5	17.5	3	17	9.5
Government services	10.5	5.5	10.5	5.5	13	10.5

Note: Data not available for Brunei Darussalam, Cambodia, Lao PDR, and Myanmar.
Source: Michigan Model.

provides an example of such estimates for five service areas in the original ASEAN countries plus Vietnam to give an idea of how extensive protection is in various sectors.[17] Protection in electricity, gas, and water is estimated to be nil, but protection in other private services, especially financial services, is relatively high for all countries, save Singapore. Protection in trade and transport is also high in the Philippines and Thailand. Thus, liberalization of trade in services within the AEC will no doubt have a significant effect on services trade, a result that we do obtain in Chapter 2.

EASE OF DOING BUSINESS

The World Bank's annual *Doing Business* ranks countries on ease of doing business by means of indicators and sub-indicators (Table 1-7). For 2009, rankings of ASEAN Member States vary widely on the overall indicator, from 1 out of 181 countries (Singapore) to 165 (Lao PDR). Thailand, Malaysia, and Brunei ranked above average and the other ASEAN countries ranked below average.

ASEAN countries rank poorly on regulations for "starting a business" (except Singapore) and "registering property" (except Thailand and Singapore), but rank well on regulatory costs of international trade (except Cambodia and Lao PDR). Singapore has the best ranking of ASEAN countries and in the world. For example, Singapore requires only 4 documents to export or import but Cambodia requires 11. It takes 3–5 days to obtain regulatory approval to export and import in Singapore but more than 20 days in several other ASEAN countries. And the cost of importing and exporting is US$439–$456 per container in Singapore and about $2,000 in Lao PDR.

FOREIGN DIRECT INVESTMENT

Reducing business costs and thereby attracting FDI is a longstanding objective of ASEAN economic cooperation. Part and parcel of production-network building in ASEAN, FDI itself attracts new flows of capital and foreign exchange, provides access to foreign markets, enables technology transfer, and tends to strengthen institutions in developing countries, stabilizing the business environment and spurring beneficial internal "policy competition."[18] The result is an attractive business environment within which multinational corporations (MNCs) can thrive and facilitate the emergence of regional MNCs. FDI inflows also expand opportunities for small- and medium-sized local suppliers through subcontracting, training, management organization, and other forms of technology transfer. In short,

Table 1-7
Ease of Doing Business in ASEAN (Rankings based on 181 economies)

	Brunei	*Cambodia*	*Indonesia*	*Lao PDR*	*Malaysia*	*Myanmar*	*Philippines*	*Singapore*	*Thailand*	*Vietnam*	*ASEAN Average*
Ease of doing business	88	135	129	165	20	n.a.	140	1	13	92	87
Starting a business	130	169	171	92	75	n.a.	155	10	44	108	106
Dealing with construction permits	72	147	80	110	104	n.a.	105	2	12	67	78
Employing workers	5	134	157	85	48	n.a.	126	1	56	90	78
Registering property	177	108	107	159	81	n.a.	97	16	5	37	87
Getting credit	109	68	109	145	1	n.a.	123	5	68	43	75
Protecting investors	113	70	53	180	4	n.a.	126	2	11	170	81
Paying taxes	35	24	116	113	21	n.a.	129	5	82	140	74
Trading across borders	42	122	37	165	29	n.a.	58	1	10	67	59
Documents to export (number)	6	11	5	9	7	n.a.	8	4	4	6	7
Time to export (days)	28	22	21	50	18	n.a.	16	5	14	24	22
Cost to export (US$ per container)	630	732	704	1,860	450	n.a.	816	456	625	734	779
Documents to import (number)	6	11	6	10	7	n.a.	8	4	3	8	7
Time to import (days)	19	30	27	50	14	n.a.	16	3	13	23	22
Cost to import(US$ per container)	706	872	660	2,040	450	n.a.	819	439	795	901	854
Enforcing contracts	157	136	140	111	59	n.a.	114	14	25	42	89
Closing a business	35	181	139	181	54	n.a.	151	2	46	124	101

Source: Compiled from World Bank, Doing Business 2009.

by enabling a local economy to enter regional and global production networks, FDI facilitates the integration of the least-developed ASEAN countries, regions, and groups.

Shares of FDI Inflows

Table 1-8 summarizes FDI inflows to ASEAN during the 1995–2006 period. It shows that world FDI inflows almost quadrupled from 1995 to reach $1.3 trillion in 2006. This global FDI is concentrated in developed countries; the United States and the EU together have consistently accounted for more than half of global FDI, except for in 2004. However, FDI inflows to ASEAN as a share of total world inflows have dropped from their highs in the mid-1990s, about 8 percent of world FDI inflows, to somewhat less than 4 percent in recent years. Still, FDI inflows into ASEAN have been robust, reaching $52 billion in 2006.

Table 1-9 shows FDI to individual ASEAN Member States during the same period. ASEAN had record years in 2005 ($41 billion) and 2006 ($52 billion). Almost half of inward FDI to ASEAN over the 1995–2006 period went to Singapore alone. Thailand and Malaysia, whose growth during the "miracle" years was fuelled in part by robust FDI inflows, saw a significant slowdown in inflows in the 2000s, though they each had impressive rebounds in 2006. Indonesia's FDI inflows were usually negative (sometimes significantly so) from the onset of the Asian financial crisis through 2004,[19] though it, too, experienced a strong rebound over the 2005–2006 period. The same is generally true

Table 1-8
World Shares of FDI Inflows to ASEAN and Selected Other Countries and Regions
(Percentage of Total World FDI Inflows, 1995–2006)

Host \ Year	1995	1996	1997	1998	1999	2000	2001	2002	2003	2004	2005	2006	% of Total (1995–2006)
United States	17.16	21.5	21.13	24.59	25.79	22.25	19.15	11.97	9.42	18.3	10.68	13.43	18.16
EU 25	38.3	31.8	29.1	39.6	45.7	49.3	45.8	49.4	45.5	27.5	51.4	40.7	42.8
Japan	0.01	0.06	0.66	0.45	1.16	0.59	0.75	1.49	1.12	1.05	0.29	-0.5	0.57
China	10.95	10.62	9.25	6.41	3.67	2.88	5.63	8.48	9.49	8.17	7.66	5.32	6.41
South Korea	0.36	0.51	0.54	0.72	0.9	0.64	0.5	0.55	0.78	1.21	0.75	0.38	0.66
East Asia	21.6	21.8	19.4	12.3	9.6	9.9	11.9	13.5	16.5	18.9	16.4	13.4	14.21
ASEAN	8.22	7.76	7.01	3.14	2.62	1.67	2.49	2.9	4.34	4.75	4.34	3.94	3.79
World (US$ million)	342,592	392,743	489,243	709,303	1,098,896	1,411,366	832,567	621,995	564,078	742,143	945,795	1,305,852	9,456,573

Notes: 1) The EU 25 include Austria, Belgium, Luxembourg, Cyprus, Czech Republic, Denmark, Estonia, Finland, France, Germany, Greece, Hungary, Ireland, Italy, Latvia, Lithuania, Luxembourg, Malta, Netherlands, Poland, Portugal, Slovakia, Slovenia, Spain, Sweden, and the UK.
2) The figures for China do not include inflows to Hong Kong and Macao.
3) East Asia includes China, Hong Kong, Lao PDR, Taiwan, South Korea, Cambodia, Indonesia, Malaysia, Myanmar, Philippines, Singapore, Thailand, and Vietnam.

Source: UNCTAD FDI Statistics Online.

Table 1-9
FDI Flows to ASEAN 1995–2006 (US$ million)

	1995	1996	1997	1998	1999	2000	2001	2002	2003	2004	2005	2006	Total
Brunei	583	654	702	573	748	549	526	1,035	3,123	212	289	434	9,427
Cambodia	151	294	168	243	232	149	149	145	84	131	381	483	2,611
Indonesia	4,346	6,194	4,678	−356	−2,745	−4,550	−3,279	145	−596	1,895	8,336	5,556	19,624
Lao PDR	88	128	86	45	52	34	24	25	20	17	28	187	734
Malaysia	5,815	7,297	6,323	2,714	3,895	3,788	554	3,203	2,473	4,624	3,965	6,060	50,711
Myanmar	318	581	879	683	304	208	192	191	291	251	236	143	4,277
Philippines	1,577	1,618	1,261	1,718	1,247	2,240	195	1,542	491	688	1,854	2,345	16,775
Singapore	11,503	9,303	13,533	7,594	16,067	16,485	15,649	7,200	11,664	19,828	15,002	24,055	167,883
Thailand	2,070	2,338	3,882	7,491	6,091	3,350	5,061	3,335	5,235	5,862	8,957	10,756	64,428
Vietnam	1,780	1,803	2,587	1,700	1,484	1,289	1,300	1,200	1,450	1,610	2,021	2,360	20,585
Total	28,231	30,209	34,099	22,406	27,375	23,541	20,372	18,023	24,235	35,117	41,068	52,380	357,054

Notes: 1) Data compiled from the respective ASEAN Central Banks and Central Statistical Offices. Unless otherwise indicated, the figures include equity and inter-company loans.
2) Figures for Brunei Darussalam, Cambodia, Malaysia (for the whole data series); figures for Indonesia (2004– 1st Q 2006); Philippines (1999–1st Q 2006) and figures for Myanmar and Vietnam (2003–2005) include reinvested earnings.
3) Figures for Singapore include reinvested earnings for the whole data series, but exclude inter-company loans for 1995–1996.
4) Cambodia's figures for 2006 are estimated figures.
5) Indonesia's figures for 2005 had been revised due to their BOP survey.
6) Myanmar's figures are by fiscal year ending in March of the following calendar year. Not available for quarter 2006 and 2007.
7) Philippine's figures for 2005 had been revised due to their BOP survey.
8) Singapore's figures from 2002–2005 had been revised due to their BOP survey.
9) Thailand's figures from 2001–2005 had been revised due to their BOP survey.
10) Vietnam's figures for 2006 only cover the data on 1st half 2006. Not available for quarter 2006 and 2007.
11) Figures for total and cumulative total are preliminary.
Source: ASEAN Secretariat — ASEAN FDI Database, 2007.

for the Philippines, which had disappointing FDI inflows through 2004 but experienced record inflows in 2006. Inflows to Vietnam have been relatively stable, generally in the $1.2 billion–$2.4 billion range. FDI inflows to the other transitional ASEAN economies (Cambodia, Lao PDR, and Myanmar) have been low.

The EU has been by far the largest supplier of FDI to ASEAN ($79 billion), 60 percent more than the value of US FDI ($49 billion) and more than twice that of Japan ($34 billion).[20] In fact, the United Kingdom alone invested slightly more than Japan. China has been only a marginal source of FDI ($1.8 billion), but the newly industrialized Asian economies (South Korea, Hong Kong, and Taiwan) invested $19 billion.

Intra-ASEAN FDI

Although it has been declining since the Asian financial crisis, intra-ASEAN FDI is important. Intra-ASEAN trade as a percentage of the region's total is 26 percent, while intra-ASEAN FDI as a share of total FDI inflows is only about 14 percent. Singapore is the source of about two-thirds of intra-ASEAN FDI, and its outflows to Malaysia and Thailand account for one-third of all intra-ASEAN FDI.

CONCLUSION

The economies of ASEAN Member States have been internationalizing and ASEAN trade has been undergoing rapid structural change characterized by rising intraregional trade, flourishing economic interaction, and more symmetric business cycles. Since AFTA, ASEAN leaders have realized that regional cooperation can facilitate efficient structural change, reduce transaction costs, boost competitiveness, create markets, close development gaps, and plug ASEAN into global production chains. The decision to create the AEC is a milestone, an extremely ambitious project to create a single market and production base, a competitive economic region integrated into the global economy, and an equitable economic region.

The goal of the AEC is not to boost trade and investment *per se* but to reduce the costs of doing business, diffuse best practices, and deepen integration with global production chains, rather than merely Southeast Asian ones. As expressed in the AEC Blueprint:

> The AEC is the realisation of the end goal of economic integration as espoused in the Vision 2020, which is based on a convergence of interests of ASEAN Member Countries to deepen and broaden economic integration through existing and new initiatives with clear timelines. In establishing the AEC, ASEAN shall act in accordance to the principles of an open, outward-looking, inclusive, and market-driven economy consistent with multilateral rules as well as adherence to rules-based systems for effective compliance and implementation of economic commitments.

It will be difficult technically and politically to implement this program. Costs are frequently cited in the press and considerable pessimism regarding political will to achieve an AEC is expressed in the media and other circles. Costs are clear — but what about the benefits? In the rest of this study we present the gains possible from the AEC in quantitative estimates and qualitative analysis. Our results are reassuring: the AEC should generate significant gains for all ASEAN Member States and ASEAN stakeholders.

NOTES

1. The European energy markets and to some degrees its financial markets are still not integrated. The EU's response to the financial crisis beginning in September 2008 revealed how continued diversity in financial sector organization impedes unified action.
2. See ADB (2008), Chapter 3, for a survey of these determinants and details on the convergence process.
3. Intra-industry trade refers to exports and imports in the same industry (e.g., electronics for electronics), as opposed to interindustry trade, which deals with trade across industries (e.g., oil for automobiles). With value chains, discussed at length below and in other chapters, trade across countries is intra-industry: for example, value-added across an international electronics production chain will involve countries exchanging electronic components as they build their final good.
4. See Rana (2006).
5. Plummer (2008).
6. By "ranking" here, we mean ranking according to export value, with the largest being first and the smallest last (we include a cutoff of $500,000). We do this at a very disaggregated level, as there is obviously a potential aggregation bias.
7. Brunei's SRCC coefficient at 0.33 is actually the lowest. However, Brunei is somewhat of an exception in this analysis because 90 percent of its exports are petroleum related. But these exports only occupy a relatively few commodities in the 5-digit SITC line-up, and since the SRCC is non-parametric, this leads to a bias.

8. This type of normalization is done by dividing the intraregional trade shares by the shares of ASEAN trade in global trade.
9. ADB (2008) gives a survey of these studies.
10. Note that tariff data are not available for Cambodia, Lao PDR, and Myanmar in this dataset.
11. Bora, Kuwahara and Laird (2002)
12. See, for example, sectoral studies on NTBs in priority sectors in ASEAN, which are discussed in the next section.
13. ASEAN-6 and Vietnam.
14. Clemes, et al. (2003).
15. Data on the direction, composition, and patterns of trade in services are far less comprehensive than for trade in goods. Hence, trade analysis is somewhat more difficult.
16. Findlay (2007).
17. These data were provided by the "Michigan Model," the trade model at the University of Michigan. We thank Alan Deardorf, Robert Stern and Kozo Kiyoto for providing these data to us.
18. By "policy competition" we mean that countries in a free trade area have an incentive to adopt best practices, promote a low-cost business environment, and embrace transparency to compete for FDI flows.
19. These negative figures are due in part to huge repayments of intracompany loans by foreign affiliates. Accounting for FDI inflows in Indonesia is tricky, especially for the petroleum sector, where there is a large foreign presence but FDI inflows are not counted generally as FDI (but part of "product sharing" agreements). Moreover, because there was a large depreciation of the rupiah during this period, end-year valuations of the change in FDI stocks generally would have a strong negative effect on the numbers.
20. The data summarized in the paragraph come from the ASEAN Secretariat, *Statistics on Foreign Direct Investment in ASEAN*, Eight Edition, 2006.

2
Regional Market for Goods, Services, and Skilled Labor

Zakariah Rashid, Fan Zhai, Peter A. Petri, Michael G. Plummer, and Chia Siow Yue

The AEC Blueprint calls for creating a single market and production base by achieving a free flow of goods, services, and skilled labor. AFTA had done much to integrate ASEAN's goods market but far less has been done for services and skilled labor. Goals of the AEC include reducing transaction costs associated with trade in goods and services, attracting FDI through nondiscrimination and best practices, and enabling the free movement of skilled labor throughout the region. These are ambitious goals but potentially well worth the effort. If they are met the private sector will benefit from an integrated regional market, rather than a series of individual national ones.

This chapter will delineate various measures required to complete the task of establishing free flow of goods, services and skilled labor as articulated in the AEC, evaluate the likely economic effects that will derive from a successful implementation of these measures, and consider how they will affect various stakeholders and their likely impact on the success of the AEC itself. We conclude that extending AFTA to include the elimination of NTBs and trade facilitation measures should generate considerable economic benefits — on the order of 5.3 percent of ASEAN GDP (under conservative assumptions). It is difficult to quantify the likely effects of the free flow of skilled labor, but theory suggests that rationalizing the division of labor in ASEAN and enabling skilled labor to function as input for FDI promises considerable economic gain.

FREE FLOWS OF GOODS: A SURVEY OF THE ISSUES

Following the principle of economic theory that benefits accrue if goods and services cross borders uninhibited by artificial barriers, the AEC aims to create a single market and production base in which transaction costs are minimized and trade gains maximized. A trading region so unified will facilitate development of production networks, exploit fragmented trade opportunities, and become a global production center or at least central to global supply chains. The AEC builds on AFTA, taking it beyond tariffs to nontariff barriers, trade facilitation, and related areas. In the following paragraphs we explore the stakes involved in liberalizing trade in goods.

Trade and Growth in ASEAN

Economists tend to agree that trade openness has an important role in economic growth. Openness refers to a lack of barriers to international trade and investment (e.g., tariffs and nontariff barriers) and trade as a percentage of economic activity (e.g., relative to GDP). Obviously, the two are related; fewer barriers will increase trade as a percentage of GDP. Trade influences growth through many channels: access to a global market, absorption of new technologies, greater competition, attraction of capital and especially FDI, incentives for investment in infrastructure, and better management techniques.

The wisdom of an outward-oriented industrialization policy is echoed throughout the academic literature. The World Bank (1993) underscores export promotion and outward orientation as key to the success of the East Asian miracle economies. Radelet, Sachs and Lee (2001) verify that integration with the global economy over the liberalization period in East Asia (1960s to the mid-1990s) led to structural change in favor of labor-intensive manufactures and largely explains why East Asian countries grew faster than the rest of the world. ADB (2008) underscores how the outward-orientation of Asian developing economies in general and ASEAN in particular has not only contributed to strong economic growth and vibrant export sectors but also has put these countries in cutting-edge production networks, generating efficient inflows of FDI and associated technology transfer. The World Bank's "East Asian Renaissance" study (2008) shows how Asia is using regional trading agreements to reinforce regionally-oriented market trends. ASEAN is at the center of these initiatives.

Through AFTA, ASEAN has done much to remove intraregional tariff barriers. As noted in Chapter 1, trade as a percentage of GDP has increased impressively in recent years. The strong performance of ASEAN countries before the 2008–2009 global economic crisis derived in no small part from AFTA and its liberalization and facilitation measures. With the exception of the Asian Financial Crisis period, GDP growth in ASEAN Member States has been higher than the world average since the beginning of AFTA implementation in 1993, and economic growth has been particularly strong since 2003, when ASEAN leaders began to consider the AEC program in earnest. Of course, this does not prove causality, but it is strong prima facie evidence of a clear link. Moreover, the literature suggests that there is an "anticipatory effect" created by the announcement of the formation of deeper economic integration (see, for example, Freunde and McLaren 1999); it would be consistent with the experience of other regional groupings that economic agents have already been anticipating the AEC.

Disaggregated Trade: Signs of ASEAN Production Network-Building

Chapter 1 considered ASEAN trade at the aggregate level. Table 2-1 presents the most important ASEAN exports to other ASEAN countries at a relatively high level of disaggregation and by absolute value and shares of regional exports in global exports for 1993 (beginning of AFTA), 2003 (beginning of AEC drive), and 2006 (latest year).

The top intraregional exports are transistors, semiconductor devices and valves, automatic data processing machines, parts and accessories for office, petroleum and oils products, and

Table 2-1
Top Five Product Exports for the ASEAN Member States, 1993, 2003, 2006

Products (3-digit SITC)	Value of Exports ($ billions)			Share of Regional Trade (%)		
	1993	2003	2006	1993	2003	2006
INDONESIA						
Transistors, semi-conductors devices, valves etc. (776)	19.27	395.60	704.12	39.35	54.87	57.34
Automatic data processing machines (752)	55.8	152.75	355.69	62.7	17.79	19.91
Parts and accessories for office (759)	36.86	757.59	529.95	78.3	79.38	89.74
Petroleum oils and products (334)	80.3	322.59	901.25	8.7	21.07	32.01
Telecommunications equipment, NES & parts (764)	124.8	511.72	608.23	48.5	36.43	49.89
MALAYSIA						
Transistors, semi-conductors devices, valves etc. (776)	1,597.68	6,165.3	7,092.19	21.92	27.52	27.80
Automatic data processing machines (752)	39.30	488.44	848.72	8.75	5.79	5.19
Parts and accessories for office (759)	1,169.50	2,666.37	3,105.05	43.9	32.03	27.18
Petroleum oils and products (334)	388.80	1,132.00	2,109.98	77.0	51.28	72.21
Telecommunications equipment, NES & parts (764)	879.90	997.53	3,778.97	39.78	19.07	23
PHILIPPINES						
Transistors, semi-conductors devices, valves etc. (776)	93.6	3,817.6	4,337.6	11.6	24.0	25.6
Automatic data processing machines (752)	15.1	223.4	499.0	8.0	5.4	10.7
Parts and accessories for office (759)	11.4	678.9	763.6	42.5	24.5	22.4
Petroleum oils and products (334)	6.33	144.8	64.0	6.12	18.6	11.2
Telecommunications equipment, NES & parts (764)	11.1	144.7	63.6	2.8	18.6	7.52
THAILAND						
Transistors, semi-conductors devices, valves etc. (776)	611.9	1,226.8	1,782.5	35.8	19.5	21.5
Automatic data processing machines (752)	517.8		919.7	54.6		8.5
Parts and accessories for office (759)	1,165.8	1,508.7	733.8	44.6	39.7	47.3
Petroleum oils and products (334)	160.7	719.1	2,733.0	56.5	70.4	68.5
Telecommunications equipment, NES & parts (764)	181.4	704.8	223.2	19.8	25.1	8.24
SINGAPORE						
Transistors, semi-conductors devices, valves etc. (776)	1,670.4	10,945.4	15,147.2	24.4	29.6	22.3
Automatic data processing machines (752)	289.9	1,324.3	2,125.9	2.4	8.3	16.4
Parts and accessories for office (759)	618.4	2,685.3	4,936.3	15.2	25.6	25.9
Petroleum oils and products (334)	1,364.3	3,652.1	11,526.1	15.5	28.7	34.1
Telecommunications equipment, NES & parts (764)	1,105.7	3,858.3	5,332.1	28.1	46.7	33.7
BRUNEI						
Transistors, semi-conductors devices, valves etc. (776)	—	0.02	0.02	—	66.05	99.98
Automatic data processing machines (752)	—	0.44	0.42	—	91.19	52.1
Parts and accessories for office (759)	—	0.45	0.29	—	61.96	72.59
Petroleum oils and products (334)	0.3	7.95	0.14	0.4	48.49	97.7
Telecommunications equipment, NES & parts (764)	—	8.04	4.33	—	83.38	68.59

VIETNAM						
Transistors, semi-conductors devices, valves etc. (776)	—	3.99	26.1	—	5.6	12.9
Automatic data processing machines (752)	—	4.1	95.6	—	2.7	14.2
Parts and accessories for office (759)	—	223.9	455.9	—	70.8	90.03
Petroleum oils and products (334)	—	114.6	387.1	—	81.6	80.8
Telecommunications equipment, NES & parts (764)	—	9.62	8.75	—	7.3	6.1

Source: UN-COMTRADE and calculations by MIER.

telecommunications equipment. These products tend to have the same importance across the region, and have a high concentration of shares in total world exports. In 2006, the share of regional exports of selected products was even greater than 70 percent in some countries (e.g., in Indonesia, office parts and accessories; Malaysia, petroleum oils and products). Most of these involve electronics and are part of the fragmented trade inherent in the formation of value chains (see Chapters 4–6) and petroleum trade. Intra-ASEAN exports increased from 1993 to 2006 in almost all of these product categories except automatic data processing machines. It seems odd that Singapore, the only country to commit fully to abolishing tariffs on intraregional trade in AFTA, has a low share of regional exports in these products compared to other ASEAN Member States. But this is no doubt because it is a center of entrepot trade generally, not just for ASEAN. For the other countries, the shares of regional export are quite high in the same product categories.

How have intraregional product exports changed over time relative to ASEAN trade with the rest of the world? Answering this question might afford us even more insight into the dynamics of intraregional trade. To begin, we calculate a simple orientation index that permits us to gauge these trends. Our index is expressed as the share of commodity k in ASEAN country j's exports to the region, relative to the share of commodity k in non-regional exports. If the index exceeds unity, the country is said to have a higher propensity to export product k to regional markets. Changes in the index (1993–2005) refer to growing or declining shares for regional markets (Table 2-2).

Overall, manufacturing products exhibit a growing regional orientation in ASEAN Member States, except Brunei. Similarly, for machinery and transport equipment the index rises over the period in the range of 0.12–2.83, save for Malaysia (–0.1) and Thailand (–0.25). Malaysia's regional orientation has been declining in almost all product categories except manufacturing and miscellaneous manufacturing products. Even with its larger presence in international trade at the global level, Singapore's regional reorientation index grew in all categories except fuel and lubricants (–0.09), chemicals (–0.26), and goods not classified (–0.78).

Effects of ASEAN Integration: Extant Studies

Regional trade agreements (RTAs) have positive and negative economic effects; positive effects derive from a more efficient internal division of labor (trade creation) and negative ones from discrimination against nonmember countries (trade diversion). This is why economists stress that RTAs should be outward-oriented to minimize distortions against non-partner countries. This "second best" nature of RTAs has provoked many studies of their actual effects on efficiency and growth, including models that

Table 2-2
ASEAN Regional Orientation Indices for Major Product Groups, 1993–2006 (SITC 1-Digit)

	Year	Food & Feeds	Beverages & Tobacco	Crude Materials, Inedible, Except Fuels	Fuels, Lubricants, etc	Animal & Vegetable oil	Chemicals	Manufacturers classified by materials	Machinery & Transport Equipment	Misc Manufactured	Goods not classified by kind
Brunei	1993	0	0	1	0.26	0	1	19.3	0	0	0
	2006	0.27	—	10.29	0.31	—	4.64	4.32	2.83	0.38	0.39
	Δ 93–06	0.27		9.29	0.05		3.64	−14.98	2.83	0.38	0.389
Indonesia	1993	0.18	1.12	0.18	0.03	0.02	0.65	0.19	0.48	0.12	3.53
	2006	0.24	1.25	0.06	0.12	0.16	0.36	0.33	0.71	0.07	0.09
	Δ 93–06	0.06	0.13	0.12	0.09	0.14	−0.29	0.14	0.23	−0.05	−3.44
Malaysia	1993	0.83	3.30	0.14	0.80	0.16	0.72	0.41	0.39	0.25	1.38
	2006	0.64	3.03	0.12	0.56	0.11	0.53	0.43	0.29	0.25	0.64
	Δ 93–06	−0.19	−0.27	−0.02	−0.24	−0.05	−0.19	0.02	−0.1	0	−0.74
Philippines	1993	0.03	0.05	0.06	0.13	0.09	0.60	0.08	0.10	0.01	0.08
	2006	0.12	1.51	0.12	0.87	0.08	0.14	0.29	0.22	0.04	0.03
	Δ 93–06	0.09	1.46	0.006	0.74	−0.01	−0.46	0.21	0.12	0.03	−0.05
Singapore	1993	0.37	0.27	0.27	0.48	0.18	0.62	1.09	0.25	0.20	0.31
	2006	0.59	1.18	0.69	0.39	0.32	0.36	1.10	1.08	0.44	0.10
	Δ 93–06	0.22	0.91	0.42	−0.09	0.14	−0.26	0.01	0.83	0.24	−0.21
Thailand	1993	0.08	0.26	0.06	0.16	0.18	0.42	0.16	0.46	0.07	0.84
	2006	0.13	1.78	0.25	1.31	1.41	0.43	0.23	0.21	0.08	0.06
	Δ 93–06	0.05	1.52	0.19	1.15	1.23	0.01	0.07	−0.25	0.01	−0.78
Vietnam	2006	0.16	0.66	0.03	0.48	0.31	0.39	0.24	0.27	0.02	0.13

Source: UN-COMTRADE and calculations by MIER.

project effects *ex ante* and those designed to establish what efficiency actually occurred *ex post*. Economic widening and deepening in Europe has been studied the most, but just about all RTAs have been considered as well, including AFTA.

The literature suggests that RTAs have had a positive effect on efficiency and welfare and that their ultimate impact depends on how comprehensive and open they are (e.g., shallow agreements and "fortresses" do not perform well). Salutary agreements include the EU itself and NAFTA; less salutary agreements include the inward-looking Latin America Free-Trade Area and Mercosur.

Other studies investigate the effect of Asian regional economic integration using multiple regions and sectors in computational general equilibrium (CGE) models. These studies include Adams and Park (1995), Park (1998 and 2008), Diao and Somwaru (2000), Hosoe (2001), Hadad et al. (2002), Lee, Roland-Holst and Mensbrugghe (2004), and Brown et al. (2004). Such studies tend to find positive but small effects, partly because of the downward-biases characteristic of these types of models.

Lee, Roland-Host and van der Mensbrugghe (2001) estimate the likely impact of APEC trade liberalization on real GDP, sectoral output, exports and imports. Their model predicts that real GDP would increase by about $42 billion for developed APEC members and $83 billion for developing APEC members. Overall, APEC trade liberalization would produce trade expansion in most product categories. Park (2008) considers the impact of potential East Asian RTA strategies. He models several scenarios, including AFTA and ASEAN agreements with Northeast Asian partners. He finds that AFTA generates a positive effect for ASEAN Member States, but that gains from trade would rise if it were to couple ASEAN integration with other Asian RTAs. In a very recent work, Manchin and Pelkmans-Balaoing (2008) use a gravity model to estimate directly the impact of AFTA to date, and find that, in fact, AFTA preferential tariffs do matter for a range of products, particularly where the most-favored nation (MFN) tariff and the AFTA preference tariff differ by a "critical" amount.

In addition to participating in the WTO,[1] more and more ASEAN Member States are engaging in RTAs with non-partners, especially in the form of free-trade areas (FTAs) (Table 2-3).[2] Singapore has aggressively pursued trade partnerships with other countries throughout the world.

Table 2-3
Major RTAs including ASEAN Member States as of June 2009

Implemented (year)	Signed (year of signing)	Under Negotiation	Under Consideration
ASEAN			
China (2005), Japan (2008), Korea (2007)	Australia and, New Zealand (2008), India (2009)		ASEAN+3, ASEAN+6, EU
BRUNEI			
ASEAN (1992), Japan (2007), Trans-Pacific (P4, 2006)		Pakistan	
CAMBODIA			
ASEAN (1999)			
INDONESIA			
ASEAN (1992), Japan (2007)	Group of 8 (2008)	Pakistan	India, Australia, European, US
LAO PDR			
ASEAN (1997), APTA (revised, 2006))			
MALAYSIA			
ASEAN (1992), Japan (2006), Pakistan (2007)	Group of 8 (2008)	Australia, Chile, India, New Zealand, US, Islamic Conference	Korea

continued on next page

Table 2-3 — *cont'd*

Implemented (year)	Signed (year of signing)	Under Negotiation	Under Consideration
		MYANMAR	
ASEAN (1997)			
		PHILIPPINES	
ASEAN (1992), Japan (2006)			Pakistan, US
		SINGAPORE	
ASEAN (1992), EFTA (2003), India (2005), Japan (2002), Korea (2006), New Zealand (2000), Australia (2003), Jordan (2005), Panama (2006), US (2004), Trans-Pacific (P4, 2006)	China (2008), GCC (2008), Peru (2008)	Canada, Pakistan, Egypt, Kuwait, Mexico, Qatar, Ukraine	Sri Lanka, UAE
		THAILAND	
ASEAN (1992) Japan (2007) Australia (2006) New Zealand (2005)		India, Bay of Bengal, Bahrain, Peru, EFTA, US	Korea, Pakistan, Chile, Mercosur
		VIETNAM	
ASEAN (1995)	Japan (2008)	Chile	

Notes: GCC (Gulf Cooperation Council); ASEAN+3 (ASEAN plus China, Japan, Korea); ASEAN+6 (ASEAN+3 plus Australia, New Zealand, India); Group of 8 (Group of Eight Developing Countries); Islamic Conference (Organization of Islamic Conference); EFTA (European Free Trade Association); APTA (Asia-Pacific Trade Agreement).
Source: www.aric.adb.org.

In the next section, we estimate the effects of the AEC using a unique CGE model that employs cutting-edge techniques and up-to-date data. In our model, we consider, inter alia, the potential effects of extending ASEAN-centric FTAs to other regions. We find that keeping the AEC open will be extremely important in ensuring maximum gains from the AEC as ASEAN relies so much on the rest of the world for its trade. We also stress that the "revealed" interest in FTAs with non-ASEAN partners underscores the importance of deepening intra-ASEAN integration. It would behoove ASEAN to be the "hub" of a system of FTAs, rather than a "spoke" attached to other hubs.

AFTA as a First Step Toward the AEC

Chapter 1, Figure 1-4 and Appendix A offer details on the applied tariff structures of the ASEAN Member States as of 2007/2008. The tariffs applied on *intraregional trade* in ASEAN have come down significantly due to AFTA. The average tariff for the ASEAN-6 in 1993 (after AFTA was launched) was about 11 percent; by 2003, it had fallen to 2.4 percent.[3] Among the ASEAN-6, Singapore has been tariff-free (except for six tariff lines on alcoholic beverages) and the others have gradually reduced tariffs such that their average CEPT tariff was 1.7 percent in 2006 (4.7 percent for the CLMV). This would suggest considerable progress due to AFTA; however, the region continues to fall short of a complete FTA. Under the AEC Blueprint, all tariffs will be reduced to zero, and NTBs will be eliminated.

The AEC aims to create a single market and production base encompassing all goods, while accelerating liberalization and integration of 12 goods and services sectors:

1. Agro-based products
2. Air travel
3. Automotives
4. E-ASEAN
5. Electronics
6. Fisheries
7. Healthcare products
8. Rubber-based products
9. Textiles and apparel
10. Tourism
11. Wood-based products
12. Logistics

These sectors are slated to be integrated more rapidly through the CEPT framework by reducing tariffs to zero rates and removing NTBs over a shorter time-frame.

Thus, it may be instructive to evaluate progress on the priority goods sectors. Except for certain sectors in Cambodia, Myanmar and Vietnam, the lion's share of CEPT tariffs in ASEAN Member States are extremely low or zero (Table 2-4). And margin of preferences for member states tend to be fairly significant in percentages, except perhaps in healthcare, in which the MFN rates are also low. The original member states and Brunei Darussalam have reduced CEPT tariff rates in priority sectors to the range of 0–4 percent. Among the CLMV countries, Lao PDR has the lowest CEPT rates (1.2–2.7 percent), followed by Vietnam (1.4–4.2), Myanmar (2.0–5.8 percent), and Cambodia (3.3–12.6 percent).

Among the priority sectors, healthcare products have been liberalized the most at the multilateral and CEPT levels; all member states have reduced their tariff rates to be in line with the required CEPT level. As for agro-based and fisheries sectors, most member states have reduced their tariffs significantly, especially Lao PDR, Vietnam, Thailand, and the Philippines. In the rubber-based products and ICT sectors, all member states except Cambodia have committed to close to zero tariffs. For the wood-based and textiles sectors, members have reduced their tariff rates significantly, except Cambodia and Myanmar. Even the automotive sector has experienced significant intraregional liberalization under the CEPT scheme: Vietnam, Thailand, Malaysia, and the Lao PDR have offered the most impressive liberalizations in this sector.

Rules of Origin and Trade Facilitation

Rules of origin constitute an essential feature of any FTA in order to avoid trade deflection, i.e., trade being diverted to the lowest-tariff country and then re-exported to a take advantage of the FTA. But rules of origin have been criticized for making RTAs sub-optimal, perhaps even detrimental to growth.

Table 2-4
Average Tariffs by Priority Sectors, 2007

Sector	MFN	CEPT07	MFN	CEPT07	MFN	CEPT07	MFN	CEPT07	MFN	CEPT07
	Indonesia		Malaysia		Singapore		Thailand		Philippines	
Electronics	4.75	1.22	6.6	0.47	0.00	0.00	5.26	0.84	3.63	0.12
Automotives	17.8	3.39	19.74	1.18	0.00	0.00	27.44	0.94	14.6	1.54
Textiles and garments	10.75	1.42	12.53	0.00	0.00	0.00	17.0	0.03	10.67	0.37
Agro-based	3.81	0.30	2.49	0.74	0.00	0.00	17.37	2.04	17.0	1.59
Fisheries	5.7	0.49	2.42	0.39	0.00	0.00	12.34	0.55	8.78	0.38
Healthcare	4.32	1.33	1.37	0.17	0.00	0.00	5.45	0.92	3.16	0.17
Rubber-based	11.29	3.63	18.35	1.33	0.00	0.00	10.86	0.84	7.4	0.57
Wood-based	3.59	0.28	9.29	0.53	0.00	0.00	10.62	1.14	8.66	0.41
ICT	3.71	1.07	4.91	0.39	0.00	0.00	3.71	0.51	2.94	0.08
	Brunei		Cambodia		Lao PDR		Myanmar		Vietnam	
Electronics	10.14	1.3	18.73	7.08	8.03	1.52	4.42	2.67	15.05	2.18
Automotives	18.07	0.58	21.18	12.57	22.23	2.21	11.35	5.16	39.82	4.12
Textiles and garments	0.67	0.00	15.97	6.24	9.45	1.17	11.8	5.83	36.62	4.19
Agro-based	0.00	0.00	11.5	6.7	19.67	2.01	4.31	3.14	25.56	2.61
Fisheries	0.00	0.00	18.8	11.8	13.76	1.56	7.89	4.05	32.49	4.83
Healthcare	1.48	0.27	9.01	3.3	7.6	2.03	2.78	2.02	7.78	1.37
Rubber-based	9.70	1.48	18.4	6.87	8.67	1.71	4.71	3.96	18.61	2.19
Wood-based	13.52	1.0	14.32	10.27	27.64	2.71	13.12	5.63	12.05	2.03
ICT	9.90	0.68	18.31	6.39	7.76	1.62	4.31	2.51	9.01	2.07

Source: ASEAN Secretariat.

In NAFTA, for example, the rules of origin come to 62.5 percent in automobiles and essentially 100 percent in many textile products (under the "yarn forward" rule).

Nevertheless, research as to how much compliance with rules of origin taxes efficiency is difficult to find. One estimate (Estevadeordal and Suominen 2003) calculates the cost to be in the range of 3 percent to 5 percent of the f.o.b. value of the exported goods.[4] Augier, et al. (2005) estimate that EU rules of origin (on extra-EU trade with partners) have reduced the region's trade with outside countries 10 percent to 70 percent, suggesting significant trade and investment distortions. Harmonized and liberal rules of origin can reduce the potential costs associated with rules of origin in the context of a trade agreement like AFTA or the AEC.

ASEAN is fully cognizant that eliminating tariffs in ASEAN will not be sufficient to achieve a single market and production base. Rules of origin regimes that enable trade are also needed. Indeed, the AEC Blueprint explicitly mandates continuous reforms to

> enhance the CEPT RoO to respond to changes in regional production processes, including making necessary adjustments such as the introduction of advance rulings and improvements to the RoO and simplify the Operational Certification Procedures for the CEPT RoO and ensure its continuous enhancement, including the introduction of facilitative processes such as the electronic processing of certificates of origin, and harmonisation or alignment of national procedures to the extent possible.

Along these lines, there have been efforts to liberalize and simplify rules of origin, particularly with regard to the screening and procedural aspects of acquiring certificates of origin. There is agreement that the regime should move toward simpler and unrestrictive rules. Simpler rules will promote regional trade and competitiveness by lowering compliance costs, reducing administrative burdens such as trade and customs procedures, and facilitating fragmented trade and production networks.

Toward Simplification

Very early on in the formation of AFTA, it was recognized that textile and textile products might be hard put to meet the 40 percent ASEAN origin rule. In 1995, it was therefore decided that ASEAN textile and garment exporters could use either the percentage value-added or the substantial transformation rule. Rules were adjusted again in 2003, when operational procedures were clarified and simplified and it was decided that a Change in Tariff Heading (CTH) rule should be adopted for determining origin as a general alternative rule. As of 2006, the CTH was fully endorsed for four sectors: wheat-flour, wood-based products, aluminum products, and iron and steel. These reforms are indeed heading toward simplification and less restriction. AFTA has introduced CTH as a substitute criterion for an increasing number of products. ASEAN has also introduced product-specific rules when the value added or the CTH rules appears harder to meet.

Cumulation and Economies of Scale

Another reform lies in the use of cumulation-type rules of origin. By allowing advanced countries to outsource labor-intensive production to low-wage partners, full cumulation encourages regional production networks. With already simple rules of origin, full cumulation will make it easier for regional firms to exploit economies of scale. ASEAN is further refining its rules of origin by developing a "partial" cumulation rule such that even goods of "partial" origin not having satisfied the 40 percent threshold can be cumulated as part of regional value content.[5] The advantages and disadvantages of various approaches to rules of origin are summarized in Table 2-5.

Simpler Procedures and Trade Facilitation

The WTO (1998) defines trade facilitation as the "simplification and harmonization of international trade procedures," where trade procedures are the "activities, practices and formalities involved in collecting, presenting, communicating and processing data required for the movement of goods in international trade." Practitioners view trade facilitation as the simplification, harmonization, standardization, and modernization of trade procedures. In defining trade facilitation the AEC Blueprint notes that

> Simple, harmonized and standardized trade and customs, processes, procedures and related information flows are expected to reduce transaction cost to enhance export competitiveness and facilitate the integration of ASEAN into a single market for goods, services and investments and a single production base.

As trade volume increases particularly across the ASEAN Member States, customs administrations must assume more responsibilities and challenging tasks. Trade facilitation is therefore intended to assist customs administrations in carrying out and simplifying their duties (Grainger 2007).

Table 2-5
Approaches to Rules of Origin

Rule	Advantages	Disadvantages	Key Issues
Change of tariff classification in the Harmonized System (CTH)	Consistent with nonpreferential rules of origin Once defined, unambiguous and easy to learn Relatively straightforward to implement	System not designed for conferring origin: many product-specific rules can be influenced by domestic industries Documentary requirements may be difficult to comply with Conflicts over goods classification can introduce uncertainty over market areas	Level of classification at which change required: the higher the level, the more restrictive Can be positive (which imported inputs allowed) or negative (cases in which change of classification won't confer origin) test: negative test more restrictive
Regional Value Content (RVC)	Simple to specify and unambiguous Allows for general rather than product-specific rules	Complex to apply: requires firms to have sophisticated accounting systems Uncertainty due to sensitivity to changes in exchange rates, wages, commodity prices, etc.	The level of value-added required to confer origin The valuation method for imported materials: methods that assign a higher value (e.g. CIF) will be more restrictive on the use of imported inputs
Specific manufacturing process (PSR)	Once defined, unambiguous Provides for certainty if rules can be complied with	Documentary requirements can be burdensome and difficult to comply with Leads to product-specific rules Can quickly become obsolete due to technological progress and require frequent modification	Formulation of specific processes required: the more procedures required, the more restrictive Should test be negative (processes or inputs that can't be used) or positive (what can be used)?

Source: Adopted from Brenton, Paul and Hiroshi Imagawa, "Rules of Origin, Trade and Customs," Chapter 9 in De Wulf, Luc and José B. Sokol, Customs Modernization Handbook (Washington, D.C.: World Bank, 2005), Annex 9.A.

ASEAN has undertaken various measures to reduce transaction costs: the ASEAN Customs Agreement of 1997, the ASEAN Framework Agreement on the Facilitation of Goods in Transit, ASEAN Framework Agreement on Multimodal Transport and the implementation of the ASEAN Framework Agreement on Mutual Recognition Agreement. The ASEAN Single Window Agreement (discussed below) is the most significant and far-reaching for trade facilitation.

The AEC envisages reductions in transaction costs through reforms in member states. A broad range of regional and national activities are being undertaken to facilitate trade but there are no baseline indicators by which to measure progress. Thus, ASEAN Economic Ministers (AEM) endorsed a proposal to develop an ASEAN Trade Facilitation Work Program (ATFWP) for 2007–2015. Now a part of the ASEAN Trade in Goods Agreement, the purpose of the program is to reduce transaction costs in ASEAN to enhance export competitiveness and help unify markets for goods, services, and investments. The program will enable ASEAN to undertake trade facilitation reforms and reduce trade transaction costs.[6]

All ASEAN Member States agreed to adopt the ASEAN Harmonized Tariff Nomenclature (AHTN), a system of tariff classification in January 2002. AHTN has an 8-digit commodity nomenclature based on the Harmonized System (HS) and involves aligning national tariff nomenclatures of ASEAN Member States with HS 2002. The AHTN constitutes a milestone in ASEAN Customs integration through the promotion of a uniform and consistent classification of goods, which should facilitate trade in the region considerably.

ASEAN integration appears to be lowering trade costs, a trend that should deepen as the AEC is implemented. According to Taylor and Wilson (2008) the trade costs of Southeast Asian countries are already low. For instance, costs associated with paperwork and time required to complete cross-border transactions have fallen significantly. Pomfret and Sourdin (2009) show that costs for ASEAN exports to Australia — a good proxy country — fell from over 10 percent in 1990 to less than 4 percent in 2007. This is significantly better than the drop in costs on overall imports to Australia; ASEAN's trade costs went from being higher than the world average in 1990 to being lower in 2007, a testament to trade facilitation in ASEAN both in absolute and relative terms. The authors note that for the original ASEAN countries, the biggest reduction in costs occurred during the AFTA-implementation phase prior to 2002, and for Vietnam and Myanmar after they joined ASEAN and began implementing AFTA in the late 1990s.

Nevertheless, more needs to be done. The World Bank (2009) shows that trade costs for many ASEAN countries continue to be high, at least relative to best practices.[7] For example, the "time to export" for the OECD averages 10.7 days, whereas it takes 22 days for Cambodia, 21 for Indonesia, 16 for the Philippines, and 24 for Vietnam. The number of documents needed for trade (especially imports) also tends to be considerably higher in ASEAN than for the OECD, and the "time for export" is significantly higher, up to 50 days for Lao PDR compared to 11 days for the OECD. Still, ASEAN performs well in the "cost to export" and "cost to import" categories (some member states even have lower costs than the OECD average).

Customs administration and procedures can drive up costs, a fact that has motivated considerable action on ASEAN cooperation. For example, with respect to customs harmonization, the Hanoi Plan of Action specifies (2.1.2, "Customs Harmonisation") that ASEAN should:

- Enhance trade facilitation in customs by simplifying customs procedures, expanding the Green Lane to cover all ASEAN products and implementing an ASEAN Harmonized Tariff Nomenclature by the year 2000;
- Promote transparency, consistency and uniformity in the classification of goods traded within ASEAN and enhance trade facilitation through the provision of facilities for obtaining pre-entry classification rulings/decisions at national and regional levels by the year 2003;
- Promote the use of transparent, consistent and uniform valuation methods and rulings through the implementation of the WTO Valuation Agreement by the year 2000;
- Operationalize and strengthen regional guidelines on mutual assistance by the year 2003 to ensure the proper application of customs laws, within the competence of the customs administrations and subject to their national laws;
- Fully operationalize the ASEAN Customs Training Network by the year 2000; and
- Undertake customs reform and modernization, in particular to implement risk management and post-importation audit by the year 2003.

ASEAN has made good progress in all these areas. Building on the Hanoi Action Plan, the ASEAN Single Window (ASW) Agreement was signed in 2005 to expedite clearance of imports and achieve an average cargo release time of 30 minutes by interconnecting national single windows. NSWs for the ASEAN-6 were to be finalized by 2008, and the CLMV have until 2012.

Nontariff Barriers

Nontariff barriers are the most significant barriers to global trade. They tend to be far more opaque, complicated, and distorting than tariffs. And as tariffs have faded in significance NTBs have become more prominent. Liberalizing trade in goods by 2015 will require eliminating NTBs by having member states abide by the Protocol on Notification procedure, set up effective surveillance mechanisms and the like, and abide by their commitment to "standstill and roll-back" NTBs. Under the AEC, Brunei, Indonesia, Malaysia, Thailand, and Singapore will eliminate NTBs by 2010; the Philippines by 2012; and the CLMV by 2015 (with some flexibilities to 2018). In addition, the region will work to create regional rules and regulations consistent with international best practices.

In sum, while ASEAN is to be commended for eliminating tariffs through AFTA-CEPT, a step that paid for itself in strong growth, it must now eliminate NTBs, a step that will likely have a greater positive effect on efficiency and growth. Indeed, MFN applied rates and CEPT preferential rates for imports are already low and any further gains from complete removal in the context of the AEC will be small. Removing NTBs will do much more. Dean, Feinberg, Signoret, Ferrantino and Ludema (2006) estimate that NTBs in five major ASEAN countries have increased prices significantly (e.g., in the range of 73 percent to 205 percent in fruits and vegetables; 82 percent to 109 percent in bovine meat; and 93 percent to 112 percent in processed food). Removing these barriers could lower business costs and consumer prices significantly. Our empirical model presented in the next section is one of the few to include NTB elimination at the sectoral level. Our simulations show the large gains from removing NTBs.

A CGE APPROACH TO ESTIMATING THE EFFECTS OF THE AEC

The AEC constitutes an important change in the depth of economic integration. As noted earlier, empirical evidence in the literature suggests that economic integration through AFTA and other regional measures has had a positive if modest effect on trade and growth in ASEAN. Impediments to intraregional trade and investment such as NTBs, border controls, and so forth, continue to limit the potential of that integration. By creating a single market and production base, the AEC will go a long way in freeing the region of these limits; we argue above and in other chapters that the effects of these measures should be significant in spurring intraregional trade, FDI, and growth. We might already be seeing this; the anticipatory effect of the AEC noted above may have helped the strong growth in GDP, trade, and FDI in the ASEAN region since 2003,[8] when ASEAN leaders declared their intention to create an AEC. Much remains to be done before 2015. However, the AEC Blueprint details the type of measures that the region requires to move toward its potential.

Once the AEC is functioning how will it affect regional welfare? To date, no study has tried to estimate the potential effects of implementing AEC Blueprint measures in this regard. We attempt to do this here. We begin with a brief summary of studies related to our analysis then present our CGE model and the results from our simulations.

CGE Literature on Potential of Deep Integration

AFTA and other economic initiatives have already had an important effect on trade and welfare. Estimating the effects of an FTA is straightforward: reduce tariffs on intraregional trade (and in some cases NTBs) and trace the effects on trade, structural change, welfare, and returns to the factors of production using, for example, a CGE simulation. The AEC builds on AFTA but the complicated measures articulated in the AEC Blueprint to create a single market, such as trade facilitation, are notoriously difficult to quantify. Yet, doing so is necessary to see how the AEC could affect trade in goods.

To show the differences between "traditional estimates" — induced by liberalization of tariff and tariff-equivalent NTBs — of gains due to trade liberalization in Asia (Scenario 1) and more general trade-cost reduction effects such as improving customs clearance, lower transaction costs, and facilitation of international market access (Scenario 2), Brooks, Roland-Holst and Zhai (2005) run simulations to compare the aggregate impact on real income, exports, and terms of trade.[9] They assume that trade costs not related to policy are around 120 percent and are cut by half over a 20-year period for East Asia, Southeast Asia and South Asia.[10] The results are illuminating. Under Scenario 1, real income rises 0.9 percent to 2.9 percent for East Asia, 1.9 percent to 6.6 percent for Southeast Asia, and 0.3 percent to 0.6 percent for South Asia. Such magnitudes are fairly standard in the literature. Under Scenario 2, the gains are many times as large, 8.1 percent to 53.8 percent, 35.5 percent to 116.6 percent, and 10.4 percent to 22.4 percent, respectively. The AEC aims at efficiency increases of the type modeled in Scenario 2; by this comparison, we could see the AEC building significantly on AFTA and enhancing gains by many times the mere FTA scenario.

Other studies on benefits from trade facilitation also show large attendant gains, though not to the extent of Brooks et al. (2005). For example, De Dios (2006) estimates that a 10 percent savings in transport costs will increase trade by approximately 6 percent. Wilson and Shepherd (2008) show that the gains from trade facilitation will yield far greater gains than comparable tariff reforms. For example, improving port facilities alone in ASEAN should expand trade by 7.5 percent, or $22 billion. Estimates of the effects of improvements in infrastructure development noted in the AEC Blueprint on Indonesia, Malaysia, the Philippines, and Thailand should increase per capita GDP in these countries by 2 percent to 12 percent.[11]

One "natural experiment" by which to estimate potential benefits would be the EC's Single Market Program, which did not focus on best practices but on improving efficiency by harmonizing the types of policies included in this section. The EC at the time was already a customs union, but it did not have a common commercial policy[12] and its markets were segmented in many ways. The famous "Cecchini Report" (Cecchini 1988) estimated that the ultimate effect of the Single Market Program would be to increase EC GDP in the range of 2.4–6.5 percent. This is in addition to integration measures already in place after 30 years of regional cooperation. Economies of scale, one of the main advantages of creating the EC single market and production base, alone accounted for a 2 percent increase in EC GDP. Now, these estimates included some measures that go well beyond what the AEC entails. Still, ASEAN was not as integrated as the EC was at the time of the Single Market, and the AEC does focus more on best practices than mere national treatment, which was the overarching goal of the EC. While one would expect to see large effects in the EC case in some areas, the AEC might well generate significantly larger benefits in others.

Hertel, Walmsley, and Itakura (2001) analyze the potential gains from the Japan — Singapore FTA, which is interesting for our purposes because it is a "new age" deep-integration agreement inclusive of many of the measures outlined in the AEC Blueprint. Moreover, since Japan's average tariff is less than 2 percent in manufactures and Singapore essentially has a zero average tariff, these effects are insignificant in the modeling exercise, making it somewhat comparable to ASEAN under AFTA.[13] They essentially develop a dynamic CGE/GTAP-based model using an *ex ante* simulation but with some *ex post* features in estimating some "dynamic" and policy-related changes that one would expect from a deep-integration accord such as the Japan — Singapore FTA. Thus, they add to traditional trade barrier effects the harmonization of e-commerce standards, liberalizing rules in trade in services, automating customs services in Japan (to be consistent with Singapore), and investment flows. Interestingly, given the nature of this new age agreement, *all* regions of the world gain, including, of course, Japan and Singapore. Fully 70 percent of the gains accrue to Japan (a good share of which due to improved customs services). Hertel, et al. stress that it is precisely the "new age features" that drive positive results for all.

CGE Model of the AEC[14]

Our CGE model is a version of a global general equilibrium model developed by Mensbrugghe (2005) and Zhai (2008). The model has its intellectual roots in the group of multicountry, applied general equilibrium models used over the past two decades to analyze the impact of trade policy reform (Shoven and Whalley, 1992; Hertel, 1997). Many of the CGE studies cited above are grounded in this tradition. A novel feature of the model is its incorporation of recent heterogeneous-firms trade theory into an empirical global CGE framework. The model features intra-industry firm heterogeneity in productivity and fixed cost of exporting, which enables us to investigate the intra-industry reallocation of resources and the exporting decision by firms, and thereby capture both the intensive and extensive margin of trade. Such an approach is more realistic than the usual assumption of homogeneous firms and is a special advantage in the context of an outward-oriented region like ASEAN. The model is calibrated to the GTAP (version 7) global database, which was released in November 2008 and uses 2004 as the base year. It includes 22 country/regions, including all ASEAN countries, and 21 sectors, giving us a fairly good breakdown of sectors. All results are for 2015 under IMF growth projections for the baseline.

In Appendix B we outline the key features of the model.[15] Suffice it to note here that our model endeavors to capture the "value added" of the AEC through a variety of innovative channels:

- In addition to allowing for the complete removal of tariffs within ASEAN, the model allows for the elimination of NTBs. Because NTB data are not in the GTAP database we use disaggregated trade restrictiveness data available through the World Bank to match up NTBs with our sectoral disaggregation.[16]
- To include the FDI effects, we use our estimates of AEC-induced changes in FDI (Chapter 4). Hence, while FDI is exogenous in this model, we do estimate these changes separately.
- We include five service sectors: utilities, construction, trade transport, private services (including financial services), and government services. Moreover, we include ad valorem equivalents of barriers to trade in services (Table 1-6 in Chapter 1), calculated by the Michigan Model team.[17]
- We assume that trade costs will fall by 5 percent in the AEC. This is an extremely conservative assumption. However, in this modeling exercise we strive to generate "lower bound" estimates in order to be on the safe side. This fall in trade costs is modeled using an "iceberg" approach, which has become a traditional technique.

Results

In our modeling exercises, we have five scenarios:

- *Scenario 1 (AFTA)*: removal of all remaining tariffs in ASEAN (i.e., completion of AFTA).
- *Scenario 2 (AFTA+)*: Scenario 1 plus the removal of NTBs and a 5 percent reduction in trade costs (i.e., as a percentage of trade values).
- *Scenario 3 (AEC)*: Scenario 2 plus FDI effects.
- *Scenario 4 (AEC Spoke 1 FTAs)*: Scenario 3 plus an FTA with the rest of the East Asian Summit countries (i.e., Australia, New Zealand, India, Japan, China, and South Korea). Note: this scenario does not assume that the "+6" countries eliminate barriers to trade between themselves.
- *Scenario 5 (AEC Spoke 2 FTAs)*: Scenario 4 plus FTAs with the United States and EU.

The estimated welfare effects of these scenarios are presented in Table 2-6, with section A giving results in US$ billions and section B in percent change in GDP.[18] The results are illuminating.

Table 2-6
Welfare Gains in 2015

	A. US$ billions, 2004 price, EV					B. Percent of baseline GDP, EV				
	AFTA	AFTA+	AEC	AEC+ S1	AEC+ S2	AFTA	AFTA+	AEC	AEC+ S1	AEC+ S2
ASEAN	10.1	38.0	69.4	115.6	151.0	0.8	2.9	5.3	8.9	11.6
Brunei	0.2	0.4	0.5	0.6	0.7	2.6	5.4	7.0	9.3	10.6
Cambodia	0.3	0.5	0.6	0.7	1.2	2.7	5.4	6.3	7.2	12.3
Indonesia	1.0	6.2	27.6	36.5	43.2	0.2	1.4	6.2	8.2	9.7
Lao PDR	0.0	0.1	0.2	0.2	0.2	0.6	2.5	3.6	3.8	4.6
Malaysia	2.7	2.9	5.7	21.1	27.9	1.4	1.5	3.0	11.2	14.7
Myanmar	0.0	0.2	0.6	0.7	1.4	0.3	1.2	4.4	4.8	9.3
Philippines	0.9	2.2	4.5	4.4	5.9	0.6	1.6	3.2	3.2	4.3
Singapore	2.6	14.0	15.1	18.1	19.0	1.6	9.0	9.7	11.6	12.2
Thailand	1.6	9.8	12.2	19.5	25.8	0.6	3.9	4.9	7.8	10.4
Vietnam	0.9	1.6	2.4	13.8	25.7	1.1	1.8	2.8	16.0	29.8
Partners (Spoke 1)										
China	0.4	−4.6	−7.8	−6.5	−12.2	0.0	−0.1	−0.2	−0.1	−0.3
Japan	0.1	−1.3	−1.6	9.2	7.3	0.0	0.0	0.0	0.2	0.1
Korea	−0.2	−1.4	−2.7	10.6	9.1	0.0	−0.1	−0.3	1.1	0.9
India	0.8	0.1	−0.8	23.9	23.5	0.1	0.0	−0.1	1.7	1.6
Australia	−0.0	−0.2	0.2	0.3	0.1	0.0	0.0	0.0	0.0	0.0
New Zealand	−0.1	−0.1	−0.1	−0.1	−0.2	0.0	−0.1	−0.1	0.0	−0.1
Partners (Spoke 2)										
US	0.2	−2.8	−1.8	−3.7	−3.6	0.0	0.0	0.0	0.0	0.0
Europe	−0.3	−7.1	−2.3	−5.4	−6.2	0.0	0.0	0.0	0.0	0.0
Other economies						0.0	0.0	0.0	0.0	0.0
Hong Kong (China)	0.0	0.3	−0.2	0.3	0.3	0.0	0.1	−0.1	0.1	0.1
Taiwan (China)	−0.1	−0.8	−1.4	−3.2	−3.6	0.0	−0.2	−0.3	−0.8	−0.9
Canada	0.0	−0.1	0.4	0.8	0.7	0.0	0.0	0.0	0.1	0.1
Rest of World	0.4	−0.5	1.4	1.6	0.4	0.0	0.0	0.0	0.0	0.0
World	11.4	19.4	52.7	143.4	166.8		0.0	0.0	0.1	0.3

- First, the overall increase in ASEAN real income (relative to the baseline) of the AEC comes to $69 billion, or 5.3 percent of ASEAN GDP — a large increase especially given the conservative underlying assumptions. They increase the potential gains in ASEAN of completing the AFTA by more than fivefold.
- Second, all ASEAN Member States gain from the AEC, though obviously some gain more than others. The range of gains runs from a 2.8 percent increase in real income (Vietnam) to 9.7 percent (Singapore).[19] Cambodia gains the most out of the CLMV countries, with real income rising by 6.3 percent.
- Third, considerable gains are generated by extending the AEC to include ASEAN's East Asian partners and the United States/EU. This underscores the importance of keeping the AEC open and testifies to the wisdom of the "integration into the global economy" pillar of the AEC (see Chapter 6). For example, adding FTAs with East Asia, the United States and the EU to the AEC more than doubles the gains. Here, Vietnam is perhaps the most notable; while it gains the least from the AEC, it gains by far the most from the AEC-Spoke 2 scenario, with an estimated increase in its GDP of almost 30 percent, better than 10 times its potential gains from the AEC alone.

Next, we consider the implications for international trade. Table 2-7 summarizes the impact of our five scenarios on ASEAN exports and imports. Clearly, ASEAN trade is expected to boom with the AEC: exports grow at a rate that is 43 percent above the baseline, and imports by slightly less (35 percent), suggesting a modest improvement in the trade balance but a significant rise in the internationalization of the economies. Given the potential productivity spillovers associated with international trade (generally excluded in this model), the secondary effects of the strong increase in trade could be extremely important in making member states more competitive. The CLMV do particularly well in this regard; Lao PDR exports are expected to better than double and Cambodian exports should rise by more than three-fourths due to the AEC.

At the sectoral level, we note that the AEC should have important structural implications for the ASEAN economies. In general, primary materials tend to contract, whereas manufacturing output booms. Electrical equipment is expected to grow by the most (35.9 percent), followed closely by machinery (34.3 percent) and metals (31.9 percent). All service sectors also gain — particularly utilities (8.6 percent) and construction (7.3 percent) — with the exception of government services, which contracts slightly (0.9 percent). See Table 2-8.

Finally, we examine estimated changes in the sectoral composition of international trade due to the AEC. Exports of grains (163 percent), metals (140 percent), and food (113 percent) each better than double due to the AEC (Table 2-9). Vehicles (86 percent) and machinery (59 percent) also increase significantly. In terms of services exports, only construction exports rise (33 percent). Imports of food increase impressively (196 percent), as does paddy rice (144 percent). All service categories experience a significant increase in imports due to the AEC. See Table 2-10.

In short, the "value added" of the AEC should be large. It should generate considerable gains in efficiency due to the removal of barriers to intraregional trade and other aspects of the "single market and production base" endeavor. It should enhance structural change throughout the region and lead to a significant increase in international trade, with its associated spillover effects on productivity and economic dynamism.

However, our modeling exercise also points out the crucial importance of keeping the AEC open; it is clearly in ASEAN's interest to create a "hub and spoke" system in which ASEAN itself constitutes the hub.

Table 2-7
Effects on International Trade as Percent Change from Baseline, 2015

	Exports					Imports				
	AFTA	AFTA+	AEC	AEC+ S1	AEC+ S2	AFTA	AFTA+	AEC	AEC+ S1	AEC+ S2
ASEAN	6.5	31.2	42.6	70.9	88.9	7.0	32.7	35.4	67.8	86.4
Brunei	2.1	9.8	10.4	8.6	13.7	6.1	28.1	30.1	27.2	41.8
Cambodia	37.0	70.3	77.6	86.8	113.9	39.5	76.5	82.0	93.4	135.3
Indonesia	6.5	22.5	53.6	84.0	109.5	7.1	24.3	17.6	60.0	86.0
Lao PDR	41.0	85.0	101.1	103.6	110.3	32.8	70.0	73.3	75.7	82.3
Malaysia	4.5	26.4	35.6	56.3	65.4	6.0	34.2	40.6	70.9	81.4
Myanmar	8.7	43.9	65.8	100.7	163.2	7.8	39.7	45.1	78.9	132.9
Philippines	2.9	25.4	45.4	67.3	82.4	3.0	27.2	34.0	55.8	69.9
Singapore	4.5	39.7	43.7	61.1	64.9	4.4	34.5	38.1	54.5	58.1
Thailand	8.8	27.8	33.6	63.5	85.5	9.8	31.5	34.7	72.2	97.8
Vietnam	15.4	49.0	55.4	160.1	239.5	14.3	43.1	47.1	129.8	197.4
Partners (Spoke 1)										
China	0.0	−0.7	−0.8	7.5	6.9	0.0	−0.8	−0.8	7.7	6.9
Japan	−0.1	−0.6	−0.5	8.4	7.6	0.0	−0.5	0.1	10.8	9.9
Korea	−0.2	−1.1	−1.5	7.1	6.6	−0.1	−0.9	−1.2	8.1	7.6
India	0.1	−0.1	−0.3	57.4	57.0	0.1	0.0	−0.2	40.8	40.8
Australia	−0.1	−0.5	−1.0	5.3	4.4	−0.1	−0.4	0.3	7.5	6.6
New Zealand	−0.3	−0.5	−0.6	6.1	5.1	−0.4	−0.5	−0.3	8.4	7.3
Partners (Spoke 2)										
US	0.0	−0.3	−0.8	−1.4	2.9	0.0	−0.1	0.2	0.3	3.3
Europe	−0.1	−0.3	−0.9	−1.3	0.6	0.0	−0.1	0.1	0.4	2.4
Other economies										
Hong Kong (China)	0.0	−0.2	−3.0	−3.7	−4.1	0.0	0.3	0.2	0.7	0.6
Taiwan (China)	−0.1	−0.9	−1.4	−3.3	−3.7	−0.2	−1.1	−1.4	−3.8	−4.3
Canada	0.0	−0.2	−0.8	−1.1	−1.3	0.0	−0.1	0.1	0.2	0.0
Rest of World	−0.1	−0.2	−0.6	−1.0	−1.4	0.0	−0.1	0.2	0.4	0.1
World	0.4	1.8	2.1	6.4	8.4	0.4	1.8	2.2	6.6	8.6

FREE FLOW OF SERVICES

During the past three decades, the world economy has undergone rapid structural transformation. One major change is the rising importance of the services sector, in part a function of the rising importance of information communication technology (ICT), finance, and telecommunications (OECD 2002). In many countries the services sector itself has now become the largest economic sector as well as the most important source of jobs. Over the 1990–2005 period, the growth rate of services in Southeast Asia was relatively robust compared to other major components of GDP, in the 5 percent to 9 percent range on average per year (Figure 2-1). Over the 1995–2007 period, services as a percentage of total output in Southeast Asia grew in most countries, and in Cambodia, Indonesia, Malaysia, Singapore, and Thailand, the share came to 40 percent or higher (Figure 2-2). The share of trade in services as a percentage of total trade grew in half of the ASEAN countries over 2000–2007 (Figure 2-3), which is especially significant given the large increase in total trade over that period.

Table 2-8
Changes in Sectoral Output (% change from baseline, 2015)

	AFTA	AFTA+	AEC	AEC+S1	AEC+S2
PRIMARY MATERIALS					
Paddy rice	−1.2	−3.5	−4.6	−3.8	−1.6
Grains, other	−2.7	0.7	−5.0	−13.4	−24.5
Crops, other	0.0	−1.0	−2.8	4.3	1.6
Livestock	1.8	0.1	−0.2	5.8	6.5
Natural resources	−0.3	−2.5	−3.1	−4.1	−5.3
Mining	0.1	−0.5	−1.1	−2.3	−2.8
MANUFACTURING					
Food	8.6	9.8	12.8	53.7	50.8
Textiles	5.8	8.2	27.3	35.4	81.4
Wood products	1.8	−4.7	3.0	−11.1	−16.7
Apparel	5.7	9.0	18.4	90.0	194.3
Chemicals	2.0	4.1	12.6	13.8	13.4
Metals	1.1	18.2	31.9	4.1	9.2
Electrical equipment	−1.9	23.4	35.9	47.0	51.8
Machinery	1.2	21.3	34.3	39.2	37.7
Vehicles	3.6	13.9	22.8	−5.7	−6.8
Other manufactures	0.3	2.3	10.3	7.3	7.0
SERVICES					
Utilities	0.4	1.4	8.6	4.9	5.7
Construction	0.2	3.6	7.3	13.0	14.5
Trade, transport	−0.7	−3.2	1.9	0.3	0.3
Private services	−1.5	−7.7	1.7	−3.9	−9.4
Government services	0.0	−0.6	−0.9	−1.0	−1.0

Several factors contribute to this trend: rapid urbanization, public sector expansion, and rising demand for intermediate services used as inputs to other sectors and for final consumer services. Moreover, global trade in services has been growing even faster than merchandise trade (Arkell 2001). For example, global trade in commercial services has grown steadily by about 6 percent per annum over the 1990–2000 period (WTO 2005). The service sector also accounts for some 40 percent of the global annual stock of FDI (WTO Annual Report 2001).

The vital role of the services sector in the domestic economy is reflected at the international level as well. Until the Uruguay Round of GATT, services trade was not part of multilateral trade negotiations. The Uruguay Round established the General Agreement on Trade in Services (GATS), which went into effect in 1995. The objective of GATS is to promote trade in services and liberalization of such trade through negotiations, transparency in rules and regulations, and increasing participation of developing countries. The GATS covers all services except those supplied by a governmental authority on non-commercial basis and not in competition with other service suppliers (Chanda 2002; Hilbert 2003).

Besides reform at the multilateral level under GATS, liberalization has become an important part of RTA negotiations. For instance, the members of ASEAN concluded the ASEAN Framework Agreement on Services (AFAS), and Australia and New Zealand have concluded the Closer Economic Relations Agreement (CER) covering services trade. Meanwhile, Southern Cone Common Market

Table 2-9
Changes in Sectoral Exports (% change from baseline, 2015)

	AFTA	AFTA+	AEC	AEC+S1	AEC+S2
PRIMARY MATERIALS					
Paddy rice	11.1	19.7	17.9	30.6	49.2
Grains, other	8.1	171.2	163.4	40.9	14.4
Crops, other	7.0	22.7	10.3	48.2	45.8
Livestock	8.3	24.4	13.3	1.5	8.4
Natural resources	0.4	−1.1	−10.0	−17.9	−20.7
Mining	−0.1	0.6	−10.8	−6.1	−8.3
MANUFACTURING					
Food	71.7	105.8	113.1	278.4	285.5
Textiles	14.4	26.5	56.3	128.1	240.2
Wood products	8.5	5.5	16.3	3.2	−1.1
Apparel	10.3	17.6	31.8	185.0	389.5
Chemicals	7.4	26.9	34.3	69.3	70.8
Metals	4.9	114.7	139.7	83.6	104.5
Electrical equipment	−2.2	29.9	45.7	61.4	68.9
Machinery	2.5	42.4	59.0	76.9	76.9
Vehicles	18.6	70.1	85.7	83.3	88.5
Other manufactures	1.6	12.7	29.6	41.0	44.2
SERVICES					
Utilities	−2.5	−16.4	−2.7	−22.4	−28.3
Construction	−1.8	16.1	32.9	39.5	52.7
Trade, transport	−4.7	−21.8	−16.6	−20.5	−0.2
Private services	−7.2	−27.9	−22.5	−35.4	−13.5
Government services	−1.0	−11.7	−17.2	−23.7	−10.4

(Mercosur) member countries of Latin America have chosen to follow the GATS-type approach to open their services market gradually.

The inclusion of services in global trade liberalization creates opportunities and challenges for economies and businesses. In this regard, the services sector in ASEAN countries must respond rapidly and flexibly to demands for competitiveness, efficiency, and productivity to achieve the objectives outlined in the AEC Blueprint. In the following subsections we focus on the services sector as a whole, including an overview of the objectives of the AEC for services liberalization, the definition and classifications of the services sector, the development of the services sector in ASEAN, and services liberalization under AFAS. We conclude by suggesting policies to help achieve a free flow of services trade under the framework of the AEC.

Services Definitions and Classifications

Among economists there is no widely accepted definition of services or consensus on how they should be defined. This has hampered the compilation and disaggregation of services data (Sieh, Mahani and Loke 2000). Generally, data on the sector in most countries are highly aggregated, often inconsistent, and tend to underestimate the output of the services sector (Sieh, Mahani and Loke 2000).

Table 2-10
Changes in Sectoral Imports of ASEAN (% change from baseline, 2015)

	AFTA	AFTA+	AEC	AEC+S1	AEC+S2
PRIMARY MATERIALS					
Paddy rice	52.6	133.2	144.4	141.8	162.5
Grains, other	0.8	3.9	12.3	80.8	92.2
Crops, other	6.9	19.1	26.8	74.3	109.0
Livestock	2.2	8.9	12.3	62.9	90.5
Natural resources	3.5	5.1	6.4	19.3	20.4
Mining	2.4	9.3	15.7	20.9	22.4
MANUFACTURING					
Food	116.2	188.7	196.9	295.9	340.2
Textiles	10.8	26.3	31.9	157.5	267.8
Wood products	12.6	36.0	38.5	80.0	97.8
Apparel	6.2	20.7	21.5	147.7	247.7
Chemicals	5.5	26.1	27.8	62.9	75.9
Metals	3.0	49.5	53.2	67.2	71.3
Electrical equipment	−0.9	23.0	30.8	47.9	51.6
Machinery	1.5	20.1	24.7	42.2	44.2
Vehicles	5.9	24.4	24.7	74.5	79.9
Other manufactures	3.1	31.0	30.9	85.8	107.9
SERVICES					
Utilities	4.6	26.4	27.6	35.4	41.0
Construction	4.4	31.4	22.7	73.1	142.8
Trade, transport	4.7	37.5	35.9	77.7	124.1
Private services	3.2	33.2	18.1	54.6	120.0
Government services	1.6	11.2	14.5	26.1	40.2

Modern economic theory suggests that there may be no need to separate economic analysis of trade in services from that of trade in goods (Delunay and Gadrey 1992).[20] But frequently cited distinguishing features of services are that they are intangible, invisible and perishable, which requires simultaneous production and consumption. Many services share these features but some have tangible outputs. For instance, photographs produced by photographers and internet banking do not require direct contact between customer and suppliers, and software programs can be stored on diskettes and transmitted.

In most ASEAN Member States, the services sector comprises final services for consumption, such as hotels and restaurants, the wholesale and retail trade, and intermediate services, including business and professional services, transport and communications, finance, insurance, information technology and computer services. Some have reclassified these services subsectors broadly into three subgroups: producer, public, and other (Economic Report 1991/1992). Producer services comprise transport, storage and communications and the finance, insurance, real estate and business services subsectors. This group provides the ancillary services and financing requirements for the leading sectors of the economy such as agriculture, mining, manufacturing, and construction. Meanwhile, public services are generally provided by the public sector such as health and education, defense and security, water and

Figure 2-1
Average Annual Services Growth Rate, 1990–2004 (%)

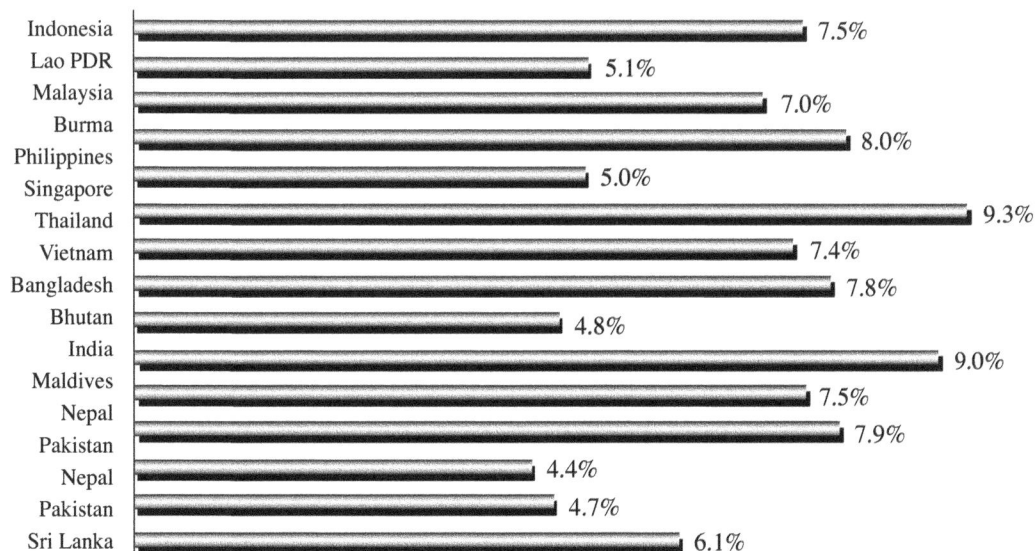

Country	Growth Rate
Indonesia	7.5%
Lao PDR	5.1%
Malaysia	7.0%
Burma	8.0%
Philippines	5.0%
Singapore	
Thailand	9.3%
Vietnam	7.4%
Bangladesh	7.8%
Bhutan	4.8%
India	9.0%
Maldives	7.5%
Nepal	7.9%
Pakistan	
Nepal	4.4%
Pakistan	4.7%
Sri Lanka	6.1%

Source: Karthikeyan (2007).

Figure 2-2
Share of Services in GDP (Selected Years, %)

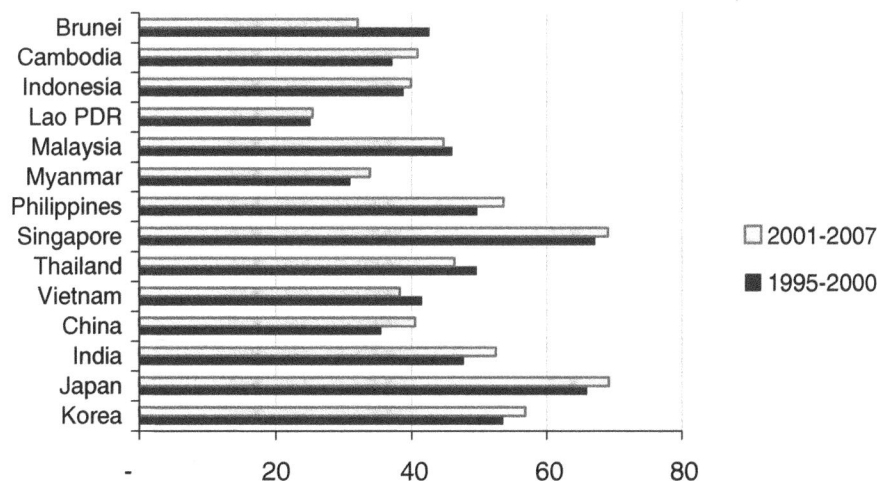

Brunei, Cambodia, Indonesia, Lao PDR, Malaysia, Myanmar, Philippines, Singapore, Thailand, Vietnam, China, India, Japan, Korea

☐ 2001-2007 ■ 1995-2000

Note: Japan, Lao PDR data available only until 2006; for Myanmar, only until 2005.
Source: ADB Key Indicators.

electricity supplies as well as sanitary services. Finally, the other services subgroup comprises the wholesale and retail trade, hotels and restaurants and the other services subsectors. Most countries classify their services sector based on the standard criteria provided by the United Nations Provisional Central Product Classifications (CPC) for the purpose of national accounting.

Figure 2-3
Share of Trade in Services in Total Trade (Selected Years, %)

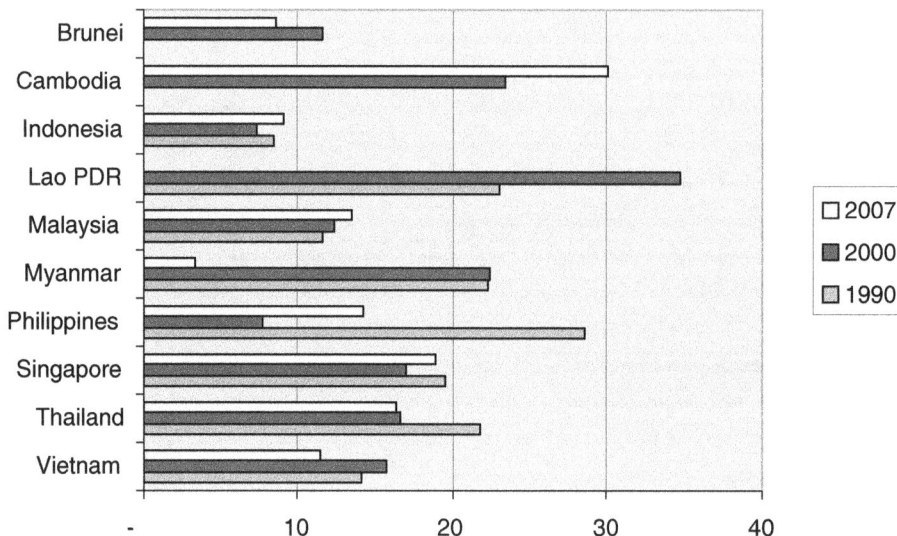

Note: Data for Brunei Darussalam are for 2001 and 2006. Data for 2007 are estimates for all ASEAN economies except Singapore, whose 2007 figure is provisional.
Source: UNCTAD, Handbook of Statistics, 2008.

It is also difficult to define "trade in services." Since there is a need for producers and consumers to interact for a service to be rendered, this influences how international transactions in services are conducted (Arkell 2001). With this in mind, scholars have attempted to define services trade as clearly as possible. Trade in services has been conventionally classified on the basis of the location of the service providers according to the following typology.

*   *Mode 1, Cross-border Supply*, is similar to trade in goods and occurs when a service crosses a national boundary (e.g., access to international telecommunications).
*   *Mode 2, Consumption Abroad* occurs when the consumer travels to the territory of the service supplier (e.g. education, tourism and health services/medical patients).
*   *Mode 3, Commercial Presence* occurs when a foreign company establishes a subsidiary or branch abroad to provide services in another country (e.g. foreign retailers, foreign banks or telecommunication firms setting up operations in a foreign country). This mode is the most closely related to FDI.
*   *Mode 4, Presence of Natural Persons*, which involves individuals traveling from their own country to supply services in another (e.g. consultants, design or software engineers, or the temporary transfer abroad of employees of a multinational). Mode 4 comes up frequently in debates on immigration.

AEC Framework on Services Liberalization

Liberalization of trade in services is a key element of the AEC program, which intends to provide substantial freedom to ASEAN services suppliers and facilitate cross-border interaction in ASEAN, subject to domestic regulations. According to the Coordinating Committee on Services, there will be no back-loading of commitments in liberalizing services in the AEC; pre-agreed flexibility will be accorded to all member states. To achieve free flow of services by 2015, ASEAN is working toward mutual recognition of professional qualifications (see discussion of free flow of skilled workers below). To meet goals for liberalizing services under the AEC, member states must do the following:

1. Remove all restrictions on trade in services for air transport, e-ASEAN, healthcare and tourism (four priority sectors) by 2010 and for logistics services by 2013.
2. Remove all restrictions on trade in services for all other services sectors by 2015.
3. Undertake liberalization through consecutive rounds timed every two years until 2015 (i.e. 2008, 2010, 2012, 2014, and 2015).
4. Schedule a minimum number of new subsectors for each round (10 subsectors in 2008; 15 in 2010; 20 in 2012; 20 in 2014 and 7 in 2015) based on GATS W/120 classification.
5. Schedule packages of commitments for every round, according to the following parameters:
   — No restrictions for Modes 1 and 2, with exceptions due to bona fide regulatory reasons (such as public safety), which are subject to agreement by all ASEAN Member States on a case-by-case basis.
   — Allow for foreign (ASEAN) equity participation of not less than 52 percent by 2008, and 70 percent by 2010 for the four priority services sectors; not less than 49 percent by 2008, 51 percent by 2010, and 70 percent by 2013 for logistics services; and not less than 49 percent by 2008, 51 percent by 2010, and 70 percent by 2015 for other services sectors.
   — Progressively remove other Mode 3 market access limitations by 2015.
6. Set the parameters of liberalization for national treatment limitations, Mode 4 and limitations in the horizontal commitments for each round by 2009.
7. Schedule commitments according to agreed parameters for national treatment limitations, Mode 4 and limitations in the horizontal commitments set in 2009.
8. Complete an inventory of barriers to services by August 2008.
9. Complete mutual recognition arrangements (MRAs) currently under negotiation (architectural services, accountancy services, surveying qualifications, medical practitioners) by 2009.
10. Implement MRAs expeditiously according to the provisions of each MRA.
11. Identify and develop MRAs for other professional services by 2012 and complete them by 2015.
12. Strengthen human resource development and capacity building in services.

For financial services, liberalization measures should allow members to ensure orderly development of the sector and maintenance of financial and socioeconomic stability. Member states are to be guided by the following principles in pacing liberalization:

• Liberalization through ASEAN Minus X formula, where countries that are ready to liberalize can proceed first and be joined by others later; and
• The process of liberalization should take place with due respect for national policy objectives and the level of economic and financial sector development of the individual members.

This is an ambitious agenda indeed. It will take considerable effort to implement these measures on a timely basis. However, as we point out below, the expected returns should be high.

Services and ASEAN Development

The view that services are important only when an economy reaches an advanced stage of development is being challenged by evidence that services are a prerequisite for development (Wahba and Mohieldin 1998; Kanapathy 2003). In many developing countries adequate provision of services is important for dynamic growth (Kanapathy 2003). Growth of services is strongly associated with income growth and economic modernization (Francois and Reinert 1996). Economists have long shown that as incomes grow so does the demand for services (e.g., tourism, education, health), which contributes to the rising importance of this sector in the economy (Tucker and Sundberg 1988; Sieh and Yap 1989; OECD 2002; Kanapathy 2003). Although demand for services is income-elastic, its productivity growth is said to be lower than in the manufacturing and agricultural sectors. This is due to the difficulty of substituting capital for labor in the production of some services such as hotels, restaurants, and transport (WTO 2000). Even though the expansion of the sector is associated with a rise in per capita income, its development varies across countries.

The expansion of the service sector seems crucial in the economic development of the ASEAN economies, as services generally bind the other sectors such as manufacturing and agriculture. The sector is a sizeable component of GDP in all ASEAN countries and it has been rising in most since 1995 (Figure 2-2). The share of employment in this sector has been rising in all ASEAN economies for which there are data since 1990 (Table 2-11), contributing 40 percent to 50 percent of GDP on average in ASEAN countries. The sector's contribution to GDP and employment has been substantial for most member states, especially Singapore, Thailand, Philippines, Malaysia, and Indonesia. Except for Brunei and Lao PDR, the share of the sector in GDP was more than 30 percent in 2005. Singapore's services sector registered the highest shares in GDP as well as employment. With a comparative advantage in services, Singapore could become a major exporter of business and professional services, banking and financial services, and computer services. The increasing share of employment in the services sector generally indicates that the sector is largely labor-intensive, especially for skilled labor (OECD 2002).

Table 2-11
Share of Services in Employment, 1990–2007 (%)

	1990	1995	2000	2001	2002	2003	2004	2005	2006	2007
Brunei	...	...	...	77	...	...	...	...	...	...
Cambodia	...	...	18	19	...	...	...	...	...	...
Indonesia	30	38	37	38	37	36	39	38	...	...
Lao PDR	...	11	...	...	...	...	...	...	...	...
Malaysia	47	48	50	52	53	54	55	...	...	...
Myanmar	21	...	...	...	...	...	...	...	...	...
Philippines	40	40	47	47	47	47	48	48	...	...
Singapore	...	68	66	74	75	76	76	70	...	...
Thailand	22	28	32	35	34	35	37	37	...	...
Vietnam	...	...	22	22	23	24	25	...	...	...

Source: Asia Development Bank.

A study by UNCTAD (1998) shows that the increasing share of employment in the sector in industrial countries has been accompanied by changes in the workforce, including greater participation by women, a shift to white-collar jobs, and an increase in skills and wages.[21] Thus, as the sector grows in importance, it will lead to a higher rate of labor force participation in addition to generating more highly skilled and better paying jobs.

Trade in Services

The importance of services is also evident in trade as measured by the export and imports of services. Since the mid-1980s many services considered nontradable have been traded. Tradability is defined as the possibility for the cross-border delivery of final services or of individual components in the services production chain without the movement of the producer or the customers (UNCTAD 1994). The rapid increase in traded services is related closely to globalization and technological progress in information and communications services (Sieh and Yap 1989; Arkell 2001; Cuadrado-Roura 2002; OECD 2002). Trade in commercial services, which encompasses transport, travel, insurance and financial services, has grown faster than trade in merchandise trade over the past decade.

From 1990 to 2007 the share of services exports to and imports from the world as a percentage of total trade was volatile in most ASEAN countries and only increased in Cambodia and Malaysia (Figure 2-3). But it constituted more than 10 percent of total trade in almost all ASEAN countries in 2007. For ASEAN as a whole, the estimate of the 2006 export and import levels are US$120.9 billion and US$150.3 billion, respectively.[22] Another significant trend is that imports of services exceed exports for all ASEAN Member States, save Lao PDR and Cambodia. Within the trade in services categories, transport, travel and other business services constitute the largest sectors in the ASEAN Member States, with the travel subsector accounting for the largest share.

Services Liberalization Under GATS and AFAS

Developing countries' interest in services liberalization emerged after the Uruguay Round and has heightened as most RTAs include services in negotiations. For instance, in the Asia-Pacific, the Australia — New Zealand Closer Economic Relations Trade Agreements (ANCERTA) in 1988 included services. A decade later, AFAS was agreed to by ASEAN. The GATS framework was used as the basis for negotiations under AFAS. Signed in 1995, the AFAS aimed to improve cooperation in the service sector by eliminating intraregional trade restrictions and expanding liberalization in services ("GATS plus"). Under AFAS, negotiations focused on financial services, transport, telecommunications, tourism, and professional business services. ASEAN has concluded seven packages of commitments through successive rounds of negotiations since January 1, 1996.[23] The final destination of ASEAN liberalization is the removal of all trade barriers by 2015 as called for by the AEC.

The "Roadmap for the Integration of ASEAN" has identified MRAs for professional services as essential for the free flow of professional services. MRAs, the most recent development in ASEAN cooperation in trade in services, enable the qualifications of professional services suppliers to be mutually recognized by signatory member states, hence facilitating the free flow of professional services. A number of areas are being negotiated and considered for MRAs, and ASEAN has concluded MRAs for engineering, architectural, accountancy, surveying, nursing, and medical and dental practitioner services.

Table 2-12
Shares of Services Exports and Imports as Percentage of Country's Total Trade, 1980–2004 (%)

		1980	1985	1990	1995	2000	2001	2002	2003	2004
World	Exports	17.21	18.43	20.02	19.63	19.48	20.24	20.48	20.18	19.79
	Imports	18.92	19.24	20.71	20	19.32	20.06	20.42	20.08	19.47
Developed economies	Exports	19.38	19.72	21.16	20.82	21.76	22.36	23	22.94	22.6
	Imports	17.47	18.25	20.71	20.53	19.84	20.56	21.14	21.06	20.52
Developing economies	Exports	11.66	14.92	16.14	17.05	14.9	15.81	15.23	14.47	14.42
	Imports	23.19	22.65	20.07	18.77	17.96	18.68	18.47	17.57	16.95
ASEAN										
Brunei	Exports	—	—	—	—	4.48	—	—	—	—
	Imports	—	—	—	—	38.45	—	—	—	—
Cambodia	Exports	—	—	—	11.76	23.42	25.03	25.66	20.45	—
	Imports	—	—	—	13.67	14.46	14.23	13.91	13.18	—
Indonesia	Exports	—	4.36	8.49	10.33	7.38	8.75	10.12	7.72	18.44
	Imports	—	28.78	22.01	24.86	27.92	31.42	32.35	30.56	34.37
Lao PDR	Exports	—	28.44	23.14	23.74	34.72	34.8	31.47	22.45	—
	Imports	—	18.17	12.46	16.25	7.44	5.65	1.2	1.05	—
Malaysia	Exports	8.05	11.26	11.81	13.92	12.41	14.11	13.74	11.45	12.53
	Imports	21.86	25.16	17.27	17.25	17.75	19.31	17.94	18.11	15.39
Myanmar	Exports	10.86	17.69	29.58	27.89	22.34	14.36	12.97	10.69	11.23
	Imports	8.51	13.75	12.13	12.19	13.16	13.24	12.95	15.53	12.85
Philippines	Exports	20	32.56	28.38	34.89	9.63	9.15	8.16	8.54	9.58
	Imports	15.7	14.5	12.61	20.79	16.05	13.98	10.7	10.96	10.66
Singapore	Exports	19.99	16.82	18.98	17.68	16.46	17.87	17.91	16.29	19.17
	Imports	11.5	12.58	13.3	14.47	16.73	19.38	20.2	18.71	20.43
Thailand	Exports	18.76	22.43	21.96	21.12	16.96	17.11	18.89	16.83	16.54
	Imports	16.45	17.78	17.59	22.87	21.58	21.13	22.68	21.36	21.45
Vietnam	Exports	..	..	7.04	28.27	15.76	15.75	15	..	..
	Imports	..	..	4.38	19.55	18.77	18.86	17.23	..	..

Source: UNCTAD (2006).

Gains from Services Liberalization: A Review of the Literature

Most trade literature has focused on trade in goods and the literature on services trade is in its infancy. Thus, the welfare implications of liberalization of trade in services are not as well understood. Early work by Colin Clark (1940) and Hill (1977) stressed the importance of the services sector and its potential role in economies. Scholars then focused on comparative advantage, on international patterns of services, and on determining whether the pattern of trade in services could be explained by the same factors as trade in goods (e.g. Waelbroeck et al. 1985; Tucker, K. and Sundberg, M. 1988; Bano and Lane 1995). Now services liberalization has become prominent, especially since the Uruguay Round. Numerous studies were undertaken to assess the theoretical and empirical rationale for liberalization of the trade for developed and developing countries. In general, these studies cover the impact of liberalization or examine sectoral liberalization, such as telecommunications (Knudsen J.S. 2002) and transport, education, and financial services (Wahba, J. and Mohieldin, M. 1998).

Modeling studies show that the global gains from services trade and investment liberalization are likely to be substantial, and to be shared evenly between developed and developing economies. Brown et al. (1996) simulate the impact of a 25 percent reduction in the ad valorem tariff equivalents of services barriers under various assumptions about variety, scale, and competition. Liberalization is trade-enhancing for all countries. Similarly, Chadha (2000) studies the effects of a reduction of 25 percent in the ad valorem tariff equivalent on the services sector using a dataset composed of three Asian developing countries and regions (India; Rest of South Asia; Indonesia, Malaysia, the Philippines, and Thailand; and NIE-4) and three developed countries/regions (EU, Japan, and US). The estimated welfare gains are relatively large and characterized by larger relative gains for Asian developing countries than for developed countries. Welfare effects from liberalizing trade in services results in a change of 0.7 percent for India, 0.9 percent for the rest of South Asia (including Bangladesh, Bhutan, Maldives, Nepal, Pakistan and Sri Lanka), 1.8 percent for Indonesia, Malaysia, the Philippines and Thailand, and 1.7 percent for the NIE-4 (Hong Kong, Singapore, South Republic of Korea and Chinese Taipei). Increasing the cut to a 33 percent reduction in tariff equivalents and greater country disaggregation, Chadha et al. (2001) estimate large welfare gains for ASEAN countries, especially for Thailand (4.2 percent of GDP).

Dee and Hanslow (2000) confirm the relative importance of services trade in the global economy by estimating that services sector liberalization in a multilateral setting would increase global GDP by US$130 billion. These gains would be concentrated in developing countries where there are currently the greatest barriers to services trade. Another study by the Productivity Commission (Verikios and Zhang 2001) assesses the effects of liberalization in the financial services and telecommunications sectors and suggests that economies gain by removing barriers to the establishment of new operations and by liberalizing existing operations. For the world as a whole, the one-off gains are estimated to be at least 0.2 percent of combined GNP, or about US$50 billion.

In sum, these and other studies show that the *gains from services liberalization accrue to the countries implementing reforms*. Unilateral reforms provide the main gains: lower priced services, access to badly needed foreign investment and technology for infrastructure development, better ways of organizing business, and better risk management capacity through foreign participation in financial services (Drake-Brockman 2003). Rajan and Bird (2002) assess the state of services liberalization and the policy environment of the financial and telecommunications sectors in five Asian economies, including Malaysia and Thailand, and stress the theoretical expectation of a beneficial impact of an appropriately timed and sequenced liberalization of the telecommunications and financial service sectors on overall growth and welfare. The results suggest that the greatest gains come from "complete liberalization," especially from removing impediments to market access for "establishment" rather than "operations."

Matto and Fink (2004) analyze the effects of preferential versus MFN-based liberalization of trade in services. Preferential liberalization brings about static welfare gains. The key difference is that protection in services does not generate fiscal revenue, as do tariffs on imported goods. Thus, the trade diversion effect associated with preferential liberalization in services does not lead to any loss in government revenue that can lead to negative welfare effects as is the case with goods. Hence, the case for RTAs in trade in services is stronger than that for trade in goods. But, of course, MFN liberalization generally yields greater welfare gains than preferential liberalization, as it promotes entry of the most efficient service providers, greater economies of scale, and knowledge spillovers.

Our CGE Model Estimates for Services

In our modeling exercise above, we do not generate large changes in the growth of output due to services liberalization, though some structural change does take place at the sectoral level. Note, however, that our simulations cover only liberalized estimates of existing ad valorem equivalents of barriers to trade in services. These barriers actually were not very high; in only one sector in one country (Indonesia, private services) did the ad valorem equivalent exceed one-fifth (21 percent), and most were under 10 percent (Table 1-6). We did not include some of the benefits that should derive through the AEC discussed above (e.g., MRAs, foreign equity restrictions, and the like). As they are not included in our modeling exercise, the likely dynamic effects of the AEC on services are probably significantly underestimated.

In terms of structural change, Table 2-13 summarizes our CGE results for services categories at the country level. Construction expands in every member state due to the AEC. Trade and transportation output increases in most ASEAN countries and in some countries the effect is large, especially in Myanmar. Private services, which include financial services, expands significantly in Myanmar (38 percent) and Indonesia (22 percent) and contracts substantially in Singapore (21 percent) and Malaysia (11 percent). There are small output effects in the other countries. Output effects in government services tend to be small, with most countries experiencing either no change or a slightly negative effect, with the exception of Lao PDR.

Trade in Services, Welfare, and Competitiveness

There is growing evidence that services liberalization is a major potential source of welfare gains, and that the performance of service sectors (or services policies) may be an important determinant of trade volumes, the distributional effects of trade, and economy-wide growth (Hoekman 2006). Market opening may be perceived less threatening by service providers among smaller groups of countries for some sectors, suggesting that liberalization is easier in a regional context (Stephenson 2001). The empirical evidence on ASEAN Member States emphasizes that there are significant economic gains from liberalization of services, though the gains may be unevenly distributed across countries. Services liberalization could involve short-term adjustment costs, which need to be appreciated and managed. Services liberalization in particular requires that the institutional and regulatory environment be strengthened before and during liberalization.

The main benefits of services liberalization are enlarged services export markets; improved service competitiveness and efficiency that contribute to the competitiveness of goods; and MRAs that improve service delivery by foreign suppliers. There are winners and losers. Winners include local SMEs who gain from market expansion and improved competitiveness; workers employed in a growing variety of services; governments who collect more revenue thanks to growth in service sectors; and consumers accessing cheaper services under various modes. Losers include inefficient service sectors, as part of the "trade creation" process, with uncompetitive services, such as SMEs, losing out to foreign competition.

Table 2-13
AEC Effects on Services Output and Trade
(CGE Model Estimates, % change from baseline, 2015)

		Output		Exports		Imports	
		AFTA	AEC	AFTA	AEC	AFTA	AEC
Brunei	Utilities	−0.4	−1.7	−1.7	−17.1	0.5	8.7
	Construction	−4.6	7.9	−0.7	−18.9	−5.0	43.7
	Trade & Transport	1.1	0.6	14.3	0.5	−11.7	7.2
	Priv. Services*	−0.2	−2.9	1.2	−14.4	−1.5	22.6
	Government	−0.2	−0.6	3.1	−8.5	−1.8	5.3
Cambodia	Utilities	−4.0	−8.0	0.4	3.7	−4.3	−8.3
	Construction	4.9	15.8	7.9	66.3	0.4	−9.5
	Trade & Transport	−2.4	−3.7	−9.7	−22.4	14.6	51.7
	Priv. Services*	−2.3	−4.4	−12.4	−24.9	13.0	47.7
	Government	−1.1	−3.3	−6.3	−19.0	3.0	11.2
Indonesia	Utilities	0.4	20.5	0.6	32.3	0.4	7.5
	Construction	0.0	7.8	1.9	62.4	−1.8	−12.8
	Trade & Transport	0.2	11.5	2.9	27.7	−2.7	3.0
	Priv. Services*	−0.1	21.6	−0.2	107.0	−0.1	−28.5
	Government	−0.1	−1.0	0.4	−18.2	−0.3	11.4
Lao PDR	Utilities	1.0	9.1	15.1	36.8	−6.3	−4.8
	Construction	1.6	5.8	44.4	326.9	−29.4	−75.0
	Trade & Transport	2.8	11.6	23.8	64.8	−27.6	−38.9
	Priv. Services*	0.9	13.1	24.3	99.4	−28.2	−51.1
	Government	5.8	7.1	13.1	15.9	−6.1	−6.6
Malaysia	Utilities	−0.5	−0.2	−6.4	−22.3	3.3	18.1
	Construction	0.8	5.0	−3.1	47.5	4.9	−18.9
	Trade & Transport	−1.3	−3.0	−5.6	−29.0	4.7	55.0
	Priv. Services*	−1.8	−11.2	−5.7	−25.4	4.4	29.4
	Government	−0.1	−0.5	−2.1	−26.6	1.0	17.9
Myanmar	Utilities	0.3	17.9	1.2	68.1	−0.1	−7.6
	Construction	−1.0	5.4	5.8	150.6	−7.1	−58.5
	Trade & Transport	1.3	30.8	4.3	83.9	−5.0	−35.5
	Priv. Services*	−0.4	38.1	1.9	172.8	−2.8	−42.6
	Government	0.1	0.1	1.2	−0.5	−0.7	1.2
Philippines	Utilities	1.0	4.3	−2.4	−5.1	2.3	8.0
	Construction	0.6	4.3	−6.0	−9.0	7.5	52.3
	Trade & Transport	−0.2	7.4	−3.4	9.7	3.6	13.7
	Priv. Services*	−0.1	1.5	−4.4	−3.1	4.6	19.8
	Government	0.2	−1.7	−3.0	−19.3	1.8	11.4
Singapore	Utilities	3.2	11.6	−8.1	−34.5	7.6	39.0
	Construction	0.5	6.1	−14.6	−46.5	18.8	129.4
	Trade & Transport	−2.5	−11.0	−10.0	−35.5	8.8	47.1
	Priv. Services*	−6.4	−21.3	−13.3	−42.4	8.2	53.6
	Government	0.3	0.5	−6.3	−26.0	3.8	19.1
Thailand	Utilities	−0.1	6.1	−3.4	−17.0	1.7	17.2
	Construction	0.3	7.0	−2.2	−6.2	2.8	46.2
	Trade & Transport	−0.6	−0.7	−3.8	−17.4	3.7	38.1
	Priv. Services*	0.0	−1.2	−0.8	−13.6	0.8	31.4
	Government	−0.2	−1.1	−2.8	−18.4	1.3	11.5
Vietnam	Utilities	0.3	0.1	2.9	−17.3	−0.9	13.0
	Construction	−0.1	11.1	12.0	159.2	−11.0	−50.3
	Trade & Transport	6.1	19.5	15.3	46.2	−9.8	−10.0
	Priv. Services*	2.6	−2.1	8.8	−2.7	−6.2	11.3
	Government	−0.7	−4.1	2.6	−11.8	−2.2	3.8

Note: *Private Services includes financial services.
Source: Authors' model results.

FREE FLOW OF SKILLED WORKERS

If the economic literature focuses more on trade in goods than on trade in services, it fails even more in considering the economic effects of removing restrictions on immigrant labor in general and skilled labor in particular. But as the free flow of skilled labor has important implications for services trade, FDI, and productivity growth, leaving this key aspect of the AEC out of our economic estimates will certainly produce a significant downward bias in terms of what we can expect from the AEC program. In this section, we consider some of these potential effects.

Domestic Demand and Supply and Movement of Skilled Workers

ASEAN includes member states that are natural exporters and importers of skilled labor. Manning and Sidrorenko (2007) divide the ten member states into three groups:

- *Group I — Singapore, Brunei (high income) and Malaysia and Thailand.* Countries in this group all have relatively open regimes with regard to the import of professional manpower, and are major suppliers of healthcare services through Mode 2 (consumption abroad) and to a lesser extent Mode 3 (investment abroad). All have strategies to become major exporters of IT services.
- *Group II — Philippines, Indonesia and Vietnam (middle to low-income).* These countries have regimes protective of professional manpower. Their domestically oriented IT industries rely little if at all on temporary in-migration of professionals. The Philippines is the major exporter of skilled and unskilled labor in the region. Indonesia and Vietnam also export labor on temporary contracts, but these flows consist largely of unskilled workers. All are heavily involved in, or seek to expand, the export of nurses.
- *Group III — Cambodia, Lao PDR and Myanmar (low income).* These countries import a relatively small number of professional workers. Cambodia is more open with regard to the import of professionals, mainly associated with FDI. All export unskilled manpower to Thailand, and Myanmar exports a small number of professionals in the region, partly related to better English language skills.

In 2004, the Group I countries hosted a significant number of unskilled and skilled migrants. In professional manpower, high levels of FDI and slower development of national talents (than, for example, in Taiwan or Korea) help explain an imbalance between the domestic demand and supply of manpower, exacerbated by some out-migration in Singapore and Malaysia. All other countries in the region were net labor exporters, mainly of unskilled labor. The deployment of professional manpower from abroad was limited partly by lack of demand in more capital and skill-intensive industries, and partly by stringent regulations governing the employment of foreign manpower. The one outstanding case of out-migration of skilled manpower has been the Philippines in the ASEAN region (ASEAN-ANU Migration Research Team 2005).

Rapid economic growth and a high-income elasticity of demand have created excess demand for healthcare and IT professionals throughout the region. Regarding the former, three of the four Group I economies — Singapore, Malaysia and to a lesser extent Brunei — are significant importers of skilled manpower in the health sector. In contrast, the low-income countries rely almost exclusively on domestic supply for manpower in the healthcare sector. The Philippines is by far the largest supplier of nurses in ASEAN and beyond (ASEAN-ANU Migration Research Team 2005). With respect to IT, all countries tend to have more open regimes with regard to the movement of workers than in healthcare. Among the Group I countries, Singapore's regulations on in-migration are relatively generous for skilled workers. In Malaysia, the domestic demand for IT is linked to the Multimedia Super Corridor (MSC) status operations overviewed by Multimedia Development Corporation (MDC). Although the Thai government has not played such a proactive role in promoting the IT industry, it is estimated that the demand for IT professionals will increase rapidly.

The Philippines has comparative advantage relative to other middle-income ASEAN countries, especially in English language skills, and almost all of these IT services are provided by Filipino nationals at home. Even though they hold IT-related diplomas and degrees, few Indonesians and very few Vietnamese IT workers are employed overseas.

Demand for IT services and professionals among Group III countries has not risen as dramatically but there have been important developments. In Myanmar, for example, the movement of IT professionals to and from Myanmar appears to have picked up with the easing of restrictions on Internet use (ASEAN-ANU Migration Research Team 2005; Manning and Sidrorenko 2007)

Economic Effects of Labor Mobility

A review of the literature on welfare economics of labor mobility suggests that there are many benefits to mobility — production specialization, human capital acquisition, knowledge creation, cross-border spillovers, and risk redistribution — but that the distribution of benefits is likely to be uneven. In addition, some sending countries may incur costs in the short run and possibly in the long run, including loss in human capital spillovers, reduced capacity for knowledge absorption, and widening gaps in innovation (Gera et al. 2004).

Remittances are an important economic effect of labor mobility of skilled and unskilled workers alike. According to Labor and Social Trends in ASEAN 2007, ASEAN's remittance inflows were an estimated US$26 billion in 2005, of which Indonesia accounted for 8 percent, the Philippines 62 percent, Thailand 9 percent, and Vietnam 15 percent. The figures are probably underestimated because a substantial portion of remittances go through informal channels. The 2005 amount of remittances was more than 7 times that of the 1990 figure (US$3 billion), and more than twice that of 2000 (US$10.3 billion).

Barriers To and Regulations for Labor Mobility

While differences in development among the ASEAN Member States present a challenge to regional integration in general, they are a driving force in intraregional mobility of skilled labor. Tullao and Cortez (2006) note several factors that influence the cross-border flows of skilled workers, including globalization, the rise of ICT, and stiff competition among firms. Member states have responded favorably by liberalizing their trade and investment regimes and have experienced substantial increases in FDI and enhanced global production networks especially in recent years. The expansion of FDI inflows has attracted even more skilled and professional workers.

The "movement of natural persons" in ASEAN increasingly consists of temporary movements of skilled and professional workers between more developed and less-developed regions. However, in 2005 only 39 percent were migrants from within ASEAN; 61 percent were from outside ASEAN, especially from the United States and the EU. Filipino and Vietnamese migrants went mainly to the United

States. Widening wage differentials for professional workers between ASEAN and developed countries have contributed to these movements, even when sending countries suffer a comparative scarcity of skilled labor at home. Filipino nurses, for instance, earn US$3,000–US$4,000 monthly in the United States compared to US$75–US$200 in the Philippines (IHPDS 2005).

Barriers to the inward mobility of professionals include

- Visa requirements and procedures,
- Minimum education/job experience requirements,
- Levies on employment of foreign workers,
- Employment restricted to a specific firm/geographic location/office,
- Economic test to justify the need for employment of a foreign professional,
- Lack of recognition of professional training and experience obtained in a foreign country,
- Licensing regulations of professional associations.

When deciding to move to another country for temporary employment, professionals balance the costs of language barriers, cultural differences, and adapting to a new environment against the benefits of higher wages and better job prospects. For doctors and nurses, language requirements are often a major barrier to the recognition of training, even if standards of clinical care are similar. An extreme form of national treatment discrimination includes a citizenship requirement to practice an occupation, such as for professionals in the Philippines. Examples of the preference for labor from "traditional sources" abound in the region (especially in Brunei and Malaysia), and several countries impose quantitative restrictions (ASEAN-ANU Migration Research Team 2005).

Furthermore, the international market for professional labor is mediated by recruitment and headhunting agencies and overseas employment boards. Some of these may be able to gain power in certain market segments and act as gatekeepers for foreign entry. These are largely unregulated activities, and the market power results in high fees charged to the individual foreign professionals.

Recommendations Regarding Free Flow of Skilled Labor

Flows of skilled workers in ASEAN will likely increase significantly as a result of economic and social forces, especially increases in FDI and free flows of services. The AEC stipulates that ASEAN will become a region within which skilled labor will flow freely. Under certain conditions labor-receiving and labor-sending countries will benefit from this development. Receiving countries will enjoy a "brain gain" and labor productivity gains, and be better able to upgrade their economies, although local professionals will face competition for jobs. Sending countries will face "brain drain" in the short term but this could be offset by remittances and a reverse brain drain in the medium and long term as returnees bring wealth, skills and experiences, and their business and social networks back home (Chia 2008).

Skilled labor migration is a complex and politically sensitive matter but these benefits more than justify the political hurdles and other costs that will have to be overcome. In any event, it is hard to envision a single market and production base without the free flow of skilled labor, which is complementary to other freedoms, especially FDI and services. To enable the free flow of workers, the AEC Blueprint stresses three categories of actions:

1. Enhance cooperation among ASEAN University Network (AUN) members to increase mobility of students and staff.
2. Develop core competencies and qualifications for job/occupational and trainers skills required in priority service sectors by 2009 and in other services sectors (2010 to 2015).
3. Strengthen the ability of each member state to promote skills, job placement, and develop labor market information networks.

If worker mobility is going to benefit all member states — and even become a new comparative advantage — it should be regularized through MRAs for various occupations and qualifications, facilitation of foreign registration of qualifications, encouragement of language proficiency, and greater transparency in and information on labor markets and hiring requirements.

Furthermore, regional economic communities and other institutions should redouble their efforts to achieve cooperation and integration in education. They should aim to harmonize educational and technical standards in areas relevant to MRAs and to adopt policies across countries that will facilitate the exchange of students and teachers and, later, the mobility of skilled workers. It would be useful if ASEAN adopted concerted approaches to improve the efficacy of their education systems in providing the necessary skills for the labor markets. Productive dialogue among member states' workers, employers, governments, and educators appears to be the critical ingredient for achieving national and regional consensus on policies for human resource and labor market development.

SUMMARY OF RESULTS

The free flow of goods, services, and skilled labor are the backbone of the single market and production base envisaged under the AEC. Estimating the quantitative effects of liberalized trade in services and especially of skilled labor is difficult and where we could not estimate explicitly the likely effects of the AEC we were still able to make a strong qualitative case as to why it should generate substantial benefits. Our CGE model, however, allowed us to quantify many economic effects, most importantly, perhaps, a rise in economic welfare of 5.3 percent, or $69 billion — more than six times the estimated effect of completing AFTA (Figure 2-4). Table 2-14 summarizes our predicted structural effects on sectoral output and trade.

We also conclude that

- All member states will gain from an AEC, though some will gain more than others.
- Trade in goods will expand, with exports outpacing imports in all but three manufacturing sectors and offering opportunities to integrate the region into global production chains.
- Imports of services trade in most sectors will grow at a more rapid pace than exports, which will contract in several sectors (Table 2-13).
- Extending the AEC to include "+1" agreements with its East Asian neighbors will increase the aggregate welfare benefits to ASEAN by two-thirds, and by an additional one-third if the United States and the EU are added.

Note that our estimates are conservative and exclude many measures that will no doubt generate significant efficiency effects, some of which are considered in subsequent chapters. Finally, Table 2-15

Figure 2-4
Summary of Estimates of the Welfare Effects of AFTA and the AEC

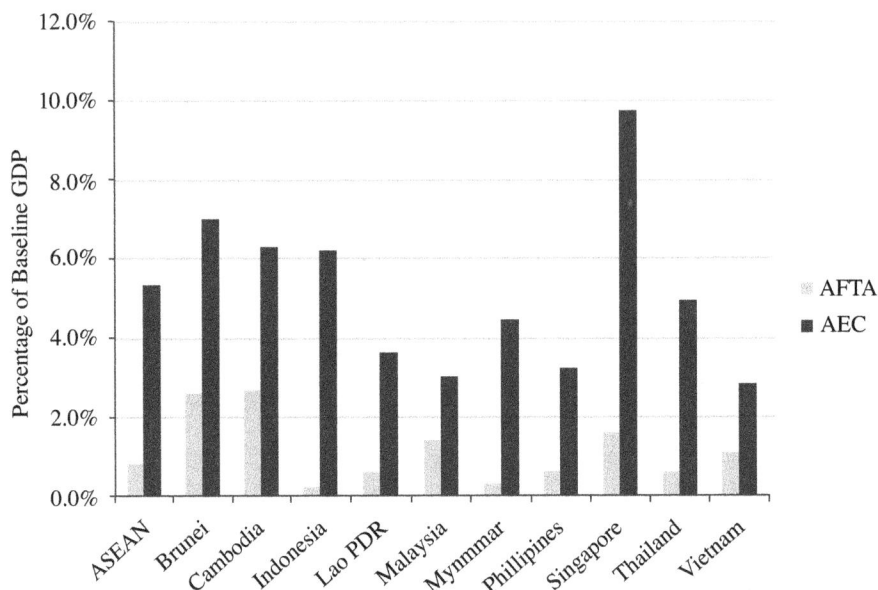

Table 2-14
Structural Effects of AFTA and AEC

ASEAN	Output		Exports		Imports	
	AFTA	*AEC*	*AFTA*	*AEC*	*AFTA*	*AEC*
Paddy rice	−1.2	−4.6	11.1	17.9	52.6	144.4
Grains, other	−2.7	−5.0	8.1	163.4	0.8	12.3
Crops, other	0.0	−2.8	7.0	10.3	6.9	26.8
Livestock	1.8	−0.2	8.3	13.3	2.2	12.3
Natural resources	−0.3	−3.1	0.4	−10.0	3.5	6.4
Mining	0.1	−1.1	−0.1	−10.8	2.4	15.7
Food	8.6	12.8	71.7	113.1	116.2	196.9
Textiles	5.8	27.3	14.4	56.3	10.8	31.9
Wood products	1.8	3.0	8.5	16.3	12.6	38.5
Apparel	5.7	18.4	10.3	31.8	6.2	21.5
Chemicals	2.0	12.6	7.4	34.3	5.5	27.8
Metals	1.1	31.9	4.9	139.7	3.0	53.2
Electrical equipment	−1.9	35.9	−2.2	45.7	−0.9	30.8
Machinery	1.2	34.3	2.5	59.0	1.5	24.7
Vehicles	3.6	22.8	18.6	85.7	5.9	24.7
Other manufactures	0.3	10.3	1.6	29.6	3.1	30.9
Utilities	0.4	8.6	−2.5	−2.7	4.6	27.6
Construction	0.2	7.3	−1.8	32.9	4.4	22.7
Trade, transport	−0.7	1.9	−4.7	−16.6	4.7	35.9
Private services	−1.5	1.7	−7.2	−22.5	3.2	18.1
Government services	0.0	−0.9	−1.0	−17.2	1.6	14.5

Table 2-15
Summary of AEC Benefits for Stakeholders: Free Flow of Goods, Services, and Skilled Labor

Stakeholders	AEC Process	AEC Major Benefits
1. ASEAN as a regional grouping	Creates a single market and production base, making ASEAN a unified market. Sets stage for even deeper integration. Will require considerable political will to implement.	ASEAN real income should rise by at least 5.3 percent under conservative assumptions. Increased productivity through rise in trade should enhance estimates significantly. Free flows of skilled labor will add additional efficiencies. Benefits from ASEAN centrality only possible with such an integrated market.
2. ASEAN Member States	Will allow for specialization in comparative advantage industries, reduced transaction costs, enhanced participation in production chains, and benefits extended negotiating clout through an integrated entity.	All ASEAN Member States gain from AEC, though some gain more than others. Trade of member states should boom, particularly in manufactures, food. Structural change will be in direction of comparative advantage. More efficient distribution of skilled labor should increase efficiencies in all member states, including as a complement to FDI inflows and services. Gains through more efficient customs services and other forms of trade facilitation should be large particularly for the lower-income countries.
3. CLMV countries	In addition to (2), better integration with rest of ASEAN, harmonization, better position to integrate and take advantage of global economy.	All CLMV countries gain from AEC, some significantly (especially Cambodia). Adoption of "best practices" should generate the greatest gains to CLMV. Structural change will render economies more efficient, with comparative advantage goods expanding. As AEC increases attractiveness of region in terms of production networks, CLMV countries will gain through increased trade and FDI. Shortage of skilled labor will be improved.
4. ASEAN businesses including SMEs	Same as (2) above. Requires firms to restructure to take advantage of market opportunities and to overcome import and supplier challenges presented by AEC.	Businesses will gain through higher rates of market growth, greater macroeconomic stability necessary to make the AEC work, fewer obstacles to trade, lower bureaucratic costs, greater harmonization of business-related measures, removal of bottlenecks in terms of skilled labor, fewer obstacles to business expansion.
5. ASEAN investors	Same as (4).	Same as (4).
6. ASEAN labor including professionals	Same as (2), but particularly free flow of services and of skilled labor, and MRAs for professional qualifications.	Labor of expanding industries, services and firms benefit from increased employment and higher wages, while those adversely affected by AEC competition suffer potential unemployment necessitating adjustment assistance. Free regional mobility of skilled labor benefit countries having skills shortages, and professionals and skilled workers are able to find better employment opportunities and earnings; complement to FDI.
7. ASEAN consumers	Same as (2).	Consumers tend to be the biggest beneficiaries of trade liberalization, as a greater diversity of products are available at lower prices. Services liberalization will be particularly important in this regard, given that it continues to be more restricted in ASEAN than trade in goods.

continued on next page

Table 2-15 — *cont'd*

Stakeholders	AEC Process	AEC Major Benefits
8. ASEAN's global partners	AEC focuses on open regionalism; strong incentives to be non-discriminatory.	AEC rejects the idea that ASEAN could be a block; policy emphasis is on inclusion rather than exclusion. Gains from the AEC are magnified considerably when undertaken together with initiatives in East Asia and the US/EU. By acting with a single voice (only possible with a single market and production base), ASEAN can take a larger role in advocating global economic liberalization.

summarizes the likely implications of a free flow of goods, services, and skilled labor for various stakeholders in ASEAN.

NOTES

1. All ASEAN Member States are WTO Members save the Lao PDR, which is at a relatively advanced state of negotiations for accession; a WTO Working Party was established in February 1998 and it has held four meetings, the last in July 2008.
2. For a real-time list of FTAs by ASEAN countries and the Asian region more generally, see www.aric.adb.org.
3. These data come from the ASEAN Secretariat.
4. This study is available on the PECC website: http://www.pecc.net/trade_washington.htm.
5. Previously only components which themselves had ASEAN content of 40 percent or more counted. Thus the valued addition to products that did not meet the 40 percent threshold could not be included in the origin determination.
6. The quantum of costs reduction will be determined during the course of implementing the ATFWP.
7. All data obtained from: http://www.doingbusiness.org/ExploreTopics/TradingAcrossBorders/, accessed June 14, 2009.
8. At least up to the current global economic crisis, which arguably began in September 2008.
9. Brooks, Roland-Holst and Zhai model the Scenario 2 liberalization as an "iceberg effect," in which a fraction of goods and services "melt away in transit due to the trade costs" (p. 4, fn 4).
10. Note that this value is a guesstimate and is not derived systematically or empirically.
11. As discussed in Chapter 5, this assumes convergence to the level of efficiency of the best performing ASEAN countries in this regard (Singapore). While 2–12 percent is a wide range (which is to be expected, given the difficulties associated with measuring efficient in this context), even the most conservative results are large: a 2 percent increase in per capita income is greater than estimates of the effects of AFTA, for example.
12. It did have a Common External Tariff, of course, but NTBs and other controls varied widely across member countries. For example, while Italy and Germany applied the same tariff on Japanese auto imports, at the time the later only allow in less than 3,000 Japanese cars per year, whereas Germany had no quantitative restrictions at all. Obviously, this type of diversity leads to significant market segmentation.
13. Of course, this does not make them completely comparable, as external tariffs are greater than zero in the post-AFTA commercial policy regimes of the ASEAN Member States. Still, the point here is that tariff changes are insignificant for the simulation results.
14. Fan Zhai and Peter Petri developed the model and conducted simulation exercises at the ADB Institute.
15. A detailed specification of the model can be found in Zhai (2008).

16. http://econ.worldbank.org/WBSITE/EXTERNAL/EXTDEC/EXTRESEARCH/0,,contentMDK: 21085342~pagePK:64214825~piPK:64214943~theSitePK:469382,00.html.

17. We are grateful to Alan Deardorf, Robert Stern, and Kozo Kiyota for supplying these data to us.

18. All numbers are based on an "equivalent variation" approach to estimating the changes in welfare.

19. Given that Singapore is already an open economy, this large effect deserves an explanation. It derives from three factors: (1) given the openness of the Singaporean economy, the reduction in trade costs accounts for 41 percent of the total gain of 9.7 percent; (2) NTB removal comes second, as Singapore's NTBs in agriculture come to 13.2 percent and to 4.5 percent in manufacturing (34 percent of the total gain); and the comprehensive tariff removal under AFTA, due to increased market access and a related terms of trade improvement (16 percent of the total gain).

20. For detailed analyses of the difference between goods and services, see Victor R. Fuchs (1968), T.P Hill (1977), Bhagwati (1984) and Riddle (1986). Meanwhile for the history of economic thought on services refer to Delunay and Gadrey (1992).

21. See also OECD (2002); Martin (2006).

22. All data cited in this paragraph are taken from UNCTAD (2006).

23. Round 1, 1996–1998; Round 2, 1999–2001; Round 3, 2002–2004; Round 4, 2005–2006; Round 5, 2007–2009.

3
Competition Policy, Infrastructure, and Intellectual Property Rights

Wisarn Pupphavesa, Santi Chaisrisawatsuk, Sasatra Sudsawasd, and Sumet Ongkittikul

Under the AEC Blueprint, ASEAN is to embody a "competitive economic region" by 2015. Achieving this will require ASEAN Member States to adjust policies and practices related to competition, infrastructure development, intellectual property rights, and other related matters.

Currently, member states vary considerably in the sophistication of their competition policies, and some have only rudimentary or negligible policies in place. Strengthening competition policy in individual member states and harmonizing policies across the region could yield important economic benefits, in addition to ensuring an efficient and robust AEC. As we show in this chapter, empirical estimates of the potential benefits of a competitive economic region indicate that gains could be considerable, particularly for developing member states. GDP per capita for Indonesia, Malaysia, the Philippines, and Thailand could grow 3 percent and up to 15 percent more because of AEC-related competition policies, and by 2 percent to 12 percent more because of AEC-related infrastructure development. And FDI inflows to Indonesia, Malaysia, the Philippines, and Thailand as a percent of GDP could increase 10 to 14 percent. In sum, the gains from achieving a competitive economic region will likely far exceed those expected from, for example, liberalizing tariffs and nontariff barriers.

In this chapter, we evaluate the status of competition policy in ASEAN and the potential contributions of regional harmonization through the AEC; explore issues related to intellectual property protection; review infrastructure issues identified in the AEC Blueprint; and assess the state of consumer protection in the ASEAN region. We then present a quantitative assessment of the AEC competitive economic region using "extreme bound analysis" and the implications of that assessment for policy.

COMPETITION POLICY AND THE AEC

ASEAN aims to foster a culture of fair competition in Southeast Asia. Currently only Indonesia, Singapore, Thailand, and Vietnam have competition laws and regulatory bodies. ASEAN does not have either an official body for cooperative work on competition policy and law (CPL) or relevant bodies to exchange policy experiences and institutional norms pertinent to CPL.[1] Hence, the AEC Blueprint calls for member states to (1) introduce competition policy by 2015; (2) establish a network of authorities for discussing and coordinating competition policies; (3) build capacity to develop national competition policy; and (4) develop a regional guideline on competition policy by 2010.

National Competition Policy Framework

ASEAN Member States need well-designed national CPL to (1) secure and enhance the economic and social benefits of trade and investment liberalization, and (2) counter the potential anticompetitive behavior of domestic and multinational firms. In this they are not alone. The purpose of any CPL is to foster free and effective competition and to maintain and facilitate the competitive process (World Bank and OECD 1999). A CPL is not an end in itself but a means to improve economic efficiency, economic growth and development, and consumer welfare. *Inter alia*, it endeavors to do this by

- Restricting the use anticompetitive agreements between firms;
- Preventing the abuse of dominant positions in product and factor markets;
- Precluding substantial erosion of competition through mergers or acquisitions;
- Deterring misleading, deceptive, or unconscionable conduct by firms; and
- Removing government regulations that unnecessarily restrict competition or confer a competitive advantage to a government-owned business.

While trade and investment liberalization has resulted in increased competition in domestic and international markets, and has acted to some extent as a substitute for a national CPL framework, it might have also spawned anticompetitive activity. For example, to take advantage of cross-border and cross-firm economies of scale and scope firms may merge or form joint ventures, strategic alliances, research consortia, and producer–supplier networks, some of which can have anticompetitive consequences.[2] In recent decades the number of international mergers has risen, and some markets in industrialized and developing countries are now characterized by market concentration and dominance. Thus, policymakers must be vigilant with regard to the possibility of restrictive business practices by transnational corporations as such practices may hurt consumers and efficiency in developing countries.

Regional Cooperation and Guidelines on Competition Policy

As more firms locate in multiple countries it becomes ever more difficult to detect and punish anticompetitive behavior. Therefore, ensuring an effective national CPL increasingly requires international and regional cooperation on competition matters.

A regional cooperation mechanism in ASEAN will have a number of benefits. First, it can help ensure that anticompetitive practices do not impede regional economic integration. Second, national competition regulatory bodies will be able to curb administrative costs by pooling and sharing information, experiences, and resources. Third, it will help ensure that the consequences of anticompetitive practices (e.g. collusion, horizontal or vertical exclusion/foreclosure and mergers) are dealt with explicitly and that individual governments do not tacitly condone such practices among domestic firms to the detriment of firms in other member states (Brussick, P., A. Alvarez and L. Cernat 2005, viii).

Fourth, regional guidelines for competition policy will help make CPL consistent among member states, and this consistency will deepen the benefits of regional economic integration. For example, in allowing businesses to operate under roughly the same rules region-wide, a harmonized CPL will lower transaction costs for cross-border trade and investment, further rationalize resource allocation, bring a wider range of goods and services to market, and allow businesses and consumers alike to expect the same standards in all member states. As horizontal and vertical barriers to entry and trade are removed and regional resources are allocated efficiently, the region will gain productive and dynamic efficiency. It follows that individual member states and the region as a whole will enjoy larger markets, more trade and investment opportunities, expansion of economic activities, improved consumer welfare, and increases in employment, export earnings, and disposable income.

Less-developed member states who are concerned that they have few resources to design, implement, or enforce CPL have the most to gain from a regionally harmonized CPL and an effective national CPL framework. Participating in the development of regional cooperation on competition policy will help them ensure a level playing field and help their competition regulatory bodies learn from other member states as information, experiences, and resources are pooled.

Diversity and Harmonization

Only Indonesia, Singapore, Thailand, and Vietnam have national CPLs, each with differences in objectives, coverage, rules and processes, and exemptions (Table 3-1). Their "horizontal agreements," regarding, for example, prohibitions on price fixing and bid rigging, have some similarities but are still distinct as are their "vertical agreements" regarding fixing dealerships, conditions, or practices in purchases or distribution and the misuse of market power (Tables 3-2 and 3-3).

Table 3-1
Exemptions from Application of National Competition Law in ASEAN

Reason for Exemption	Indonesia	Singapore	Thailand	Vietnam
Improving production or distribution	✓	✓		✓
Promoting technical or economic progress	✓	✓		✓
Promoting SMEs	✓			✓
Promoting exports or competitiveness of domestic firm in international market	✓			✓
Cooperatives	✓			
Farmer cooperatives			✓	
State enterprises or government action		✓	✓	
IPR related	✓			
International contracts ratified by government	✓	✓		
Safeguarding foreign trade and foreign economic cooperation		✓		✓
Contracts related to franchise	✓			

Sources: Law of the Republic of Indonesia No. 5 of 1999 concerning the ban on monopolistic practices and unfair business competition; Singapore's Competition Act; Thailand's Competition Act, B.E. 2542 (1999); Vietnam's Law on Competition.

Table 3-2
Prohibited Horizontal Agreements in National CPLs

Prohibited Agreement/Conduct	Indonesia	Singapore	Thailand	Vietnam
Price fixing	✓	✓	✓	✓
Production restriction	✓	✓	✓	✓
Sale restriction	✓	✓	✓	✓
Bid rigging	✓		✓	✓
Exclusive geographical areas	✓	✓	✓	✓
Quality reduction			✓	
Exclusive dealership			✓	
Market control	✓	✓	✓	✓
Technical development restriction		✓		✓
Investment restriction		✓		✓
Dissimilar conditions to different parties	✓	✓		
Obligation irrelevant to the contract subject	✓	✓		✓
Boycotting	✓			✓

Sources: Law of the Republic of Indonesia No. 5 of 1999 concerning the ban on monopolistic practices and unfair business competition; Singapore's Competition Act; Thailand's Competition Act, B.E. 2542 (1999); Vietnam's Law on Competition.

Table 3-3
Prohibited Misuse of Market Power in National CPLs

Prohibited Conduct	Indonesia	Singapore	Thailand	Vietnam
Predatory behavior towards competitors	✓	✓		✓
Price fixing			✓	✓
Production restriction		✓	✓	✓
Market restriction	✓	✓	✓	✓
Distribution restriction			✓	✓
Technical development restriction	✓	✓		✓
Dissimilar conditions to different parties		✓		✓
Obligation irrelevant to the contract subject		✓		✓
Preventing entry	✓			✓

Sources: Law of the Republic of Indonesia No. 5 of 1999 concerning the ban on monopolistic practices and unfair business competition; Singapore's Competition Act; Thailand's Competition Act, B.E. 2542 (1999); Vietnam's Law on Competition.

These national CPLs have only three objectives in common: promote and protect fair competition, promote and protect economic efficiency, and advance the public interest. Singapore's CPL also aims to enhance productivity and innovation, for which relevant prohibited agreements may be exempted if necessary (Competition Commission of Singapore, 2007, paragraph 2. 24). And Vietnam and Indonesia allow exemptions from prohibited agreements in favor of technological advances. Vietnam's CPL has other objectives as well, such as promoting the competitiveness of SMEs and of Vietnamese enterprises in international markets.

This diversity could lead to unequal competition among firms of different member states and compromise the integrity of a unified market. Hence, to realize a competitive economic region, member states need to carefully develop a harmonized and effective set of objectives.

INTELLECTUAL PROPERTY RIGHTS

The AEC Blueprint focuses on the creation, commercialization, and protection of intellectual property. At present IPR legal coverage and depth in member states varies widely (Table 3-4).

The ASEAN-6 seem to have more coverage and depth than the CLMV for most types of assets (e.g., copyright, patent, trade mark, and design) and have regulatory bodies. Despite the existence of regulatory bodies, laws and regulations put in place long ago have never been updated. The Copyright Act in Myanmar dates back as far as 1914; the Patent Act in Thailand to 1979 and in Malaysia to 1983. In addition, the regulations themselves differ considerably, which will pose a significant challenge when harmonizing policies and practices, whether for IPR registration processes or protection through enforcement.

To move toward an AEC in which intellectual property enhances competitiveness, many gaps in development and in incentives will have to be bridged, particularly between original and newer ASEAN members. Less developed countries, which tend to be net consumers rather than net creators of intellectual property, are less inclined to enforce IP rights. Furthermore, some have argued that least-developed member states would do well to have implicit subsidies to promote use of intellectual property assets, enhance competitiveness in the New ASEAN, facilitate the catching-up process, and permit these countries to become IP-asset creators at a later date.

Creation of IP Assets

IP asset creation involves incentives to innovate, capability to innovate, and the registration of IP rights. The AEC Blueprint recognizes that activities related to innovation need to be improved to boost regional competitiveness. Patent productivity in ASEAN, a proxy indicator of innovation as measured by patents granted to residents and R&D personnel in business, varies among member states and is disappointing even when the performance of Singapore, Malaysia, and Thailand is factored in. Since 1997, ASEAN as a whole has had significantly less patent productivity than Japan or Korea (Tables 3-5, 3-6, and 3-7).

Another indicator — scientific research supported by legislation — suggests that Malaysia and Singapore lead member states and that governments in most developing economies in ASEAN are little involved in supporting IP asset creation, a likely reflection of the fact that such support requires significant public infrastructure (Table 3-8). Thus, for some developing and least-developed countries, international trade and investment and the scientific research that gets transferred through them is crucial for IP-related development.

To support the creation of IP assets and lower the cost of IPR registration, the AEC Blueprint calls for making registration processes effective and convenient and for harmonizing processes. Narrowing the economic development gap (as described in Chapter 5 of this volume) would, of course, expedite harmonization. Private sector contributions are equally important. To achieve the IPR goals outlined in the AEC Blueprint, scientific research cannot be viewed as a uniquely public good. In fact, the private sector in the more developed member states has been facilitating scientific research and R&D and thereby providing an environment conducive to IP asset creation.

Table 3-4
Summary of ASEAN Member States IPR Laws and Regulations by IP Asset Types

IP Asset	ASEAN Member States				
	Singapore	Thailand	Malaysia	Indonesia	Philippines
Copyright	Copyright Act (effective 1987), latest revision 2006	Copyright Act B.E. 2537 (1994)	Copyright Act (1987)	Law No. 19 of 2002 regarding Copyrights	Republic Act No. 8293 (the Intellectual Property Code of the Philippines) (1998)
Patent	Patent Act (effective 1994), latest revision 2005	Patent Act B.E. 2522 (1979)	Patent Act (1983)	Law No. 14 of 2001 regarding Patents	Republic Act No. 8293 (the Intellectual Property Code of the Philippines) (1998), as amended by Republic Act No. 9502 (Universally Accessible Cheaper and Quality Medicines Act of 2008)
Trade Mark	Trade Mark Act (effective 1998), latest revision 2005	Trade Mark Act B.E. 2534 (1991)	Trade Mark Act (1976)	Law No. 15 of 2001 regarding Marks	Republic Act No. 8293 (the Intellectual Property Code of the Philippines) (1998), as amended by Republic Act No. 9502 (Universally Accessible Cheaper and Quality Medicines Act of 2008)
Design	Registered Designs Act (effective 2000), latest revision 2005	Patent Act B.E 2522 (1979) (Patent for Design)	Industrial Design Act (1996) Layout Designs of Integrated Circuited Act (2000)	Law No. 31 of 2000 regarding Industrial Design Law No. 32 of 2000 regarding Lay-out Design of Integrated Circuit	Republic Act No. 8293 (the Intellectual Property Code of the Philippines) (1998)
Trade Secret	NA	Trade Secret Act B.E. 2545 (2002)	NA	Law No. 30 of 2000 regarding Trade Secret	Republic Act No. 8293 (the Intellectual Property Code of the Philippines) (1998)
Geographical Indication	Geographical Indications Act (effective 1998), latest revision 1999	Protection of Geographical Indications Act B.E. 2546 (2003)	Geographical Indications Act (2000)	Government Regulation No. 51 of 2007 regarding Geographical Indication	Republic Act No. 8293 (the Intellectual Property Code of the Philippines) (1998)

continued on next page

Table 3-4 — *cont'd*

IP Asset	ASEAN Member States				
	Singapore	Thailand	Malaysia	Indonesia	Philippines
Plant Varieties	Plant Varieties Protection Act (effective 2004), latest revision 2006	Plant Varieties Protection Act, B.E. 2542 (1999)	Plant Varieties Act (2004)	Law No. 29 of 2000 regarding Plant Variety	Republic Act No. 9168 (An Act to Provide Protection to New Plant Varieties, Establishing National Plant Variety Protection Board, June 2002.
Others	Layout-designs of Integrated Circuits Act (effective 1999), latest revision 2000	Optical Disc Production Act B.E. 2548 (2005) Protection of Layout Design of Integrated Circuit Act B.E. 2543 (2000) Protection and Promotion of Thai Traditional Medicine Knowledge ACT B.E. 1999 (2542)	Optical Discs Act 2000 (Act 606)	NA	Republic Act No. 9150, providing for Protection of Layout Designs (Topographies) of Integrated Circuits, amending certain sections of Republic Act 8293 (Intellectual Property Code of the Philippines) Republic Act No. 9329 (The Optical Media Act of 2003)

IP Asset	ASEAN Member States				
	Brunei	Cambodia	Lao PDR	Myanmar	Vietnam
Copyright	Emergency (Copyright) Order, 1999 (effective May 1, 2000)	Law on Copyright and Related Rights (2003)	The Intellectual Property Law (2007)	Copyright Act of 1914	The Intellectual Property Law (2005) and (revised 2009)
Patent	Invention Act (Chapter 72) (effective since 1925)	Law on Patent, Utility Model Certificate and	The Intellectual Property Law (2007)	NA	NA

	Emergency (Patent) Order, 1999 (gazetted but not enforced yet awaiting enactment of Patent Regulations)	Industrial Design (2003)	NA	NA	NA
Trade Mark	– Trade Mark Act – Trade Mark Rules – Trade Mark (Importation of Infringing Goods) Regulations, 2000 (effective June 1, 2000)	Law on Marks, Trade Name and Acts of Unfair Competition (2002)	The Intellectual Property Law (2007)	NA	NA
Design	Emergency (Industrial Designs) Order, 1999 Industrial Designs Rules, 2000 Emergency (Layout-Designs) Order, 1999 (effective May 1, 2000)	Law on Patent, Utility Model Certificate and Industrial Design (2003)	The Intellectual Property Law (2007)	NA	NA
Trade Secret	NA	Draft Law on Trade Secret and Undisclosed Information	The Intellectual Property Law (2007)	NA	NA
Geographical Indication	NA	Draft Law on Geographical Indication	The Intellectual Property Law (2007)	NA	NA
Plant Varieties	NA	Law on Seed Management and Breeder Right (2008)	The Intellectual Property Law (2007)	NA	NA
Others	NA	NA	NA	NA	NA

Source: Tabulated by authors from official data provided by the ASEAN Member States, including the governments of Singapore, Thailand, Malaysia, Indonesia, the Philippines, Brunei, Cambodia, Lao PDR, Myanmar, and Vietnam.

Table 3-5
Patent Productivity (Patents Granted to Residents/R&D Personnel in Business ('000s))

Country	1997	1998	1999	2000	2001	2002	2003	2004	2005	2006
Japan	221.68	205.01	221.59	192.02	193.44	195.25	190.89	191.56	182.17	n.a.
Korea	160.31	460.82	514.84	263.19	186.35	249.96	237.66	266.25	348.23	n.a.
Indonesia	n.a.	n.a.	n.a.	n.a.	n.a.	n.a.	n.a.	n.a.	n.a.	n.a.
Malaysia	n.a.	10.52	n.a.	7.15	n.a.	7.50	n.a.	3.92	n.a.	33.23
Philippines	n.a.	n.a.	n.a.	n.a.	n.a.	n.a.	n.a.	2.99	n.a.	n.a.
Singapore	2.52	3.44	4.97	9.96	17.12	21.21	13.98	26.95	32.50	24.89
Thailand	11.49	n.a.	5.48	n.a.	8.34	5.41	8.56	8.40	8.00	n.a.

Source: World Intellectual Property Organization; The WIPO Patent Report, 2007 Edition (http://www.wipo.int/ipstats/fr/statistics/patents); OECD Main Science and Technology Indicators 2/2007; UNESCO Web; National sources.

Table 3-6
Number of Patents Granted to Residents (average 2004–2006)

Country	1997	1998	1999	2000	2001	2002	2003	2004	2005	2006
Japan	129,937.00	125,704.00	129,832.00	123,788.00	118,107.00	109,625.33	109,337.00	110,625.67	111,483.33	116,806.33
Korea	14,496.00	35,880.00	39,581.50	34,030.00	29,338.67	24,969.33	27,502.00	31,994.67	39,742.67	59,335.33
Indonesia	n.a.	n.a.	n.a.	n.a.	n.a.	n.a.	n.a.	n.a.	n.a.	n.a.
Malaysia	52.00	21.00	30.00	28.00	27.00	24.67	27.00	29.00	30.67	82.67
Philippines	25.00	6.00	5.50	6.33	n.a.	n.a.	n.a.	16.00	n.a.	n.a.
Singapore	20.00	30.00	39.00	60.00	106.67	171.67	196.00	272.67	376.67	464.33
Thailand	28.00	43.00	36.00	39.00	44.00	47.33	52.33	52.00	59.67	n.a.

Source: World Intellectual Property Organization; The WIPO Patent Report, 2007 Edition (http://www.wipo.int/ipstats/fr/statistics/patents).

Table 3-7
Number of Patents in Force per 100,000 Inhabitants

Country	1997	1998	1999	2000	2001	2002	2003	2004	2005	2006
Japan	690.83	740.34	793.76	820.22	847.36	860.09	n.a.	865.12	879.03	n.a.
Korea	n.a.	n.a.	n.a.	595.11	660.92	688.81	690.57	689.93	874.37	964.84
Indonesia	0.51	0.68	0.63	0.52	n.a.	n.a.	n.a.	n.a.	n.a.	n.a.
Malaysia	36.10	25.35	31.47	24.69	23.32	24.87	26.75	27.37	34.06	35.66
Philippines	2.23	0.79	n.a.	n.a.	n.a.	n.a.	n.a.	n.a.	n.a.	n.a.
Singapore	432.06	383.63	457.20	548.15	703.07	862.74	930.64	948.16	1,008.58	970.15
Thailand	3.26	4.26	1.78	2.63	n.a.	n.a.	n.a.	n.a.	n.a.	n.a.

Source: The WIPO Patent Report, 2007 Edition (http://www.wipo.int/ipstats/fr/statistics/patents).

Table 3-8
Scientific Research Supported by Legislation (0–10 index)

Country	2004	2005	2006	2007	2008
Japan	6.59	6.35	6.85	6.47	6.45
Korea	5.71	6.18	5.01	6.47	4.68
Indonesia	3.51	3.71	3.72	3.79	4.15
Malaysia	6.67	6.19	6.74	6.86	6.35
Philippines	4.75	4.98	4.73	3.07	3.66
Singapore	8.48	8.20	8.44	8.55	8.69
Thailand	5.62	5.00	5.49	4.04	4.64

Source: IMD WCY Executive Opinion Survey based on an index from 0 to 10. The number closer to 10 implies a greater degree of scientific research supported by legislation.

Commercialization of IP

The tangible benefits of commercialization encourage innovation but also burden the user of an IP asset. For example, how does one determine the "right price" for an asset? Can the market function well enough or is there a role for government due to, for example, an existing externality? Does the relationship between creation, commercialization, and protection imply that commercialization should be harmonized across ASEAN to achieve goals for regional competitiveness? We have argued that harmonizing laws and regulations, filing procedures, and enforcement mechanisms will be important in using IP to enhance competitiveness. The ASEAN IPR Action Plan 2004–2010 endorsed by the AEC Blueprint is seen as a step toward a fully functional regional IPR system. But with so many differences in IPR laws and regulations, levels of protection and enforcement capability, and stages of economic development across member states, harmonization poses a Herculean challenge to ASEAN: it will take significant political will to achieve this objective.

Protection of IP

Preserving the value of IP assets requires an effective system of protection, one in which the costs of protection do not exceed the benefits. Where such assets are crucial for a country's catching-up process, for example, providing protection is perceived as a drag on competitiveness. Patent and copyright infringement are common in developing economies, and IP protection is a critical issue in economic relations between developing countries, which tend to be net consumers of intellectual property, and developed countries, which tend to be net creators as well as consumers.

The AEC Blueprint endeavors to improve the effectiveness of IPR protection among member states by providing for sustained consultation and information exchange among national enforcement agencies dealing with protection. As we have noted, member states have widely varying enforcement capabilities and the diversity of laws and their application will make regional initiatives and harmonization challenging at best. The IPR enforcement index scores presented in Table 3-9 indicate the diverse, yet generally poor, performance of member states in providing protection. Only Singapore and, perhaps, Malaysia appear to be effective.

Table 3-9
IPR Enforcement Survey Index (max. score=10)

Country	1999	2000	2001	2002	2003	2004	2005	2006	2007	2008
Japan	7.40	7.39	7.50	6.76	7.11	6.56	6.44	7.07	7.03	6.97
Korea	4.61	6.91	6.00	5.82	5.18	5.63	5.62	5.03	5.20	4.99
Indonesia	3.40	3.96	3.53	2.52	2.53	2.87	2.71	3.05	3.86	3.81
Malaysia	5.92	5.97	5.11	6.23	5.87	6.20	5.24	6.21	6.65	6.12
Philippines	6.22	5.79	5.16	3.65	4.29	3.82	3.52	3.80	3.56	4.33
Singapore	7.97	8.13	8.06	7.87	7.91	8.24	7.90	8.19	8.54	8.36
Thailand	5.16	5.63	5.42	4.89	4.92	5.10	4.72	4.66	3.49	4.58

Source: IMD WCY Executive Opinion Survey based on an index from 0 to 10 (indicating better IPR enforcement).

In sum, since all countries are potential IP creators, registration and enforcement are important to competitiveness. But while net producers of IP see strong registration systems and enforcement mechanisms as essential, net consumers see them as impediments in the economic "catching up" process. Bridging this asymmetry of interests is an important objective of the AEC.

INFRASTRUCTURE DEVELOPMENT

The potential of many AEC initiatives depends on having the right infrastructure in place. The AEC Blueprint highlights seven areas of special concern:

1. Transport cooperation
2. Land transport
3. Maritime and air transport
4. Information infrastructure
5. Energy cooperation
6. Mining cooperation
7. Financing of infrastructure projects

Transport cooperation requires implementing several ASEAN framework agreements (i.e., on multimodal transport, on the facilitation of goods in transit, on the facilitation of inter-state transport). Progress on land transport requires completing the Singapore-Kunming Rail Link (SKRL) and improving road safety in general. The Blueprint recommends creation of a roadmap for "integrated and competitive maritime transport in ASEAN" to strengthen intra-ASEAN shipping markets and services, as well as roadmaps for integration of the air travel sector and proposes an ASEAN Single Aviation Market. It also advances information infrastructure initiatives, including

- Implementing the ASEAN Telecommunications Regulators Council;
- Promoting and deepening regional policy and a regulatory framework to deal with "Next Generation Networks," including interoperability issues;
- Developing a framework for coordinated e-government programs for efficient delivery of public services, and facilitating regional trade, investment and other business activities; and
- Activating the ASEAN e-Government Forum to identify public services for ICT applications.

Cooperation on the trans-ASEAN gas pipelines and the ASEAN power grid projects will optimize the region's energy resources for greater security. Below we describe the Infrastructure Development Program (IDP) of the AEC Blueprint and discuss related policy issues and problems.

AEC and Transport Infrastructure

The purpose of infrastructure development and improvement as expressed in the AEC IDP is to achieve efficient, secure, and integrated transport networks in ASEAN. According to the ASEAN Secretariat, activities as early as 2003 were geared toward greater and deeper regional integration in infrastructure development. A major challenge has been identifying where action on an ASEAN-wide basis is required or advisable. Transport, for example, is crucial to nearly all economic interactions. The transport action agenda adopted in the Hanoi Plan of Action, 1998 (and the Successor Plan of Action in Transport 1999–2004) called for:

- Progressive liberalization of trade in services, notably through adoption of alternative approaches to liberalization;
- Development of the trans-ASEAN transportation network, including civil aviation, major road and rail corridors, principal ports and sea lanes, and inland waterways;
- Implementation of the ASEAN Framework Agreement on Multimodal Transport; and
- Adoption of harmonized vehicle standards and regulations.

A trans-ASEAN transport network plan has been completed, and pertains to 28 major highways, 6 rail lines, 46 seaports, and 51 airports.

Roads

ASEAN Member States have done project preparation studies for the ASEAN highway network and inland freight terminal development. There has been considerable progress on ASEAN agreements on multimodal transport and the ASEAN Agreement on the Facilitation of Goods in Transit. Progress has also been made in the adoption and implementation of harmonized vehicle standards and regulations.

Rail

ASEAN leaders have endorsed the broad thrust of the feasibility study on the Singapore-Kunming Railway Link (SKRL) project, which has been accorded priority status. ASEAN leaders have endorsed the routes agreed to by the transport ministers.

Maritime

The offers of individual ASEAN Member States on maritime transport liberalization were incorporated into the Third Package of Commitments under the ASEAN Framework Agreement on Services (2001). An ASEAN Cruise Development Study has been completed, and a study of maritime transport sector development has been commissioned. Training programs for vessel masters and chief engineers have been held and pilot courses in port management and infrastructure management developed. ALMEC

Corporation's (2002) study of maritime sector development proposed a policy and development framework plan for 2003–2008, but the plan has been slow to take shape. Soesastro (2005) suggests that lack of political will has stalled the plan.

Logistics

In Appendix C, we review infrastructure development issues in logistics and aviation. We note here that logistics is one of the most important aspects of infrastructure and economic integration. Efficient cross-regional coordination will be the basis of an effective logistics system. Barriers to coordination include customs, foreign investment, and mode-specific constraints. In assessing the logistics performance of ASEAN Member States, De Sauza et al. (2007) conclude that Singapore performs very well, followed by Brunei and Thailand.

Aviation

In surveying the aviation policies of ASEAN Member States, Forsyth et al. (2004) found that only the more developed countries have advanced policies and clear policy objectives for the sector. For example, Singapore's aviation policy aims to promote Singapore as an aviation hub. Forsyth et al. also suggest that regional liberalization will generate two types of benefits. First, passengers will gain from lower fares and better service. Second, airlines will gain from falling costs and access to new markets. Liberalization of the sector will also affect government revenue, foreign exchange, employment, and business communications — with costs and benefits in each area depending on a number of circumstances (Forsyth et al. 2004).

Roles and Objectives of Cooperation

The development programs described above pertain to physical or "hard infrastructure" measures, regulatory or "soft infrastructure" measures, or the financing of infrastructure projects. The AEC infrastructure development program can be categorized as shown in Table 3-10.

The Singapore-Kunming Rail Link (SKRL) stands out in the AEC Blueprint; it is part of the Trans-Asian Railway Network. Valautham (2007) observes that activities to develop the network in ASEAN have mostly been carried out within the framework of the SKRL project pursued by the ASEAN Secretariat since 1995. Under the project, the governments and railway organizations of the countries concerned have discussed construction of the missing links to complete the three route options between the two cities. Related feasibility studies have been carried out either by the countries themselves or through the technical assistance of donor countries/agencies, such as the Korea International Cooperation Agency for the missing link between Myanmar and Thailand; or by China for the Cambodian section of the missing link between Cambodia and Vietnam.

Completion of the missing link will allow rail to play a part in economic integration by extending the reach of the container land-bridge currently operating between Malaysia and Thailand to a range of destinations in other countries such as Cambodia, the Lao PDR, and Vietnam.

For road infrastructure, the AEC Blueprint highlights the ASEAN Highway Network (AHN) projects, in particular road construction/improvement of transit transport routes. This will support

Table 3-10
ASEAN Infrastructure Initiatives

Physical or "Hard Infrastructure" Measures	Regulatory or "Soft Infrastructure" Measures
TRANSPORT	

Land Transport
   Singapore-Kunming Rail Link
   ASEAN Highway Network
   Road Safety
Maritime Transport
Air Transport
	The ASEAN Framework Agreement on the Facilitation of Goods in Transit
	The ASEAN Framework Agreement on Multimodal Transport
	The ASEAN Framework Agreement on the Facilitation of Interstate Transport
	Roadmap for Integrated and Competitive Maritime Transport in ASEAN
	Roadmap for Integration of the Air Travel Sector
	ASEAN Single Aviation Market

INFORMATION INFRASTRUCTURE	
	Implement the ASEAN Telecommunications Regulators Council Promote and deepen regional policy and regulatory framework to deal with the opportunities and challenges in the area of Next Generation Networks Develop a general framework or guideline for coordinated ASEAN e-government programs
ENERGY COOPERATION	
Trans-ASEAN Gas Pipelines (TAGP) ASEAN Power Grid (APG)	
FINANCING INFRASTRUCTURE	
SKRL, TAGP, and APG	

Source: ASEAN Secretariat.

AEC policies relative to the free flow of goods within ASEAN and will complement the railway network as a multimodal transport system in ASEAN.

Full use of this infrastructure requires appropriate regulatory measures, such as the framework agreements on multimodal transport, facilitation of goods in transit, and facilitation of inter-state transport. Once infrastructure projects are complete, road transport rules and regulations will have to be harmonized. Harmonization should cover technical aspects (e.g., infrastructure standards, vehicle standards, road signs and signaling, road safety standards) and economic aspects (e.g., road taxes, fuel taxes, and infrastructure charges). In addition, harmonization and liberalization of transport regulations facilitates trade and economic integration, as the European experience shows (see Appendix C for a brief discussion of European air transport).

Policy Issues and Problems

Implementation of agreements, liberalization of the transport services, and transnational infrastructure investment has been difficult in ASEAN, as it has been in other regions. Key agreements are the

ASEAN framework agreements on multimodal transport, on the facilitation of goods in transit, and on the facilitation of inter-state transport.

In raising concerns about implementation, Nikomborirak (2005) notes these agreements were originally proposed because services liberalization was too slow. To facilitate intraregional trade — suffering from cumbersome border procedures and incompatible regulatory standards — ASEAN chose instead to focus on frameworks for transport-related cooperation and coordination. Soesastro (2005) suggests that implementation of detailed action plans for cooperation in transport and in energy lags because of a lack of political will. Making progress in these areas requires building regional constituencies, possibly through new institutional arrangements.

Transport services must be liberalized because implementation of agreements, however difficult, will not guarantee an efficient regional transport system. The transport sector is highly protected in each ASEAN Member State, and transport operators are usually highly subsidized, state-owned enterprises. In this regard, the European experience can be instructive. The European Commission's policy document — *European transport policy for 2010: time to decide* — presented a systematic approach to policy integration covering four themes: shifting the balance between modes of transport, eliminating bottlenecks, placing users at the heart of transport policy, and managing the globalization of transport. Although the AEC is not as ambitious or comprehensive as the EU, some lessons can be borrowed. For example, the railway sectors in EU countries have been liberalized over the past 15 years, enabling healthy competition between modes of transport and between countries. Some infrastructure projects have also been launched at the regional level. This success reflects the fact that railway *policy* has been just as coherent as the physical *infrastructure* has been functional. In ASEAN, not only the railway sector but also road haulage and airline industries could all benefit from similar liberalization. In sum, to enhance efficiency, national transport markets need to be more open to the region, so that operators from different countries can compete.

While the AEC Blueprint IDP concentrates on cooperation projects, a market-oriented approach to infrastructure use is also important (i.e., less state intervention and more liberalization of transport services). An "open sky policy" for example can produce considerable returns in the aviation sector (Appendix C). The same should be encouraged in other sectors, such as road freight transport and the railway sector.

Curtotti et al. (2006) review ASEAN energy cooperation, an area in which member states, under the ASEAN Plan of Action in energy cooperation (APAEC), 2004–2009, are implementing short-, medium- and long-term policy responses to address supply sustainability risks. They indicate that ASEAN is intensifying cooperation in

- Development and exploration of energy sources and supplies;
- Diversification of the energy mix and promotion of alternative fuel sources;
- Facilitation of energy efficiency and conservation;
- Promotion of renewable energy; and
- Enhancement of emergency response coordination and preparedness to minimize risks associated with energy (oil) supply disruptions.

They conclude that cooperation in creating the trans-ASEAN gas pipeline and ASEAN power grid projects between ASEAN members and partners will enhance energy security in the region.

CONSUMER PROTECTION

Currently, consumer protection in most member states is weak and varies widely in coverage (Table 3-11.) As with IPR, it is not always clear how consumer protection laws are enforced. Empirical literature on consumer protection in the member states is lacking. Still, consumer protection will no doubt become prominent as regional integration intensifies and as increasingly prosperous consumers become more aware of protection issues.

Table 3-11
Consumer Protection in Cambodia, Indonesia and Thailand

Area of Protection	Cambodia	Indonesia	Thailand
Advertisement	✓	✓	✓
Contract		✓	✓
Label		✓	✓
Safety	✓		✓

Source: Authors' survey results. For this study, we surveyed the consumer protection laws of various ASEAN Member States. Full survey results are available upon request.

To advance consumer protection, the AEC Blueprint calls for an ASEAN Coordinating Committee on Consumer Protection, a network of consumer protection agencies to facilitate information exchange, and courses for consumer protection officials and consumer leaders in preparation for an integrated ASEAN market.

QUANTITATIVE ESTIMATES OF AEC BENEFITS AND COSTS

As observed in Chapter 1, generating support for the AEC's ambitious programs requires identifying and, where possible, quantifying potential benefits. In this section we provide an empirical assessment of the potential impact of various aspects of the "competitive economic region" called for in the AEC Blueprint. A full assessment would be a lengthy endeavor, so we limit our scope to impacts on economic growth and foreign direct investment, as these are key to regional prosperity (see Chapters 1 and 4).

The relationship between competition and growth is unclear theoretically and empirically (Dutz and Hayri 2000). The same is true with the relationship between competition and investment: competition can easily increase investment, but it may also dampen innovation and the investment activity of dominant firms under certain conditions. In the short run, the relationship between competition and FDI is also ambiguous, underscoring the need for empirical analysis. Despite these ambiguous relationships, no study has attempted to evaluate the impact of AEC competition policy on ASEAN Member States, making this study crucial.

Our analysis uses panel data (i.e., cross-sectional and time-series data) compiled for more than 100 countries beginning in 1980. We employ 26 indicators of AEC "competitive economic region"-related policies. Some of them are beyond the current scope of the AEC, at least as specified in the AEC Blueprint. Nevertheless, they may be identified as critical factors for AEC success. A test based on extreme-bound analysis (EBA) is performed to identify all relevant robust measures associated with the AEC-related policies.

Based on robust measures, the potential impact on economic growth and FDI inflows for Indonesia, Malaysia, the Philippines, Singapore, and Thailand are evaluated by assuming that the goal of the AEC is to improve competitiveness of member states such that they converge toward the most competitive country in the region. This type of approach is also employed in Chapter 4; it gives us a good idea of the "envelope" potential inherent in best practices. The findings will hopefully provide useful information to policymakers and other stakeholders in supporting the AEC, as well as in choosing appropriate policies to improve the competitiveness of each member state.

Methodology

This study follows the influential work of Leamer (1983) and the EBA approach developed by Levine and Renelt (1992) to provide a test of robust partial correlations of various "competitive economic region" policy indicators with economic growth and FDI inflows. Basically, the model is of the simple form:

$$Y = \beta_X X + \beta_M M + \beta_Z Z + \varepsilon,$$

where Y is the dependent variable; X is a set of variables always included; M is a set of policy variables of interest; Z is a set of optional variables that have been identified previously as potential important explanatory variables; β is an estimated coefficient; and ε is an error term.

Since a correct specification of a set of the Z-variables is generally unknown, regressions with all possible subsets of the Z-variables are estimated to provide extreme upper and lower bounds for the estimated coefficient of policy variables (i.e., M-variables). The extreme upper (lower) bound is identified by the highest (lowest) estimated coefficient of the variables of interest, β_M, plus (minus) two standard deviations. If the estimate remains significant and has the same sign within both bounds, the EBA results are considered to be "robust"; otherwise, the results are considered to be "fragile."

For growth and FDI model specifications, a slight variant of the Levine and Renelt (1992) and Sudsawasd and Moore (2006) approaches is applied.[3] Y is either the natural log of GDP per capita (in GDPPC) or the share of FDI in GDP (FDI). In a growth regression, a set of X variables includes the share of investment in GDP (INV), the 5-year lag of real GDP per capita (IGDPPC), the annual rate of population growth (POPG), higher education achievement rate (HEDU), and the secondary school enrollment rate (ENROLL). The X-variable is the export share in GDP, and the M-variables are a set of indicators of the AEC competitive economic region policies, which will be discussed in the next subsection. Due to time constraints, this study is restricted to a set of at most three Z-variables, which are the share of government expenditure in GDP (GOV), the inflation rate (INF), and the growth rate of domestic credit (GDPC).

Data are mainly from three sources: the IMD World Competitiveness Yearbook 2008, the IMF International Financial Statistics, and the World Bank World Development Indictors. The dataset is a panel of over 100 countries with observations covering the 1980–2006 time period. The Hausman (1978) specification test is performed to examine whether a fixed or random effects model specification is appropriate for this study. The results suggest that a random effects model is more appropriate given our data. In addition, this study employs a model with the robust covariance matrix estimator. Only estimation results from the random effects models with robust covariance matrix are reported and discussed.

Note that this study is not the first to apply the EBA to analyze the impact of competition policy on growth. Dutz and Hayri (2000) examine the cross-country relationship between the intensity of competition and growth. They find a strong correlation between growth and effective enforcement of antitrust and competition policy. Unfortunately, the Dutz and Hayri model is characterized by several weaknesses. For instance, their estimation is based on cross-sectional data; time variation is ignored. With a limited dataset, they do not examine the differences between developed and developing economies, for which the results can diverge significantly (see below).

Since it is not appropriate to impose such an assumption, this study takes the analysis a step further by using panel data, and with this richer dataset we can estimate the impact of competition policy in the context of both developing and developed countries. In addition, we extend the scope of the study to include the impact on FDI inflows. Since none of the existing literature examines this relationship, the findings of this study will provide fresh information to policymakers.

Indicators Related to AEC Competitive Economic Region Policies

The objective of this chapter is to evaluate the economic effects of policies related to achievement of a competitive economic region. Those policies focus on competition policy, intellectual property rights, and infrastructure development.[4] Since there is no consensus on indictors that can perfectly capture each element of the AEC in this context, we start by compiling relevant quantitative and qualitative indicators, arriving at the 26 presented in Table 3-12.[5] Fifteen relate to competition policy. They are either direct or indirect measures of the quality and intensity of competition. Some (such as the "Legal and regulatory" indicator) are beyond the scope of the AEC strategic plan, as stated in the AEC Blueprint. However, it is in the interests of this study to explore all relevant competition policy measures that could affect efficiency and the economy. After all, the AEC aims for best practices in this area.

The first indicator, *Openness*, is constructed based on the suggestion of Ariff (2008). Intuitively, in a market that is highly open and faces global competition, firms find it difficult to discriminate between the domestic and global markets. Hence, they become more competitive in pricing. For other competition policy indicators, they are basically qualitative data drawn from the IMD survey. However, like all data of this nature, these qualitative indicators have shortcomings and should be interpreted with caution.[6]

Five indicators pertain to IPR. Four of them are based on hard data. Except for an *Intellectual property rights* indicator, the data are based on a survey opinion on the adequate enforcement of IPR. As discussed above, the effects of the strength of IPR on economic growth and FDI inflows are complex. This leaves us the important task to examine empirically this relationship.

This study classifies infrastructure development indictors into three categories: general infrastructure, telecommunication, and energy infrastructure. For general infrastructure indicators, *Customs' authorities* and *Distribution infrastructure* are qualitative, reflecting responses to the following questions: Do customs' authorities facilitate the efficient transit of goods? Is the distribution infrastructure of goods and services generally efficient? The rest are quantitative indicators. We include two measures for

Table 3-12
Policy Indicators Defined

Indicators	Definition
COMPETITION POLICY	
1. Openness	Export plus import share of real GDP.
2. Legal and regulatory	The legal and regulatory framework encourages the competitiveness of enterprises.
3. Protectionism	Protectionism does not impair the conduct of your business.
4. Public sector contracts	Public sector contracts are sufficiently open to foreign bidders.
5. International transactions	International transactions can be freely negotiated with foreign partners.
6. Foreign investors	Foreign investors are free to acquire control in domestic companies.
7. Subsidies	Subsidies do not distort fair competition and economic development.
8. Competition legislation	Competition legislation is efficient in preventing unfair competition.
9. Product legislation	Product and service legislation does not deter business activity.
10. Value system	The value system in your society supports competitiveness.
11. Capital markets	Capital markets (foreign and domestic) are easily accessible.
12. Immigration laws	Immigration laws do not prevent your company from employing foreign labor.
13. Bureaucracy	Bureaucracy does not hinder business activity.
14. Transparency	Transparency of government policy is satisfactory.
15. Price controls	Price controls do not affect pricing of products in most industries.
INTELLECTUAL PROPERTY RIGHTS	
16. Patents granted to residents	Number of patents granted to residents (average 2004–2006).
17. Securing patents abroad	Number of patents secured abroad by country residents.
18. Intellectual property rights	Intellectual property rights are adequately enforced.
19. Number of patents in force	Per 100,000 inhabitants.
20. Patent productivity	Patents granted to residents/R&D personnel in business ('000s).
INFRASTRUCTURES/GENERAL INFRASTRUCTURE	
21. Customs' authorities	Customs' authorities do facilitate the efficient transit of goods.
22. Distribution infrastructure	The distribution infrastructure of goods and services is generally efficient.
23. Roads	Density of the network, km per square km.
24. Air transportation	Number of passengers carried by main companies, thousands.
TECHNOLOGY	
25. Technological cooperation	Technological cooperation between companies is developed.
ENERGY	
26. Energy infrastructure	Energy infrastructure is adequate and efficient.

Source: Data are obtained from the IMD's World Competitiveness Yearbook 2008, except that the "Openness" data are from the IMF's IFS CD-ROM 2008 and the World Bank's WDI online accessed on July 15, 2008.

telecommunication and energy infrastructure: *Technological cooperation* refers to the extent to which technological cooperation between companies is developed and *Energy infrastructure* relates to adequate and efficient energy infrastructure. In general, all of these infrastructure development indicators are expected to have a positive impact on economic growth and FDI inflows.

The recent data for the original ASEAN countries (Indonesia, Malaysia, the Philippines, Singapore, and Thailand) concerning each indicator are presented in Table 3-13. Singapore holds the highest rank

Table 3-13
Competition Policy Indicators: Indonesia, Malaysia, the Philippines, Singapore, and Thailand

Indicators/Country	Indonesia	Malaysia	Philippines	Singapore	Thailand	Mean	S.D.
Competition Policy							
Legal and regulatory	4.29 (25)	5.35 (16)	3.28 (42)	8.65 (1)	3.78 (34)	5.07	2.14
Protectionism	4.91 (39)	5.28 (35)	3.70 (51)	7.42 (6)	5.45 (33)	5.35	1.34
Public sector contracts	5.30 (35)	4.54 (47)	5.29 (36)	8.23 (1)	6.05 (27)	5.88	1.42
International transactions	6.45 (43)	6.62 (39)	6.22 (44)	9.13 (2)	6.51 (42)	6.98	1.21
Foreign investors	6.30 (40)	4.64 (52)	5.18 (50)	8.63 (10)	5.33 (48)	6.01	1.58
Subsidies	4.00 (48)	5.02 (31)	4.27 (43)	7.07 (4)	5.25 (25)	5.12	1.20
Competition legislation	4.85 (37)	5.42 (31)	3.55 (51)	7.33 (2)	4.44 (41)	5.12	1.41
Product and service legislation	5.22 (45)	6.19 (22)	4.54 (51)	8.12 (1)	5.28 (42)	5.87	1.39
Value system	5.02 (41)	6.92 (10)	5.49 (33)	8.67 (1)	5.66 (29)	6.35	1.47
Capital markets	6.22 (39)	6.34 (37)	5.25 (48)	8.79 (2)	6.58 (35)	6.64	1.31
Immigration laws	4.29 (47)	6.08 (23)	6.36 (16)	7.96 (1)	5.88 (29)	6.11	1.31
Bureaucracy	2.96 (24)	3.85 (15)	1.28 (50)	6.93 (1)	3.11 (21)	3.63	2.07
Transparency	3.63 (37)	4.53 (22)	1.58 (53)	7.70 (2)	2.70 (46)	4.03	2.33
Price controls	5.59 (43)	5.55 (44)	4.90 (49)	7.85 (9)	4.82 (50)	5.74	1.23
Intellectual Property Rights							
Patents granted to residents (2006)	n.a.	83.00 (35)	16.00 (46)	464.00 (22)	60.00 (38)	155.75	207.37
Securing patents abroad (2005)	11.00 (50)	100.00 (35)	18 (46)	388.00 (26)	(22)	107.80	167.68
Intellectual property rights	3.81 (48)	6.12 (27)	4.33 (46)	8.36 (2)	4.58 (42)	5.44	1.85
Number of patents in force (2006)	n.a.	36.00 (38)	n.a.	970.00 (4)	n.a.	503.00	467.00
Patent productivity (2006)	n.a.	33.20 (16)	3.00 (41)	24.90 (21)	8.00 (36)	17.28	14.16
General Infrastructures							
Customs' authorities	2.58 (52)	5.66 (31)	2.72 (51)	8.68 (1)	4.99 (37)	4.93	2.50
Distribution infrastructure	4.00 (53)	7.70 (18)	4.45 (51)	9.44 (1)	6.41 (37)	6.40	2.26
Roads (2005)	0.20 (44)	0.30 (37)	0.67 (31)	4.63 (2)	0.1 (51)	1.18	1.94
Air transportation (2005)	26,836 (16)	20,369 (20)	8,057 (34)	17,744 (23)	18,903 (22)	18,382	6,758.37
Technology							
Technological cooperation	4.47 (48)	6.81 (16)	5.36 (32)	7.50 (2)	5.27 (35)	5.88	1.24
Energy							
Energy infrastructure	3.48 (50)	7.31 (16)	4.60 (43)	9.43 (1)	6.58 (22)	6.28	2.33

Note: Countries' rank orders are in parentheses. Unless specified, the data are 2008 data. n.a. is not available.
Source: IMD's World Competitiveness Yearbook 2008.

for most indicators in the ASEAN region and sometimes in the world. Singapore is ranked first in the world for many indicators, while many of the other original ASEAN countries are ranked almost at the bottom. In addition, it appears that existing policy variation in the Indonesia, Malaysia, the Philippines, and Thailand group is quite large.

Policy variation provides valuable information. It suggests, for example, how difficult it will be to establish AEC competition-related measures and policies. In this study, policy variation is simply measured by a standard deviation from the regional average, shown in Table 3-14. Within the original ASEAN countries, a *Transparency* indicator has the highest variation of all competition policy indicators, whereas, a *Subsidies* indicator has the lowest variation. Thus, this may suggest that, comparing the AEC objective pertinent to transparency, the policy related to subsidies may be easier to get approval from its members. However, this example by no means suggests that policy variation is the only factor influencing policy formulation in the context of the AEC. Other factors (e.g., political perceptions, domestic supports) will contribute to the success of the AEC as well but are outside the scope of this empirical estimation.

Empirical Results

Our empirical study groups data into three broad groups: all country data, developing country data, and developed country data.[7] Regressions without Z-variables are referred to as "base" regressions.[8] Because there are a large number of potential AEC-related policy measures (*M*-variables), the EBA test helps to identify robust measures from the growth and FDI models. Summaries of the EBA tests from growth models for each group of data are presented in Appendix C (Tables C-1 and C-2) and the EBA tests from FDI models are reported in Tables C-3 to 3-4.

The findings are remarkable. When the "all country" dataset is used, the estimated coefficients of six policy measures are robust with respect to growth: *Foreign investors, Price controls, Intellectual property rights, Customs' authorities, Distribution infrastructure*, and *Roads*" (Appendix C, Table C-1), whereas only the Price controls measure is shown as having a robust correlation with FDI inflows

Table 3-14
Summary of Estimated Impacts of AEC Policy on GDP per capita (% change)

Measures/Countries	Indonesia	Malaysia	Philippines	Thailand
COMPETITION POLICY				
Legal and regulatory	6.56	4.94	8.14	7.35
Protectionism (decrease)	4.68	3.97	7.01	3.66
Foreign investors	8.06	14.17	12.13	11.60
Bureaucracy	7.39	5.68	10.67	7.10
INFRASTRUCTURE DEVELOPMENT				
Customs' authorities	11.84	5.70	11.56	7.01
Distribution infrastructure	7.64	2.39	6.99	4.19

Note: Only robust policy indicators are employed. The study considers the case in which the selected ASEAN countries are as competitive as Singapore.

(Table C-3). *As all variables are highly correlated with growth and/or FDI, the evidence generally suggests strong positive effects associated with strengthening competition policies.* In addition, it shortens the list of robust policy-related measures for a closer look from policymakers.

Next, the EBA test is performed with the dataset restricted to developing countries. The list of robust measures related to growth changes significantly. The six robust policy measures become *Legal and regulatory, Protectionism, Foreign investors, Bureaucracy, Customs' authorities,* and *Distribution infrastructure* (Table C-2), though the results for FDI are the same as in the case of the full sample pooling (Table C-4). Note that the findings confirm the hypothesis that the relationship between policy measures and growth may vary significantly, depending upon a country's level of development. Thus, policy recommendations for developing ASEAN countries should be guided to some degree by this empirical evidence.

Finally, the EBA results from the developed country dataset (not shown, due to space constraints) reveal that none of the competitive policy measures is robustly correlated with growth. These results suggest that most of the benefits from strengthening competition and infrastructure development policies are to be found in developing countries, not developed countries.

AEC Policy Evaluation

In this section, we evaluate the quantitative impact of AEC policies on growth and FDI inflows for Indonesia, Malaysia, the Philippines, and Thailand ("Selected ASEAN"). For evaluation methods, first, the target of the AEC is assumed to be improvement in competitiveness for all member states, such that each converges to the same level as the most competitive country in the region, our "best practices" assumption (Chapter 4 uses a related approach regarding changes in FDI stocks). In addition, only the robust policy-related indicators are considered, for which Singapore is found to be the most competitive.

Since the Selected ASEAN group is composed of all developing countries, the estimated coefficients of the "base" regression using a panel of the developing-country dataset are employed. The difference between the actual and Singapore-target level of each robust indicator is calculated. Given all this information, the impacts of AEC policies on growth and FDI inflows can be assessed. The results are presented in Tables 3-14 and 3-15.

The results indicate that the Selected ASEAN group (Indonesia, Malaysia, the Philippines, and Thailand) will benefit from the AEC in economic growth and FDI inflows. In terms of GDP per capita growth, Selected ASEAN is expected to grow around 3 to 15 percent more due to AEC competition policies. If infrastructure development in the Selected ASEAN countries converges to that of Singapore, growth in GDP per capita of the group will likely increase by 2 to 12 percent. In addition, the Selected

Table 3-15
Summary of Estimated Impacts of AEC policy on FDI Share of GDP (% change)

Measures/Countries	Indonesia	Malaysia	Philippines	Thailand
COMPETITION POLICY				
Price controls	10.10	10.30	13.22	13.56

Note: Only robust policy indicators are employed. The study considers the case in which the selected ASEAN countries are as competitive as Singapore.

ASEAN countries will become more attractive destinations for FDI with the elimination of price controls. The estimation suggests around 10 to 14 percent increases in the share of FDI inflows as a percentage of GDP.

One might wonder whether the estimated impacts of the AEC policies on all member states are too high. These are certainly impressive numbers. However, considering all the effects we are taking into consideration, these large changes are not counterintuitive. First — as was noted in Chapter 1 with the World Bank "Ease of Doing Business" indicators as well as the survey in this chapter — ASEAN Member States vary widely in levels of competitiveness and related measures. According to the World Bank and other sources, Singapore is the world's most business-friendly country. Hence, as we are assuming that the Selected ASEAN group will converge to best-practice levels, the impact of the AEC policies are naturally going to be large. Second, the estimations assume full realization of AEC policies, which may, realistically, take a long time as it did for the EU Single Market. If it takes 10 years for each member state to converge at the same level as Singapore today, the estimated impact in each year during this period would be approximately around one tenth of the numbers cited above. Finally, the AEC Blueprint policies may go a long way in helping the Selected ASEAN countries approach best practices; however, full implementation of regional best-practices is beyond what the AEC Blueprint has set out to do. Hence, the actual impact for each member state will likely be smaller, at least given the current ambitions of the AEC Blueprint.

In sum, our findings suggest that economic integration in ASEAN would do well to emphasize policies aimed at improving the "Legal and regulatory" framework, (reducing) "Protectionism," enhancing measures *vis-à-vis* "Foreign investors," reducing "Bureaucracy," improving efficiency of "Customs' authorities," and implementing "Distribution infrastructure" measures. To be specific, first, the AEC might extend its cooperation to include the legal and regulatory frameworks that encourage the competitiveness of firms in its member states. Second, all protectionist policies in the member states, including tariff barriers and state aid to enterprises, should be eliminated to improve market efficiency and economic growth. Third, foreign investors should be freer to acquire control in domestic corporations for both privately owned and state-owned enterprises to promote economy-wide competition. Fourth, since bureaucracy could hinder business activity and economic growth, policies that improve the efficiency and transparency of bureaucratic measures could stimulate economic growth considerably. The findings confirm that the efficiency of customs' authorities and distribution infrastructure of goods and services play important roles in promoting regional prosperity. Finally, a primary AEC focus should be on the elimination of price controls used throughout the member states to increase FDI into the region.

SUMMARY AND CONCLUSIONS

Our analysis of the "competitive economic region" component of the AEC argues strongly that effective implementation of measures already stipulated in the AEC Blueprint — and related measures that might be considered in the future — will generate significant economic gains to ASEAN in general and to its less-developed members in particular. The likely implications of the AEC on various ASEAN stakeholders are summarized in Table 3-16.

We have considered the economic effects of measures related to competition policy, infrastructure, energy, and IPR as articulated in the AEC Blueprint. In the first part of the chapter, we found that a great deal of diversity exists in these areas, and make a strong case for improving competition policy in

Table 3-16
Summary of AEC Benefits for Stakeholders: Competitive Economic Region

Stakeholders	AEC Process	AEC Major Benefits
1. ASEAN as a regional grouping	Creates links necessary to foster regional integration	Stronger infrastructure links; less policy divergence in competition and IPR; more behind-the-border cooperation consistent with deep integration and necessary for a single market and production base.
2. ASEAN Member States	Improve national policy regimes regarding competitive-economic-region policies; stimulate significantly economic growth and development	Create a roadmap to best practices in competition policy, infrastructure development, and IPR; enhance efficiency; protect consumers and increase safety, from consumer products to road safety; increase per capita GDP by 2–12 percent.
3. CLMV countries	In addition to (2), reduce policy disparities and infrastructural gaps, improve interconnectedness with rest of ASEAN	As these are the least developed, closing the policy and "best practices" gaps will lead to the greatest gains; infrastructure improvements will arguably help the CLMV the most; implementing AEC policies will strengthen policy regimes in all CLMV countries, as AFTA has in the area of trade; better inter-linkages and creation of single market will expand fragmented trade and, hence, benefit SMEs.
4. ASEAN businesses including SMEs	Same as (2) but also will improve supply chains and production networks of which SMEs in particular can benefit	Better competition policy will create a more level playing field; adoption of best practices will reduce costs associated with regulation and bureaucracy; better infrastructure will lower business costs and improve opportunities; better IPR protection will stimulate innovation; strong growth effects will improve significantly business environment; better inter-linkages and creation of single market will expand fragmented trade and, hence, benefit SMEs.
5. ASEAN investors	Same as (2), including improvement in regulatory regimes and investment opportunities	With rapid development in ASEAN, infrastructure investments will continue to offer important opportunities; greater efficiencies will lower project costs and increase investments; policy harmonization and upgrading will enhance stability, lower risk.
6. ASEAN consumers	Focus for first time on protecting ASEAN consumers in the integration process	Rise in consumer awareness as the region becomes more prosperous; better competition policy will help consumers; regional norms will improve quality and safety.
8. ASEAN's global partners	AEC embraces nondiscrimination and best practices	Measures and policies included in competitive economic region are nondiscriminatory: FDI will gain the same efficiencies as local firms, perhaps even more as logistics, for example, are more important for foreign firms; enhanced IPR will help foreign innovation exporters; reduction in policy dispersion in favor of best practices will make global harmonization, where relevant, easier.

individual member states as well as harmonizing policies across the region. We also emphasize that improving IPR laws and their implementation will help stimulate innovation and attract FDI. Infrastructure development is also considered at length; without dedicated efforts to improve transportation infrastructure the potential of the AEC will be restricted.

In the second part of the chapter, we presented an empirical estimation of the impact of several AEC-related policies on economic growth and FDI inflows. Our estimates indicate that the correlations are robust and that developing countries will benefit the most from increasing competition and from infrastructure development. In terms of GDP per capita, the Indonesia, Malaysia, the Philippines, and Thailand are expected to grow around 3 to 15 percent more due to AEC competition policies and by around by 2 to 12 percent more due to infrastructure improvements. In addition, the share of FDI inflows to these member states as a percent of GDP is expected to increase around 10 to 14 percent with the improvement in "price controls." These findings suggest large positive effects and give weight to the merit of implementing AEC policies for creating a competitive economic region.

We again emphasize that some of the policies identified in this study go beyond the scope of those in the AEC Blueprint. Nevertheless, they are consistent with the goals of the AEC (i.e., to increase regional economic efficiency and remove barriers to regional economic integration). Moreover, the findings are based on strong underlying assumptions (e.g., that all member states target the level of competitiveness to be consistent with the regional leader, a difficult prospect given large existing regional policy divergences). Therefore, the actual impact of AEC-related policies could be much smaller and the estimated impacts derived in this study should be considered as upper bounds.

NOTES

1. The exception would be the recently established ASEAN Experts Group on Competition, which held its first meeting in March 2008.
2. See Neven, D. and P. Seabright, 1997 and Utton, M.A., 2006.
3. Levine and Renelt (1992) use the EBA to investigate cross-country linkages between various economic policy indicators and growth and investment. Likewise, Sudsawasd and Moore (2006) use the EBA to examine the linkage between trade policy uncertainty and investment by using panel data.
4. It is unfortunate that we are unable to find indicators closely related to consumer protection measures, another important element of the AEC Blueprint in this area.
5. One useful data source is the IMD World Competitiveness Yearbook. It has the comprehensive global data on competitiveness, in which data of 55 countries based on 331 criteria are collected. Around two-thirds of the measures are based on hard data collection and the remaining one-third derives from an executive opinion survey.
6. For instance, the "Competition legislation" variable is based on the following question: "Is competition legislation efficient in preventing unfair competition?" The responses from large corporations that hold some monopoly power may give high marks to this question even if the market structure is highly concentrated. Consequently, this indicator could have a reverse relation with competition. Since a relationship between competition policy indicators and the intensity of competition is unclear, it becomes even more difficult to identify the true relationship with economic growth and FDI inflows.
7. Developing and developed countries are classified according to the World Bank classification.
8. Although the estimation results are not reported in this paper, they are available upon request.

4
The AEC and Investment and Capital Flows

Rafaelita M. Aldaba, Josef T. Yap, and Peter A. Petri

As agreed in the AEC Blueprint, ASEAN is committed to achieving "free flow of investment" and "freer flow of capital" among its member states by 2015. ASEAN is focusing mainly on FDI inflows but is also concerned with regional financial integration, which entails opening the financial services industry and liberalizing capital flows among member states. Of the six dimensions of financial liberalization identified by Williamson and Mahar (1998), ASEAN is committed to two that are key to global financial integration: free entry into the financial services industry and liberalization of international capital flows. The other four — elimination of credit controls, deregulation of interest rates, bank autonomy, and private ownership of banks — are considered largely of national interest.

In theory, investment flows are part of capital flows but issues related to investment flows are distinct from those related to other capital flows. This is reflected in the objectives of the AEC wherein "free" is associated with investment and "freer" with capital. The structure of this chapter is based on this distinction. We first describe FDI inflows, the status of financial liberalization and integration in ASEAN, and the trade — investment nexus and production networks. We then survey the literature on the empirical effects of regional economic integration on FDI flows and the impact of financial liberalization. We also provide quantitative estimates of the impact of the AEC on FDI inflows and discuss the qualitative effects of AEC-related policy measures on FDI and capital flows.

INVESTMENT FLOWS AND CAPITAL FLOWS IN ASEAN

As Table 4-1 shows, the composition of capital flows to emerging markets and developing countries has changed over time, with inflows of FDI making up a growing share. This trend held true in ASEAN Member States until the 1997 financial crisis, after which the share fell sharply, from a 35 percent

Table 4-1
Composition of Gross Inflows to ASEAN, Emerging Markets, and Other Developing Countries

	1980–84	1985–89	1990–94	1995–99	2000–04	2000–06
ASEAN (US$ billion)	23.1	35.1	51.3	75.6	89.9	113.2
Share of FDI	13.0	13.6	27.3	35.0	25.9	25.7
Share of Equity and Portfolio	4.5	3.4	6.9	8.2	5.7	9.3
Share of Debt	82.5	82.9	65.8	56.8	68.4	65.0
Emerging markets (US$ billion)	66	60	194	328	288	n.a.
Share of FDI	15.5	27.3	24.4	40.7	48.6	n.a.
Share of Equity and Portfolio	1.5	3.4	11.7	11.0	12.1	n.a.
Share of Debt	83.0	69.3	63.9	48.2	39.3	n.a.
Other developing countries (US$ billion)	6	4	7	13	16	n.a.
Share of FDI	15.1	17.2	27.7	40.9	44.2	n.a.
Share of Equity and Portfolio	1.1	0.6	0.5	0.5	0.4	n.a.
Share of Debt	83.8	82.2	71.8	58.6	55.4	n.a.

Note: Data for ASEAN exclude Brunei, Lao PDR, and Vietnam, which do not submit IIP Statements to the IMF.
Source: ASEAN data, IMF Financial Statistics; IMF Balance of Payments Statistics and International Investment Position (IIP); Emerging Markets and Other developing countries, Table 1 of Prasad and Rajan (2008).

average in 1995–1999 to an average share of 25.7 percent for the period 2000–2006. Developing countries' share of external debt has declined over time as well, but this trend also reversed for ASEAN as a group after the 1997 crisis. This reversal was largely due to the assistance from official creditors required to address liquidity problems. The share of equity and portfolio flows has increased steadily for emerging markets, which includes the majority of ASEAN Member States. For "other developing countries," however, portfolio and equity flows have stagnated, reflecting the relatively poor investment climate in these countries.

AEC and Free Flow of Investment

Investment cooperation and protection in ASEAN is currently implemented through the 1998 Framework Agreement on the ASEAN Investment Area (AIA) and the 1987 ASEAN Agreement for the Promotion and Protection of Investment. The AIA originally covered liberalization of five sectors and their related services: manufacturing, agriculture, fishery, forestry, and mining and quarrying. In 2003 it was amended to cover education, healthcare, telecommunications, tourism, banking and finance, insurance, trading, e-commerce, distribution and logistics, transportation and warehousing, and professional services such as accounting, engineering, and advertising. The AIA grants national treatment to investors at the pre-establishment and post-establishment stages, with some exceptions identified in temporary exclusion lists (TELs) and sensitive lists (SLs). The TELs will be phased out based on agreed timelines and the SLs will be reviewed periodically, though it has no timeline for phase out (Table 4-2).

Under the AEC Blueprint, the AIA and related agreements will be enhanced through the ASEAN Comprehensive Investment Agreement (ACIA), signed on February 26, 2009 and to come into force

Table 4-2
Schedule of Temporary Exclusion List Phase Out for ASEAN Investment under the AIA

End Date	Manufacturing	Agriculture, Fishery, Forestry & Mining and Services incidental to the five sectors
1 Jan 2003	ASEAN-6: Brunei, Indonesia, Malaysia, Philippines, Singapore, and Thailand	
Myanmar		
1 Jan 2010	Vietnam, Lao PDR, and Cambodia	ASEAN-6, Cambodia
1 Jan 2013		Vietnam
1 Jan 2015		Lao PDR, Myanmar

Source: ASEAN Secretariat.

within six months of signing. The ACIA, which takes into account international best practices, is based on four pillars: liberalization, protection, facilitation, and promotion (Exhibit 4-1). Like most "new age" FTAs, the AEC Blueprint includes deeper integration provisions vital to investment. These cover services, standards, competition law, customs cooperation, intellectual property rights, and dispute

---

Exhibit 4-1
Four Pillars of the ASEAN Comprehensive Investment Agreement

LIBERALIZATION ASEAN Member States will progressively liberalize their investment regimes until they achieve free and open investment by 2015. Member states are committed to extending nondiscriminatory treatment, including national treatment and most favored treatment, to investors in ASEAN with few, if any, exceptions; to reducing and, where possible, removing restrictions to entry for investments in Priority Integration Sectors covering goods; and reducing and, where possible, removing restrictive measures and other impediments, including performance requirements.

PROTECTION The ACIA provides enhanced protection for all investors and investments, regardless of nationality. It has provisions on investor and state dispute settlement mechanisms; transfer and repatriation of capital, profits, dividends, etc; transparent coverage on the expropriation and compensation; full protection and security; and treatment of compensation for losses resulting from strife.

INVESTMENT FACILITATION The ACIA provides for more transparent, consistent, and predictable investment rules, regulations, policies, and procedures. ASEAN Member States are committed to harmonizing investment policies to achieve industrial complementation and economic integration simplifying procedures for investment application and approval; disseminating information on investment rules, regulations, policies and procedures, including developing one-stop investment centers or investment promotion boards; strengthening databases on all forms of investments covering goods and services; strengthening coordination among ministries and agencies; consulting with ASEAN private sectors to facilitate investment; and working toward areas of complementation ASEAN-wide as well as bilateral economic integration.

PROMOTION The ACIA also commits member states to promoting (1) ASEAN as an integrated investment area and production network; (2) intra-ASEAN investments, particularly investments from the ASEAN-6 to the CLMV countries; (3) the growth and development of small and medium-sized enterprises and multinational corporations; (4) industrial complementation and production networks among MNCs in ASEAN; (5) joint investment missions for regional clusters and production networks; and (5) a network of bilateral agreements on avoidance of double taxation among ASEAN countries.

settlement, all of which are crucial in reducing transaction costs and in attracting efficiency-oriented FDI. (These topics are considered in-depth in other chapters.)

The AEC Blueprint is committed to open regionalism, national treatment, and MFN treatment of investors. It also recognizes the importance of creating an integrated production base to capture FDI and hone the region's competitive edge as a globally oriented manufacturing base. FDI has encouraged the growth of regional production networks in ASEAN and East Asia. Those networks are at the heart of intraregional trade and investment flows and are key drivers of economic growth in ASEAN together with its integration with the East Asian region. The new ACIA provides clear timelines for investment liberalization in line with the AEC; extends benefits to foreign-owned ASEAN-based investors; and offers a more liberal, facilitative, transparent, and competitive investment environment. Hence, we expect that the AEC should generate significant dividends for the region and will set the stage for a single market and production base.

AEC and Freer Flow of Capital

Freer flow of capital is an integral part of the ASEAN Roadmap for Monetary and Financial Integration adopted in 2003. During the 12th ASEAN Finance Ministers Meeting in Danang, Vietnam, in April 2008 the elements of the roadmap were highlighted in the joint ministerial statement (Exhibit 4-2).

ASEAN FDI and Production Networks

As shown in Figure 4-1, all ASEAN Member States except Indonesia experienced rising average shares of FDI to GDP in the 2000–2006 period as compared to the 1990s.

ASEAN FDI Stocks

ASEAN today attracts 3.5 percent of the world's FDI, and its inward FDI stocks are equal to about one-third of its GDP (Table 4-3). This is reasonably high by world standards, but not so by the region's own historical standards. ASEAN's share of world foreign investment used to be one-third larger in the early1990s, when its share of world income was lower. Since then, ASEAN's popularity among investors has declined in relative terms, reflecting some combination of increased perception of risk (caused by the 1997–98 Asian financial crisis), less expansionary macroeconomic policies, competition from China and India, and the region's somewhat deteriorated rankings in world investment indices.

Of course, these generalizations hide much variation. Vietnam, for example, has attracted exceptional amounts of foreign capital, even as its macroeconomic challenges put future flows at risk. In addition, FDI inflows into the region have been rising gradually as ASEAN adjusts to the emergence of China and the risks of another financial crisis recede. But foreign investment rates are still far below reasonable expectations in some countries, especially Indonesia and the Philippines.[1]

The promise of the AEC is to return ASEAN to a trajectory of rapid investment growth once the current economic uncertainties are resolved. This should involve intraregional investments as well as new FDI inflows, which are especially desirable for expanding regional production networks. A variety of studies have analyzed the role of ASEAN as a production hub, and view the region very positively as a destination for vertical FDI (Fukao et al. 2003, Urata 2001). The AEC can be expected to affect investment through several channels. Some sections of the AEC Blueprint,

---

Exhibit 4-2
Excerpts from Joint Ministerial Statement of 12ᵗʰ ASEAN Finance Ministers Meeting
Regarding ASEAN Roadmap for Monetary and Financial Integration

DEEPENING CAPITAL MARKETS
To support the AEC goals of freer capital flows and our vision for an interlinked ASEAN securities market, our officials have been engaging the private sector to distill the key issues that impede capital markets development in ASEAN. To this end, we agreed to establish a Medium Term Strategic Framework that systematically maps out action items to strengthen market linkages, market access and market liquidity.

In particular, on establishing market linkages, we agreed on the usefulness of working with bond information providers to facilitate the widest possible dissemination of ASEAN bond markets data to enhance international investors' interests. We also supported the promotion of alliances among ASEAN Exchanges and welcomed the exploration of greater collaborative efforts towards enhancing market linkages and liquidity in the region. We will also look at how best to achieve a more conducive environment for regional cross border financial flows in ASEAN.

We noted the harmonization initiatives to develop ASEAN and Plus Standards to facilitate greater efficiency in cross border issuance of equity and debt securities to strengthen the attractiveness and competitiveness of ASEAN as a fund-raising centre.

We agreed to strengthen our dialogue mechanisms with key market participants operating in ASEAN capital markets. This will enable us to keep abreast of capital market developments, and ensure that our markets remain responsive to the needs of issuers, investors and financial intermediaries.

REINFORCING FINANCIAL SERVICES LIBERALIZATION
We have committed to liberalize key financial services sectors by 2015, towards our Leaders' objective of achieving the AEC. Our officials will assess the feasibility of further expanding the scope and pace of liberalization. We reiterated our commitment to facilitate intraregional trade and investment by progressively opening up our financial services sector to one another.

In this regard, we are pleased with the conclusion of the Fourth Round of financial services liberalization negotiations under the ASEAN Framework Agreement on Services (AFAS) and have signed the Protocol to Implement the Fourth Package of Financial Services Commitments this afternoon. We agreed to launch the Fifth Round of negotiations which will conclude by 2010. Our officials will continue to facilitate financial services negotiations with our Dialogue Partners.

CAPITAL ACCOUNT LIBERALIZATION
Capital Account liberalization is important to promote growth and to support regional economic integration. We therefore reaffirmed our commitments to further liberalize capital account at a pace that will ensure the maximization of the benefits while providing adequate safeguards against macroeconomic instability.

---

especially Sections A3 and A4 on the free flow of investment and freer flow of capital, are designed to facilitate the flow of capital into and within the region. And the general integration of ASEAN, with concomitant improvements in the region's productivity, will provide inducement for companies to invest in ASEAN production sites.

ASEAN FDI Inflows

Table 4-4 presents FDI flows to the region by source country and by sector during the period 1999–2006. The cumulative flows to the ASEAN Member States amounted to US$194 billion.[2] The largest source of FDI is the EU (36 percent of the total), followed by Japan (17 percent), and the United States (13 percent). Intra-ASEAN investment, which reached a cumulative total of about US$23 billion,

Rafaelita M. Aldaba, Josef T. Yap, and Peter A. Petri

Figure 4-1
FDI Stock as Share of GDP (%)

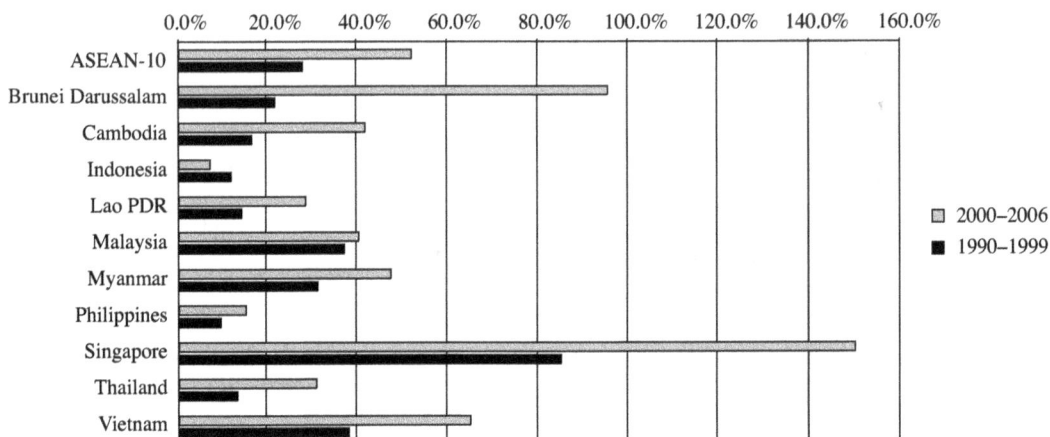

Sources: IMF-World Economic Outlook, 2007; UNCTAD FDI Statistics Online.

Table 4-3
ASEAN's Share of World FDI Stocks

	Stock ($ millions)			Distribution of World Stock (%)			Annual Growth Rate (%)	
	1990	*2000*	*2006*	*1990*	*2000*	*2006*	*1990–2000*	*2000–06*
World total	1,779,198	5,810,189	11,998,838	100.00	100.00	100.00	12.6	12.8
ASEAN	63,165	263,349	420,025	3.55	4.53	3.50	15.3	8.1
Brunei Darussalam	33	3,868	9,861	0.00	0.07	0.08	61.0	16.9
Cambodia	38	1,580	2,954	0.00	0.03	0.02	45.3	11.0
Indonesia	8,855	24,780	19,056	0.50	0.43	0.16	10.8	−4.3
Lao PDR	13	556	856	0.00	0.01	0.01	46.1	7.5
Malaysia	10,318	52,747	53,575	0.58	0.91	0.45	17.7	0.3
Myanmar	281	3,865	5,005	0.02	0.07	0.04	30.0	4.4
Philippines	3,268	12,810	17,120	0.18	0.22	0.14	14.6	5.0
Singapore	30,468	112,633	210,089	1.71	1.94	1.75	14.0	10.9
Thailand	8,242	29,915	68,058	0.46	0.51	0.57	13.8	14.7
Vietnam	1,650	20,596	33,451	0.09	0.35	0.28	28.7	8.4
Major emerging regions	166,942	1,164,577	2,207,352	9.38	20.04	18.40	21.4	11.2
China	20,691	193,348	292,559	1.16	3.33	2.44	25.0	7.1
India	1,657	17,517	50,680	0.09	0.30	0.42	26.6	19.4
Hong Kong, China	45,073	455,469	769,029	2.53	7.84	6.41	26.0	9.1
Eastern Europe	2,988	93,443	331,750	0.17	1.61	2.76	41.1	23.5
Latin America	96,533	404,800	763,335	5.43	6.97	6.36	15.4	11.2
Major developed	1,144,749	3,437,584	7,223,416	64.34	59.16	60.20	11.6	13.2
European Union	749,838	2,180,717	5,434,329	42.14	37.53	45.29	11.3	16.4
United States	394,911	1,256,867	1,789,087	22.20	21.63	14.91	12.3	6.1

Source: UNCTAD FDI online database.

Table 4-4
FDI Flows to ASEAN, by Source Country and Sector 1999–2006 (US$ million)

Sector	Japan	US	EU	ROK	HK	Taiwan	PRC	ASEAN	Others	Total
Agriculture, fishery & forestry	–40	166	336	220	–50	104	26	503	24	1,290
Mining & quarrying	124	–197	6,119	201	245	87	807	2,421	1,003	10,810
Manufacturing	19,369	939	33,625	1,229	987	2,189	259	8,119	7,869	74,584
Construction	195	–339	248	–213	27	79	8	277	109	391
Trade/commerce	5,701	5,646	6,403	614	812	80	419	2,914	3,127	25,717
Financial intermediation	6,173	11,896	13,639	152	732	2,249	–48	2,864	4,672	42,329
Real estate	–82	1,310	3,150	640	431	193	419	4,257	751	11,069
Services	2,183	2,337	4,158	423	226	465	122	2,818	4,306	17,039
Others	1	2,732	1,931	203	927	161	–5	–1,657	4,384	8,677
Total	33,624	24,489	69,609	3,470	4,337	5,606	2,008	22,515	26,246	19,3987

Note: The total includes adjustments on Cambodian and Philippine data.
Source: ASEAN Secretariat.

accounted for 12 percent. The emerging economies of East Asia contributed about 8 percent (Taiwan, 3 percent; Korea, 2 percent; China, 1 percent; Hong Kong, 2 percent). The manufacturing sector received the bulk of the flows (38 percent of the total cumulative flows for the period), followed by financial services (22 percent), and trade/commerce (13 percent). Other services accounted for 8 percent while real estate and mining and quarrying registered equal shares of about 6 percent each. Except for the United States, FDI from all source countries was concentrated in manufacturing. During this period, US FDI was highest in financial services.

The biggest source of intra-ASEAN investment for the period 1999 to 2006 was Singapore, which accounted for 64 percent of the total cumulative flows for the period (Table 4-5). Malaysia followed with a share of 21 percent and Indonesia with a share of 11 percent. Manufacturing accounted for 36 percent of the total intraregional FDI flows. Trade and commerce, financial services, and other services had a combined share of 39 percent, while real estate accounted for 18 percent.

For the period 2002 to 2006, Thailand received the largest share of intraregional FDI flows (35 percent), followed by Singapore and Indonesia (22 percent each), Vietnam (5 percent), Cambodia (2 percent), Lao PDR (0.16 percent), and Myanmar (0.6 percent).

FDI — Trade Nexus

Trade flows are treated at length in other chapters. It suffices here to note that ASEAN exports and imports are heavily concentrated in the machinery sector, which consists of the following commodity groups:

- Non-electrical machinery, including plant and capital equipment
- Office machinery and computers

Rafaelita M. Aldaba, Josef T. Yap, and Peter A. Petri

Table 4-5
Intra-ASEAN FDI Cumulative Flows by Source Country and Sector, 1999–2006 (US$ million)

Sector	BD	Cam	Ind	Lao PDR	Mal	Myan	Phil	Sing	Thai	Viet	Total
Agriculture, fishery & forestry	—	1	–3	—	201	3	22	192	89	0	503
Mining & quarrying	0	—	22	—	198	0	18	2,178	3	1	2,421
Manufacturing	16	1	37	8	401	2	148	7,343	156	7	8,119
Construction	3	—	–20	0	112	0	3	137	41	0	277
Trade/commerce	85	6	115	0	–176	27	10	2,807	31	10	2,914
Financial intermediation	–7	0	431	1	1,048	–1	124	1,782	–514	0	2,864
Real estate	4	4	1,776	1	1,995	45	81	337	–2	18	4,257
Services	10	0	81	0	845	11	3	1,463	397	8	2,818
Others	5	7	92	0	91	1	13	–1,890	21	4	–1,657
Total	116	18	2,530	11	4,714	87	421	14,349	220	48	22,515

Source: ASEAN Secretariat.

Table 4-6
Intra-ASEAN FDI Flows: 2002–2006 by Host Country (US$ million)

Host Country	2002	2003	2004	2005	2006	Total
Brunei Darussalam	21.23	36.79	19.66	19.43	9.71	106.82
Cambodia	8.52	19.88	31.92	129.18	155.54	345.04
Indonesia	1,296.62	383.46	204.25	883.32	1,524.53	4,292.18
Lao PDR	2.92	2.98	7.75	6.68	10.56	30.9
Malaysia	0.02	251.12	980.17	572.91	467.82	2,272.05
Myanmar	25.11	24.28	9.31	38.35	27.79	124.84
Philippines	87.44	175.37	71.11	12.69	−95.56	251.06
Singapore	762.3	699.2	548	1,175.60	1,137.70	4,322.80
Thailand	1,408.29	1,060.42	688.71	762.22	2,822.12	6,741.76
Vietnam	200.43	100.4	242.87	164.72	181.89	890.31
TOTAL ASEAN	3,812.89	2,753.90	2,803.75	3,765.11	6,242.09	19,377.75

Source: ASEAN Secretariat.

- Electrical machinery, including television receivers, sound recorders and reproducers, and telecommunications equipment
- Transportation machinery vehicles and parts.

These commodity groups comprised 46.5 percent of ASEAN trade in 2006 (Table 4-7). Within the ASEAN region these groups accounted for about 46 percent of the total and outside the region they made up almost 47 percent of the total. That a large part of intra-industry trade in ASEAN and East Asia is vertical is attributed to (1) diversity in the level of economic development among East Asian economies; and (2) the emerging regional production networks through which parts and components of different quality and characteristics are being traded for the production of finished goods.

Intra-industry trade is closely associated with FDI flows and the establishment of regional production networks. Foreign investment flows usually precede the onset of joint production between developed and developing economies. Multinational corporations fragment their production processes into sub-processes located on the basis of comparative advantage, giving rise to specialization in production (Kawai 2005). Thailand, for example, has become the regional hub for Toyota and the world's other large automakers such as Mitsubishi, Honda, Auto Alliance (Ford and Mazda), GM, and Isuzu (Exhibit 4-3). As of 2002, Thailand had 1,800 locally based suppliers providing engines, engine components, body parts, brake systems, steering systems, suspensions, transmissions and electronics. With a strong supplier base, Thai-based automakers source almost 90 percent of their parts domestically. In 2005, the assembly and parts sectors contributed 42.4 percent of Thailand's total manufacturing value added.

Production Networks and FDI in Manufacturing

There are two major motives for FDI in manufacturing: serve the domestic market and obtain cheaper inputs (Shatz and Venables 2000). The former, often referred to as "horizontal FDI," occurs when a firm decides to duplicate production facilities and sell in two or more markets in different locations

Table 4-7
ASEAN Machinery Imports and Exports, 2006 (% of total)

HS	Description	Intra-ASEAN	Extra-ASEAN	Total ASEAN
84	Non-electrical machinery (inc plant & capital equipment, office machinery & computers)	14.40	15.30	15.07
85	Electrical machinery (inc television receivers, sound recorders & reproducers, & telecommunications equipment)	27.86	27.49	27.58
86–89	Transportation machinery (vehicles & parts)	3.72	3.91	3.86
Total		45.98	46.70	46.51
Exports (US$ million)		189,176.5	561,530.8	750,707.3
Imports (US$ million)		163,594.9	490,503.5	654,098.4
Total Trade (US$ million)		352,771.4	1,052,034.3	1,404,805.7

Source: ASEAN Secretariat, ASEAN Trade Database.

because of tariffs and other barriers to trade. As such, horizontal FDI and trade are substitutes, since parent firms replace exports with local production.

The search for low-cost inputs is known as "vertical FDI." This entails slicing the vertical chain of production into many stages and locating links in different countries where costs are lower. Vertical FDI usually creates trade since goods at different stages of production are transported between locations. This is known as cross-border production sharing or fragmentation of production. With vertical specialization a slight reduction in trade costs can lead to large trade in intermediate goods due to the multiple border-crossings of sequentially finished goods. Under this production strategy, labor-intensive processes are located in labor-abundant countries like ASEAN Member States and China. This phenomenon is common in the automotive and electronics sectors.

Drawing on fragmentation theory, a number of authors have developed models to explain production fragmentation, which has emerged not only in East Asia but also in the United States and Mexico/Costa Rica, and between Germany and the Czech Republic, Slovakia, Hungary, and Poland (Kimura 2008). Before fragmentation, a firm handles all production processes from upstream to downstream. Fragmentation allows a firm to separate processes into two or more components and locate in different areas. Jones and Kierzkowski (1990) characterize fragmentation as a series of production blocks (PB) connected by service links (Figure 4-2).

Technological advances and declining costs of services also affect the rise of fragmentation and production networks (Jones and Kierzkowsky 2001; Arndt 2003). Significant declines in transportation, communication, and coordination costs have enabled multinational corporations to fragment production internationally within the firm and take advantage of differences in technologies and factor prices among countries. These have created new opportunities for the production sharing that has been exploited profitably by the countries of East Asia. Jones and Kierzkowsky (2004) emphasize that

Exhibit 4-3
Toyota's Innovative Multipurpose Vehicle Project

The automotive industry is global, high-tech, and capital-intensive, requiring economies of scale to make operations profitable. To maintain competitiveness, automakers fragment production by separating the capital-intensive segments from the labor-intensive ones and transferring labor-intensive segments to developing countries that have large domestic markets.

Toyota's Innovative Multi-Purpose Vehicle (IMV) Project exemplifies this process. Under the project, Toyota upgraded and expanded plants in Thailand (Toyota Motor Thailand or TMT), Indonesia (PT Toyota Motor Manufacturing Indonesia or TMMIN), Argentina, and South Africa and turned them into assembly and export bases for a line of innovative IMVs. The project also aims to increase imported components sourced from Toyota plants and suppliers in Asian and Latin America countries outside Japan.

Thailand is regarded as the base. TMT has a production capacity of 280,000 units and is expected to export 140,000 units of pick-up trucks and SUVs. Indonesia has a capacity of 80,000 units with 10,000 units for export; South Africa has 60,000 units with 30,000 units for export and

Argentina has 60,000 units with 45,000 units for export.

Historically, Toyota established R&D centers only in Japan, the United States, and Western Europe. In 2005, it opened its first R&D center in an emerging market, the Toyota Technical Center Asia Pacific Thailand Co. Ltd. The center operates like those in developed countries, taking platforms and models developed in Japan to suit the needs of different emerging markets. In March 2005, Toyota established an R&D center in Australia to gain better understanding of local needs in Asia and Oceania.

Aside from its stable macroeconomic environment, good infrastructure, relatively large domestic market, and extensive network of components manufacturers, Thailand's success in integrating with global production networks of foreign automakers is the result of long years of policy reform. Like many developing countries, Thailand followed an import-substitution policy from 1970 up to the mid-1980s. Since then, it has managed its trade and industrial policy quite well; as such, it was able to shift successfully from a highly protected industry toward an export-oriented one in the early 1990s.

Figure 4-2
Fragmentation of Production

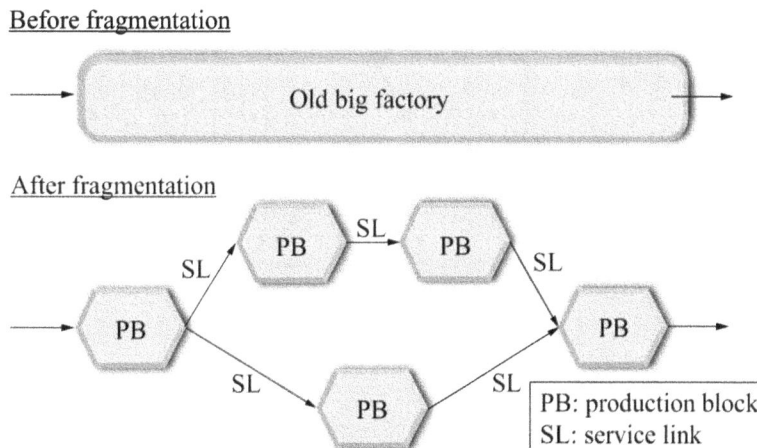

Source: Ando and Kimura (2008).

- The optimal degree of fragmentation depends on the size of the market.
- Economic growth encourages fragmentation and trade in parts and components.
- The lowering of service links costs promotes fragmentation and outsourcing of output.

Recent research indicates that deep fragmented production magnifies trade by causing a rise in intermediate goods trade per se and multiple border-crossings of sequentially finished goods with value added at each stage of production (Yi 2003). In turn, the share of final goods trade in overall trade gets smaller as the international fragmentation of production rises (Egger and Pfaffermayr 2005).

More recently, fragmentation analysis has incorporated new economic geography, particularly to address issues such as agglomeration and spatial location of economic activity. Jones (2006) notes that increases in the outsourcing of economic activity, whether national or global, may lead to new forms of agglomeration. Combining fragmentation theory with new economic geography, Ando and Kimura (2005) provide a useful tool for understanding the mechanics of international production and distribution networks that have emerged in East Asia. Their framework is characterized by both intra- and inter-firm transactions across countries in a particular region, which reflects the more complex operations of production networks in East Asia. As Figure 4-3 shows, the production networks that evolved in East

Figure 4-3
Production Networks in NAFTA and East Asia

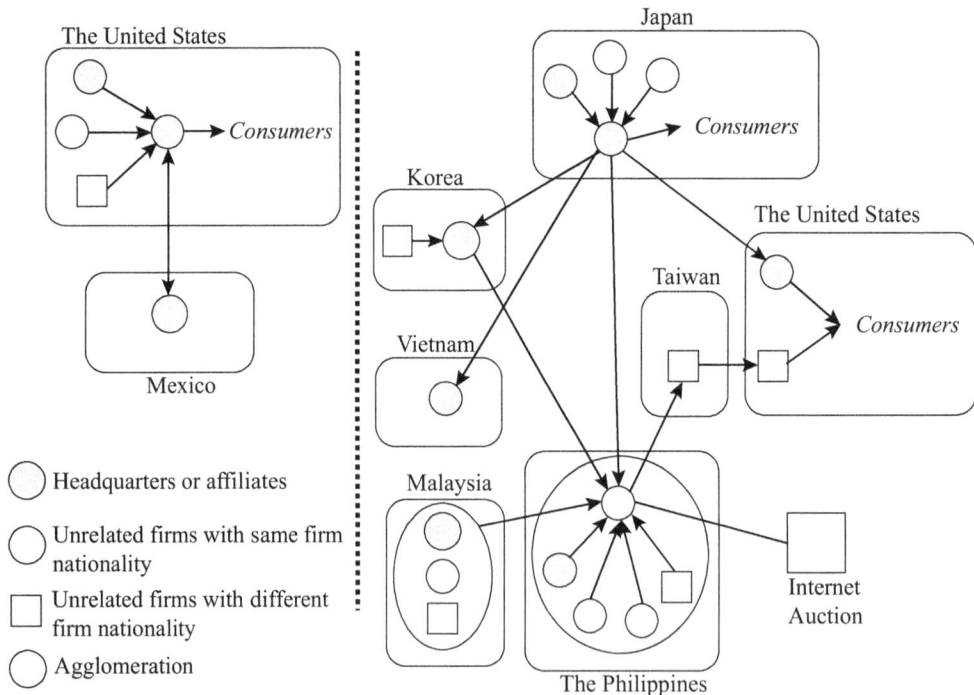

Source: Ando and Kimura (2008).

Asia go beyond the simple intra-firm fragmentation accompanied by back-and-forth transactions observed in the United States and Mexico.

According to Ando and Kimura (2008), three elements make fragmentation possible:

- Production cost saving in fragmented production blocks.
- Acceptable cost for service links that connect remotely located production blocks.
- Low cost to set up the network.

Fragmentation theory suggests that in the right policy environment — one that enables low service link and network set up costs — differences in development stages may hasten fragmentation and FDI at the production process level (Kimura 2008). Securing such a policy environment entails liberalizing and facilitating trade and investment, pursuing reforms that lower transaction costs, and strengthening institutions and economic infrastructure to improve the investment and business environment. Kimura suggests that a stable legal system and the creation or upgrading of industrial estates, one-stop shops for foreign investors, and logistics infrastructure can quickly improve the investment climate in developing countries.

Ando and Kimura (2008) characterize East Asia's production and distribution networks as complex cross-border production sharing that involves intra- and inter-firm back-and-forth transactions across a number of countries. As noted earlier, networks have enabled developing countries to take advantage of their comparative advantage at a greater level of specialization. Haddad (2007) indicates that a substantial portion of exports from Malaysia, Philippines, Thailand, and Vietnam are accounted for by vertical specialization. She notes that between 1998 and 2004, Malaysia, the Philippines, and Thailand performed exceptionally well in exports of finished or assembled machinery. Japan absorbs more than half of East Asia's machinery exports. Haddad notes as well that the networks that initially linked Japan vertically with Korea and Taiwan in low-skill assembly activities have gradually moved to lower-wage countries such as Malaysia, the Philippines, and Thailand. These networks are now moving to China and Vietnam.

China is often viewed as a major competitor of ASEAN in attracting FDI and in integrating regional production chains. As China improves its industrial capabilities, ASEAN's competitive cost advantage may be eroded and investors may shift operations to China. For instance, in the past decade China's semiconductor industry, particularly its foundry sector, has caught up with those of Japan, Malaysia, and Taiwan. China's decision to open up to foreign investors was critical in stimulating a large inflow of investment and managerial and engineering personnel from Taiwan and accelerated the catch-up process (ADB 2008).

To address the China challenge, ASEAN Member States need to pursue further liberalization and deeper reforms to improve their competitiveness, attract more investment, and make ASEAN a single investment area. The AEC Blueprint emphasizes the importance of regional cooperation to facilitate efficiency-seeking FDI and intensifying the region's participation in regional and global production networks.

Financial Integration in ASEAN and East Asia

The law of "one price" implies that price convergence will accompany financial integration. Fully integrated financial markets imply that traders can perform transactions freely anywhere within an area.

In a financially integrated region, therefore, prices for similar financial assets (i.e. those with similar expected adjusted-returns) should converge. Arbitrage will tend to erode price differentials that may have arisen due to market power, different regulations, and imperfect flows of information. Financial integration therefore implies greater co-movement of prices in the region and is typically accompanied by an increase in financial assets traded in the region and that held by regional participants.[3]

One can examine as well the relationship of consumption growth and income growth. Economic theory suggests that if a region is financially integrated then consumption growth in a member economy will be more closely related to regional consumption growth than to its own income growth. The ability to borrow from other member economies facilitates consumption risk-sharing.

Several studies have evaluated the extent of financial integration in East Asia. Applying a gravity model of cross-border portfolio asset and bank claim holdings, Kim, Lee and Shin (2007) found that East Asia tends to be relatively more integrated with global markets than with regional markets, particularly when compared with Europe. Their consumption risk-sharing model also indicated that East Asia tends to have relatively weaker regional risk-sharing arrangements, but stronger global risk-sharing arrangements compared to Europe.

By calculating the standard deviation of various interest rates, the ADB (2008) observed declining interbank rate differentials and converging bond yields among 10 East Asian economies. However, the interbank rate differentials still remained higher than comparable figures for the EU prior to the introduction of the euro. Meanwhile, Garcia-Herrero and Wooldridge (2007) assessed the progress of global and regional economic integration in emerging markets in three regions: Europe, Asia, and Latin America. Their results, which are based largely on the methodologies described above, are summarized in the concluding section of their study:

> The multifaceted nature of financial integration makes it hard to compare the progress of different emerging regions. That being said, available data point to significant integration over the past decade. The new EU members have reached a very high level of financial integration […] At the same time, the geographical reach of integration in the new EU members is relatively limited; their integration almost entirely reflects the deepening of links with their neighboring financial bloc.

> By contrast, in Latin America the geographical reach of integration is broader than in the new EU members, involving neighboring countries as well as those farther afield. Yet the progress of integration has been much less rapid. Overall, financial integration in Latin America lags behind that in the new EU members.

> The situation in Asia is somewhere between those of Europe and Latin America. Geographical links are broader than among the new EU members. One respect in which Asia stands out from other emerging regions is that it has the largest share of foreign investment financed within the region. Indeed, intraregional links are more important than those with the largest neighboring financial centre, Japan, although still secondary to links to global markets. Nevertheless, the progress of integration is closer to that of Latin America: for example, capital mobility continues to be restricted in several countries.

While all these studies examined a mixture of ASEAN Member States and other Asian countries, Bilas (2007) considered ASEAN separately and evaluated financial integration in NAFTA, the EU, Mercosur, and ASEAN on the basis of movements in real interest rates. He concluded that NAFTA and the EU-25 show similar values of real interest rates among their members while the situation with Mercosur and ASEAN Member States is the opposite. This implies that capital is more mobile in NAFTA and EU-25 than in Mercosur and ASEAN.

A stylized fact that emerges is that ASEAN is among the least financially integrated with the rest of the world. Financial integration among member states is also relatively weak, particularly when compared to Europe. This phenomenon, which is generally true across East Asia, has been analyzed extensively (Eichengreen and Park 2004; Park, Lee, and Shin 2007; ADB 2008).

Why Financial Integration is Weak in East Asia

A significant reason for weak financial integration in East Asia is disparities in economic development, particularly when compared with Europe:

> Asia's legacy of underdeveloped national financial markets and institutions is perhaps the biggest impediment to greater financial integration and intermediation. While some economies have more developed financial sectors than others, and all have huge progress over the past decade, the traditional dependence on bank financing and the legacy of financial repression have stunted the growth of equity and bond markets in many economies (ADB 2008).

Controls on capital account transactions have a persistent effect on the volume of cross-border claims, and their impact is longest where those controls were maintained for the greatest number of years (Eichengreen and Park 2004). Similarly, inadequate deregulation and the limited openness of national financial markets impede their development. Capital controls, inadequate deregulation, and restricted national financial markets hinder the issuance of local currency bonds, limit investment in foreign bonds by domestic investors, and prevent foreign borrowers from issuing bonds denominated in different currencies in Asian markets (ADB 2008).

Statistical evidence suggests that East Asian economies have no incentive to diversify their portfolio holdings within the region because of the homogeneity of the economies in terms of the correlations of their output growth with output growth of the global economy (Park, Lee and Shin 2007). Countries with different structures, subject to different economic shocks, and low business cycle correlation, will find it more advantageous to develop closer financial links with one another. The opposite case is generally true in East Asia. Other related reasons for the absence of a "regional bias" have been offered: investing in East Asia may involve higher costs since most East Asian countries are developing economies with under-developed financial markets; information sharing may be more difficult among East Asian countries; and economic agents in these countries may have better information about financial markets of developed countries like the United States.

The divergence of macroeconomic policies in East Asia may also hamper financial integration. Different exchange rate regimes lead to greater exchange-rate volatility between currencies. This can be contrasted to the experience of European countries that adopted the euro. Weak fiscal positions in some countries also prevent their involvement in regional financial cooperation.

Policy Approaches to Strengthen Financial Integration

The reasons for weak financial integration indicate which policy issues must be addressed. For example, should ASEAN pursue greater financial liberalization, including further financial integration? (The appropriate policy would depend largely on the impact of further integration on the real economy). If yes, then what is the "optimal sequence" for reform?

Some have proposed the standard process suggested by McKinnon (1993): start with fiscal balance; proceed with domestic financial liberalization and development of prudential bank regulation, accompanied by current account liberalization; end with capital account liberalization, with long-term capital flows such as FDI preceding short-term flows. Others cite the indirect benefits that accrue to a country's governance and institutions when it opens up to cross-border capital flows (Prasad and Rajan 2008), implying that some aspects of financial liberalization feed on each other. This is related to the proposal for "optimal cascading." Chow et al. (2006) argue that it is not necessarily the case that all three dimensions of liberalization — domestic financial sector development, exchange rate flexibility, capital openness — occur sequentially. Instead, it may be more effective if all three are determined together as a holistic set of interrelated policy decisions. If so, then it is important to recognize that policymakers desirous of maintaining financial stability while embarking on a liberalization program should not focus on optimal sequencing but on optimal cascading.

Once financial integration is pursued, the balance between global integration and regional integration and their relationship must be determined. A case in point is the use of the foreign exchange reserves of East Asian economies. The limited development of regional financial markets and their small and fragmented nature have led to a large part of Asian savings being intermediated outside the region. Asia recycles its capital inflows by purchasing US dollar-denominated investment products such as US Treasuries, and the funds return to Asia through US direct and portfolio investment. Fostering domestic financial markets and regional financial integration is important because it facilitates the intermediation of Asian savings in the region and attracts foreign investment in instruments denominated in the domestic currency (Chow et al. 2006). Such alternative sources of funding would reduce Asia's reliance on foreign currency borrowing and, concomitantly, its exposure to maturity and currency mismatch risks.

The question is whether it would be beneficial to encourage intraregional financial intermediation, which would certainly reduce global financial integration. East Asia — particularly through the ASEAN+3 process — has been promoting regional financial integration. However, some analysts believe that any trade-off is short-term and that regional and global integration are complementary in the medium- to long-term (Garcia-Herrero and Wooldridge 2007).

IMPACT OF FREE INVESTMENT FLOWS AND FREER CAPITAL FLOWS IN THE AEC

Impact of Regional Integration on Investment Flows — Empirical Evidence

Table 4-8 summarizes the findings of studies that examine the impact of the EU, NAFTA, and Mercosur on FDI inflows.

European Union. Studies on European economic integration generally provide empirical support for the proposition that integration attracts FDI. This suggests that integration influenced the rise of investment in Europe, as well changing patterns and flows of investment. Some studies suggest otherwise, but these focused more on the differing impact of the two stages of integration and the nature of flows (i.e. inward and outward). The EU experience shows that regional economic integration is imperative and feasible. The European model is a combination of ambitious goals and a step-by-step approach. Its overarching principle is that an integrated region, which can provide one production platform and efficient supply chain, has more weight in international trade negotiations. From the start of the integration process, EU Member States achieved rapid economic growth and gained considerable

Table 4-8
Summary of Studies on Regional Integration and its Impact on FDI

Author (Year)	Impact of Regional Integration on FDI
THE EUROPEAN UNION (EU)	
Franko (1976), Pelkmans (1984)	Provided evidence of investment diversion caused by integration.
Lipsey (1990)	Locational changes of fixed investment by US multinational firms were relatively small after the 1992 program.
Molle and Morsink (1991)	Intra-EC trade and intra-EC investment are complementary to each other, but only above a certain level of trade intensity.
Thomsen and Nicolaides (1991), Dunning (1992), Balasubramanyam and Greenaway (1992)	Positive impact as evidenced by surge in American and Japanese investment in Europe in response to opportunities and threat created by integration.
Blomstrom and Kokko (1997)	Positive impact; the common market had attracted investments from the US that might otherwise have been located in other European countries.
Barrell and Pain (1997)	Significantly affected the pattern and level of FDI in Europe and considered a major vehicle for competition and productivity.
Sekkat and Galgau (2001)	Creation of European Single Market did not significantly affect FDI inflows from non-EU Member States.
Barrell and Choy (2003)	Increased integration involved increased internal trade as the customs union was perfected, but that increased trade integration has not been as important since 1980.
De Sousa and Lochard (2004)	First EU enlargement in 1986 was not beneficial; second in 1995 was positive.
Kyrkilis and Pantelidis (2004)	Enlargement after 1980 had no significant effect on intraregional FDI.
NORTH AMERICAN FREE TRADE AGREEMENT (NAFTA)	
Blomstrom and Kokko (1997)	Bulk of inflows of FDI to Mexico was directed to the local market because of the country's improving economic and institutional environment and not mainly because of the removal of trade barriers.
Monge-Naranjo (2002)	NAFTA gave a significant advantage compared to other Central American countries with respect to attracting FDI.
Robertson (2006)	Provided indirect evidence that post-NAFTA FDI tends to be vertical.
Waldkirch (2008)	Confirmed commonly held perceptions that the US is the most important source of FDI in Mexico and provided evidence of positive effect of FDI on productivity, in particular, total factor productivity (TFP).
Feils and Rahman (2008)	Positive but selective effect on FDI inflows into the region.
MERCADO COMMON DEL SUR (MERCOSUR)	
Blomström and Kokko (1997)	Significant changes in trade and investment rules resulted in relatively strong FDI effects.
UNCTAD (2000)	Above-average growth in FDI inflows attributed to a few exceptionally large acquisitions, rather than a permanent change toward Mercosur in the composition of FDI flows.
Yeyati et al. (2003)	Market size has a significant effect in attracting FDI as evidenced by the booming of FDI inflows.
Ciravegna (2003)	Provides empirical evidence, to a limited degree, that regional integration can create the appropriate conditions for multinationals to upgrade their operations in developing countries, given that the region is also gradually being inserted into global networks.
Kubney et al. (2008)	Developments at the level of individual Mercosur-member countries suggest that regional integration has been just one, and possibly even a minor, factor driving FDI inflows.

economic strength. The region achieved a more or less borderless economy in 1999 that culminated in adoption of the euro in 1999.

North American Free Trade Agreement. On the whole, the literature suggests that the impact of NAFTA on FDI has been positive. The NAFTA experience shows the institutionalization of integration in bilateral and multilateral agreements of various scopes and the sheer weight of the United States in the integration process.

Mercosur. Mercosur is a customs union whose members are obliged to adopt common external tariff structures and to harmonize their trade and foreign affairs policies. This facilitates a flow of capital and investment into member countries. Studies of the impact of Mercosur are ambiguous about the union's attractiveness for FDI and the distribution of FDI among members. Factors such as trade and investment rules (Kubney et al. 2008), market size (Blomström and Kokko 1997; Yeyati et al. 2003), and economic conditions (UNCTAD 2000 in Kubney et al. 2008) have varying impact on the integration process. Moreover, the union has a large number of exceptions, suggesting that it is not necessarily a good example of the implications of regional economic cooperation for FDI.

Potential Impact of the AEC on Investment Flows

A distinct feature of the AEC Blueprint is its recognition of the importance of regional cooperation in facilitating efficiency-seeking FDI and deepening the region's participation in dynamic production networks. Another important feature is the adoption of open regionalism. The key impacts of the AEC on FDI flows are presented in Table 4-9, which classifies impacts on the basis of the transmission channels: investment provisions, deep integration provisions, FDI inflows, market size, and growth effects.

Investment Provisions

The ACIA is more comprehensive than its predecessors. It has provisions on investment liberalization, promotion, facilitation, and protection; provisions reaffirming national treatment and most-favored-nation treatment; a provision on compensatory adjustment to deal with modification of commitments; improved provisions on investment disputes between an investor and member states, transfer, and treatment of investments; and new provisions on special and differential (S&D) treatment through technical assistance, capacity building and facilitation. It offers flexible treatment, taking into account individual countries' sensitivities (granting S&D treatment for the newer ASEAN Member States).

The ACIA adopts a single negative list approach on reservations (progressive reduction or elimination of reservations in accordance with the strategic schedule of AEC in three phases: 2008–2010, 2011–2013, 2014–2015) and its Article on Scope of Application allows for inclusion of any other sector as may be agreed upon by all member states. ASEAN investors as well as foreign-owned ASEAN-based investors will enjoy benefits of the ACIA. It prohibits performance requirements and its provisions on senior management and boards of directors aim to encourage inflows of foreign and senior managers. Specific concerns of member states may be addressed in the ACIA as appropriate.

Provisions allowing for greater participation of foreign investors in domestic firms will generally lead to more FDI as new sectors are opened up, foreign ownership restrictions are relaxed, and performance requirements are abolished.

Table 4-9
Potential Impact of AEC Blueprint on FDI

Transmission Channel	Expected Change in FDI & Capital Flows	Notes
FTA investment provisions	Positive	Investment liberalization; most-favored-nation treatment and national treatment; investment protection, promotion and facilitation
Other "deep integration" provisions that improve host country's investment climate	Positive	Services, Standards, Competition, Customs Cooperation, IPR, Dispute Settlement
Trade and FDI Horizontal FDI Vertical FDI	Positive due to the expected shift from horizontal to vertical FDI and increase in horizontal FDI for services	With productions networks, FDI and trade are complements Singapore, Malaysia, Thailand, Philippines and Indonesia are already important participants in complex regional production networks Services liberalization is expected to increase horizontal FDI
Market size (extended common market hypothesis)	Positive	In the literature, market size is the most robust determinant of FDI, suggesting a positive relationship between market size and FDI
Dynamic/growth effects	Positive	FDI is positively associated with economic growth, though direction of causation is unclear.

Source: The transmission channels are based on Medvedev (2006).

Third-wave Investment Provisions Affecting the Investment Climate

The AEC includes deeper integration features such as trade in services, setting and harmonization of standards, competition law, customs cooperation, intellectual property rights, and dispute settlement. These will improve the host economy's investment environment and are likely to attract FDI inflows particularly in services. From 1999 to 2006, financial services accounted for 22 percent and trade and commerce 13 percent of total cumulative FDI inflows.

ASEAN Member States are committed to lifting all restrictions on trade in services in air transport, e-ASEAN, education services, healthcare, telecommunications, tourism, banking and finance, insurance, trading, e-commerce, distribution and logistics, transportation and warehousing, and professional services such as accounting, engineering, and advertising. This liberalization will eliminate restrictions on Mode 1 (cross-border delivery) and Mode 2 (consumption abroad) and progressively remove Mode 3 (commercial presence) market access limitations by 2015.

In a study of the EU, Barrel and Pain (1997)[4] conclude that implementation of the EU Single Market Program facilitated the mobility of capital and generated a significant change in investment patterns and levels of FDI in manufacturing and services. In general there has been an increase in FDI flows in Europe, and the stock of FDI as a percent of GDP rose markedly in the four large European economies between 1989 and 2000.

Trade Flows and FDI Effects

The theoretical and empirical literature on trade and investment are ambiguous on the relationship between trade and FDI, as each seems to determine the other simultaneously. The magnitude of the impact of preferential trade liberalization on FDI flows could be positive or negative depending on the type of FDI, industry characteristics, and the MNC's capacity to undertake new investment projects.

For horizontal FDI — which is based on a tariff-jumping perspective with trade and FDI as substitutes — intraregional FDI flows are expected, at least in theory, to decline because trade liberalization makes exporting from the home country relatively more attractive than FDI as a way to serve the regional market. But this effect would be significant only for regions such as the EU and NAFTA. Most FDI inflows to ASEAN Member States come from outside the region and are directed to services and vertically integrated manufactures. For vertically integrated FDI — where the operations of MNCs in different affiliates are specialized — regional integration is expected to increase regional flows. This is the most likely effect of the AEC.

Our analysis of trade and investment in ASEAN and East Asia described the importance of trade in parts and components, the fragmentation of production, and the development of complex networks. Singapore, Malaysia, Thailand, the Philippines, and Indonesia are key participants in international production sharing and production networks. Vietnam is also increasingly involved while Cambodia, Lao PDR, and Myanmar are just starting to take part. The AEC can accelerate the participation of these countries in regional production networks.

The AEC aims to deepen ASEAN integration into the global economy and make ASEAN a more dynamic participant in regional and global production networks. This is expected to lead to net increases in FDI inflows arising from vertical FDI inflows. As Arndt (2003) indicates, an FTA that is clearly trade-diverting under traditional circumstances becomes trade-creating when carried out within the context of deeper integration, where preferential liberalization is accompanied by production sharing. As noted in other chapters, average tariffs in ASEAN are already relatively low, even with respect to peak tariffs. This implies that tariff-hopping FDI will not be significant in most sectors.

Plummer (2007) notes that trade and investment reforms under the AEC are expected to cause a shift from horizontal to vertical FDI flows to the region as MNCs take advantage of opportunities associated with vertically integrated, specialized plants across the diverse ASEAN region. There will be less horizontal FDI as horizontal production activities are consolidated. According to the ASEAN Secretariat (as cited in ADB 2008, 62), the AICO Scheme has promoted regional production networks particularly for the automotive and electronics industries by (1) reducing preferential tariff rates to 0–5 percent, (2) liberalizing foreign equity restrictions, and (3) establishing dispute settlement mechanisms. Trade integration has deepened international production networks in the automotive industry particularly. Audi, for example, uses its Hungarian plant to manufacture engines, a relatively labor-intensive part. The plant has been Hungary's biggest exporter and one of its highest-revenue companies for a number of years (Dieter 2007). AFTA, launched in ASEAN in 1992, reduced tariffs to 0 to 5 percent by 2003 and made the integration of production in the region attractive. This led to the systematic creation of regional production networks by Japanese automakers through FDI. See Exhibit 4-4.

Exhibit 4-4
Regional Integration and the Deepening of Production Networks:
The Automotive Industry in the EU and ASEAN

Both the European and ASEAN experiences have shown the importance of integration in facilitating regional production networks. This is best illustrated by the dramatic transformation of the automotive industry over the past decade.

The auto industry has been a leading driver of change in the industrial development of Eastern Europe. The development of the car and component industry was led by Western European companies like Volkswagen, General Motors/Opel, Fiat and Renault. In recent years, manufacturers from East Asia like Toyota, Kia, and Hyundai have started to manufacture vehicles in Eastern Europe. Specialization and outsourcing in Europe have been supported by the presence of a pool of specialized SMEs.

After the creation of an FTA between the EU and Hungary (which became operational in March 1992), Audi, a German auto manufacturer, decided to relocate its entire engine manufacturing to Hungary. Today, the Audi Hungarian Motor Kft., located in Győr, is one of the most important suppliers of engines for Audi and the rest of the Volkswagen Group. The company was founded in Hungary in February 1993 after potential production locations had been compared all over Europe. Note that Hungary was in a good position to engage in component manufacturing because the country was supplying components to the USSR car manufacturers for decades.

The plant site covers an area of about 1.7 million square meters and has a workforce of 5,000 employees.

The plant has been Hungary's largest exporter and one of the highest-revenue companies in the country. Almost everything in the Audi plant is subcontracted out to local suppliers. In 2005, the plant produced a total of 1.69 million engines. A tool-making shop with total investment of 40 million euros was added in 2005.

In ASEAN, trade liberalization through the ASEAN Free Trade Area (AFTA) has made the integration of production in the region attractive. This gave automakers unrestricted access to Southeast Asian markets, which is essential in achieving economies of scale and for the development of full production (instead of, for example, the assembly of completely-knocked-down kits). Previously, ASEAN had the Brand-to-Brand Complementation Scheme which was signed in 1988 allowing intraregional tariff preferences and local content accreditation. This was replaced by the AICO Scheme effective November 1, 1996. On January 28, 1992, the ASEAN Member Countries agreed to remove barriers to intra-ASEAN trade by creating the AFTA. Its main mechanism was the Common Effective Preferential Tariffs, which would reduce tariffs to a range of 3 to 5% by the year 2003 for the automotive industry.

With the creation of AFTA, Japanese auto makers systematically created production networks through accelerated FDI. These changes did not only improve the competitiveness of Japanese firms, but also contributed to the de facto integration processes in Asia and to the regionalization of production.

Sources: Dieter (2007) and Toyota Motor Corporation.

In a study of determinants of intraregional flows to Asia using a gravity model, Rajan (2008) found that exports and FDI appear to be complementary: higher exports stimulate future FDI flows. This is suggestive of vertical specialization and production integration between Asian economies as characterized by Ando and Kimura (2005). Liberalization and removal of barriers to trade in services are expected to increase horizontal FDI particularly in Mode 3 services (commercial presence).

Market Size

Theoretically, preferential trading agreements expand markets and therefore increase FDI. Thus, a large regional market should create a more attractive investment site for foreign MNCs than national markets do separately. After formation of the EU Single Market, the EU's share in global FDI inflows rose from about 30 percent in the 1980s to about 50 percent in the 1990s and has remained there since (Table 4-3 and UNCTAD 2006). After joining NAFTA Mexico experienced a sharp increase in its FDI inflows, which rose from an average of US$12 billion during the 1991–1993 period to US$54 billion in the period 2000–2002 (Kose et al. 2004 as cited in Kumar 2008). Note, however, that an FTA-extended common market effect is not automatic; its size depends on the economic and geographic proximity of the partners (Medvedev 2006).

Long-term Growth Effects

Studies on FDI and growth/dynamic effects indicate that regional integration may affect FDI by generating growth. This positive relationship is attributed to FDI's growth-enhancing knowledge and spillovers. The direction of causation, however, is not clear. For instance, Rodrik (1999) suggests that FDI tends to be located in more productive and faster-growing economies. Medvedev (2006) further indicates that while the positive FDI — growth link is well established, the connection between regional integration agreements and growth is ambiguous, which makes the hypothesis about regional integration, growth, and FDI uncertain.

In sum, FDI is crucial to the success of economic integration in ASEAN. Apart from attracting new capital and foreign exchange, making it easier to reach foreign markets, and transferring technology, FDI can strengthen institutions and stabilize the business environment (Plummer 2007). UNCTAD (2006) also notes that liberalization is vital in facilitating efficiency-seeking industrial restructuring. This process facilitates creation of supply capabilities in less-developed countries. FDI is also the least volatile of capital flows, making countries less susceptible to sudden stops or reversals of flows. There have been few theoretical discussions of the impact of regional integration on FDI (Medvedev 2006) and none provides a general prediction of the impact (Blomström and Kokko 1997). Theoretical models identify investment-creating and investment-diverting effects of regional integration but leave the question of which effects dominate to empirical studies.

Calculating the Effects of AEC on FDI Flows

How much foreign investment can be expected from the AEC? An empirical estimate of the potential for enhancing ASEAN foreign investment inflows could be developed in two ways. The simpler method — the one feasible within the time constraints of this study — is to ask how ASEAN compares to "frontier" foreign investment levels, that is, to FDI levels that prevail in the world's most successful FDI-attracting economies. A more complex (but likely more accurate) method would involve estimating a structural model of FDI inflows that attributes variations in determinants that are likely to be affected by the AEC, including, for example, the region's effective scale, ranking on business indicators, and openness to trade.

In any case, our current analysis is limited to estimating frontier investment with reference to the global distribution of FDI stocks. To make the concept of the "frontier" operational, we estimated three different measures of state-of-the-art performance, all expressed in terms of the ratio of FDI stock to GDP. These measures are

- The average of the three highest years of FDI/GDP ratios experienced by a particular economy in the past;

- The 75th percentile of the global distribution of FDI/GDP ratios; and
- The point half-way between the economy's current ratio and the 90th percentile of the global distribution.

In all cases, economies with the actual ratios exceeding the frontier estimate were assumed to remain at their higher ratios.

The results of applying these alternative measures of the frontier are reported in Table 4-10. The differences are substantial, ranging from 28 percent to 63 percent of baseline FDI stocks. Relative to actual 2006 inward FDI stocks, these would amount to a range of $117–$264 billion of additional stocks. Increases are especially large for Indonesia and the Philippines — both big economies that do not perform especially well with respect to FDI and could gain substantial productivity and credibility from deeper integration into ASEAN. All economies would gain FDI by moving to the frontier. The exception is Singapore under some measures as its inward FDI stocks are already near the very top of the global distribution.

What could be the welfare gains associated with such increases in FDI stocks? Answering this question requires making further assumptions. The key point is that much of the return of FDI-invested companies represents gains that accrue to foreign investors rather than to the host economy. But the host economy will benefit too — through higher tax collections, technology transfers, human capital investments, connections to foreign markets, and possibly a wage premium that is often associated with foreign companies. Upstream or downstream links by the foreign-invested firm may generate further opportunities for income and profit in the host country. Overall a rough estimate might be that host-economy benefits amount to an annual 5 percent return on FDI stocks. Given this, the benefits associated with the FDI increases calculated in Table 4-10 will be in the annual $6–$13 billion range, or in the range of 0.5–1 percent of annual ASEAN GDP.

Table 4-10
How Integration Might Increase ASEAN's FDI Stocks (US$ million)

	Actual Inward FDI Stock 2006	*Potential Inward Stock (Hypothetical 2006)*		
		[1] Top 3 years	*[2] 75th percentile*	*[3] 1/2 to 90th percentile*
ASEAN	420,025	536,993	684,178	643,649
Brunei Darussalam	9,861	19,057	15,312	15,312
Cambodia	2,954	3,245	3,481	3,969
Indonesia	19,056	77,545	178,794	134,655
Lao PDR	856	1,209	1,686	1,599
Malaysia	53,575	90,704	73,067	78,074
Myanmar	5,005	7,165	6,378	7,280
Philippines	17,120	17,849	57,364	48,757
Singapore	210,089	211,070	210,521	210,521
Thailand	68,058	68,928	101,180	104,599
Vietnam	33,451	40,221	36,395	38,883

Source: Authors' calculations based on UNCTAD FDI online database.

The dynamic effects of serving as a magnet for FDI might be greater. Sustained connections with leading foreign companies and markets are likely to increase not just current productivity but also the rate of productivity growth. They should also ensure an increased flow of "economic intelligence" that is, information that might help the region adapt more rapidly to changing markets and technologies around the world. And close links with foreign companies could also help to cement the region's relations with their source economies, helping to ward off the bouts of criticism and protectionism that sometimes accompany intense commercial relationships.

Adjustment Issues and Recommended Measures for FDI Flows

The removal of regulatory and legal barriers to international capital flows and the participation of foreign investors in domestic firms and financial markets will lead to more FDI, but significant increases in FDI can be realized only if the most important sectors are opened up and member states improve their core business environment. This requires that member states implement complementary policies that help improve the investment climate.

Individual ASEAN countries are facing the huge challenge of improving their competitiveness. As UNCTAD (1999) and many others have noted, a large market is a powerful draw for investors, but MNCs serving global markets increasingly look for world-class infrastructure, skilled and productive workers, innovative capabilities, and an agglomeration of efficient suppliers, competitors, support institutions and services. To be successful, implementation of the AEC must be accompanied by complementary policies and programs, especially at the national level. For example, member states would do well to

* Continue implementing reforms under the AEC/ACIA commensurate with improvements in their domestic business environment, including economic regulations, corporate governance, and labor policies.
* Develop logistics infrastructure and strengthen legal systems to increase FDI inflows.
* Devise, unilaterally and collectively, structural adjustment and reform assistance programs as well as capacity-building measures to help those who could be adversely affected by reforms.

Kimura (2008) notes that policies and recommendations to deepen the participation of ASEAN Member States in global and regional production networks, should take into account a country's level of development and level of participation in regional production networks. For example, policy for Cambodia, Myanmar, and Lao PDR should focus on how to attract a first wave of production fragmentation from industrial agglomeration that has formed nearby. For these countries, the removal of tariffs, trade and investment facilitation, as well as institution building for investment climate and industrial zones are critical.

For Thailand, the Philippines, Malaysia, and Indonesia — which are facing competition from lower and higher-income countries — policies designed to upgrade the industrial structure and human capital will be vital, as well as policies to form industrial agglomeration. For the Philippines and Indonesia, human-resource development and overall improvement in the business environment are particularly important. For Singapore, a major source and recipient of FDI, policy should focus on improving and advancing the country's technological and innovative capabilities and diversifying into new areas of services development.

In a comprehensive study of the impact of the AIA on FDI inflows to ASEAN, Plummer (2007) concludes that the AIA has had a generally positive effect and has helped open up sectors and reduce barriers to investment. To strengthen and enhance the AIA, the author proposes the following actions:

- Introduce collective measures to be taken by all ASEAN Member States and encourage individual member states to lower transaction costs and strengthen market factors to facilitate investment and promote regional production networks.
- Widen the scope of industries by transferring Mode 3 services from the ASEAN Framework Agreement on Services (AFAS) to the AIA.
- Combine the AIA, the 1987 Agreement for the Promotion and Protection of Investments, and appropriate provisions of bilateral investment treaties into a comprehensive "AIA-Plus" agreement.
- Harmonize national provisions on equity ownership, land tenure, nondiscriminatory taxation, movement of skilled labor, and financial flows at the ASEAN regional level to ensure national treatment.
- Consolidate timeframes for actions.
- Identify and then remove investment impediments using specific procedures and within a specific timeframe.
- Reduce the number of industries and sectors under the sensitive list and review those covered with a view toward a phase out.
- Make the AIA-Plus an integral part of the AEC as its provisions would cover investments, services, capital flows, and skilled labor associated with investment.
- Establish a mechanism for monitoring progress.
- Expand the mandate of the ASEAN Secretariat and strengthen its technical and analytical capabilities.

Soesastro (2008) and Lim (2008) point out the need to develop a new scheme that can promote the region's dynamic involvement in regional and international production networks. Pupphavesa (2008) suggests the following to make investment liberalization more effective:

- Strengthen commitments to collective approaches and common time frames for trade and investment liberalization. The current mechanism of accession to other countries' investment liberalization is conditional on ASEAN-X basis; while this encourages voluntary reciprocal liberalization and discourages free riding, it allows X countries to fall behind in liberalization. This weakens the regional force of attracting investment and reduces the benefits of induced investment.
- Remove impediments to inward FDI as soon as possible. ASEAN Member States should classify impediments (e.g., administrative, market access and national treatment standards, incentives, operational restrictions), analyze their causes or rationales, and remove as many as possible.
- Harmonize tax incentives, or better still, eliminate them.
- Adopt an unconditional MFN approach in liberalizing investment to better attract FDI and form a competitive production base.
- Liberalize trade and investment in tandem, minimizing and eliminating as soon as possible the TEL and SL in trade in goods and services.
- Facilitate restructuring by accompanying trade and investment liberalization with structural adjustment measures. As noted, ASEAN Member States need to come up with structural adjustment and reform assistance and capacity building measures to help those adversely affected by reforms.

Sudsawasad (2008) suggests that the absence of a comprehensive network of tax treaty agreements in ASEAN may raise business costs and impede regional integration. While there seems to be insufficient evidence that corporate income tax rates have a significant impact on FDI flows to East Asia, the author finds that bilateral income tax treaties increase FDI inflows to the original ASEAN countries. This finding would support the rationale for tax treaty formation as a means of increasing FDI. While Singapore and Indonesia have extensive bilateral tax treaty networks, others like Brunei, Lao PDR, and Myanmar have very limited networks with other East Asian countries. For example, except with Thailand, Cambodia has hardly any tax treaty agreements with East Asian countries. Several ASEAN Member States also offer more favorable treaty agreements to non-ASEAN members than they do to ASEAN Member States (Farrow and Jogarajan 2006 as cited in Sudsawasad 2008). Some treaties were also concluded many years ago and could be out of date. Hence, it is important that the AEC develop a regional tax regime and a standard tax treaty framework for the region.

Finally, ASEAN countries should learn from the experience of China and successful ASEAN partners in harnessing the benefits of FDI. Firm-level competitiveness is primarily a function of technology and technological capability, the development of which can help overcome constraints to regional economic integration. One practical measure is the Local Industries Upgrading Program described in Exhibit 4-5. This program can be implemented at the ASEAN level, with Thai firms, for example, being the source of technology and CLMV firms being the recipients.

Impact of Capital Account Liberalization — Empirical Evidence

Despite the theoretical and intuitive arguments in favor of capital mobility, the benefits have to be determined empirically. Two general issues must be addressed: the impact of global financial integration and whether regional financial integration should be pursued ahead of greater global financial integration.

A comprehensive review by Obstfeld (2007) covers the major empirical studies of the past decade. He finds that at the macro level in particular, it is difficult to find unambiguous evidence that financial opening yields a net improvement in economic performance for emerging countries. This does not imply, however, that financial liberalization, or specifically capital account liberalization, must be abandoned. There are plausible explanations why empirical work does not unambiguously show that capital account liberalization is beneficial on a net basis.

- First, there may be threshold levels of institutional development only above which the benefits exceed the costs. This could also explain why the correlation between growth and the use of foreign capital is strongly positive for industrial countries but not for low-income countries.
- Second, collateral benefits of openness to foreign capital are greater at higher levels of development while the associated costs and risks are greater at lower levels of development.
- Third, crude quantity-based measures of the use of foreign finance, such as the current account deficit or gross inflows, may not capture the influence of foreign capital.

Hence, Obstfeld argues that despite the skimpy direct evidence that developing countries gain from financial globalization, they should nonetheless proceed in a cautious incremental manner. There is strong evidence that domestic financial development spurs growth under the right conditions, and these conditions — plus domestic financial development itself — are likely to make capital inflows

---

Exhibit 4-5
Capacity-building Spillovers from FDI

Direct interfaces between domestic and foreign knowledge subsystems may take myriad forms: FDI, joint ventures, licensing, OEM, original design manufacturing, original brand manufacturing, subcontracting, franchising, management, marketing, technical service and turnkey contracts, overseas training, overseas acquisition of overseas investments, strategic partnership or alliances, for technology, R&D contracts, bilateral cooperative technology agreements, and material sub-assembly.

FDI is expected to infuse a host economy with advanced skills and technology. Direct effects of FDI inflows include higher productivity, upgraded technological and managerial practices, R&D, employment, and training. Indirect effects or spillovers occur through collaboration with local R&D institutions, technology transfer to local downstream and upstream operations, and turnover of trained personnel.

The literature often assumes that FDI leads to substantial capacity-building spillovers through horizontal and vertical linkages. Local firms' ability to benefit from such spillovers, however, depends on their capacity to absorb them. The empirical evidence on productivity, wages, and export spillovers in developing, developed, and transitional economies reveals that it is far easier to identify potential spillovers in theory than to verify them empirically.

In Singapore, the government promoted the development of absorptive capacity, using FDI spillovers to turn domestic SMEs into attractive input and service suppliers. Through the Local Industries Upgrading Program (LIUP), launched in 1986, it encouraged transnational corporations to transfer technology and skills to a selected group of SMEs. The program covered the salary of a full-time procurement expert to work for specific periods with the SMEs to help them upgrade production and management to international standards and precision norms.

For SMEs, the LIUP had three phases: (1) improve operational efficiency, such as production planning and inventory control; (2) launch new products or processes; and (3) join product, process R&D activities with TNC partners.

Thus, Singapore first created a critical mass of trained technical workers then offered local and foreign enterprises grants to spur R&D investment. This stimulated strong demand for innovation, particularly in activities serving foreign markets.

Source: Adopted from UNIDO 2005 Industrial Development Report, p. 75, Box 6.6.

---

from abroad more productive. Moreover, in the long-term, an internationally open financial system is likely to be more competitive, transparent, and efficient than a closed one.

Several studies support the case for regional financial integration. The 1988 Cecchini Report, which focused on the benefits of the European Single Market Program, cautioned that fully liberalizing capital movements will increase the risk of exchange rate instability. The report proposed ensuring the benefits of economic integration by increasing cooperation on monetary policy through a strengthened European Monetary System (EMS). This eventually led to the establishment of the euro area.

A study by London Economics (2002) examined the quantitative impact of European financial integration focusing on the EU-15. The empirical work suggests that trading costs could fall sharply as a result of full European financial market integration. Schiavo (2005) finds robust and consistent evidence that monetary integration enhances capital market integration, which in turn feeds back into the system and results in closer business cycle synchronization. This feed-back mechanism supports financial integration and, coupled with the trade channel, lends credit to the hypothesis that countries are better candidates to join a monetary union *ex post* rather than *ex ante*. This process creates a virtuous cycle and enables the emerging markets of Europe to integrate seamlessly into the EU.

UFJ Institute (2003) estimates the impact of East Asian regional trade integration on the volume of cross-border capital flows. Simulations using a simple model showed the following: (1) a stable and continuous inflow of export-oriented FDI is needed to sustain the targeted growth of the regional economy; (2) cross-border loans will result from stable economic growth; and (3) inflows of portfolio investment are affected by the size of the domestic capital market and the presence of foreign investors but the volatility of such flows and limited data preclude robust estimates. The findings are consistent with the empirical result of Park and Eichengreen (2004), which showed that lack of formal trade integration has limited regional financial integration in East Asia.

Benefits of Financial Integration

Financial integration centers on capital mobility, which is generally viewed as advantageous to economic development. The benefits of global financial integration are well understood. Capital flows to emerging market economies have eased the domestic savings constraint, which in turn has increased investment and boosted economic growth. To the extent that real returns to marginal investment are lower in capital-rich than in capital-scarce countries, the movement of capital from developed to emerging market economies improves the efficiency of world resource allocation. Having international capital available also helps smooth expenditures, especially when a country experiences adverse exogenous shocks. Meanwhile, an open capital account for developed and emerging market economies allows for greater portfolio diversification and better management of risk on the part of investors. This is one of the more common arguments at the microeconomic level for capital account liberalization.

While these points build the case for global financial integration, the case for regional financial integration is nuanced (ADB 2008). For one thing, regional integration is less likely than global to foster risk-sharing, insofar as business cycles tend to be more closely correlated among neighboring countries than among distant ones. There is evidence that financial integration facilitates better diversification of risk when countries are more specialized (Garcia-Herrero and Wooldridge 2007).

The argument for regional integration usually highlights the institutional dimension. Experience in Europe and more recently in Asia shows that peer pressure has promoted better and harmonized local practices in financial systems, including accounting, tax treatment and even regulation and supervision. Regional institutions can apply peer pressure and foster the dialogue and information-sharing that promote financial development and integration, as well as best practices in financial regulation and supervision (ADB 2008).

The importance of local information and common time zones for financial markets can add to the benefits of regional integration. In particular, information asymmetries or differences in investment styles could cause investors in neighboring countries to act differently from those in distant countries, and so regional integration might help to diversify the global investor base (Garcia-Herrero and Wooldridge 2007).

Adjustment Issues and Recommended Measures for Capital Flows

An effective policy agenda for financial liberalization focuses on maximizing the gains and minimizing the risks associated with financial development. Such an agenda would entail adoption of policy measures at all levels: domestic, regional, and international. A major issue in this chapter is how regional financial cooperation can facilitate the transition to financial openness, including capital account liberalization. The ADB (2008) identifies the major weaknesses in any given financial regime to be

- Insufficient market opening and capital account liberalization;
- Limited and varying degrees of transparency, financial regulation, financial supervision, and governance;
- Inadequacies in risk management in financial firms and markets; and
- The heterogeneity of supervisory, accounting, and auditing rules and regulatory frameworks across countries.

A prioritized agenda for countries deepening their financial development would include (1) strengthening the banking sector primarily by improving its regulation and supervision; (2) adoption of international norms and standards; and (3) promotion of capital markets, especially local currency bond markets, to create the liquidity and innovative financial products required to attract a broader and more diversified investor base (Chow et al. 2006, ADB 2008, Erskine 2004).

Can regional financial cooperation in ASEAN advance the development of member states' financial systems and if so, how? The most important mechanism may be the Policy Dialogue and Surveillance Process (PDSP). At present, the PDSP is carried out through the ASEAN+3 Economic Review and Policy Dialogue (ERPD) and the ASEAN Surveillance Process (ASP). A common component is a peer pressure mechanism intended to induce appropriate policy responses and reforms in the financial sector. The ERPD and ASP also have a common weakness, namely their inability to ensure forthright and effective discussion of policy. The primary source of this weakness is the absence of an independent, professional organization that can prepare relevant analyses, and the "ASEAN way," which respects "consensus and non-interference in others' domestic affairs."

Whether under the purview of ASEAN or ASEAN+3, the PDSP must be transparent, comprehensive, and open in order to be effective. One way for the PDSP to attain these qualities is through restructured objectives. Thus, instead of being confined to anticipating a crisis and minimizing its impact, the PDSP could also

- Coalesce common interests in the region and project them in a global rules setting;
- Support domestic policymaking by providing mechanisms for frank and useful discussion of economic issues and problems in a constructive and supportive environment, and by creating peer pressure for policymakers in less well performing countries; and
- Provide necessary inputs for regional economic cooperation.

In addition to supporting domestic reforms, regional financial cooperation can give ASEAN Member States a stronger voice in advocating reforms of the international financial architecture to reduce the volatility and risks associated with capital flows. While capital account liberalization may be inevitable, an ASEAN unified position would be useful to ensure that the international economic environment is conducive to positive outcomes. Such an approach could be effective in setting global rules but would arguably be more effective at the ASEAN+3 level. A case in point is the insertion of collective action clauses in loan contracts or even the proposal for a Sovereign Debt Restructuring Mechanism.

Regional cooperation can also make the application of a capital-control mechanism (e.g., reserve requirements to manage surges in capital inflows) more effective. International endorsement of such a mechanism, for example by the IMF, would give it weight (Grenville 2007) and could be offered alongside operational guidelines and a weighing of advantages and disadvantages in application. Even if a capital-control mechanism does not gain international endorsement, applying it on a regional level will be more effective than applying it only at the national level (as Thailand did ineffectively in December 2006).

Other examples of regional approaches to cooperation in this area include fostering the growth of regional bond markets, strengthening the Chiang-Mai Initiative, strengthening exchange-rate coordination, and building market infrastructure such as regional clearing houses, payment and settlement systems, credit rating agencies, research and training facilities, and databases. The usefulness and progress of these efforts, particularly for regional financial integration, have been discussed extensively in other studies (e.g., ADB 2008).

The last major issue is optimal sequencing or optimal cascading, as may be the case. If one accepts the notion that a minimum threshold of institutional development must be crossed before financial liberalization or even capital openness can be effective, how does one recognize the threshold? This "threshold" notion may lead to tautological policy recommendations such as "in order to develop, the country must be developed." At present, it would be best for ASEAN to focus on developing the financial systems of its member states. Regional financial integration can then adopt a multi-track and multi-speed approach.

CONCLUSION AND RECOMMENDATIONS

There are compelling reasons to believe that the AEC Blueprint's goals of open FDI and freer flows of capital will enhance competitiveness and increase welfare in ASEAN. Studies of other regional groupings underscore the importance of regional integration in attracting FDI. The EU Single Market Program led to significant increases in FDI in manufacturing and services. Internal EU trade seems to be complementary to intraregional FDI as economic liberalization facilitates the relocation of economic activities and the formation of production and distribution networks. NAFTA's experience indicates large increases in FDI inflows since the creation of NAFTA for Mexico, with post-NAFTA FDI from the United States being characterized as vertical. The empirical results for Mercosur are quite mixed, probably because regional integration has been partial and member countries have faced numerous shocks (e.g., the Brazilian devaluation in 1999, the Argentine economic crisis of 2001–2002) that have inhibited creation of a truly unified market. Our own calculations above suggest that the rise in FDI stocks could be large.

Economic studies emphasize that regional economic integration is a significant determinant of FDI inflows and facilitates it considerably. *The AEC, which aims to create a single ASEAN market and single production base, is expected to lead to greater economies of scale and other dynamic effects that would improve its competitiveness and make it more attractive to investors.* The AEC is committed to the principles of open regionalism, national treatment, and MFN treatment of investors. It also recognizes the importance of creating an integrated production base to capture FDI as well as honing the region's competitive edge as a globally oriented manufacturing base.

In this regard, the ACIA provides clear timelines for investment liberalization in line with the AEC, extends benefits to foreign-owned ASEAN-based investors, and offers a more liberal, facilitative, transparent and competitive investment environment. We expect that a net positive impact on FDI in manufacturing and services will be realized through the following channels:

- ACIA provisions that allow greater participation of foreign investors in domestic firms.
- AEC deep integration features that will improve investment environments. Deep integration affects trade in services, standards setting and harmonization, competition law, customs cooperation, IPR, and dispute settlement.
- Liberalization and facilitation that deepen ASEAN's global integration and participation in regional and global production networks and increase vertical FDI inflows. Horizontal FDI in differentiated products as well as in service-related FDI is also expected to go up especially in Mode 3.
- Development of a large regional market more attractive to foreign MNCs than separate, national markets.
- The virtuous cycle of economic growth due to regional integration attracting more FDI.

As ASEAN Member States deepen their economic integration through the AEC, strengthening the ACIA will be crucial. Following Plummer (2007) and others, we suggest the following to bolster the ACIA and make it more effective in achieving the objectives of the AEC:

- Introduce collective measures to be taken by all ASEAN Member States and encourage individual members to lower transaction costs and strengthen market factors to facilitate investment and promote regional production networks.
- Widen the scope of industries by transferring Mode 3 of services from the AFAS to the ACIA.
- Adopt a common timeframe and specific procedures for liberalizing trade and investment.
- Develop a regional tax regime and a standard treaty framework for ASEAN (Sudsawasad 2008) to prevent the "noodle bowl" effect of overlapping BITS and bilateral trade and economic partnership agreements.

Though a large domestic market remains a powerful magnet for investors, MNCs serving global markets increasingly look for world-class infrastructure, skilled and productive workers, innovative capabilities, and an agglomeration of efficient suppliers, competitors, support institutions and services. Thus, the AEC should be accompanied by complementary policies and programs especially at the national level. Member states should continue to implement their investment and trade reforms in line with the ACIA and improve their domestic business environment, including economic regulations, corporate governance, and labor laws. They should also develop their logistics infrastructure and stable legal and economic systems to increase FDI inflows.

ASEAN Member States also need to come up with, unilaterally and collectively, structural adjustment and reform assistance and capacity building measures to help those who may be adversely affected by reforms. Additionally they should devise policies — taking into account each country's level of development — that deepen involvement in production networks. Deepening that involvement entails continuing to liberalize and facilitate trade and investment, pursuing reforms that lower transactions costs, strengthening institutions and developing economic infrastructures to improve the investment climate, and reducing service link costs.

Applying a methodology based on three measures of state-of-the-art performance in FDI stock/GDP ratios, we estimate above gains in FDI due to the AEC that vary between 28 percent to 63 percent

Table 4-11
Summary of AEC Benefits for Stakeholders: Investment and Capital Flows

Stakeholders	AEC Process	AEC Major Benefits
1. ASEAN as a regional grouping	Necessary component of "single market and production base". Exemplary of outward-orientation of AEC program.	Estimated increase in FDI stocks of up to $265 billion and increase in ASEAN welfare of 1% per annum under conservative assumptions; enhanced attractiveness for production networks and fragmented trade; potentially lower cost of capital.
2. ASEAN Member States	Large boost to FDI inflows will generate significant benefits in terms of capital/forex inflows, technology transfer, links to global production chains, and trade flows.	Our estimates of increases in FDI as the member states approach the "frontier" tend to be significant for all countries, though some countries gain more than others. Chapter 2 CGE estimates showed that including FDI into the welfare estimates of the effects of the AEC increases significantly potential gains for most.
3. CLMV countries	Same as (2); "best practices" and related provisions should help improve FDI legal and institutional framework, as well as develop financial institutions.	Increases in FDI flows have helped economic development in all ASEAN Member States to date; the CLMV should gain significantly from the likely large boost in FDI to most of their markets (both extra-ASEAN and from the more developed ASEAN countries), with FDI stocks rising from about one-tenth to one-third of GDP due to AEC. The CLMV will have more to gain from access to production chains, technology spillovers, and improved capital markets.
4. ASEAN businesses including SMEs	Same as (2); allows for greater rationalization of production, economies of scale, and inclusion of SMEs in the regional integration process due to production chains.	Large benefits for business due to higher economic growth, lower transactions costs to doing business in the region, greater partnering opportunities with foreign firms and easier plug-in to production networks, and easier access to foreign markets. Greater stability in ASEAN, stronger financial markets, potentially lower cost of capital, should also generate large gains to all ASEAN businesses, particularly SMEs.
5. ASEAN investors	Same as (4).	Same as (4). Investment and capital liberalization would encourage intra-ASEAN investment flows and partnerships and improve opportunities of developing ASEAN MNCs.
6. ASEAN labor including professionals	Free flow of FDI dovetails with free flow of skilled labor in Chapter 2.	Through greater FDI (and services liberalization), there should be an increase in demand for skilled and unskilled labor in the member states. Employment should rise. MNCs tend to pay higher wages than national firms. Technology transfer should help improve skill sets and productivity.
7. ASEAN consumers	Same as (4).	Greater economic efficiencies and import liberalization should lower prices and improve range of products and services available in member states; greater economic growth will boost purchasing power.
8. ASEAN's global partners	FDI is a key variable in FTA negotiations; integrated market makes negotiations easier.	Same as (4). Outward-orientation will improve the economic and investment status of ASEAN in Asia and the world, particularly as competing investment destinations *vis-à-vis* China and India.

of baseline FDI stocks, or a range of $117–264 billion of additional FDI stock. The welfare gains of this increased FDI amount conservatively to $6–$13 billion or 0.5–1 percent of annual ASEAN GDP. And the dynamic effects of serving as a magnet for FDI might be even greater. Sustained relationships with foreign companies and markets are likely to increase productivity and the rate of productivity growth; forge a channel for "economic intelligence," information that helps the region adapt readily to changing markets and technologies; and cement relations with source economies, helping to ward off the bouts of criticism and protectionism that sometimes accompany intense commercial relationships

The case for "freer" capital flows is not as straightforward for ASEAN Member States as is the case for free investment flows. Regional financial integration should be less of a priority than regional financial cooperation primarily because of the risks involved. Regional cooperation can facilitate the development of national financial systems through a more effective PDSP. Still, greater global financial integration in the medium- to long-term will be beneficial for ASEAN Member States. In this context, regional financial cooperation will be useful in reducing risks. ASEAN Member States can be the focal point in East Asia in advocating for reform of the international financial architecture. Joint action in crafting measures to manage capital inflows will also be worthwhile.

In terms of sequencing, it would be prudent to address the disparity in the level of development of the national financial systems. As stated earlier, many recommendations along this line have already been laid out in various studies and it is a matter of consolidating the proposed measures. Table 4-11 summarizes the likely effects of the AEC on ASEAN stakeholders due to the "investment and capital flows" outlined in the AEC Blueprint.

NOTES

1. The spillover effects of the US financial crisis are largely seen in the sharp falls in ASEAN stock markets and export demand. So far the ASEAN financial institutions have not been seriously affected, as the ASEAN financial sectors have been strengthened since the Asian financial crisis. The sharp falls in export demand are affecting economic growth in the ASEAN region and prospects for investment inflows.
2. Table 4-4 presents a cumulative total of FDI inflows from 1999 to 2006 from the ASEAN Secretariat database. The UNCTAD database does not have FDI by sector, hence the ASEAN Secretariat database is used instead.
3. From ADB (2008), p. 122.
4. As cited in Barrel and Choy (2003).

5

Narrowing the Development Gap in ASEAN

Dionisius Narjoko, Pratiwi Kartika, and Teguh Wicaksono

Regional economic integration has become very important for ASEAN. ASEAN Vision 2020 envisages an integrated Southeast Asian region characterized by equitable economic development and fewer socioeconomic disparities. The Hanoi Action Plan in 1998 declared ASEAN's intention to create a prosperous and highly competitive region characterized by free movement of goods, services, investments, skilled labor and freer flow of capital. The 2003 Declaration of ASEAN Concord II called for establishment of an ASEAN Economic Community (AEC) that would "turn the diversity that characterizes the region into opportunities for business complementation making it a more dynamic and stronger segment of the global supply chain."[1]

Achieving an AEC poses myriad challenges for ASEAN and ASEAN Member States. One of the most important is narrowing the development gap between the older member states and the ones that joined ASEAN in the latter 1990s — Cambodia, Lao PDR, Myanmar, and Vietnam (CLMV). These transitional economies, in which agriculture is still the major contributor to GDP, have significantly lower per capita GDP and rank much lower on socioeconomic indicators than original members (Chia 2007)[2] (Table 5-1).

To narrow the development gap, ASEAN's main instrument has been the Initiative for ASEAN Integration (IAI). The IAI aims to enhance the productive capacity of the CLMV countries and make them more competitive (Chia 2007). Many projects have been implemented under the IAI's 2002–2008 work plan, which designates infrastructure, human resources, information and communication technology, and assistance with and promotion of regional economic integration as top priorities. IAI projects have had positive outcomes but the work plan's narrow focus, insufficient interagency coordination, and weak ownership in the CLMV countries have hampered progress (Chia 2007).[3] The

Table 5-1
Some Development Indicators for ASEAN Countries

	GDP (US$ billion) 2004	Population (million) 2005	Per Capita GDP (US$) 2004	Share of Industry in GDP, 2003	Human Development Index (Rank) (2003)
Brunei	5.2	0.4	13,879	58.4	33
Cambodia	4.9	13.9	358	27.9	130
Indonesia	258.0	219.0	1,193	45.0	110
Lao PDR	2.4	5.9	423	24.6	133
Malaysia	118.0	26.2	4,625	42.1	61
Myanmar	9.1	56.0	166	17.3	129
Philippines	86.1	84.2	1,042	33.5	84
Singapore	106.9	4.3	25,207	31.1	25
Thailand	163.5	65.0	2,537	45.8	73
Vietnam	45.4	83.1	554	38.5	108

Source: *ASEAN Yearbook of Statistics*, various issues, cited by Salazar and Das (2007).

AEC Blueprint calls for improving the IAI and mandates its continuation. More important, it recognizes the significant role of external economic factors and mandates that IAI-related activities take into account global regulations.

In this chapter we explore how the AEC's "equitable economic development" initiative will benefit ASEAN. In particular, how deeper economic integration will affect the region's development gap, the conditions or policy initiatives that should be embraced to narrow the gap, and what can be learned from experience in ASEAN and elsewhere. In doing so, we adopt an eclectic approach, distilling what we know from previous studies and producing some fresh evidence from statistical data. We discuss findings from previous studies on the impact of economic integration on the development gap; examine income inequality and poverty, presenting an empirical analysis of income distribution in some major ASEAN Member States (where data are available); review the literature on the SMEs in ASEAN, particularly with regard to international production networks in Southeast Asia; and discuss ASEAN's initiatives for narrowing the development gap. Throughout, we present the implications for policy and offer recommendations for solving problems.

Before beginning, we summarize three salient points supported in this chapter. First, all member states will experience gains due to ASEAN and "ASEAN+" initiatives but gains will likely vary across countries. Ensuring that CLMV countries gain equitably requires putting in place policies to advance education and health, infrastructure, trade and investment facilitation (especially services), and domestic economic reform. The AEC can help by supporting these reforms through best practices and concerted liberalization across the region.

Second, enhancing welfare and income distribution across member states requires focusing on SMEs and their role in international production networks. The CLMV countries have the most to gain in entering such networks. In encouraging deeper linkages and greater participation in networks, AEC-related activities will significantly narrow the development gap.

Finally, narrowing the development gap will be crucial to the success of the AEC itself. Should they materialize, unbalanced gains accruing through integration could undermine political support for the

AEC — and without political support it will be difficult to implement the reforms necessary for a truly unified market. Other successful integration programs, such as in Europe, recognize this and have developed accommodating approaches. Hence, the AEC's emphasis on creating an "equitable economic region" is both appropriate and wise.

IMPACT OF ECONOMIC INTEGRATION IN ASEAN: LITERATURE REVIEW

The goal of economic development is to increase real per capita income over a long period of time, subject to the condition that the number of people living below the poverty line does not increase and the distribution of income does not deteriorate (Meir 2000). In so far as regional integration contributes to this goal it is a valid means of economic development. Therefore regional integration initiatives should address a wide range of social issues and aim for public policies that create opportunities for everyone, especially the poorest.

In the following survey of literature on the impact of regional integration on growth, income distribution, and poverty, we consider the likely impact of the AEC in the context of wider East Asia initiatives. The AEC is being formed as FTAs and Economic Partnership Agreements (EPAs) spread rapidly in East Asia (e.g. ASEAN–China and ASEAN–Korea, ASEAN–Japan), and there are concerns over the costs of multiple and overlapping FTAs and integration initiatives, such as the much discussed ASEAN+3 or ASEAN+6 FTAs.

In their literature survey, Kawai and Wignaraja (2007) summarize recent CGE-based studies of East Asian FTAs. They find that one strand of literature focuses on formation of an ASEAN+3 FTA or a variant like ASEAN+4 (i.e., including India). GTAP simulations by Urata and Kiyota (2003) indicate that an ASEAN+3 FTA will generate welfare gains for all members, ranging from highs of 12.5 percent of GDP for Thailand and 6.6 percent for Vietnam, to lows of 0.19 percent for Japan and 0.64 percent for the PRC. They also report modest welfare losses for non-members such as the EU (–0.02 percent) and the United States (–0.09 percent). GTAP simulations by Zhang et al. (2006) confirm these findings: an ASEAN+3 FTA is estimated to increase the overall GDP of East Asian countries by 1.2 percent and economic welfare by $105 billion, as well as raising every member's GDP in excess of 1.7 percent, with the exception of Japan. In a similar vein and based on GTAP, Mohanty et al. (2004) find that an ASEAN+4 FTA will bring gains to members of between $147 billion (liberalization of trade barriers only) to $210 billion (liberalization of barriers to trade, investment, and labor).

Another strand of literature comparing FTA scenarios provides additional insight on their costs and benefits. Using GTAP, Gilbert et al. (2004) find that an ASEAN+3 FTA will produce greater welfare gains for members than a narrower PRC–Japan–Korea FTA, suggesting that broadening FTAs in East Asia brings more benefits. Based on a GTAP model that includes capital accumulation, Cheong (2005) reports that all members reap larger gains from an ASEAN+3 FTA than a series of bilateral arrangements between East Asian economies, and that ASEAN and Japan are expected to benefit the most. Bchir and Fouquin (2006) use the CEPII Mirage Model to create several scenarios of economic integration based on a hub and spoke approach (ASEAN+1) and a regional approach (ASEAN+4 (including India). They find that ASEAN would be better off with a series of bilateral agreements than ASEAN+4 as this would allow them to better exploit their comparative advantage in agriculture, which is much more protected than manufactures in the region. Drawing on GEMAT simulations for an FTA involving goods only, Plummer and Wignaraja (2006) report that the current wave of bilateral FTAs is inferior to any of the major FTA proposals in East Asia, including ASEAN+3, ASEAN+6, or an APEC FTA. They find that an ASEAN+6 FTA will bring larger global welfare gains than an ASEAN+3 FTA. Their study provides a preliminary assessment of the economic effects of an ASEAN+3 and ASEAN+6 FTA even though services trade, trade facilitation, and other aspects of agreements are excluded from the exercise.

As these studies tend to focus on goods, Kawai and Wignaraja (2007) extend their analysis to cover the impact of liberalization of services trade and trade facilitation, including better trade-related infrastructure as well as the impact of regional tariff elimination. As shown in Table 5-2, ASEAN+3 and ASEAN+6 offer larger gains in national income for ASEAN Member States than any of the three ASEAN+1 scenarios. Estimates in the table also indicate that any scenario is Pareto optimal for ASEAN, that is, no member state is worse off as a result of the FTAs. But gains from FTAs vary, with Vietnam and Thailand gaining the most and Cambodia (among others) gaining the least.

Table 5-3 presents the wage effects for unskilled workers as a rough measure of the distributional impact of ASEAN+3 and ASEAN+6. In contrast to the universally positive impact on national income

Table 5-2
Impacts of FTA Scenarios on National Income (% change compared to 2017 baseline in constant 2001 dollars)

	ASEAN+ PRC	*ASEAN+ Japan*	*ASEAN+ Korea*	*ASEAN+3*	*ASEAN+6*
ASEAN	3.72	2.43	0.68	5.23	5.66
Cambodia	0.75	0.33	0.16	1.20	1.21
Indonesia	2.30	0.94	0.49	2.62	2.86
Malaysia	4.02	2.37	0.71	5.54	6.33
Philippines	2.13	1.59	0.52	2.40	2.85
Singapore	4.13	1.91	0.48	4.79	5.43
Thailand	7.39	6.39	1.20	12.10	12.84
Vietnam	4.68	2.94	1.58	7.35	7.63
Others	0.50	0.18	0.05	0.59	0.33

Source: ADB estimates, cited by Kawai and Wignaraja (2007).

Table 5-3
Impacts of FTA Scenarios on Wages of Unskilled Workers
(% change compared to 2017 baseline in constant 2001 dollars)

	ASEAN+3	*ASEAN+6*
Cambodia	−1.07	−1.14
Indonesia	1.67	1.53
Malaysia	4.91	5
Philippines	0.65	0.69
Singapore	4.64	5.58
Thailand	11.07	11.95
Vietnam	7.96	8.24
Others	−0.53	−1.41

Source: ADB estimates, cited by Kawai and Wignaraja (2007).

shown in Table 5-2, we see here that the impact on wages for unskilled workers is negative for some countries, notably Cambodia. This impact seems related to the income gains under the alternative scenarios. Under ASEAN+6, Thailand, Korea, Vietnam, Singapore and Malaysia — with relatively large income effects — experience increases in unskilled wages of 5 percent to 12 percent. Several other countries (such as Japan, PRC, Indonesia, Philippines and India) — with relatively smaller income effects — experience increases in unskilled wages of less than 2 percent. The correlation between income and distribution effects sheds light on the importance of economic growth in reducing poverty, as well as the need to increase the elasticity of poverty reduction with respect to growth as part of an inclusive growth strategy.

The second study of interest here is that of Ezaki and Nguyen (2008). Their CGE analysis includes the following features.

- Countries: ASEAN + China, Hong Kong, Taiwan, Korea, Japan (ASEAN+5)
- Free mobility of capital and labor between industries within countries
- Elastic mobility of capital is allowed across countries, and is a function of the differences in the rates of return to capital
- No international labor mobility and changes in technology and productivity.

The study does not include Cambodia, Lao PDR, or Myanmar but does complement Kawai and Wignaraja in providing the sectoral impacts of an East Asian Community. Like Kawai and Wignaraja, Ezaki and Nguyen show that Thailand, Vietnam, and Malaysia are the major gainers of an ASEAN+5 FTA (Table 5-4). Their gains materialize through higher capital formation, a finding that underscores the importance of capital movement in general and FDI in particular in spreading the benefits of regional integration.

Ezaki and Nguyen also provide a detailed distributional analysis that shows that the poor in Vietnam and Thailand are the main beneficiaries of regional integration. Keeping in mind the sectoral CGE result, we may infer that these distributional gains are realized mainly through expansion in the agriculture, food processing, and machinery industries (Thailand) (Tables 5-5 and 5-6). In contrast, Indonesia's poor distributional performance may be related to the structure of its economy; its more resource and capital-intensive industries would be the main beneficiaries of regional integration.

Table 5-4
Impacts of East Asian Community on Macroeconomy, Benchmark Year 2001
(% deviation from base run)

	Real GDP	HH Cons.	Gov't Cons.	Capital Formation	Exports	Imports
Thailand	1.8	8.0	−24.9	30.3	4.7	3.1
Vietnam	2.8	10.8	−45.1	12.7	14.4	17.5
Indonesia	0.3	1.4	−11.0	4.3	2.0	21.9
Malaysia	1.8	9.4	−63.2	18.9	4.3	4.6
Philippines	0.5	1.6	−6.2	5.3	1.6	7.5
Singapore	0.3	1.6	0.3	4.3	0.2	1.7

Source: Ezaki and Nguyen (2008).

Table 5-5
Impacts of East Asian Community on Industry, Benchmark Year 2001
(% deviation from base run)

Output	Thailand	Vietnam	Indonesia	China
crop	12.4	2.1	0.4	7.0
livestock	20.9	1.6	0.1	2.5
forestry	−5.0	−3.3	3.3	0.3
fishing	15.9	2.8	0.7	2.1
mining	−12.1	−1.3	−0.1	−0.7
processed food	27.3	0.8	0.6	4.0
beverage	4.3	0.7	1.7	2.5
wood	−9.2	−7.6	3.7	−1.5
chemical	0.3	−0.6	0.8	−1.6
automobile	−6.3	−41.7	−5.8	−10.5
transportation	23.1	−44.0	−0.6	3.6
electronics	1.1	−15.4	2.9	8.6
machine	7.2	4.4	6.4	−2.6
metal	−6.8	−14.3	−2.2	−1.2
textile	−12.0	83.0	0.0	−3.6
leather	−8.1	20.9	−2.5	6.2
other manufacturers	−7.6	−8.1	−2.4	−0.1
utility	0.7	2.3	0.2	−0.4
construction	27.8	12.2	3.7	3.6
service	−2.2	−4.6	−0.7	−2.4

Source: Ezaki and Nguyen (2008).

POVERTY AND INCOME INEQUALITY IN ASEAN

There is a consensus among economists that poverty reduction is strongly associated with economic growth. Recent studies seem to be cautious in affirming this relationship (Bourguignon 2002). Bourguignon proposes that if a decline in the number of poor people is due mainly to growth (as shown by high growth — poverty elasticity), then policy should focus exclusively on fostering growth to reduce poverty. Otherwise, one needs to address specific causes of poverty. Empirical evidence suggests that a high growth — poverty elasticity is not common yet several studies on poverty in East Asia or Southeast Asia find a strong association between significant poverty reduction and sustained growth (Quibria 2002; Warr 2006; Jomo 2006). In explaining this poverty reduction, Quibria points out two lessons from East Asia:

- Swift capital accumulation and openness have contributed to rapid transformation of economies in the region; and
- Pragmatic policies aimed at establishing market-oriented institutions have nurtured steady economic growth and brought dynamism to these economies.

Interestingly, Quibria finds no robust association between inequality and economic growth in these economies, suggesting that the economic "pies" of the region are shared inclusively by all even as the pies get bigger.

Table 5-6
Impacts of East Asian Community on Household Income
(% deviation from base run)

	Vietnam	Thailand
Rural	11.3	10.6
Urban	9.9	6.7
Rural		
1st decile	12.4	17.0
2nd decile	12.7	15.8
3rd decile	12.6	14.4
4th decile	12.9	11.1
5th decile	12.4	11.6
6th decile	11.9	11.2
7th decile	11.1	10.2
8th decile	11.8	9.4
9th decile	9.3	9.9
10th decile	9.9	9.0
Urban		
1st decile	14.2	8.4
2nd decile	11.5	8.7
3rd decile	12.1	5.3
4th decile	12.7	8.2
5th decile	12.4	6.0
6th decile	11.0	5.1
7th decile	10.1	6.2
8th decile	12.0	5.1
9th decile	10.0	6.6
10th decile	9.2	7.7

	Indonesia
AGEMPL	2.4
SMLFARM	2.4
MEDFARM	2.2
LARFARM	1.9
RURLOW	1.7
RURNLAB	1.9
RURHIGH	1.8
URBLOW	1.7
URBNLAB	1.7
URBHIGH	1.7

Key
AGEMPL = agricultural employee households
SMLFARM = small farmer households
MEDFARM = medium farmer households
LARFARM = large farmer households
RURLOW = low-income households in rural areas
RURNLAB = non-labor households in rural areas
RURHIGH = high-income households in rural areas
URBLOW = low-income households in urban areas
URBNLAB = non-labor households in urban areas
URBHIGH = high-income households in urban areas

Source: Ezaki and Nguyen (2008).

Warr (2006) observes variation among Southeast Asian countries in the relationship between inequality, poverty, and economic growth. If one juxtaposes poverty reduction achievement and inequality measured by Gini coefficients in ASEAN Member States, the results are mixed: poverty reduction is followed by rising inequality in Thailand; declining inequality in Malaysia and the Philippines; and a leveling-off (and low) effect in Indonesia, Cambodia, Lao PDR, and Vietnam. As he decomposes growth by sector in Thailand, Indonesia, Malaysia, and the Philippines, Warr finds surprising evidence that industrial growth has no effect in reducing poverty. He even concludes that industrial growth has not helped reduce poverty in Southeast Asia generally, though he notes that this may be the result of the negative effects of an import-substitution policy. Another important finding of Warr's study is that growth in services pulls people out of poverty. This suggests that poverty reduction strategies in Southeast Asia should try to foster growth in the service sector.

The ADB (2008) reports that poverty rates have declined in Asia and rapidly (Table 5-7). Key sources of this progress have been integration into the global economy and economic openness. In the pre-crisis period, the number of poor in Indonesia declined dramatically mainly because of the country's integration into the global economy, a transition that created opportunities for people at the

Table 5-7
Proportion of Population Below Poverty Line

Country	$1 (PPP) a day			National		
	1990	Latest year		1990	Latest year	
Cambodia	32.5	18.5	(2004)	39.0	34.7	(2004)
Indonesia	20.6	4.0	(2005)	15.1	16.6	(2007)
Lao PDR	53	28.8	(2002)	45.0	32.7	(2003)
Malaysia	< 2.0	< 2.0	(2004)	16.5	5.1	(2002)
Philippines	20.2	13.6	(2006)	33.0	33.0	(2006)
Thailand	10.2	< 2.0	(2002)	18.0	9.8	(2002)
Vietnam	50.8	8.4	(2004)	50.9	19.5	(2004)

Source: Key Indicators ADB 2008.

bottom of the income pyramid. In recent years, Vietnam has also been performing well. In the early 1990s, it is estimated that half of Vietnam's population lived on less than $1 a day (PPP adjusted). In 2004, less than one-tenth were living on less than $1 a day (ADB 2008).

Despite remarkable declines in poverty in ASEAN Member States, Cambodia, Lao PDR, and the Philippines lag behind. High poverty rates in Cambodia and Lao PDR may be attributed to the countries' reliance on low-productivity agriculture, a characteristic of early-stage economic development. Weak economic dynamism and disparities in access to infrastructure and social services across regions of the Philippines are main factors in the persistence of poverty in that country (Balisacan 2007).

With regard to Millennium Development Goals, ADB (2008) finds the Philippines and Cambodia progressing very slowly toward the "hunger target" while Thailand, Indonesia, Lao PDR, and Vietnam are on track. Malaysia and, surprisingly, Myanmar are ranked as early achievers. The data, moreover, show that poverty is very persistent in the CLMV region, except in Vietnam. Yet dynamic analysis of poverty would suggest that some original ASEAN Member States, for example, the Philippines and Indonesia, have experienced persistent poverty.

Income Gap Between CLMV and ASEAN-6

A major concern about ASEAN economic integration is the large variation in per capita income between the CLMV region and Brunei Darussalam, Indonesia, Malaysia, the Philippines, Singapore, and Thailand (hereafter the ASEAN-6). The average of the ASEAN-6 income per capita is ten times that of Cambodia, Lao PDR, and Vietnam (Table 5-8). This large difference is mainly due to Singapore and Brunei and there is, in fact, considerable variation within the ASEAN-6, with Indonesia and the Philippines ranking far below others.

The CLMV countries and ASEAN-6 also have very different economic structures. The ASEAN-6 have transformed themselves impressively: industry contributes about 47 percent to GDP (2006) and in Singapore services contribute more than 65 percent of GDP. In contrast, agriculture contributes 30 percent to GDP in Cambodia and 42 percent in Lao PDR. Meanwhile, manufacturing has developed as Vietnam's most important economic sector.

Table 5-8
ASEAN Macroeconomic Indicators (2006)

Country	Gross National Income per capita	Share of Agriculture	Share of Industry	Share of Services
	(US$ PPP)	(% of GDP)		
Brunei Darussalam	49,900	0.7	73.4	25.9
Cambodia	1,550	30.1	26.2	43.7
Indonesia	3,310	12.9	47.0	40.1
Lao PDR	1,740	42.0	32.5	25.5
Malaysia	12,160	8.7	49.9	41.3
Philippines	3,430	14.2	31.6	54.2
Singapore	43,300	0.1	34.7	65.2
Thailand	7,440	10.7	44.6	44.7
Vietnam	2,310	20.4	41.6	38.1

Source: World Development Indicators, World Bank 2007.

CLMV countries, however, have experienced rapid growth, ranging from 6.3 to 8.3 percent per annum, while the ASEAN-6 grew 4.6 percent to 5.3 percent per annum (Salazar and Das 2007). If this trend continues, the CLMV will likely catch-up with the ASEAN-6. However, it is worth noting that narrowing the income gap among ASEAN countries should not always be interpreted as "absolute convergence" in income. Green (2007) projected that Cambodia would have to grow 13 percent annually for ten years to raise its GDP per capita from US$390 in 2004 to US$1,000 by 2015, increasing its growth performance by 60 percent — no mean feat!

Even so, PPP-adjusted income per capita among ASEAN Member States suggests that convergence is on the rise. Figure 5-1 exhibits a dramatic convergence between the average per capita income of Cambodia, Lao PDR, and Vietnam and the ASEAN-6, though Vietnam contributes largely to lessening income dispersion with old ASEAN countries.

Socioeconomic Gap Between CLMV and the ASEAN-6

One of the important goals of economic development is to improve the well-being of people and not merely in economic terms. For example, average life expectancy in the ASEAN-6 is 70 years; in the CLMV it is 60 years (Table 5-9). Interestingly, life expectancy in Vietnam is higher than in Indonesia. Even though secondary education is far from universal among most member states, Cambodia, Lao PDR, and Myanmar lag far behind with only a third of secondary-school age children staying on at the secondary level.

Concerning inequality within countries, it seems that the CLMV perform better than the rest of ASEAN, as is observable by the low Gini index. However, this could well be because the countries are still in an early stage of development (e.g., according to the Kuznet hypotheses). Among the ASEAN-6, Indonesia seems to have the least income inequality. Many in the CLMV, especially Cambodia, are undernourished. Interestingly, the prevalence of undernourishment in Myanmar is very low, even lower than some of the ASEAN-6 countries. And prevalence is surprisingly high in Thailand — 22 percent — even though it has high per capita income. Access to affordable food and nutrition should be a concern for Thailand's human development.

Figure 5-1
Income per capita Dispersion (σ-convergence)

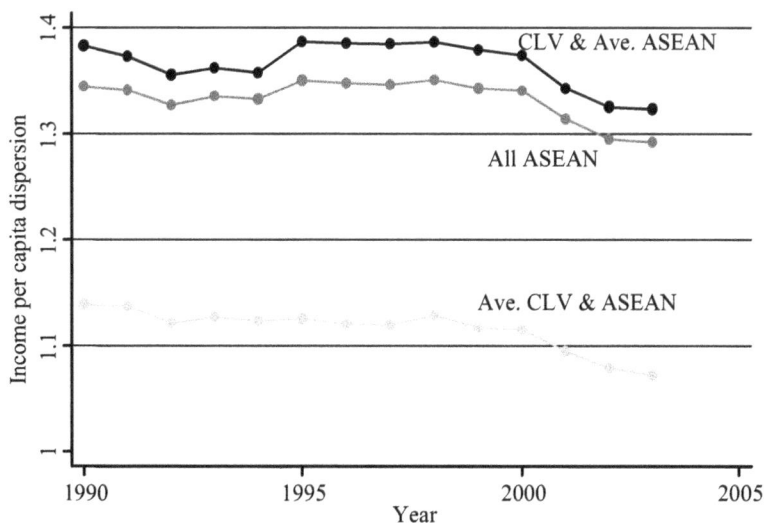

Source: Penn-World Table, Authors' calculation.

Table 5-9
ASEAN Human Development Indicators

Country	Life Expectancy at Birth (2005)	Net Enrollment, Secondary (2005)	Gini (1990–2004)	Prevalence of Undernourishment (% of pop.) (2004)
Brunei Darussalam	77.0	87.3		4
Cambodia	57.0	24.5	40.4	33
Indonesia	67.8	58.3	34.3	6
Lao PDR		37.7	34.6	19
Malaysia	73.7		49.2	3
Myanmar	61.1	37.2		5
Philippines	71.0	60.5	46.1	18
Singapore	79.7		42.5	
Thailand	70.9		42.0	22
Vietnam	70.7	69.3	37.0	16

Source: Asia-Pacific Human Development Report 2008, UNDP.

Policy Implications

Green (2007) summarizes well what should be the top priorities of ASEAN development policy. The policy should encourage sustained economic growth among ASEAN Member States. This will require general understanding and then addressing constraints to growth. For example, infrastructure, particularly in CLMV countries, must be able to meet growing demand. Inadequate infrastructure will be economically costly and will make it difficult to take advantage of myriad economic opportunities, which is exactly what happened as a result of electricity shortages in the Philippines. Other significant constraints on economic development include lack of investment in human capital. Adequate investment in health and education is a crucial determinant of growth potential. Though there is disagreement on how much should be invested, the salutary impact of education in ASEAN Member States is uncontroversial. Education, particularly secondary and tertiary, has expedited economic transformation. Among CLMV countries, the critical role of education in modernizing an economy is most evident in Vietnam.

Income Inequality in ASEAN Member States, 1994–2002

Even though per capita income analysis shows a wide income gap between the ASEAN-6 and the CLMV countries, analysis of the development process in ASEAN should also focus on income inequality within a country. A country-by-country approach could be useful in shaping policies that promote equitable development in ASEAN. In adopting individual countries as our unit of analysis, we follow Sala-i-Martin's framework and construct an ASEAN distribution of income. We pay particular attention to the CLMV countries and the distribution of income before and after they joined ASEAN.[4] After estimating a distribution of income for each member state, we construct an annual ASEAN distribution of income.[5] Data availability has us choose the 1994 and 2002 timeframe. These two-year points indicate pre- and post-periods of CLMV integration and this approach should be adequate to inform analysis about the development process and income inequalities in CLMV countries.

ASEAN Income Inequality

Figures 5-2a and 5-2b present the results of income distribution in ASEAN in 1994 and 2002, respectively. We notice that the "tallest" country distribution corresponds to Indonesia, followed by Vietnam. Moreover, it appears that a large part of individual income inequality across the ASEAN region can be explained by income differences *within* countries rather than *across* countries. This is shown in the figures since the distance between country distributions (e.g., the difference between the means of Indonesia and Vietnam) is likely to be much smaller than the differences between rich and poor Indonesians or rich and poor Vietnamese.

This general finding that the income distribution within ASEAN Member States varies more than across countries is not too surprising; we suggest that such an outcome is predictable for most regional trade groupings. For example, in the original European Economic Community countries had similar levels of economic development but greater inequality within countries than across countries. The same would be true of the "Closer Economic Relations" agreement between Australia and New Zealand, and the US-Canada Free-Trade Agreement, though NAFTA is less clear *a priori*. The differences in per capita income across ASEAN are higher than in these groupings, but the largest countries are relatively close.

The figures reveal that the income of the poor Vietnamese group has caught up with the income of the poor Philippines group in just 8 years. This shows that the strong economic growth of Vietnam in recent years has benefited the low-income group in the country. If we link the causes of strong growth to major domestic reforms and economic integration with ASEAN (and also the world), then the figures strongly support that Vietnam's economic integration program has uplifted poor Vietnamese

Figure 5-2a
ASEAN Distribution of Income and Individual Country Distribution, 1994

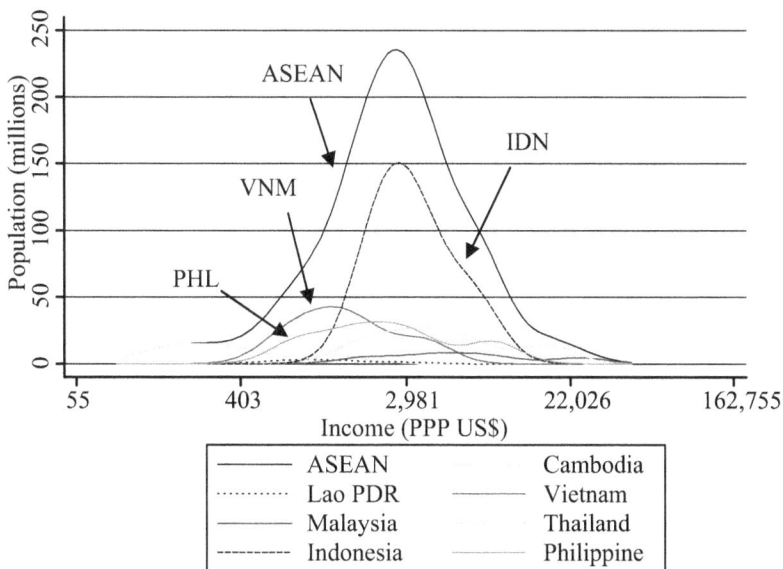

Note: IDN refers to Indonesia, VNM refers to Vietnam and PHL refers to Philippine.
Source: Penn-World Table, Authors' calculation.

Figure 5-2b
ASEAN Distribution of Income and Individual Country Distribution, 2002

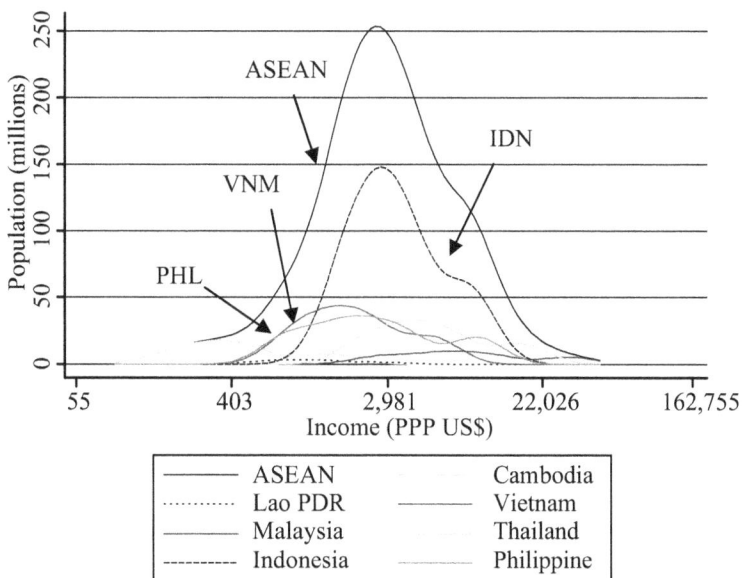

Note: IDN refers to Indonesia, VNM refers to Vietnam and PHL refers to Philippine.
Source: Penn-World Table, Authors' calculation.

considerably. However, we see an exception in Cambodia where a large share of the population is in the lowest tails between these two periods.

Figure 5-2c presents a direct comparison of income distribution in ASEAN as a whole between 1994 and 2002. One finds that income per capita seemed not to move to the right at all, suggesting that income levels in1994 and 2002 were pretty much the same. Economic crisis in 1998 and slow economic growth of major member states in the five years after the crisis are no doubt responsible for this. Still, it would appear that the wealthy did benefit over this period of slow growth (or stagnant growth).

Figure 5-2c
ASEAN Distribution of Income, 1994 and 2002

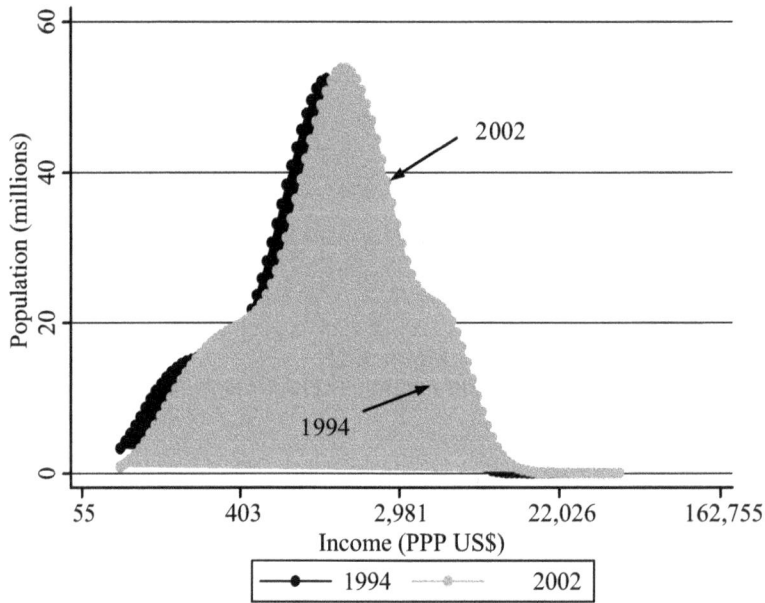

Source: Penn-World Table, Authors' calculation.

CLMV Income Inequality

Figures 5-3a and 5-3b display the distribution of income for the CLV region and the individual countries forming that group; we do not have data for Myanmar. Vietnam's income distribution contributes to a large part of income distribution in the CLV region, followed by Cambodia. Once again and as expected, inequality in the region comes largely from within-country differences rather than cross-country differences. Moreover, we find that the difference between the means of Vietnam and Cambodia is much lower than differences between poor and rich Cambodians. We also notice that in the CLV regional comparison, Cambodia and Lao PDR exhibit considerable inequalities. Income distribution in Cambodia, for example, has a considerable high variance and "two-humps"

Figure 5-3a
CLV Distribution of Income and Individual Country Distribution, 1994

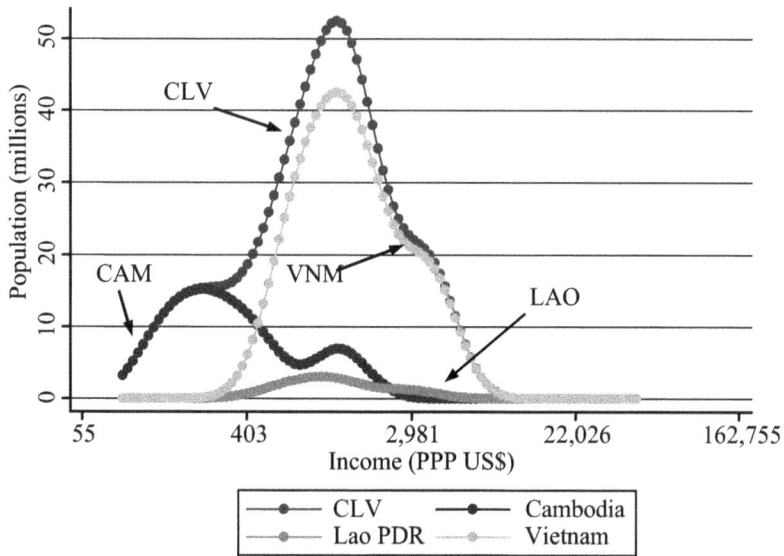

Source: Penn-World Table, Authors' calculation.

Figure 5-3b
CLV Distribution of Income and Individual Country Distribution, 2002

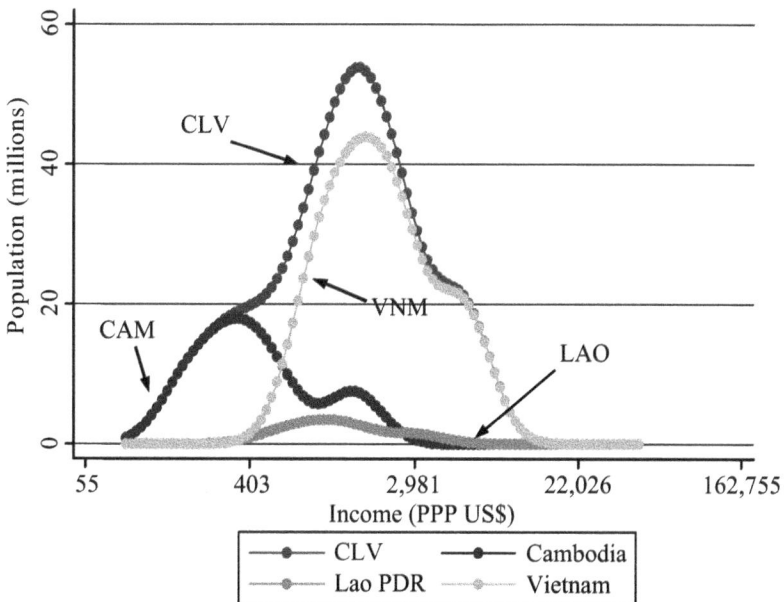

Source: Penn-World Table, Authors' calculation.

in the curve, which suggests a very high level of inequality. Lao PDR also has considerable variance in income. However, the major concern for Lao PDR is that the country seemed not to grow between 1994 and 2002.

Figure 5-3c shows that a large part of the density function shifted to the right between 1994 and 2002. This reflects that CLV average incomes have grown, particularly because of Vietnam. However, we find that the incomes of the richest group in the region improved more than the poorest group.

Figure 5-3c
CLV Distribution of Income, 1994 and 2002

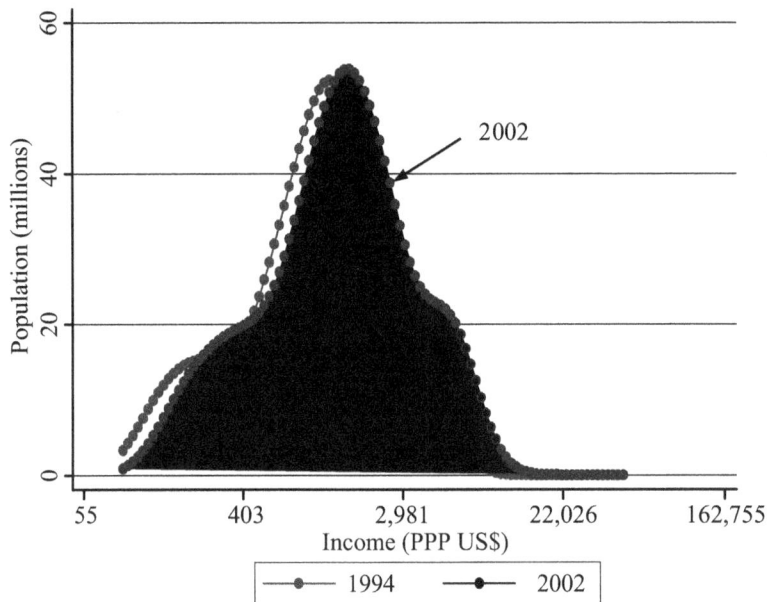

Source: Penn-World Table, Authors' calculation.

Policy Implications

Following up on the fact that inequalities in ASEAN derive significantly from within-country differences, we calculate Gini coefficients for ASEAN by weighting national coefficients by population size and organizing them into three groups: (1) ASEAN, (2) the resource-rich original ASEAN countries (Indonesia, Malaysia, the Philippines, and Thailand, hereafter IMPT), and (3) CLV. As Table 5-10 shows, income shares across citizens in ASEAN as a whole is relatively unequal: a simple average of Gini coefficients from 1993 to 2002 comes to 0.63. Yet, much of this inequality is explained by inequalities within the CLV region rather than the IMPT. Furthermore, while inequalities across the IMPT region tended to decrease the opposite occurred in the CLV.

This striking finding suggests that to narrow the development gap between ASEAN and CLV, one must attend to the *within-country* variables of the CLV, which may substantially affect inequalities

Table 5-10
ASEAN Gini Coefficients

Year	ASEAN	CLV	ASEAN-4
1993	0.60	0.61	0.47
1994	0.63	0.66	0.47
1995	0.65	0.66	0.45
1996	0.66	0.67	0.47
1997	0.63	0.68	0.47
1998	0.63	0.68	0.44
1999	0.64	0.68	0.46
2000	0.61	0.68	0.45
2001	0.62	0.68	0.42
2002	0.64	0.68	0.46
Change 1993–2002 (%)	6.82	12.41	−2.03
Average 1993–2002	0.63	0.67	0.46

Source: Authors' calculations.

among their citizens. Strengthening domestic reform and keeping borders open are examples of good policy options, and they should go hand-in-hand with encouragement from other ASEAN members for the CLMV to keep their integration with ASEAN and the world on track. As this is a key goal of the AEC, ASEAN integration should be an important protagonist in this process.

SMES AND INTERNATIONAL PRODUCTION NETWORKS IN ASEAN

In creating an integrated single market and production base the AEC can bolster the role of international production networks in member states and create opportunities for SMEs. SMEs play a vital role in the ASEAN economies.[6] In fact, more than 90 percent of firms in ASEAN Member States are SMEs and they employ from 45 to 92 percent of the workforce (Table 5-11). To be part of an international

Table 5-11
Relative Size and Employment in Nonagricultural SMEs, 2000 (est.)

Year 2000	SMEs as % of All Firms	SME Workforce as % of Total Employment
Brunei	98	92
Cambodia	99	45
Indonesia	98	88
Malaysia	84	39/m
Myanmar	96	78
Philippines	99	66
Singapore	91	52
Thailand	96	76/m
Vietnam	96	85

Note: Percentages refer to shares in national totals. /m=manufacturing only.
Source: Asasen, et al. (2003).

production network, industries and firms have to be competitive in regional production chains. Through AEC-related policies and developments SMEs should be better able to enter regional production chains, and, eventually, international production networks.

Production Networks and ASEAN Member States

As competition has intensified and transport costs have fallen economies have become more interdependent. Over time, firms have allocated segments of production to various locations according to their competitive advantage, leading to the development of international production networks. These networks are active in ASEAN Member States as indicated by the high proportion of intraregional trade in parts and components (see Chapter 1).

Older member states, for example, seem to have shifted from trade involving labor-intensive industries to trade involving capital-intensive goods. The share of trade in the electronics industry is above 40 percent for Malaysia, Philippines, Singapore, and Thailand. The CLMV still concentrate on trade in labor-intensive sectors while Indonesia is somewhat in the middle. But where data are available, they suggest that newer member states are catching-up in participating in regional production networks. The rate of growth in Cambodia's and Vietnam's exports of electronics has been much higher than rates in older member states.

Hence, a convergence of older ASEAN Member States and the CLMV in their participation in regional production networks is evident, and this is happening as AFTA is put in place. Under the AEC, priority sectors include electronics and automotives, which often involve production value chains as well as air travel and logistics services that support the networks. Achieving the AEC should deepen the involvement of the CLMV countries in regional production networks and help narrow the development gap.

SMEs and Networks: Analytical Framework

As shown in Figure 5-4, Romero and Santos (2007) postulate a typology for SMEs. The vertical axis represents areas where production can be sold, while the horizontal axis represents the location for input purchases. These two axes divide SMEs into four types:

- *Domestic SMEs* purchase inputs and sell products in a local market. They contribute to the local economy in a way that interconnects internal production systems.
- *Dependent SMEs* purchase inputs from an external market but sell to the local one. They depend on imported products and usually do not contribute much value added to the economy unless they are in high-tech industries. In ASEAN, there are few SMEs in high-tech industries.
- *Extrovert SMEs* purchase inputs from external markets, process inputs locally, and then sell the resulting products in external markets.
- *Exporting SMEs* use local resources to produce output for export. Their export orientation and backward linkages to local suppliers drives growth in a local economy. Their export potential also reflects their competitiveness in the global market.

A growth-oriented policy would concentrate on SMEs that are exporting, extrovert, and domestically oriented. In Southeast Asia, however, few SMEs export. For example, at the end of the 1990s

Figure 5-4
Enterprise Typology According to Spatial Aspect

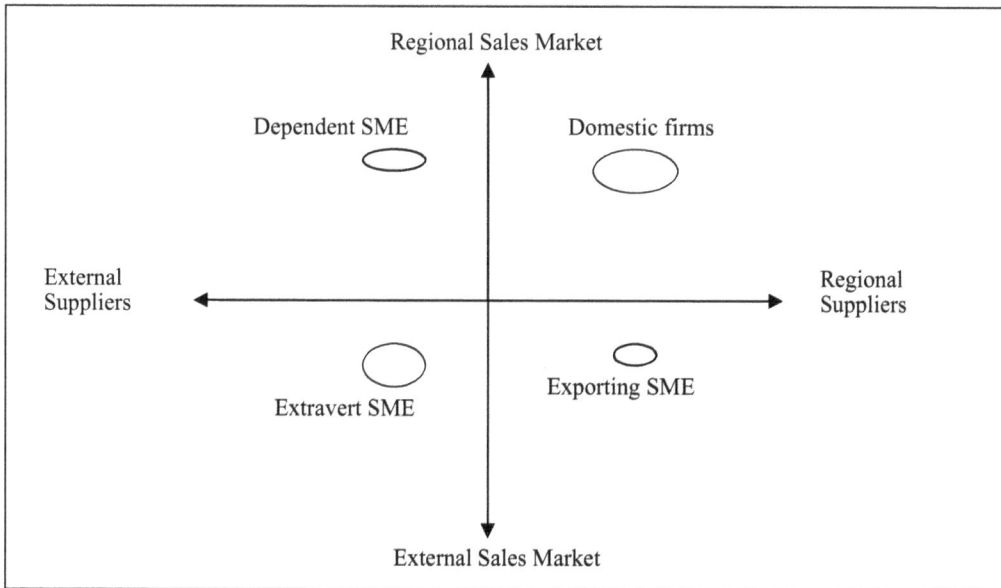

Source: Romero and Santos (2007).

Indonesian SMEs took part in only 11 percent of all non-oil and gas exports, whereas the share of Indian SMEs in total non-oil and gas exports was almost 40 percent.[7]

How does an international production network function and where do SMEs fit? A major characteristic of any network is the "flagship" company.[8] At the heart of the network, the flagship conducts many activities in which it has some comparative advantage and outsources the rest. It provides strategic and organizational leadership for resources beyond management's direct control (Rugman 1997, 182). It thus governs the position and role of firms in the network, including SMEs. In the Asian network model, two tiers of firms — high and low — supply the flagship (Ernst 2004). The major competitive value of firms in the lower tier is their low cost structure and flexibility, both prime characteristics of SMEs. Firms in the lower tier, however, are typically used as price breakers and capacity buffers, and can be dropped at short notice (Ernst 2004, 96). For example, when Compaq decided to produce and sell personal computers for under US$1,000, many small companies that manufactured personal computers in Taiwan were forced to shut down (Yusuf 2004, 40).

Being in the lower-tier suggests that an SME is expendable. Can this be changed? The role of SMEs in networks can be upgraded, broadly, by making improvements in specialization, productivity, and linkages (Hirschman 1958). This kind of upgrading requires skills, a strong base for knowledge dissemination, and strong international linkages (Ernst 2004). Two methods of upgrading are highly relevant for ASEAN integration: cluster formation and infrastructure improvement.

Industrial clusters complement production networks and nearly all SMEs participate in networks that are in clusters. Clusters are like "ports of entry" for local firms to engage with international networks. In addition, theory and empirical studies suggest that the higher the number and concentration of clusters in countries or regions, the higher the dependency-path of firms in a production network (Kuroiwa and Toh 2008). This implies that creating clusters should encourage the creation of more SMEs and engage these SMEs more fully in international production networks.

Upgrading SMEs for network participation by improving infrastructure is important for two reasons. First, infrastructure facilitates cluster development. According to the "flowchart approach" model of cluster development (Kuchiki 2005), good infrastructure facilities are necessary to attract both so-called anchor firms as well as other firms that support the anchor firm.[9] Firms that support the anchor firm are usually local SMEs. Second, SMEs are unlikely to develop their own infrastructure, except perhaps energy-generating infrastructure (Doner et al. 2004). But well-developed infrastructure, particularly for telecommunications and logistics (e.g. seaports, toll roads), is necessary to connect firms in clusters to other parts of a region or other countries involved in a network.

Policy, SMEs, and International Production Networks in ASEAN

So far we have confirmed that SMEs in ASEAN Member States can benefit from integrated production activities in Asia. Deepening SME involvement in networks through AEC-related activities and the creation of a single market and production base should promote development and improve income distribution, both important in creating an equitable economic region.

Deeper SME involvement will arguably increase the rate of job creation in less-developed member states, probably from greater greenfield entry by SMEs, and many studies in fact have demonstrated this.[10] SMEs that join labor-intensive regional networks, such as in the textile and garment sectors, are likely to benefit the most. Industrial upgrading could also result from technology and knowledge spillovers typical of SME involvement in international production. The successful experience of the Thai auto industry in integrating with the production network in Asia exemplifies the promise that networks hold for SME development (Exhibit 5-1).

Achieving these benefits will not be simple and should not depend completely on the model of flagship firms connecting SMEs. In fact, it may be much more effective to create an environment that induces flagship firms to extend their networks to all or many ASEAN Member States. In reducing costs associated with international production networks, for example, the AEC can help create the right environment. In turn, encouraging the development of industrial clusters will also help involve SMEs in networks as it is through clusters that SMEs connect to networks (Exhibit 5-2).

A minimum requirement for cluster development is well-developed infrastructure that is consistent across member states in quality and availability. Unfortunately the current situation does not encourage clusters. Levels of infrastructure development vary widely across ASEAN Member States with the performances of Lao PDR, Myanmar, and Cambodia in stark contrast to those of Malaysia, Singapore, and Brunei (Economic Research Institute for ASEAN and East Asia 2008).[11]

There are some policy actions that can be taken to accelerate infrastructure development, although some would be more effective at the country level. Private Public Partnerships (PPP) and privatization are two alternative ways to accelerate infrastructure development. We note that involving the private sector in funding infrastructure requires guarantees from the government to cover investment risks, such as exchange rate and tariff (i.e., user-fee) risk. Exchange rate risk arises from the fact that foreign currency is needed to purchase inputs while the return on investment is computed in domestic currency. The risk is higher in countries with a floating exchange rate system. Tariff risk arises from the

Exhibit 5-1
Case Study of the Thai Automotive Industry

Network-related production in ASEAN Member States has certain common elements: clusters in industrial zones, capacity building, and anchor and supporting firms (Kuchiki 2005). Network development in Thailand is instructive.

INDUSTRIAL ZONES
Thailand has at least six automotive industrial clusters, Samutprakarn being the prominent one. The clusters are in the east about 230-250 kilometers from Bangkok. The automotive industry was among five selected by the government for improvement through geographically concentrated cluster development. The private sector Thai Automotive Institute complemented these efforts by drawing up an industry master plan for equipping the cluster areas with supporting businesses. The logistic system in those areas was provided according to recommendations from Japanese consulting firms.

CAPACITY BUILDING
Institutional Reform. Thai policies related to the automotive industry developed over three periods. Before 1991, the government protected domestic industries and passed the Industrial Promotion Act, which encouraged establishment of auto assembly plants. Local content requirements were also set, which induced the emergence of local supporting industries. From 1992–1996 the government instituted tax reforms and encouraged FDI in supporting industries. Then, after the financial crisis, the government eliminated local content requirements to prop up global outsourcing. In this period, the government also encouraged trade through regional networks. In 1996, ASEAN agreed on the ASEAN Industrial Cooperation Scheme (AICO), which reduced import duty rates, local content accreditation, and export restrictions on products among participating member states. This agreement led countries to design cars for their own markets. The Toyota Soluna and Honda City are assembled in Thailand, and the Toyota Avanza is assembled in Indonesia. AICO seems to have increased intraregional trade.

Human Resource Development. Production networks in automotive supply chains support human-resource development. The relationship between the parent company and its suppliers often improves the technical and managerial skills of the suppliers. For instance, Toyota Motor Thailand as a parent company has a "Cooperative Club" with first-tier suppliers. Club activities include consultation and informal gatherings that advance their relationships with and the capabilities of suppliers.

FIRMS
Anchor Firm. The first automotive assembly plant was the Anglo-Thai Motor Company, which started in 1961 as the result of Thailand Industrial Promotion Act. Thailand now has about 12 assembly plants, 6 of which are Japanese.

Related Firms. A boom in the parts and components industry occurred in 1971, a decade after the Anglo-Thai Motor Company was established. There are now about 709 SMEs serving as first-tier suppliers to the 12 car assemblers. Of this number, 50 percent are completely Thai-owned. Serving as the second- and third-tier suppliers are about 1100 SMEs that are locally owned. The automotive industry in Thailand employs 113,512 people, 36.2 percent of them in SMEs.

Source: Chaisakul (2004).

fact that consumers often pay "administered prices" for infrastructure services. As such prices reflect political decisions not market conditions investors may encounter difficulty in adjusting rates in response to changes in production costs. For instance, raising toll road tariffs or electricity tariffs in Indonesia requires the involvement of the government and House of Representatives (*Antara News* 2007; *Jakarta Post* 2008).[12]

Mutual recognition arrangements (MRAs) could also deepen the involvement of SMEs in international production networks.[13] For example, some product standards may act as nontariff

Exhibit 5-2
Malaysian Electronics Industry

Malaysia's electronic industry joined the global production network in the early 1970s when US semiconductor firms developed offshore chip assembly in Malaysia. Then, in the 1980s, Japanese firms moved their consumer electronics production to Southeast Asian countries, including Malaysia.

Related FDI inflows resulted in impressive gains in Malaysia's production, exports, and employment. From 1990 to 2000, Malaysia's electronics industry grew at about 24 percent per annum. Over the same period, the country's exports and employment grew 25 percent and 11 percent, respectively, on an annual basis. Although impressive, recent conditions, in particular demand shifts, are altering strategic development plans for the sector. The shift is intended to overcome six structural weaknesses in Malaysia's electronics industry that define and constrain its upgrading prospects. These include an asymmetric industrial structure; a heavy dependence on imports, due to weak domestic support industries and limited Hirschman-type linkages; a heavy dependence on exports, especially to the US market; a highly concentrated composition of products, centered on low-end assembly operations; a waning capacity to generate employment; and a serious difference between the demand for and supply of skills.

The shift is expected to change fundamental parts of Malaysia's industrialization strategy. For example, Malaysia will need to transform from assembly-based to value-chain manufacturing, from sector-based to cluster-based development and from performance targets to productivity-driven growth. Accordingly, one policy initiative being implemented is the Second Industrial Master Plan. The plan has four objectives:

1. Foster the growth of leading local companies (Malaysian brands). This objective represents a concept of industrial upgrading that assumes a fixed pattern of sequencing from low-end, assembly-type subcontracting to original brand name (OBM) manufacturing.
2. Reduce dependence on imported inputs. This objective is related to whether the country succeeds in finding the right balance between reaping the benefits of imported foreign inputs and developing local backward and forward linkages.
3. Strengthen agglomeration economies by developing integrated manufacturing centers for global network flagships. This objective includes promotion of integrated manufacturing centers by the state government.
4. Develop cross-border clusters. This objective was originally driven by a desire to ease a severe shortage of IT skills by establishing joint growth triangles with neighboring countries that would attract low-cost engineers from throughout Asia.

Source: Ernst (2004).

---

barriers, but an MRA on those standards would not only facilitate SMEs' access to markets but also lower transaction costs by eliminating duplicative testing. Indeed, the ASEAN Consultative Committee on Standards and Quality (ACCSQ) has made progress on standards and mutual recognition of conformity assessments. In 1998, member states signed the ASEAN Framework Agreement on Mutual Recognition Agreements and in 2002 the MRA for Electronic and Electrical Equipment. In 2003, they agreed on the ASEAN Harmonized Cosmetic Regulatory Scheme as well. That scheme consists of Schedule A on mutual recognition of product registration approvals, and Schedule B on the ASEAN Cosmetic Directive. Despite some problems in implementation, these agreements are advancing ASEAN as a single market and production base. It is hoped that the sectoral focus on electronic and cosmetics spurs SME development in particular, since SMEs are the main business agents in these sectors.

Enforcing harmonized regulations, however, can be difficult, particularly with regard to SMEs. For example, the Indonesian cosmetic industry chose Schedule B to implement ASEAN cosmetic regulations such as Good Manufacturing Practice (GMP). Schedule B is preferred over Schedule A because it is more feasible and less costly. But seventy to 80 percent of the country's cosmetic firms are SMEs (i.e., they have fewer than 100 employees) and they are not choosing to acquire GMP certificates. In addition, the ministerial decree to apply GMP is advisory and not a compulsory requirement (Amri et al. 2007).

It appears that the main challenge of initiating and enforcing MRAs is lack of political will. There is a great deal of variation in the quality of goods produced in member states so MRA must be carefully devised to ensure that the lowest quality does not become the standard. The AEC Blueprint rightly makes MRAs a priority. In fact, harmonizing standards through MRAs may be a primary means of encouraging SMEs to export and, in turn, become involved in the region's production activities.

ASEAN INITIATIVES TO NARROW THE DEVELOPMENT GAP

ASEAN Member States have gradually overcome their reluctance to address openly the narrowing of development gaps in the region out of fear of creating a "two-tier ASEAN" (e.g., the ASEAN-6 and the CLMV). Other deep regional integration groups have had to confront this problem as well. The EU, for example, frequently struggles with the prospect of multi-tier sets of member states. And it has always made the politically difficult decision that formal members will have the same responsibilities and rights, even though transition periods are allowed to diverge.[14]

Longer Transition Periods for CLMV

In economic and policy regimes, a sort of two-tiered ASEAN already exists. Newer members have longer timeframes in which to eliminate barriers to trade and investment, something consistent with the EU approach. These timeframes are intended to ease the transition of the CLMV countries, which face greater challenges in fulfilling their integration obligations and have many more capacity constraints. But these countries do need to be fully "on board" by the end of the transition period. A two-tier ASEAN will constrain the AEC's potential as a single market and production base and will raise many questions about the true "value" of being an ASEAN Member State. The AEC envisions an additional five years for the transitional economies to adopt the AEC Blueprint measures and exigencies. Such additional time for transition should be sufficient.

As described by Chia (2007), the development gap in ASEAN involves income, human development, economic structures, market economy institutions, and infrastructure. These gaps impede economic integration because they affect the very ability to integrate. Unless these gaps are narrowed, the CLMV countries will feel disadvantaged in trying to benefit from regional integration. But, of course, lax implementation of the AEC Blueprint will only exacerbate the situation. Hence, to allow the CLMV countries to transition effectively into the new unified market, concerted action is needed to assist them in implementing AEC-consistent reforms.

Preference, Integration, and Fund Programs

In addition to the longer time frames accorded to the CLMV countries in implementing obligations under the AEC, various other measures have been introduced following the political commitments made by the group. These include the ASEAN Integrated System of Preferences (AISP), the Initiative for ASEAN Integration (IAI), and the ASEAN Development Fund (ADF).

Introduced in 2002, the AISP is a scheme by which the ASEAN-6 offer preferential tariffs to CLMV countries on a voluntary and bilateral basis. Since CLMV countries are given more time to reduce or eliminate tariffs, they cannot benefit fully from AFTA trade liberalization, which is reciprocal in nature. The AISP is meant to overcome this problem but the scheme is underused.

The purpose of the IAI is to enhance the productive capacity and competitiveness of CLMV countries through development cooperation and technical assistance. Among other things, the IAI covers infrastructure, human resource development, information and communications technology, energy, poverty reduction, and capacity building for regional economic integration. Shortcomings include weak interagency coordination, reporting mechanisms, implementation, and follow-through actions; weak ownership of the IAI projects by the CLMV countries; and poorly coordinated and too brief training programs (Chia 2007).

The ADF, established in July 2005, is managed by the ASEAN Secretariat to provide a "common pool of financial resources" to support implementation of the Vientiane Action Plan. The ADF was funded initially by equal contributions of $1 million from each member state with the further aim of leveraging funding from ASEAN Dialogue Partners and other donors. ASEAN Member States and private entities can make additional voluntary contributions. The success of this program is not clear.

In sum, these programs do not yet seem to have produced significant results, perhaps because any program to narrow multi-dimensional development gaps is a tall order. No ready measure for "narrowing gaps" has been developed to guide program implementation and without such a measure it is difficult to gauge success.

As suggested by Chia (2007), ASEAN's assistance needs to focus more on institution building and soft infrastructure. It is important to recognize the great differences in market economy institutions that exist in the ASEAN region. These differences pose real problems for regional integration.

Status and Next Steps

To develop a coherent and sustained program for narrowing the development gap, ASEAN must devise funding schemes that rely more on mobilizing its own resources. Given the comprehensive nature of the AEC project and the constraints that need to be overcome, resource mobilization is becoming urgent. At present, program funding and implementation is *ad hoc*, relying on third parties and not "owned" by the CLMV countries. These shortcomings were recognized by the ASEAN Eminent Persons Group (EPG) on the ASEAN Charter. In their recommendations, they noted the following:

> The development gap within ASEAN has to be addressed as it could otherwise adversely affect ASEAN's ability to achieve its goals. In this regard, the EPG proposes that a Special Fund be established to help narrow the development gap. For the purpose of this Special Fund, as well as to support other ASEAN regional development efforts, a new funding model with innovative mechanisms should be explored. Such mechanisms could include, *inter alia*, ASEAN's raising its own income through some forms of fixed contribution; a share of sales or excise taxes; airport taxes or visa fees collected in Member States. Given the implications of such measures, there should be further studies by financial and fiscal experts.[15]

The EPG's proposal of a new funding model seems to have been rejected by ASEAN governments, as the proposal was not in evidence in the ASEAN Charter and no initiative has been taken to undertake further studies on the matter. Lack of political will seems to be the main reason for the failure to act on EPG recommendation.[16]

One can therefore question the seriousness of efforts to narrow the development gap. It appears that ASEAN governments continue to shy away from openly discussing mechanisms for transferring resources within ASEAN. And this may be why the issue of a two-tiered ASEAN has been so long avoided. Absent political will to develop a funding mechanism, ASEAN can still systematically devise a much more focused program of development and technical cooperation, particularly for institution building and soft infrastructure. Such programs need not be confined to the CLMV countries. Expectations as to what ASEAN can do should be lowered so expectations remain realistic. For example, selecting a few strategic areas in which to implement specific programs can bring about real progress.

SUMMARY

Achieving the AEC can advance equitable economic development in ASEAN and narrow the development gap as measured by such indicators as income inequality and poverty, the performance of SMEs, and the political economy of resource transfer in ASEAN. Other studies find that ASEAN and "ASEAN+" economic integration initiatives have a robust positive impact on member states, and CGE-based studies show that integration tends to offer welfare gains for all member states and that variation in gains may be rooted in such initial conditions as commercial policy and economic development. Thus, the success of economic integration will depend in part on all member states being able to sustain economic growth. One way to encourage such growth is to support investment in human capital (i.e., education and health) and to liberalize trade in services.

As in many regional economic cooperation groups, income inequality across ASEAN Member States can be explained in part by income differences within member states.[17] Policies that focus on income distribution *within* each country could help reduce income gaps *across* countries. Such policies should be designed with specific countries' needs in mind, including the need to strengthen domestic reform. The AEC, of course, can only support this process indirectly by creating a unified market that will likely benefit the poorest countries the most, largely by deepening the involvement of SMEs in regional production chains and international production networks. Integrating SMEs is not easy, however; challenges include weak infrastructure in some ASEAN Member States and a universal lack of initiative in harmonizing regulations. The harmonization process, in turn, is largely determined by progress in creating MRAs in ASEAN, an important part of the AEC that is highlighted in the AEC Blueprint.

ASEAN has implemented some initiatives to narrow the development gap between the CLMV and older member states, but these have not yet had strong results. The longer transition periods granted to the CLMV countries to meet obligations under various ASEAN agreements do not mean that obligations need not be met or that policies to be adopted under the AEC Blueprint will not in and of themselves advance development by boosting efficiency and competitiveness in any country implementing them. But the CLMV countries will likely need a good deal more assistance and encouragement from ASEAN's more developed member states given the extent of change required and the capacity constraints impeding change.

In the EU, for example, the more developed countries have helped the less developed ones modernize and grow. Before joining the European Communities in the 1980s, Greece, Spain and Portugal were relatively poor, politically unstable, and inward looking. Since then they have performed well — especially Spain, until the 2008–2009 economic crisis — and have modernized their economies and achieved political stability. In 2004 ten former communist, transitional economies joined the EU and have since modernized and performed very well, certainly better than the EU average (suggesting a clear pattern of "catch up"). The last enlargement in 2007, in which Romania and Bulgaria joined, has been by far the most challenging. The EU, however, avers that its body of law (*acquis communautaire*) be respected in all cases, though differing implementation time horizons are possible.

Integrating these countries into the EU has improved regional and global welfare — but at a price. The EU tapped into a large budget to help modernize these countries and facilitate restructuring. What must be done to reform policies in the CLMV and achieve an AEC is far less challenging but will still require ASEAN to deploy resources. Indeed, if integration is perceived as a threat to CLMV welfare the AEC will be at risk. Therefore, steps to narrow the development gap will be essential in fostering support for integration, particularly since narrowing the gap involves behind-the-border reforms.

A coherent and sustainable program to narrow the gap should be funded using ASEAN's own resources as third-party funding tends to result in ad hoc implementation and lack of ownership among funding recipients. Our recommendations follow those in the ASEAN EPG's report, which, though applauded as a breakthrough, does not seem to have been followed up on. This indicates weak political will among member states in collectively addressing the development gap, at least at present. In the absence of necessary political will, an alternative approach is a more systematic and focused program in developing institutions and soft-infrastructure.

NOTES

1. Address by H.E. Ong Keng Yong, Secretary-General of ASEAN, to the Boao Forum for Asia Annual Conference 2003, 2 November 2003, Boao, Hainan Province, China, "Towards an ASEAN Single Market and Single Investment Destination" (http://www.aseansec.org/15365.htm).
2. See, for example, Salazar and Das (2007), as well as the other articles in the April 2007 edition of the *ASEAN Economic Bulletin*, which clearly demonstrate this.
3. Also see Severino (2007) for more detailed review of IAI implementation.
4. In constructing the distribution of income, we also employ the estimated quintile income share of each country in the region. Annual within-country data on income distribution is reported by UNU-WIDER, although only a few countries have an annual household survey. To compensate for missing data in some countries, we approximate missing values by simple linear-trending forecasted values. Once we assign income shares to each quintile for each country, we estimate a country's annual income distribution by using a nonparametric kernel-density function. To run this procedure, one should specify a key parameter, namely, the bandwidth of the kernel. In this study we follow Sala-i Martin bandwidth (0.34). After the kernel density function for each country is set up, we anchor the density so that its mean matches to PPP-adjusted GDP per capita from the Penn-World Table (PWT) and the area is in line with the population of the country.
5. We cannot estimate income distribution of Singapore, Brunei, and Myanmar for lack of data.
6. Many studies explore the role of SMEs in ASEAN. See, for example, Asasen et al. 2003 and Tambunan et al. 2007).
7. This result is consistent with the literature (e.g., Tambunan et al. 2007), which also finds limited export activities by SMEs in Southeast Asia.[0]
8. See, for example, UNIDO (2004), Ernst (2004), and Kuroiwa and Toh (2008), for discussion, explanation, and a literature review of international production networks.
9. In a model of an Asian network, the anchor firm can be considered as part of higher-tier firm that connect local suppliers with flagship companies (see the previous discussion in the text).
10. These include many case studies from some ASEAN countries reported in Kuchiki and Tsuji (2005).

11. Even less encouraging, the gap seems to have widened. See ERIA (2008) for more details.

12. Another example of political aspect in implementing PPP and privatization in Indonesia is the conflict of authority between the central and regional governments in infrastructure development. This creates another risk in addition to the general economic risk we discussed in the text, and for Indonesia in particular, infrastructure development in the country needs to warrants private investors for the risk that could be borne by the conflict, which for many reason is difficult to be quantified.

13. The EU's European Court of Justice defines the principal of mutual recognition as "Member States must allow a product lawfully produced and marketed in another Member State into their own market" (Pelkmans 2007). A product tested and certified in the exporting country does not need another conformity assessment in the importing country because of the mutually-recognized conformity assessment.

14. For example, the enlargement of the EU to include the Central and Eastern European countries occasioned many compromises on the part of the acceding countries (e.g., with respect to land ownership) and the existing members (e.g., with respect to work permits). Some suggest that Turkey be allowed to join the EU on a "special" basis (e.g., without rights associated with the free flow of labor) but the European Commission and other leaders have resisted this, as well as Turkey itself. The reason: the EU does not want to have a two-tier system.

15. See Report of the Eminent Persons Group on the ASEAN Charter, December 2006, p. 17.

16. The closed nature of the ASEAN government meeting does not allow us to elaborate on lack of will as a reason for lack of implementation, but the mechanisms proposed by the EPG could be implemented, but not without difficulty.

17. In noting the development gap between the CLMV countries and other ASEAN countries, however, one should bear in mind that Vietnam has been catching up rapidly over the past ten years.

6
Competitiveness and Leverage

Peter A. Petri

ASEAN's relations with the world economy are the heart of the fourth section of the AEC Blueprint (Appendix D). Effective integration could turn ASEAN's 10 economies into a global powerhouse — the world's third largest economy, in terms of population, behind China and India — and dramatically improve the region's ability to attract globally mobile capital and technology and develop advantageous partnerships with other economic centers. How can this potential be realized and what benefits would accrue?

The AEC Blueprint envisions an ASEAN distinct from most other regional groupings by its outward focus. This vision reflects economic realities: most ASEAN Member States conduct a majority of their trade with outside partners, have overlapping patterns of comparative advantage, and are embarked on similar, outward-oriented development trajectories (see Chapters 1 and 2). There are real benefits to be had from the internal dimensions of ASEAN integration — e.g., more competition and improved scale economies in production, greater efficiency in consumption — but the benefits of improving the region's competitive position in the world economy could be especially significant.

ASEAN's external success will depend in part on how the region responds to challenges, improves the efficiency of its production system, and manages its trade and investment relations with the rest of the world. These two aspects of integration — improving global competitiveness and using negotiating leverage — are the focal points for this analysis. In the rest of this chapter we explore the challenges posed by a rapidly changing global environment; examine solutions offered by the AEC, specifically strategies for competitiveness and leverage; and assess the benefits that could result from these strategies and how to implement them.

CHALLENGE: ASEAN'S NEW COMPETITIVE ENVIRONMENT

ASEAN has recovered from the financial crisis of 1997–1998 but, at least until recently, its performance has fallen short of its exceptional pre-crisis trajectory. As Figure 6-1 shows, ASEAN's average annual growth rate has declined from 7–8 percent to 5–6 percent and had been reaccelerating gradually before the current economic turmoil began in September 2008.[1] ASEAN's solid performance is due in part to its ability to keep pace with the rapid growth of world export markets — its share of world exports, though no longer rising, has remained stable. But at the same time, ASEAN's share of world FDI inflows has fallen by nearly half, from around 6 percent to 3–4 percent. As the current wave of shocks winds its way through the world economy, ASEAN's recent gains look increasingly precarious.

These average data in fact overstate the region's progress because they include the very rapid expansion of Cambodia, Lao PDR, Myanmar, and Vietnam (CLMV). While ASEAN's recent performance would be envied in many parts of the world, it looks less satisfactory when viewed from a historical perspective and even fragile in the context of a deteriorating world economy. Leaders are naturally seeking ways to boost performance, regionally by improving productivity and internationally by enhancing the region's competitive position. These strategies are driven by four features of the region's external environment: stiffening competition, rapidly changing markets, increased requirements for regional cooperation, and shifting policy priorities. The following subsections examine each feature in turn.

Competitors Gaining Fast

A dominant feature of ASEAN's new environment is the rise of China and India and, within the region, the CLMV countries. All are major competitors for many of ASEAN's established economies and

Figure 6-1
Can ASEAN Sustain Its Momentum?

5-Year Moving Averages

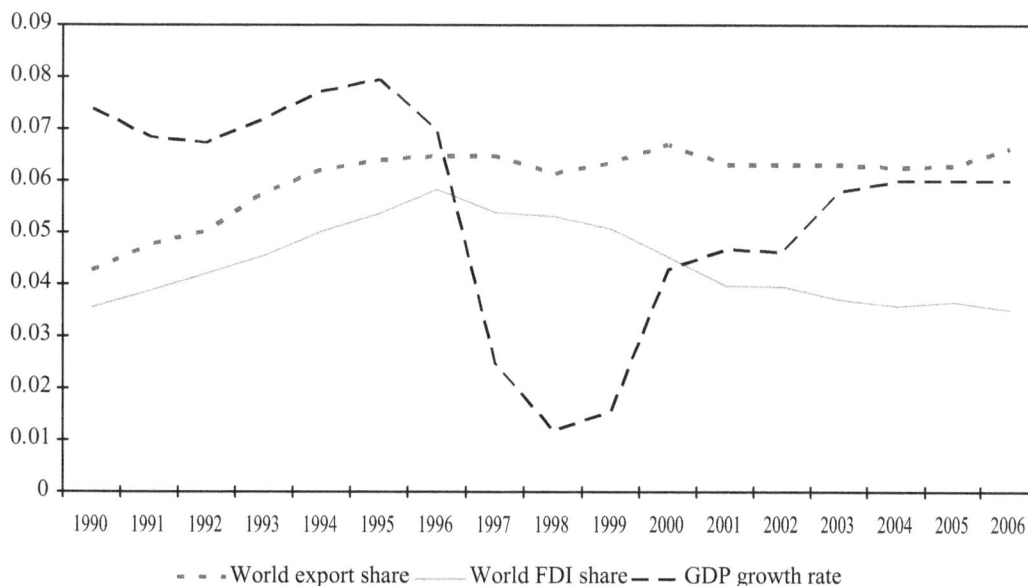

- - - World export share ——— World FDI share — — GDP growth rate

Source: Author's calculations.

industries — as well as important markets for others. On balance, how do they affect ASEAN's prospects?

After many years of exceptional progress, between 2000 and 2006 ASEAN exports barely kept pace with world export growth (Figure 6-2). There was also much variation within ASEAN, with CLMV exports growing much faster than those of Indonesia, Malaysia, and the Philippines. In 2000, China and India exported 32% *less* than ASEAN and in 2006 they exported 37% *more*. Within ASEAN, the CLMV countries increased their export share by about 40 percent. Recent research finds little evidence for the view that China and India's rise have reduced ASEAN's exports or growth rates (see for example, studies by Athukorala 2007, Busakorn et al. 2005. and Plummer and Cheong 2007), but it is hard to escape the conclusion that ASEAN exports face exceptional pressures as they adapt to this new competitive landscape.

Figure 6-2
Growth in Exports by Exporter, 2000–2006

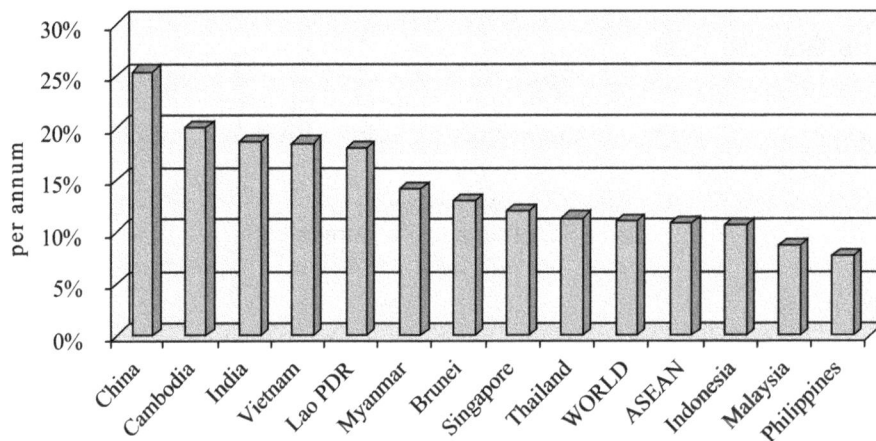

But who exactly competes with whom? Some insight can be gained from the similarity of the export structures of different economies. Table 6-1 presents correlation coefficients for the export structures of pairs of economies, calculated by Plummer (2007). The 25 percent most competitive pairs (countries with export correlations of 0.34 or higher) are in italics and the 25 percent least competitive pairs in bold (export correlations of 0.16 or below).

There is a clear pattern to the findings. Since countries usually compete most intensively with others at similar technology and development levels, we entered countries in Table 6-1 in order of income *per capita*. The italic cells of the table (high similarity) turn out to be clustered around the diagonal, that is, among countries with similar incomes. The bold cells (low similarity) tend to be far away from the diagonal, that is, in country pairs with incomes that are far apart. There are some surprises — the Philippines tends to compete "above" its income level, while Indonesia tends to compete "below" it — but most of the keenest export competition nevertheless involves economies with similar incomes. At the lower end of the income scale Cambodia and Vietnam compete with each

Table 6-1
Who Competes with Whom? Rank Correlations of Exports to OECD Countries, 2005

	ASEAN Countries								Partner Countries					
	CAM	VTN	PHL	INO	THA	MAL	BRN	SNG	IND	CHN	TWN	KOR	HKG	JPN
Cambodia	1.00	0.39	0.19	0.35	0.27	0.32	0.25	0.20	0.38	-0.03	0.23	0.17	0.20	-0.67
Vietnam	0.39	1.00	0.23	0.37	0.33	0.19	0.19	0.06	0.24	0.32	0.07	0.03	0.28	-0.12
Philippines	0.19	0.23	1.00	0.38	0.34	0.33	-0.17	0.25	0.17	0.34	0.21	0.17	0.33	0.10
Indonesia	0.35	0.37	0.38	1.00	0.41	0.29	-0.01	0.16	0.24	0.39	0.18	0.18	0.23	0.02
Thailand	0.27	0.33	0.34	0.41	1.00	0.41	0.12	0.30	0.26	0.45	0.36	0.34	0.35	0.19
Malaysia	0.32	0.19	0.33	0.29	0.41	1.00	-0.07	0.39	0.18	0.35	0.32	0.34	0.31	0.22
Brunei	0.25	0.19	-0.17	-0.01	0.12	-0.07	1.00	-0.02	0.11	0.06	-0.01	0.10	-0.07	-0.42
Singapore	0.20	0.06	0.25	0.16	0.30	0.39	-0.02	1.00	0.21	0.26	0.33	0.35	0.23	0.38

Notes: Brunei values are for 2003, Cambodia and Vietnam for 2005. Correlation includes only commodities valued at least $250,000. Light gray highlights with italic and bold highlights represent highest 25% and lowest 25% of correlations, respectively.
Source: Based on Plummer (2007) from UN-COMTRADE.

other and with Indonesia, in the middle the Philippines competes with Indonesia and Thailand, and at the upper end Malaysia and Thailand with Singapore and each other. Outside ASEAN, lower-income ASEAN countries compete with India, middle-income countries with China, and upper-income countries with Taiwan, Korea, and Hong Kong, and to a lesser extent with Japan. China's competitive shadow, in particular, extends across an unusually wide range of income levels, reaching from Indonesia up through Malaysia.

In sum, China, India, and the CLMV countries are gaining rapidly on ASEAN's established exporters. There are no shelters in this environment and every ASEAN economy faces stiff competition both inside and outside ASEAN. It is possible, to be sure, to adapt and to find new niches, and ASEAN has indeed replaced the markets it has lost so far (holding its global export share roughly stable). But there is little room for complacency as its new competitors continue to make rapid headway.

Markets Shifting to Asia

A second prominent feature of ASEAN's environment is the shift in the destination of exports from the world's developed economies to the region's emerging markets. Although the period covered by recent data was relatively prosperous for the developed world, the most rapid growth of ASEAN's markets occurred in emerging economies and especially so in Asia.

Figure 6-3 shows the annual growth rates of ASEAN exports to various markets, which together make up about 90 percent of the region's exports. The most striking difference is the 6:1 ratios of the growth rate of the Chinese market relative to that of the US market. With such different rates of growth, substantial transformations in shares can occur in a relatively short period of time. For example, in 2000 ASEAN's exports to the "plus three" countries (China, Japan, and Korea) were roughly equal to its exports to the United States, but by 2006 they were about two-thirds higher.

Figure 6-3
Growth of ASEAN Exports by Market, 2000–2006

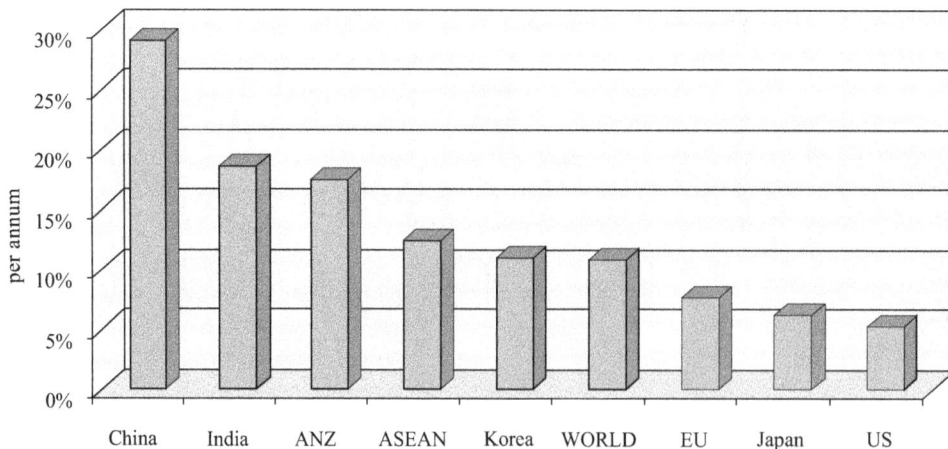

Source: Author's calculations.

ASEAN is — for now — well positioned to take advantage of Asia's rapidly growing markets because of its high presence in them. One indicator of this is the high "intensity" of ASEAN exports to Asia, as reported in Table 6-2. The intensity measure compares the share of ASEAN's exports to a particular destination with the share of total world exports to that destination — in other words, it measures the role of a market in a country's exports relative to its role in world markets. The data show that ASEAN's exports to all Asian partners and Australia and New Zealand (CER) exceed one — meaning that the share of ASEAN Member State exports to Asian economies is greater than the global norm — and are rising. By contrast, its export intensities to the United States and Europe are less than one. In short, ASEAN exports are focused on Asian markets and have managed to keep pace — indeed to increase their presence — in them as these markets have entered a period of especially rapid growth. But given the many bilateral agreements that are now emerging, ASEAN will need to actively maintain strong access to desirable markets.

Table 6-2
Export Intensities, 2006

	ASEAN	CER	China	Japan	Korea	HK	India	US	EU	World
ASEAN	4.5	3.0	1.5	2.3	1.6	2.0	2.3	0.9	0.3	1.0
Brunei	4.8	11.4	0.5	7.1	5.4	0.0	0.0	0.5	0.1	1.0
Cambodia	0.9	0.1	0.1	0.7	0.0	0.1	0.0	4.3	0.6	1.0
Indonesia	3.8	2.5	1.2	4.4	3.3	1.3	3.1	0.8	0.3	1.0
Lao PDR	10.3	2.0	0.7	0.2	0.1	0.8	0.0	0.1	0.3	1.0
Malaysia	4.7	2.6	1.1	2.0	1.5	1.9	3.1	1.3	0.3	1.0
Myanmar	9.8	0.3	0.8	1.2	0.6	0.5	11.7	—	0.2	1.0
Philippines	3.1	0.8	3.8	2.8	1.2	2.7	0.2	1.0	0.3	1.0
Singapore	5.6	3.3	1.5	1.2	1.4	2.6	2.7	0.7	0.3	1.0
Thailand	3.8	3.0	1.4	2.9	0.9	1.8	1.3	1.0	0.4	1.0
Vietnam	2.6	7.3	0.9	2.8	0.8	0.8	0.3	1.4	0.5	1.0

Source: Author's calculations based on UN trade data.

These changes are likely to be reinforced by both long-term developments and near-term adjustments in global macroeconomic conditions. In the long run, Asian growth is projected to lead the world for some time to come, as reported for example in a series of publications by Goldman Sachs (2005) and as shown in Figure 6-4.

In the shorter term, even as the economic turmoil of 2007–2009 subsides, the United States is likely to embark on a course that involves higher savings, lower current account deficits, and a relatively lower value for the dollar. Thus, US markets are likely to become less attractive destinations for Asian exports than they have been in recent decades. At the same time, as Asian economies correct their macroeconomic imbalances by raising expenditures (thus also compensating for reduced exports to the US), their demand for imports will grow. These adjustments will go hand in hand with Asian currency appreciation.

These trends need to be appreciated, but not exaggerated. In 2006, the United States and Europe accounted for about one quarter of ASEAN exports, roughly the same as ASEAN's exports to itself, and

Figure 6-4
Projected GDP Growth, 2005–2050

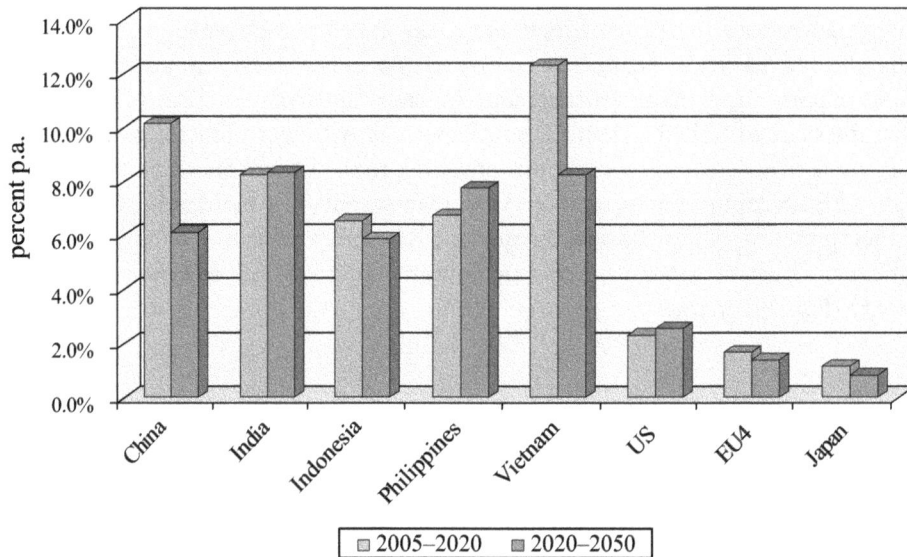

Source: Goldman Sachs (2005).

ASEAN's exports to the "plus three" countries of China, Korea and Japan (as noted in Chapter 1). Accordingly, even with slower growth, the United States and Europe will remain important markets. The implication of these trends is simply that, on the margin, they will become less attractive relative to Asian markets than they have been in the past.

Production Networks Require Regional Cooperation

A third feature is that production networks, rather than conventional trade in final goods, are becoming the engine of regional integration. Recent analyses of such networks (Kawai and Urata 2004, ADB 2008) show that they are evolving into a source of comparative advantage for Asian economies, since they put to good advantage the region's effective trading system, transport and communications links and, most important, diverse production conditions.

The complexity and importance of Asian production networks can be documented by tracing the flow of parts and components that knit together production sites throughout the region and even beyond. The share of parts and components trade has risen substantially in world trade, and especially so in Asia. Indeed, Asia has a higher share, and more rapid growth, of parts and components in trade than other regions (ADB 2008).

Surprisingly, production networks appear to reinforce regional rather than global integration. Despite the fact that falling transport and communication costs should have, if anything, a larger impact on distant (trans-regional) rather than on close-by transactions, networks appear to stimulate regional links. One possible reason is that technology has become more thoroughly diffused around the world, so that firms do not need to look as far as they used to in order to find specialized inputs or processes. Another is that activities distributed across multiple production sites require substantial human management and coordination, and personal travel is becoming relatively costly (the time involved cannot be easily reduced) across long distances and different time-zones. Whatever the reason, regional trade intensities are rising, not just in Asia, but in all major regions of the world.

The clear implication of production networks is that regional policy cooperation needs to develop in the context of "open regionalism." The payoff from integrating regional production networks is best realized in large global markets. Hence policies for regional integration should proceed in parallel with policies for deepening relations with the global economy.

Policy Moving to Regional and Bilateral Arenas

The fourth major trend is that governments, especially in Asia, are turning to regional and bilateral (rather than global) solutions to address international trade and monetary objectives. This development is sometimes attributed to the slow progress of the Doha Round and the failures of international institutions, but those may be as much symptoms as causes of the shift.

ASEAN itself is the foremost example of regional cooperation in Asia, and reflects both political and economic drivers (Bonapace 2005). ASEAN addresses demands that regional production networks place on policy — namely, the creation of regional markets, standards, and regulations. And ASEAN provides tools to exploit the cooperation opportunities generated by the rise of dynamic new economic centers such as China and India. Since the collapse of the Doha negotiations in July 2008, ASEAN has accelerated its international commercial diplomacy, and has in short time successfully concluded "plus one" trade negotiations with Japan and Australia and New Zealand (in addition to its agreements with China and South Korea). Negotiations are nearly complete with India.

But ASEAN is only one of Asia's many regional projects. ASEAN+3 (with China, Japan and Korea), the East Asian Summit (with India, Australia and New Zealand also included), APEC and ASEM are some of the "higher level" regional initiatives that surround ASEAN. At the same time, "lower level" projects emerging in ASEAN include the Greater Mekong Subregion (GMS) and other smaller efforts. The division of labor among these forums is fluid — for various reasons a multispeed, multitrack approach to cooperation is well suited to Asia's diversity and complexity (ADB 2008). Nevertheless, policies need to be coherent across the forums, and ASEAN is best equipped to play a coordinating role (Zhang 2006).

Asia is also experiencing an unprecedented wave of FTAs. Petri (2008) shows that the matrix of FTAs among all possible pairs of Asian partners is rapidly approaching completion. While there is no consensus about where these developments will lead — Petri (2008) argues that "filling the matrix" will make it easier to consolidate agreements — there is little doubt that they complicate the regional policy landscape.

The implication is that ASEAN needs a sophisticated capability to manage multiple tracks of economic policy. ASEAN's members and trading partners are active on various tracks, and ASEAN's policies must respond to (and even anticipate) developments that reflect members' interests. ASEAN will need to counter emerging threats — for example, when key partners or members consider outside preferential agreements. It will need to grasp opportunities to develop strong links with dynamic markets. And it will need to streamline past FTAs. All these are required to exploit the region's scale and negotiating clout.

STRATEGY: REGIONAL INTEGRATION AS COMPETITIVE ADVANTAGE

ASEAN's new external environment argues for a clear agenda: ASEAN needs to address increasing competition from China and other large economies, and it needs to develop tools to manage the relations of its members with outside partners. The solution will consist of stronger mechanisms of cooperation — to be sure, a prescription this is easier to propose than to implement. The region's economies will need to develop and follow more coherent policies, and its policy institutions will need to achieve confidence in planning, analyzing, and implementing joint policies and programs. As the European experience suggests, this will not be a simple or quick task. Often, it will also present a natural target for political criticism.

Nevertheless, given Asia's potential for interdependence, the region's economies should have much to gain from the implementation of the AEC, especially if this process is carefully designed — in light of the region's important global connections — to avoid the diversion of trade from efficient outside partners. Several different channels can be identified for realizing beneficial effects. Integration within ASEAN as prescribed in the AEC Blueprint will:

- Increase the scale and productivity of ASEAN industries, enabling them to capture larger markets and greater profits from global transactions.
- Raise the attractiveness of investments in ASEAN, expanding investment from abroad and the share of ASEAN savings invested regionally.
- Improve ASEAN's leverage in negotiations with "plus one" partners.
- Enhance ASEAN's influence in regional and global forums.
- Create an "ASEAN brand" to support the marketing efforts of individual countries and companies.

These developments will not only raise the efficiency of the region's economy, but they will also increase ASEAN's influence in world markets. These two types of benefits are interdependent, but it is useful to analyze them separately under the headings of competitiveness (improvements in ASEAN's productivity) and leverage (improvements in ASEAN's international bargaining position).

Economics of ASEAN Competitiveness

The positive effect of regional integration on ASEAN's competitiveness is a prime motivation for building the AEC, and the different elements of the AEC Blueprint address many of the key policies involved. Our goal here is to look more narrowly at how those policies could be shaped to maximize ASEAN's global clout, and how the results might translate into observable gains in ASEAN's economic performance.

ASEAN integration will improve the region's competitiveness by

- Increasing competitive pressures for efficient production within each economy,
- Shifting output from less to more efficient economies,
- Expanding the economies of scale achieved by producers serving the region, and
- Accelerating investments in physical capital, technology, and people.

The national and intraregional benefits that flow from these forces are discussed in other chapters — they are the main benefits that have motivated the development of single markets in Europe and elsewhere. In the following, therefore, we limit our analysis to how these effects will influence ASEAN's external economic links. As we review these links, it becomes evident that integration will not be sufficient in itself to maximize external, global benefits — *how* integration is carried out will also be important.

First, the single market and production base that ASEAN builds has to be the "right" market. To maximize the international impact of the ASEAN project, the region's internal unified market should reflect the characteristics of the region's partner markets, so that producers can easily develop products, technology, and production systems that take advantage of both intraregional and external market opportunities. This means that product and regulatory standards, financing systems, and a wide range of business procedures should mirror the state of the art in the region's principal markets. In some markets, social considerations are also important (for example, organic, "fair trade," and labor-friendly products often enjoy privileged market positions in EU and US markets). It will not always be possible to harmonize all standards with the region's most advanced economies. But as already noted many important markets are shifting to Asian countries, which have levels of development and commercial practices that are closer to those within ASEAN itself.

Second, the production systems that ASEAN develops will need to be closely linked to their foreign counterparts, especially through inflows of capital and technology. ASEAN has made large strides in becoming friendly to foreign investment, and its ability to attract investment will be magnified if companies can serve all ASEAN markets from a single ASEAN production site. But the intensity of future connections will depend on further improvements in ASEAN's environment for doing business and investing capital. According to World Bank data (World Bank 2008), such improvements are required in several countries (as discussed in earlier chapters). These will be implemented in part as countries conform to the steps outlined in the AEC Blueprint. But in addition, countries will have increased incentives to adopt business-oriented reforms on their own, in order to maximize the benefits derived from the ASEAN production platform.

Third, ASEAN will need to market its market. In the noisy global marketplace, the ASEAN brand should come to represent a wide range of characteristics that businesses and consumers prefer, which include, as noted above, regulations that ensure the safety and functionality of products, and a producer-friendly business environment. To be trusted, the ASEAN brand will need to reflect reality; that is, it will need to be backed by concrete initiatives to adopt standards and by certifications of adherence to standards by reliable research and testing agencies. A strong ASEAN brand will enhance the production and marketing efforts of (most) member states but, for the usual free-rider reasons, it will not be promoted adequately by individual members. Indeed, if members do promote the ASEAN brand, they may undermine it, since it is likely that the promotion will be by weaker companies in weaker countries. Uncoordinated promotion might confer a weaker image on the ASEAN brand than it actually represents.

Economics of ASEAN Leverage

A strong competitive position will enable ASEAN economies to benefit more from world markets, but it will not assure that benefits are maximized. Also important will be the steps that ASEAN members take individually and together to ensure access to markets around the world. ASEAN integration will increase members' ability to achieve good market access, and the region has much to gain by studying and implementing mechanisms to exploit this leverage. The economic basis of this argument is that ASEAN countries can get a better deal from other economies by working together, that is, by pursuing "ASEAN centrality." The idea is intuitive, but it is important to understand how it achieves its objective.

In most bargaining situations, potential outcomes include a range of benefit distributions. The degree to which a country achieves a favorable outcome depends on the bargaining process and on the country's options outside the process. The outcomes of bargaining games involving a few players cannot be predicted with precision, but an extensive theoretical and empirical literature helps to characterize the factors that affect the payoffs. The main conclusion of this literature is that payoffs are likely to be split among players in proportion to their base utility level, that is, the utility they would realize if they "walked away" from the game. The higher a player's fallback utility, the greater its share of additional utility distributed.

What can be said about the bargaining position of ASEAN economies? Individual ASEAN economies tend to be small compared to their major trading partners, such as the "plus three" countries and the United States and Europe. In these bargaining situations the partners have good opportunities for agreements around the world. Should they "walk away" they will experience relatively small losses and will have options for taking up negotiations with other small partners. Thus a single ASEAN Member State bargaining by itself may need to make significant concessions in order to conclude a bilateral deal.

The negotiations of individual ASEAN economies are also plagued by a "prisoner's dilemma," in which each country negotiates with a partner expecting to beat others to a better deal, even if each recognizes that its bargaining position is weaker than it would be as part of a larger group. But the benefits that the "first player" temporarily achieves by acting alone will be offset when other members conclude their agreements. Bargaining as a group could have generated a larger pool of benefits to be distributed among countries than bargaining in isolation.

Working as a group creates leverage. The most direct approach for achieving collaboration is to prohibit individual negotiations, but that is not likely to be achievable. The alternative is to permit individual negotiations to proceed, but to devise rules to constrain them in order to maximize joint advantage. This could take the form of requirements that individual FTAs concluded by ASEAN Member States extend "most favored nation" treatment to ASEAN parties not involved in the negotiations — in the most ambitious case by extending all benefits offered by either party to all ASEAN members. At a minimum, at least the ASEAN partner in an external agreement could agree to extend MFN treatment to all ASEAN members, so that the external negotiations it conducts do not undermine the value of preferences that it has already extended within ASEAN. Ideally the foreign partner would also extend MFN privileges across ASEAN — and this, in effect, would lead to its negotiating with ASEAN as a group.

Even when negotiations are jointly conducted via ASEAN, the mechanisms that now appear to be in place do not result in coherent, joint negotiations. ASEAN negotiations do seem to offer some important benefits: for example, they usually specify rules of origin that cumulate across ASEAN members, so that value added in every ASEAN economy is treated as value added by the final exporter.[2] But other aspects of ASEAN negotiations are less constructive. The present protocol of negotiations appears to result in parallel, bilateral deals between ASEAN countries and external partners. In some cases, ASEAN members appear to have very little information about the progress of negotiations by other members. Thus the possibility arises that, once negotiations are completed, ASEAN countries find themselves at a disadvantage relative to other member states due to different concessions offered by the external partner. These mechanisms create needless political friction and a potentially significant loss of leverage in the regional negotiation process.

ASEAN's emerging single market and production base is a major asset, comprising economies with more than 500 million people. It offers possibilities for great leverage. This fact is not lost on others; all of ASEAN's major partners, save the United States, are studying or negotiating FTAs with ASEAN as a group. By achieving greater "ASEAN centrality" in its negotiations, ASEAN has a powerful opportunity to improve its terms in all "ASEAN plus" agreements — including in the most important forum of all, the global WTO process.

BENEFITS OF COMPETITIVENESS AND LEVERAGE: ASEAN AS FTA HUB

The benefits of greater productivity and stronger market access are potentially very large, but difficult to estimate. Further, these benefits result from economic mechanisms both internal and external to ASEAN, so even to the extent that benefits are identified, it is difficult to isolate the extent to which they are attributable to ASEAN's own policies. In Chapter 4, we estimated the incremental rise in foreign investment that might be attracted by a more competitive ASEAN. In this section, we consider the improvements in ASEAN's access to external markets through new or better FTAs. We argue and show that this effect could yield major increases in ASEAN incomes.

ASEAN is acquiring leverage in the global trading system — as demonstrated by its recent negotiating successes with important external partners — and needs to develop a strategy for using it effectively. A key objective, of course, is to sustain the global trading system in the first place. Even as an integrated unit, ASEAN will be overshadowed by other large economies and regions, and therefore remains vulnerable to the fragmentation of the global trading system. Its prospects are ultimately best served by reliable global rules and, as a leader among developing economies, ASEAN needs to exert influence in helping to resolve the current global impasse. ASEAN policy makers must be prepared to use the bloc's increasing influence to promote — and shape — the WTO and other global institutions.

At the same time, given the global impasse, ASEAN cannot forego the benefits that might be achieved through more limited integration with its most important markets. An ambitious portfolio of "plus one" FTAs will help to liberalize ASEAN's trade neighborhood, even if the more desirable goal of full, global liberalization cannot be achieved as rapidly.

The first priority in this context is to make ASEAN into a major hub for trade agreements with its largest partners. Rapid progress has been made toward this objective in the months preceding this study, but the list of potential "spokes" will continue to provide opportunities into the future. With deals now concluded with the most obvious regional partners — Australia, China, India, Japan, Korea, and New Zealand — ASEAN can now turn to consolidating these gains and to exploring ways to leverage them by developing further partnerships with the EU and the United States (or better yet, NAFTA). If agreements are achieved with these partners as well, approximately 90 percent of total ASEAN trade will be covered by regional or "plus one" trade agreements (Appendix E lists the status of ASEAN negotiations with its dialogue partners).

The development of these FTAs so far has followed an accelerating competitive ("domino") paradigm. As ASEAN gradually accelerated its timeline of regional integration, China took an early, surprising step to cement its relations with the region. ASEAN's external agreements have gained still more momentum as ASEAN accelerated its own integration efforts, bringing forward the implementation of AFTA to 2010 (for the original 6 members) and the AEC by 2015. And as we have seen, the Doha debacle of July 2008 provided additional impetus to this process.

ASEAN's role as the hub of Asian trade agreements is based not just on economic, but also political-economic grounds. As a collection of smaller economies, ASEAN is a relatively neutral participant in the competitive structure of emerging Asia. It provides an opportunity for other larger countries to demonstrate their willingness to cooperate and create harmonious regional relations. It has good commercial ties with China, Japan, and India. And it offers a wide range of primary goods and parts and components to the more specialized manufacturing economies of the north, and it does not yet have a large constellation of global companies to link the region directly to European and North American markets. Thus much of its trade takes place in the context of networks built around Northeast Asian and Western companies. In other words, ASEAN is an important, yet non-threatening partner to many larger countries.

How will ASEAN benefit from its expanding FTA hub? While resources did not permit comprehensive new estimates for this study (except for the CGE model developed in Chapter 2), some rough estimates can be built on previous work.[3] In the most comprehensive of the studies performed on these policies, Kawai and Wignaraja (2008) estimate the benefits that would result from the establishment of several ASEAN+1 scenarios, as well as more comprehensive frameworks involving ASEAN+3 and ASEAN+6 countries. For brevity, we shall refer to this study as the KW study. (The analytical features of this model are described in detail in Francois and Wignaraja, 2008.) In addition to reporting some of their main results, we also extrapolate their work to FTAs that they did not analyze, including potential agreements with Australia and New Zealand, India, the United States, and the EU.

The KW analysis is based on CGE model simulations, but it incorporates more channels of impact than most such models do. Its unusual features include induced FDI effects, and the liberalization of services as well as trade. The model's completeness may be seen as a source of strength, making it potentially more comprehensive in estimating the benefits of serious agreements. But its broad coverage could lead some to argue that the results are inflated, reflecting features of doubtful accuracy or validity. In any case, the model provides reasonable, but upper-end estimates of the likely impacts of broad liberalization.

The results of the KW study are reported in Table 6-3. (Special note needs to be made of the fact that they calculate value estimates for the year 2017, when ASEAN income levels will be around 3/4 higher than they are today.) They show large benefits not just in value but also in percentage terms — ranging from 0.7 percent of income for ASEAN overall from the ASEAN-Korea FTA, to 3.7 percent from the ASEAN-China FTA. As a first approximation of the value of the whole hub, we add the benefits derived from the three "plus one" FTAs agreements. This amounts to 6.83 percent of ASEAN income, a substantial increase consistent with the region's openness and the relatively high barriers that still confront its trade with major partners. The benefits are especially large for Thailand, Vietnam and Malaysia — economies with strong trade connections with Northeast Asia, and with an established presence in industries that are dominated by production clusters. The benefits are smallest for other CLMV countries, whose commercial ties are focused on ASEAN trade and on primary or simple labor-intensive products, rather than ties with distant production networks.

The benefits of the ASEAN's "plus one" FTAs are mostly due to trade creation and not trade diversion. Effects on other regions are mixed, but minimal — for example, in the case of the ASEAN-China FTA, they range from 0.1 percent income gains in Africa, Europe, and Oceania to a 0.3 percent

Table 6-3
Gains from ASEAN's Regional FTA Network

	ASEAN+China		ASEAN+Japan		ASEAN+Korea		Sum: 3 FTAs		ASEAN+3		ASEAN+6	
	Value	%	Value	%	Value	%	Value	%	Value	%	Value	%
ASEAN	4,4211	3.72	28,831	2.43	8,088	0.68	81,130	6.83	62,186	5.23	67,206	5.66
Cambodia	68	0.75	30	0.33	15	0.16	113	1.24	107	1.20	109	1.21
Indonesia	6,924	2.30	2,834	0.94	1,475	0.49	11,233	3.73	7,884	2.62	8,588	2.86
Malaysia	7,551	4.02	4,453	2.37	1,339	0.71	13,343	7.10	10,391	5.54	11,869	6.33
Philippines	2,556	2.13	1,915	1.59	630	0.52	5,101	4.24	3,177	2.64	3,431	2.85
Singapore	6,854	4.13	3,171	1.91	793	0.48	10,818	6.52	7,943	4.79	9,002	5.43
Thailand	16,324	7.39	14,107	6.39	2,640	1.20	33,071	14.98	26,728	12.10	28,346	12.84
Vietnam	3,371	4.68	2,119	2.94	1,136	1.58	6,626	9.20	5,293	7.35	5,490	7.63
Others	563	0.50	203	0.18	60	0.05	826	0.73	661	0.59	370	0.33
Other Regions												
Northeast Asia	9,756	0.11	18,624	0.21	7,256	0.08	35,636	0.40	165,720	1.85	2E+05	1.93
Other East Asia	-2,676	-0.30	-1,124	-0.13	-528	-0.06	-4,328	-0.49	-11,649	-1.32	-13,530	-1.54
Oceania	1,326	0.20	-1,272	-0.19	-26	0.00	28	0.01	-2,600	-0.38	26,385	3.88
South Asia	-1,059	-0.09	-823	-0.07	-530	-0.05	-2,412	-0.21	-3,620	-0.32	17,193	1.52
Central Asia	70	0.04	-41	-0.02	-26	-0.01	3	0.01	-159	-0.09	-205	-0.11
NAFTA	9,985	0.06	-214	0.00	273	0.00	10,044	0.06	-235	0.00	-4,474	-0.03
Latin America	2,667	0.13	-109	-0.01	-303	-0.01	2,255	0.11	-2082	-0.10	-2,958	-0.14
EU27	12,921	0.11	867	0.01	253	0.00	14,041	0.12	6,786	0.06	1,806	0.02
Sub-Saharan Africa	604	0.15	68	0.02	8	0.00	680	0.17	396	0.10	457	0.12
Rest of the World	4,193	0.13	326	0.01	-292	-0.01	4,227	0.13	-824	-0.03	-4,130	-0.13
World	81,998	0.17	45,134	0.09	14,173	0.03	1E+05	0.29	213,919	0.45	3E+05	0.54

Note: The value estimates (US$ million) represent income increases in 2017.
Source: Kawai and Wignaraja (2008).

income loss in "Other East Asia" (most likely Taiwan). Overall, losses in the rest of the world are very small compared to world gains; the sum of losses ranges from 4 percent of world gains in the case of the ASEAN-China FTA to 11 percent in the case of the ASEAN-Korea FTA.

The benefits of FTAs increase significantly if they are implemented fully by ASEAN+3 and ASEAN+6. These comprehensive FTAs would differ from the ASEAN hub arrangement by also liberalizing trade *among* Northeast Asian economies. Since each of these is large, bringing their mutual links also into the FTA generates further gains — almost doubling worldwide benefits relative to the ASEAN hub concept. ASEAN's gains are likely to be somewhat smaller in a broad regional FTA than in a hub system, since in the latter ASEAN enjoys preferential access to Northeast Asian markets over Northeast Asian competitors. But ASEAN's loss is small, and the predominant gain from a broad Asian FTA is large, suggesting that the ASEAN hub will ultimately accelerate the formation of larger Asian groups. This is likely to be beneficial for Asia and the world as a whole.

ASEAN has still more to gain from agreements with major partners further away. We therefore also construct rough estimates (extrapolated from the KW simulations) for FTAs with Australia and New Zealand, India, the United States, and the European Union (Table 6-4).

A very simple methodology was used to develop these extrapolations. First, using the KW results, ratios of benefits to total bilateral trade were calculated for each ASEAN economy with each FTA examined in the simulations (for example, one of these many ratios calculated in this process was the ratio of Malaysia's benefits under the ASEAN-China FTA to its two-way trade with China). To estimate the benefits from FTAs with other FTA partners, we then multiplied the model benefit/trade ratios derived from the simulations with two-way trade between ASEAN countries and other potential FTA partners. Algebraically:

(1) $B_{ij} = \beta_{ik} T_{ij}$

Where:

B_{ij} = Benefits of country i from an FTA between ASEAN and a partner j that *was not* included in the KW study
β_{ik} = Ratio of benefits/trade, calculated for country i from an FTA between ASEAN and a partner k that *was* included in the KW study
T_{ij} = Two-way trade between country i and partner j

For example, we found from the KW study that the ASEAN-China FTA would generate $0.274 in benefits for Malaysia per dollar of Malaysia's two-way trade with China. We then applied this ratio to actual two-way trade between Malaysia and India ($6,464 million) to arrive at an estimate of $1,772 million for Malaysian gains from an ASEAN-India FTA. We used the ASEAN-China benefit/trade ratios as the model for ASEAN's potential FTA with India, and the average of the ASEAN-Japan and ASEAN-Korea benefit/trade ratios as the model for ASEAN's potential FTAs with Australia-New Zealand, the European Union, and the United States.

As Table 6-4 reports, the four additional FTAs would raise ASEAN's overall gains from its FTA hub from 6.83 percent of ASEAN income to 10.31 percent.[4] The largest overall gains would be associated with an ASEAN-US FTA (2.10 percent), but the patterns of country benefits differ. In all cases, Thailand would be the largest beneficiary, for reasons already noted. But other important pairwise gains

Table 6-4
ASEAN's Wider FTA Possibilities

	ASEAN+China		ASEAN+Japan		ASEAN+Korea		Sum: 3 FTAs		ASEAN+3		ASEAN+6	
	Value	%	Value	%	Value	%	Value	%	Value	%	Value	%
ASEAN	7,326	0.62	7,880	0.66	26,119	2.20	24,986	2.10	41,326	3.48	103,512	10.31
Cambodia	6	0.06	1	0.01	331	3.65	140	1.55	337	3.72	444	4.96
Indonesia	774	0.26	1,778	0.59	1,669	0.55	2,110	0.70	4,222	1.40	12,106	5.13
Malaysia	1,041	0.55	1,772	0.94	6,074	3.23	4,624	2.46	8,887	4.73	19,278	11.83
Philippines	215	0.18	62	0.05	2,097	1.75	1,484	1.24	2,374	1.98	5,551	6.22
Singapore	1,150	0.69	1,601	0.96	4,256	2.56	4,250	2.56	7,007	4.22	14,950	10.74
Thailand	2,897	1.31	2,209	1.00	9,468	4.29	9,800	4.44	14,575	6.60	41,303	21.58
Vietnam	1,161	1.61	263	0.37	2,182	3.03	2,501	3.47	3,606	5.01	8,899	14.21
Others	81	0.07	194	0.17	43	0.04	77	0.07	318	0.28	979	1.01

Note: Value is in US$ millions.
Source: Extrapolated by author based on regional FTA results from Kawai and Wignaraja (2008).

also stand out, including Cambodia and the United States, Malaysia and India, and Vietnam and the EU. In other words, it should not be hard to find at least one champion in ASEAN for an FTA with each of the region's key external partners.

Of course, ASEAN may not succeed in building a full hub of FTAs, despite today's favorable environment. Agreements with Europe, India, and the United States will be more difficult than with East Asian partners, since each has committed to templates and requirements consistent with its own FTA networks. Over time, other new arrangements — for example within ASEAN+3 — may make it still more difficult to complete a hub. But work on ASEAN's "plus one" FTAs already demonstrates how ASEAN integration stimulates interest in partner countries. The challenge now is to exploit the opportunities that exist, and to maintain momentum by extending liberalization to more distant (and more difficult) partners.

In sum, an ASEAN FTA hub would bring substantial benefits — as much as 10 percent of ASEAN income. But such a comprehensive hub is not a guaranteed outcome of the AEC. A more appropriate measure of the gains associated with the AEC is thus the *expected* value of gains — that is, the potential gains multiplied by the subjective probability of their realization. Even more precisely, the measure should build on the *increase* in the probability of reaching an agreement that can be attributed to ASEAN's integration effort. What is clear — if not precisely quantifiable — is that regional economic integration improves prospects for reaching agreements with significant partners, and such partnerships can generate sizable expected benefits.

IMPLEMENTATION

These findings suggest large potential gains from integrating an ASEAN single market and production base with the global economy. But this result will require overcoming many obstacles.

A basic prerequisite is regional integration as laid out in the AEC Blueprint. This will require members not only to free up trade with each other, but also to pursue deeper integration of markets and production systems. As is detailed at length in other chapters of this volume, they will need to address varied "behind the border" barriers, ranging from restrictive regulations and biased procurement practices to a variety of legal and illegal obstacles to doing business. The realization of a unified market will require — as the AEC Blueprint anticipates — demanding national reforms well beyond the liberalization of trade.[5]

But even with these challenges met and the AEC implemented, the gains from global integration — as highlighted in this chapter — will not happen automatically. These global benefits will require, in addition, a strategy for making regional integration compatible with international integration — that is, policies that incorporate the requirements of global markets into the regional policy agenda. This will be difficult in practice, since regional interest groups will promote approaches that favor regional producers over global competition. Indeed, ASEAN may be often asked to "pay for" liberalization within ASEAN by sheltering ASEAN markets from third-country competition. This is the Faustian bargain that has come to haunt European integration, and especially Europe's Common Agricultural Policy. It matters whether ASEAN integrates, and it also matters how it integrates.

Finally, ASEAN's external success will depend on its ability to forge coherent positions in international economic decisions. For the most part, ASEAN economies today still manage their international economic affairs independently of each other. Even the "ASEAN+" FTAs involve separate lists of commitments by member states. Success in integrating positions will require attention and effort, and will shape the region's ability to achieve regional and bilateral agreements that maximize long-term, regional welfare. Cooperation on external issues will also contribute to a stronger sense of community among the region's economies, and will help to increase the role of regional approaches in other areas of regional policy making.

This brief section addresses some aspects of implementation, recognizing that other chapters address the implementation of the AEC Blueprint's several functional agendas in more detail. Our limited purpose here is to highlight how implementation will interact with the region's external agenda, and thus how it can affect the gains examined above.

Targeting External Competitiveness

Throughout the development of the AEC, choices will have to be made about the shape and sequence of liberalization and regulatory initiatives. Many of these choices will affect ASEAN's preparedness for global competition. For example, it may be easier to achieve regional consensus on standards or regulations that are less restrictive than those required or advocated by more advanced economies. Thus, ASEAN decision makers may confront tradeoffs between rapid regional integration around "low" regional standards and delayed integration around "high" international standards. No general prescription can be offered on these tradeoffs — the welfare consequences will at times favor rapid harmonization, and at times slower approaches that get standards "right" for global integration. The best choice will depend on technical factors particular to products and economies, such as the cost of switching to new standards, the cost of operating with multiple standards if an industry serves different markets, and the cost of upgrading standards as countries and industries mature.

These tradeoffs will be also affected by ASEAN's external strategy. For example, if integration with Asian partners is especially rapid — because these economies provide more attractive expansion possibilities or because they prove more conducive to mutual liberalization — then ASEAN should cooperate with important Asian partners to develop compatible product standards, regulations, and legal frameworks. Of course, global practices and standards may converge in the meantime, so the effect of differences among partners may diminish over time. Still, ASEAN's policies will need to be informed by a mix of considerations that balance the interests of varied national systems within the region, and varied partners outside it.

While no easy generalizations can be offered for how such choices should be made, it is important that they be based on solid analysis, motivated by the region's long-term welfare. This will require analytical capabilities that are not generally available today. Institutes in advanced countries (or for that matter in individual ASEAN economies) may have the technical expertise necessary to propose options, but their interests will not be closely aligned with those of the ASEAN region. The AEC project, therefore, will require new types of analytical advice to support the ASEAN Secretariat and governments as they consider a wide range of complex regulatory priorities. Impartial, informed analysis will be essential to reaching a proper balance among regional political pressures and ASEAN's long-term, global interests.

Enabling Cooperation

As we have seen, cooperation in external commercial diplomacy is the second important element of a successful international agenda. Cooperation can mean many things — from consultations to collective decisions. ASEAN is at an early step on this ladder, as most ASEAN members manage their international decisions independently. As already noted, this approach fails to exploit the leverage provided by ASEAN's ambitious integration effort. The AEC Blueprint's emphasis on "ASEAN centrality" appropriately identifies rigorous cooperation in this area as a major AEC priority.

Mechanisms

Countries don't work together automatically; their natural instinct is to pursue their independent objectives without intervention from others. Yet most realize that mechanisms that constrain their individual actions could benefit them jointly. An essential step for deepening cooperation is to create mechanisms that help to identify, analyze, and ultimately align, the interests of the region's economies. For example, such mechanisms could include protocols for

- Developing templates and guidelines to ensure that new initiatives conform to best practices agreed at the regional level.
- Holding consultations, in advance, on all major new international initiatives of member states, such as the study or negotiation of a new FTA.
- Studying the impact of new initiatives by ASEAN Member States on other member states and on the AEC project.
- Monitoring the progress and results of new negotiations to ensure that they conform to ASEAN templates and guidelines (these should be featured prominently in the "scorecard" that ASEAN is now developing to monitor progress toward the AEC).

There are many ways to design such systems and to equip them with the necessary analytical capacity, and the AEC Blueprint's commitment to "ASEAN centrality" will ultimately require initiatives of this type.

Compensation

Since ASEAN's external agreements may have unequal effects on member states, it would be valuable to develop facilities to compensate countries that might be harmed by international initiatives. For example, this support could take the form of investments in technology, education, or infrastructure to enable lagging countries to take fuller advantage of international opportunities. To be sure, a large system of transfers, such as that established by the EU, is neither feasible nor desirable in ASEAN. Still, productive partnerships with third countries will lead, on occasion, to diverging results, and AEC should be able to conclude such initiatives and share benefits, rather than forego them for lack of compensation mechanisms. This topic is considered at length in Chapter 5.

Institutions

Effective cooperation requires institutional learning — that is, systems for accumulating expertise and experience in managing cooperation. Typically, this happens in institutions with long-term professional staff. To be effective, such institutions need sufficient resources to implement their mission without continually seeking external funding, authorization, and government advice. Permanent institutions are difficult to develop in ASEAN — or Asia — where states prefer to cooperate in intergovernmental forums rather than standing institutions. Nevertheless, the ambition of the AEC project implies new or expanded institutions, and specifically an expanded commercial diplomacy expertise within the ASEAN Secretariat.

ASEAN Commercial Diplomacy Unit

The ASEAN Secretariat's commercial diplomacy function should evolve along with the region's confidence in joint institutions and negotiations. To create an effective professional "home" for such efforts, the member states might consider establishing, within the Secretariat, a unit that addresses the region's expanding commercial diplomacy responsibilities.[6] Such a unit might

- Collect and maintain information on ASEAN agreements and the bilateral agreements of member states.
- Commission analytical studies on alternative approaches to the region's external trade strategy, including on the bilateral agreements of member states, and the benefits associated with them.
- Provide data and ongoing analytical support to national teams participating in ASEAN negotiations.
- Develop strategies, templates, and guidelines for plus-one agreements and for the consolidation of the various bilateral agreements of member states.

In the longer run, the unit might even evolve into offering joint negotiating capabilities, along the lines of the European Commission's Directorate-General for Trade. This last step is outside the vision of the AEC, which continues to see ASEAN as an FTA subject to the commercial policies of individual states rather than as a customs union that assumes joint control over them. In this setting, negotiating authority needs to remain with individual states, which retain control over their third-country policies. Yet rapid integration within ASEAN could lead to the harmonization of external barriers, and thus ultimately to a joint negotiating approach.

Establishing such a unit in the ASEAN Secretariat will require additional resources. Consider the size of the organizations that handle similar responsibilities in national and international organizations. For example, ASEAN's larger member economies will have perhaps 10–20 senior staff members assigned to similar commercial diplomacy functions. The WTO's trade policy review mechanism (which fulfills somewhat similar functions by reviewing trade policies and agreements) also draws on approximately 20 professionals (some delegated from other responsibilities for specific tasks). At the extreme, the European Commission's Directorate-General for Trade has approximately 600 professional staff. But as already noted, the EU's trade mission is considerably broader, since the EU is a full-fledged customs union.

Since ASEAN's trade diplomacy efforts are likely to be scaled up gradually, and for the time being will continue to play a secondary role to national capabilities, a smaller effort might be acceptable as a start. Nevertheless, it would be difficult to envision the ASEAN Secretariat playing a meaningful role in the monitoring and support (and eventually leadership) of external negotiations with a staff of fewer than, say, a half-dozen senior professionals. Even with a professional staff of this size, the ASEAN Secretariat would need to rely extensively on analytical support from regional institutions such as the Economic Research Institute for ASEAN and East Asia (ERIA) and the ADB, the region's numerous think tanks and universities, as well as international organizations with relevant expertise such as the WTO and the World Bank. (Indeed, a significant professional staff in the ASEAN Secretariat is essential for effectively using and absorbing the considerable analytical resources that are already available from external organizations.)

Measurement

The results reported here promise substantial benefits from the AEC, but of course any such projection can be wrong. Although the implementation schedule of the AEC is rapid, it does allow time for analysis of progress and even substantial course corrections, should they become necessary. For example, it might be helpful to monitor at least the following four dimensions of ASEAN's external commercial diplomacy:

- *Are individual member states making progress toward cohesive external policies?* This could be tracked through indicators such as regulatory regimes, third-country barriers, and various qualitative indicators tracked by independent ranking organizations.
- *Is integration resulting in tangible improvements in trade and investment?* In addition to the usual indicators, an effort might be made to check on progress in priority sectors and on the impact of international integration on reducing income disparities.
- *Is the region adopting the principle of ASEAN centrality?* As noted, special efforts should be made to monitor the extra-ASEAN diplomacy of member states, in part to ensure that their initiatives conform to ASEAN guidelines and best practices.
- *Is the region's influence rising in global forums?* As ASEAN grows and integrates, its interests — and nationals — should be increasingly represented in the international agencies that manage global and regional cooperation.

The AEC Blueprint's short, yet powerful commitment to global integration is confirmed by our analysis in this and other chapters of this study. The results suggest (admittedly based on early and often partial estimates) that the benefits of connecting an integrated ASEAN to world markets are potentially large — indeed, larger than those associated with gains from intraregional trade. (To be sure, the gains from increased efficiencies *within* the region's several economies could be larger than all trade-related gains.) Maximizing gains from the region's international partnerships will require difficult policies — including ambitious integration within ASEAN, the alignment of regional standards and regulations with external markets, and new institutions to facilitate cooperation within ASEAN on interactions with external partners. But if these investments help to realize the benefits estimated here, they will be among the best the region can make.

NOTES

1. See Chapter 1 for growth projections and the implications of the current global crisis for ASEAN growth in the short-term.
2. It is especially important to achieve consistent rules of origin with external partners, since this will make it easier to consolidate ASEAN agreements (or at least some key features of them) into a single region-wide agreement. For further analysis of the role of rules of origin in the Asian trading system see James (2006) and

Manchin and Pelkmans-Balaoing (2007), as well as the discussion in Chapter 2.

3. There is a substantial modeling literature on the benefits of Asian free trade areas, but many of these models focus on regional groupings that extend beyond ASEAN (for example, Cheong 2005, Bchir and Fouquin 2006). Results from studies that envision a broader FTA are not directly applicable in the present context, since they are dominated by trade liberalization among the large economies of Northeast Asia (China, Japan and Korea) rather than by the development of the ASEAN hub, that is, links between ASEAN and its "plus one" partners.

4. This calculation uses the direct sum of the FTA benefits as a basis for comparison. The sum may overstate the benefits of multiple FTAs, since a "first" FTA may produce larger gains than subsequent ones. Early FTAs create new efficiencies in imports and exports, which are then only incrementally improved by later FTAs, especially if the economic structures of later partners are similar to those of early ones. Yet KW simulations of ASEAN+3 FTA suggests that the welfare gains obtained from an FTA that encompasses several partners are not much smaller than the sum of the welfare gains obtained from individual FTAs with those partners.

5. An excellent overview of the components of the strategy is provided by Hew (2007).

6. The existing External Economic Relations Division, which has overseen ASEAN's FTA negotiations, is too small for this purpose having only an Assistant Director and two junior staff. While they receive support from the rest of the Secretariat during negotiations, this is not sufficient to act as a Commercial Diplomacy unit.

7
Benefits of the AEC

Michael G. Plummer and Chia Siow Yue

The potential economic and social gains from an AEC are considerable. Each section of the AEC Blueprint — from the single market and production base to integration in the global economy — should contribute significantly to the ultimate goal of ASEAN economic cooperation: regional prosperity, stability, and equity.

However admirable, this goal will not be easily achieved. Deep economic cooperation always faces political obstacles. For example, the European Economic Community achieved its single market nearly 40 years after it was established with the Treaty of Rome. NAFTA went through two incarnations under two US administrations and required a politically risky and bold intervention by President Clinton to be ratified (and during his presidential campaign Barak Obama even considered the need to renegotiate it). Lack of progress on the Doha Development Agenda can be traced to special interests and protectionist groups in constituent economies, and this for an agreement mild in comparison to the comprehensive measures being promulgated in the AEC. Likewise, the AEC will no doubt face opposition in the political bodies of member states. Making the political costs worth enduring will require making the likelihood of widely distributed and significant gains from the AEC compellingly clear.

To this end, our study has presented the economic implications of an AEC and used a variety of techniques and approaches, including a specially designed CGE model, to estimate gains and losses. The nature of the AEC and its many measures make exact estimates impossible but our use of the best proxies available make our estimates as realistic as possible.

We conclude that the AEC should lead to substantial gains, and that these gains should be widely distributed, though some countries and agents may benefit more than others. Our CGE estimates project a 5.3 percent increase in economic welfare relative to the baseline. This is a large impact, but we suggest that it constitutes a lower-bound estimate. Our model is not only based on conservative assumptions in terms of the drop in trade costs due to the AEC (i.e., 5 percent), but also excludes the impact of such AEC-related benefits as harmonization and standardization, free-flow of skilled labor, lower costs of capital, greater stability, etc. We conclude also that all ASEAN Member States should gain from the AEC, even if different measures affect member states differently. If, for example, some CLMV countries gain less from the liberalization of nontariff and tariff barriers, they will gain more from the reduction in transaction costs, improved production networks, and the creation of an "equitable economic region." Further, we conclude that a wide range of stakeholders in member states, from the private sector to consumers, will gain from the AEC.

In this chapter, we review the main results of our study as they apply to stakeholders — businesses, labor, and consumers; ASEAN and ASEAN Member States; and investors. We also summarize our estimates of the net economic effects of the AEC.

ANALYTICAL APPROACH

The AEC is more comprehensive than previous efforts at ASEAN economic cooperation. It is arguably the most ambitious program of economic cooperation in the developing world and one of the most advanced anywhere. Given the myriad and complicated measures associated with creating a single market and production base and other aspects of the AEC, assessing its potential economic impact is complex for two reasons.

First, because modern economies are tightly knit, the AEC has implications for the business community, workers, and consumers, as well as for income distribution. In addition, it is difficult to isolate the effects of AEC measures on specific groups or aspects of the economy. For example, trade in goods affects and is affected by trade facilitation; and trade facilitation affects and is affected by trade in services. Foreign direct investment determines in part, and is determined by, all three, and all three will be significantly affected by infrastructure, that is, policies related to "competitive economic region."

Second, limitations in data and other indicators require that some of our quantitative and qualitative estimates be direct and others indirect. We use a CGE model, for example, to arrive at a straightforward estimate of the effects of the AEC on goods and services trade (Chapter 2). Elsewhere lack of data and other limitations require a different approach. For example, we examine the economic implications of ASEAN Member States converging with a market leader in "best business practices," estimating that convergence could increase growth by up to 12 percent of GDP (Chapter 3). Now, achieving best practices is more than the AEC targets but moving towards unity in best practices is a goal of the AEC Blueprint.

In addition to rises in trade shares, our quantitative and qualitative estimates are concerned with the implications of the AEC for general welfare, income distribution, and social development. The goal of the AEC is to enhance competitiveness and plug ASEAN into the global economic community not simply to raise shares of intraregional trade and investment. That ASEAN is not a "natural" bloc because intra-ASEAN trade does not constitute a majority of its total trade, or that ASEAN integration is of limited consequence because China is an important part of the regional production chain in which ASEAN participates are misguided criticisms.[1] ASEAN leaders have stressed that the AEC should be outward-oriented and not result in "Fortress ASEAN," in which economic integration heightens intraregional trade and investment by discriminating against outsiders to the detriment of efficiency and regional welfare. Fortress ASEAN might result in very high levels of intra-ASEAN trade shares but at the expense of the region's economies and social development.

BENEFITS FOR STAKEHOLDERS

General

General benefits will arise from creation of a unified market and attendant economies of scale, deepening of macroeconomic stability, and achievement of "ASEAN centrality" and "one voice." The estimated large welfare effects of the single market and production base should boost potential GDP growth; and institutional improvements, such as in financial markets and harmonization structures, should make the government sector more efficient and provide a strong impetus for the components of aggregate demand (i.e., investment, consumption, and trade). "Fragmented trade" through production networks will allow even countries with small national markets and narrow skill sets to reap cost-reduction effects of scale economies. In addition, FDI in manufacturing tends to flow to countries with stable and predictable macroeconomic priorities and records. In its macroeconomic measures, the AEC is building on a strong foundation as ASEAN Member States, when compared to other developing regions, already have in place prudent fiscal and monetary policies.

ASEAN integration has deepened as a wave of new regional trading agreements has swept the region. Most ASEAN Member States have at least one FTA with a non-ASEAN country. Since member states maintain their own commercial policies *vis-à-vis* third countries, these agreements could exert centrifugal effects on ASEAN. The AEC, however, will help maintain ASEAN centrality and the AEC harmonization process will slowly but surely cause commercial interests relative to third countries and institutions to merge. ASEAN has underperformed relative to its potential in presenting joint positions at the WTO, as well as in various extra-regional organizations such as ASEAN+3, APEC, and ASEM. The AEC will allow it to rise to its potential. While difficult to quantify, the ability of ASEAN to project its economic interests with one voice could prove to be among its most important advantages.

Business, Labor, and Consumer Stakeholders

Benefits of Free Trade in Goods

AFTA was a significant accomplishment but it left ASEAN's economic architecture incomplete in forging an integrated market. The AEC expands, deepens, and modernizes the coverage of ASEAN integration initiatives, eliminating artificial transaction costs associated with cross-border economic activity and instituting best practices.

Implementation of the AEC Blueprint, for example, will ensure that tariffs fall to zero in all sectors of economic relevance.[2] Intra-ASEAN tariffs are already low or equal to zero in almost every sector in the ASEAN-6 countries and they will soon be removed in the CLMV. AEC measures also aim to eliminate nontariff barriers (NTBs), which are now more costly to businesses than tariffs.[3] Doing so will help unify the market and stimulate intraregional trade. Complete removal of NTBs will be difficult. The EU, for example, only began to remove NTBs in earnest 30 years after it established a customs union, and it took a good deal of time to abolish some barriers.

Removing unnecessary barriers to trade, at the border and elsewhere, will encourage the growth of regional production networks in the AEC. The production of an item once made in a single factory is now organized through a network of small, independent firms or an MNC using a region as a production base. Such fragmented production and trade related to it boosts productivity, cut costs, and enables even the least-developed economies to join the global production chain.

Rationalizing rules of origin as called for in the AEC Blueprint will also facilitate the creation of production networks, reduce costs associated with independent tariff regimes, counter the distortions arising from the plethora of ASEAN-plus and bilateral FTAs, and improve prospects for small- and medium-sized enterprises across ASEAN. The rules of origin under AFTA are relatively simple and straightforward, but small and medium-sized enterprises can be particularly disadvantaged by administrative requirements stemming from any rules of origin. The AEC Blueprint aims to ensure that as much of intra-ASEAN trade as possible qualifies for *value added and change in tariff classification* rules and to keep the costs of administration and compliance as low as possible. The "Asian noodle bowl" of complex rules of origin under multiple ASEAN-plus FTAs and bilateral FTAs can distort the sourcing strategies of multinational firms and inhibit the global production chains and trade fragmentation.

Trade operations will be easier when trade facilitation measures called for in the AEC Blueprint are fully implemented: modernization of customs facilities; integration and harmonization of customs processes through mechanisms such as the ASEAN Single Window; transparency in and effective communication of customs rules and procedures; establishment of an ASEAN Trade Facilitation Repository; and transit facilitation measures.

Instituting international best practices in devising regional rules and policies will help integrate the region more effectively into the global economy. Like other deep integration accords, the AEC Blueprint mandates national treatment in most areas; unlike others, it also calls for adoption of best practices because the goal is efficiency as well as nondiscrimination. The adoption of best practices will be important for the harmonization of standards and technical barriers to trade. Given the importance of extra-regional trade and FDI to ASEAN and the need to integrate with the global economy, these standards should embody global best practices rather than regional ones. The AEC Blueprint also provides for sectoral MRAs on conformity assessment and enhances technical infrastructure.

Benefits of Broad Integration of Services

Services constitute over one-fourth of global trade and 20 percent to 30 percent of value-added in GDP in ASEAN.[4] They have become increasingly important in global economic activity in and of themselves and as facilitators of trade in goods and FDI. Their role is growing on the demand side as consumer tastes become more sophisticated, and on the supply side as production networks rely on services as facilitating inputs. Indeed, the global production value chain relies on services to exploit a competitive division of labor in any given region. An inefficient services sector hinders participation in production networks.

Liberalization and facilitation of services trade in ASEAN was articulated in the ASEAN Framework Agreement on Trade in Services (AFAS). The AEC Blueprint sees services trade as essential to the creation of an integrated market, particularly given the likely spillover effects.[5] Services trade, however, continues to be relatively restrictive in ASEAN. Many restrictions are in the form of technical regulations and licensing and qualification requirements. Some may be discriminatory, with foreign providers having to meet more demanding or burdensome requirements than local providers. National treatment in services implies leveling the services playing field across suppliers; best international practice requires adopting the most efficient regulations. That liberalization and facilitation of services in ASEAN is less advanced than for goods suggests that the "valued added" of the AEC will be even higher.[6]

Benefits of Competition and Competitiveness

The benefits of improved competition and competitiveness in ASEAN will arise from implementation of sound competition policy, protection of intellectual property rights (IPR), improved infrastructure, and "open" regionalism. For example, a sound competition policy governing economic exchange and distribution in ASEAN should improve efficiency and income distribution. The AEC Blueprint's emphasis on consumer protection and related training, technology transfer, and education in consumers' rights will no doubt improve the living standards of all but especially for those in the lower quintile of income distribution. Some ASEAN Member States do not have a formal competition policy; the AEC, therefore, will allow them to create structures based on best international practices.

As noted in the AEC Blueprint, better protection of IPR will facilitate local innovation. Moreover, the economic literature suggests that strong protection of intellectual property is necessary for technology transfer: if MNCs feel that a country's IPR regime is not well-developed, they will be less likely to engage in innovative activities, share trade secrets and production techniques, and so forth. In addition, developing countries in general are concerned that indigenous technologies are being "expropriated" by MNCs; the AEC could lead to research collaboration among member states and the patenting of various indigenous technologies. ASEAN already has accords on IPR and nearly all member states are parties to the WTO and various international intellectual property conventions. It is only natural that joint cooperation in this area should be part of the AEC.

Liberalization will have a muted effect on welfare if not accompanied by adequate infrastructure, hard and soft. After several decades of trade-oriented growth some member states have relatively well-developed trade infrastructure; in others infrastructure development is unbalanced; and in the CLMV it is highly inadequate. FDI tends to bypass countries and regions within countries that do not have adequate infrastructure, and the least-developed regions will not be able to take advantage of economic opportunities offered by the AEC without investing in ports, roads, railways, Information and Communication Technologies (ICT), and logistics. The priority articulated in the AEC Blueprint on developing infrastructure, in partnership with dialogue partners like the ADB, is therefore essential to the success of the AEC.

Finally, regional competitiveness will require openness to nonmembers. Extra-regional competition will impose discipline in a way that intraregional competition cannot — a lesson learned in the EU Single Market Program.[7] This lesson is especially relevant to ASEAN, where national competition policies are much less advanced than in Europe.

ASEAN and ASEAN Member States

Benefits of Attracting Productivity-enhancing FDI

The diversity of economic structure in the ASEAN region makes it a strong candidate for investment cooperation. The AEC is dedicated to creating a free and open FDI regime by 2015. It builds on the AIA, which itself is based on the three pillars of liberalization, facilitation and promotion of FDI. The AIA envisions national treatment for non-partner countries as well, albeit with a different time frame, demonstrating the outward orientation of ASEAN integration. Given that more than three-fourths of FDI comes from outside the region, this is likely to be a *sine qua non* for an effective FDI strategy. Studies have shown that the impact of the AIA has likely been favorable to FDI inflows,[8] but further liberalization and facilitation measures will be necessary to convince resident and nonresident MNCs that ASEAN constitutes a sufficiently integrated market. To this end, the ASEAN Comprehensive Investment Agreement (ACIA) will form the essence of the AEC's FDI regime. All indications point to best practices as well as national treatment emerging as over-riding principles of the ACIA.

Benefits of Free Flow of Skilled Labor

Economic theory makes a strong case for freer factor flows, including labor. The decision to advocate a free flow of skilled labor in the AEC was a sound one: a free flow will make ASEAN more attractive to foreign investors and set in motion a process of mutual recognition of professional qualifications. This, in turn, will lead to mutual recognition of diplomas, degrees, training certificates, and the like. Such a process will feed on itself, bringing with it closer cooperation across the region with respect to training institutes, universities, and research institutions. It will also foster social integration, giving rise, for example to cross-ASEAN professional associations. This process will help the ASEAN Community build itself from the ground up. As ASEAN Member States become more integrated through the AEC and the other two pillars of the ASEAN Community, skilled labor flows will naturally increase. To accommodate and facilitate these flows, fiscal coordination (e.g., to avoid double taxation), which is also covered in the AEC Blueprint, will become more important.

Benefits of Narrowing the Development Gap

ASEAN may be the world's most culturally, socially, and ethnically diverse regional organization. Its members' economies are also diverse, ranging from high-, medium-, and low-income states. Narrowing the development gap will build goodwill and social cohesion in ASEAN and will help maintain the political will necessary to achieve the AEC.

Narrowing the gap requires attention at the regional and national levels. First, the more developed economies will need to assist the least-developed ones up the development ladder, particularly with regard to FDI, technology transfer, human resource development and capacity building, governance structures, and the sharing of development experiences and best practices; and The AEC Blueprint stresses that economic growth should be inclusive and reiterates ASEAN's commitment to cooperation through such mechanisms as the Initiative for ASEAN Integration (IAI). The IAI spells out a number of priority areas, including human resource development, ICT, capacity building for regional economic integration, energy, investment climate, tourism, poverty reduction, and improvement in the quality of life.

Second, existing and potential income inequality within countries must be addressed. Even as regionalization and globalization improve national income distribution, technological change and investment agglomeration could worsen income inequality. Regional cooperation, for example, could diffuse each country's growth impulses from the center to the periphery through investment and trade activities linking border areas of ASEAN Member States. Failing to address rising income inequality at home can create significant problems. Moreover, rising income equality will be blamed on the AEC, whether or not it is responsible. Such a response could reduce the political will to implement the complicated and politically difficult measures and policies inherent in the AEC. Thus, addressing income inequality makes a lot of sense from a political-economy perspective. It also makes economic sense in that income inequality can actually be detrimental to economic growth.[9]

Less-developed members could also benefit from the better negotiating leverage of the ASEAN grouping in various regional and international negotiations. This diversity has important advantages for the AEC: as transborder transactions costs fall investors will be able to use the diversity in factor endowments and cost levels and structures to establish production value chains.

ASEAN Member States and Investors

Benefits of Financial and Capital Market Development

Since the Asian Crisis of 1997–1998, ASEAN Member States have sought to improve domestic capital markets and enhance cooperation at the regional and ASEAN+3 levels. Interest in stock market integration arises primarily because an integrated regional stock market is more efficient than segmented national capital markets. Specifically, ASEAN Member States want to reduce firms' traditional dependence on bank loans and offer alternative financing through bond and stock issuances, while also seeking capital from outside the region. And savers would welcome a greater choice of investment opportunities.

As financial markets become more integrated, investors from all member states will be able to allocate capital to where it is most productive. This should especially benefit the least-developed countries where the rate of return on investment should be highest. With more cross-border flows of funds, additional trading in individual securities will improve the liquidity of the stock and bond markets, which will in turn lower the cost of capital for firms seeking capital and lower transaction costs. These effects suggest more efficient allocation of capital in the region. With respect to fixed-income markets, the development of bond markets is a natural priority given the need to finance infrastructure projects, business expansion, and budget deficits in some member states. Bond markets are also important in establishing risk benchmarks in the economy.

The AEC Blueprint stresses the importance of facilitating capital market development and cross-border trade in assets.[10] As facilitation proceeds, efficiency will rise and the cost of capital will fall. The result should be more robust investment, which has been somewhat problematic in recent years: the fall in GDP growth in ASEAN from a pre-Crisis level of approximately 8 percent to 5 percent post-Crisis can mostly be explained by the drop in investment's share of GDP from one-third to one-fifth.[11] As FDI tends to gravitate to markets with strong financial institutions, concerted liberalization, development, and regional cooperation in this area should have significant secondary effects on development in most other sectors.

Given the nature of the ongoing financial crisis, the region may tend to shy away from capital-market development. This would be a mistake. The current crisis, which originated in the United States, stems from a number of factors, most of which did not apply in the ASEAN region: persistent and unsustainable macroeconomic imbalances, excess credit expansion, asset-market bubbles, lack of financial supervision, shortcomings in the structure of financial regulation, inadequate value-at-risk models, and unethical and even fraudulent bookkeeping. Closer cooperation could mitigate the effects of the global contagion and, alongside concerted financial development, help avoid crises or at least minimize their impact.

Benefits Summary

The global economy and Asia constantly produce challenges and opportunities for ASEAN and its member states, which do well to advance together lest they fall behind, particularly given the stiff competition with China and India for markets, investments, and resources. The AEC is a bold step in concerted economic reform.

Achieving a single market and production base will allow ASEAN to benefit from efficiency and economies of scale in value-chain processes. Indeed, the benefits of the AEC for various stakeholders should foster a stronger, more vibrant, and more deeply integrated region (Table 7-1). The AEC should generate significant and widely distributed economic benefits that deepen political and macroeconomic stability and give ASEAN a potent voice in international fora. The success of the AEC requires achieving the "equitable economic region" called for in the AEC Blueprint, and in this regard some stakeholders may need assistance to adjust to structural change so they do not bear the costs of change disproportionately. Above all, success requires mustering political will to implement the AEC Blueprint by 2015 and sustaining that political will for years many years to come.[12] The benefits of the AEC as described here and as realized through implementation should strengthen political will.

EMPIRICAL ESTIMATES OF AEC ECONOMIC IMPACTS

The following are our salient conclusions regarding the potential economic impact of the AEC. The AEC will or is likely to

- *Increase ASEAN real income significantly.* Our CGE model estimates that ASEAN economic welfare should rise by 5.3 percent or $69 billion relative to the baseline — more than six times the estimated effect of completing AFTA. All ASEAN Member States gain as well.
- *Lead to a robust expansion in ASEAN trade in goods.* Exports will outpace imports in all but three manufacturing sectors, and many of these areas offer opportunities to enter global production chains.
- *Boost welfare through its policy of openness.* Extending the AEC to include "+1" agreements with East Asian neighbors increases aggregate welfare benefits to ASEAN by two-thirds and by an additional one-third if the United States and the EU are added.
- *Attract FDI in a variety of ways.* FDI will likely be attracted by greater economic dynamism, fewer barriers to production networks, and the policy measures of the ASEAN Comprehensive Investment Area. Production networks, in turn, will be particularly advantageous to SMEs throughout ASEAN and in CLMV countries in particular.
- *Increase baseline FDI stocks by 28 percent to 63 percent.* Relative to 2006 inward FDI stocks, these increases represent $117 to $264 billion. The potential gain to annual income growth will (conservatively) be on the order of 0.5 percent to 1.0 percent of GDP per annum. Moreover, given the diversity of ASEAN and the potential for its entering production value chains, this effect should be large.
- *Boost per capita GDP through best practices.* Instituting competition policy best practices alone could raise per capita GDP by 26 percent to 38 percent in the resource-rich original ASEAN Member States, including an increase of 8 percent to 14 percent due to rising foreign investment due to policy reform.[13] These figures are on par with estimates of the economic impact of new EU Member States in joining the EU (39 percent, estimated by Lejour et al. 2007).
- *Help the CLMV countries continue converging with the rest of ASEAN.* The CLMV countries should be able to keep "catching up" through the many opportunities for production networks created by an AEC and the productivity enhancing effects of AEC's emphasis on best practices.

Table 7-1
Summary of AEC Benefits for Stakeholders

Stakeholders	AEC Process	Major Benefits
1. ASEAN	Deeper and speedier economic integration. Requires political will, commitments, and AEC compliance.	Consolidates ASEAN centrality; affects shift in economic gravity northwards; promotes dynamic, equitable, and sustainable economic growth in region; anchors production networks in region through FDI inflows; promotes macroeconomic stability and financial cooperation.
2. ASEAN Member States	Free flows of goods, services, investment, and skilled labor; freer flow of capital; competitive economic region; equitable economic development; and integration into global economy. Requires domestic economic reforms and structural reforms, and compliance on AEC commitments.	Faster economic growth, employment creation, larger FDI inflows, and improvements in productivity and competitiveness through improved resource allocation, scale economies, and fragmented production. Access to larger regional market and beyond and to more technological and human resources. Encourages intraregional trade and investment; more efficient international standards and best practices adopted; greater participation in production networks and global value chains. IPR protection will encourage technology-intensive FDI and R&D activities. Ability to use the AEC to undertake politically sensitive domestic reforms. Increased tax revenue from economic expansion offsets loss of tariff revenue. One ASEAN voice provides clout in regional and international forums. Economic gains through ASEAN Hub FTAs as opposed to bilateral FTAs.
3. CLMV countries	In addition to (2) above, specific measures to narrow development gaps, such as through IAI, learning from ASEAN countries' best practices. Requires domestic economic reforms and structural adjustments, and compliance on AEC commitments.	Could gain the most from liberalization and reforms to improve efficiency and competitiveness and play catch-up. Access to ASEAN capital, investment, technology, technical assistance, development experience and best practices. Better able through single market to participate in global production networks and value chains. Gain clout in regional and international negotiations. Better able to undertake politically sensitive domestic reforms through the AEC.
4. Businesses including SMEs	Same as (2). Requires firms to restructure to take advantage of market opportunities and to overcome import and supplier challenges presented by AEC.	Larger market access and lower input costs and transaction costs through elimination of tariffs and NTBs on goods and improved regulatory environment on services. Lower trade-related costs and easier trade operations due to improvements in customs, logistics, transportation connectivity, and ICT and well as rationalized rules of origin and harmonized product and technical standards.
5. Investors	Same as (2), but particularly free flows of investment and freer flow of capital. Requires good corporate governance and accountability.	Stronger investment rights (with exceptions), national treatment, improved investment protection and dispute settlement; deepening capital markets and financial services liberalization. Local investors can enter into joint

		ventures with foreign investors to exploit local and foreign markets. Smooth flow of skilled labor improves management options.
6. Labor including professionals	Same as (2), but particularly free flow of services and of skilled labor, and MRAs for professional qualifications.	Expanding industries, services, and firms create jobs and offer higher wages, (those adversely affected by AEC competition could lose jobs and require adjustment assistance). Free flow of skilled labor benefits countries with skills shortages, and professionals and skilled workers are able to find better jobs and earn more. Complement to FDI.
7. Consumers	Same as (2), but particularly free imports and introduction of competition law/policy.	Access to cheaper and wider range of imported goods and services, a more competitive domestic market environment, and consumer protection.
8. ASEAN's global partners	AEC's open regionalism	Little trade and investment diversion; a dynamic and economically resilient region is an advantage for the global economy. ASEAN can play a positive role in international forums such as WTO, IMF, World Bank, and in regional forums such as APEC and ASEM.

- *Improve labor markets and labor management by allowing free flow of skilled labor.* The free flow of labor will attract foreign investors and complement FDI; stimulate mutual recognition of professional qualifications, deepening regional cooperation among training institutes, universities, research institutions, and the like; be especially beneficial for countries with labor shortages; and help professionals and skilled workers find better jobs and earn more money.
- *Benefit consumers, the forgotten stakeholder.* Consumers will have access to a cheaper and wider range of imported goods and services and enjoy more extensive consumer protection.

Our research suggests that the net benefits of the AEC should be large, well beyond the 5.3 percent increase in economic welfare due to "AEC value added" that we derive in our conservative CGE model. Other gains that would bolster the economic impetus of the AEC but not specifically modeled include

- Lower cost of capital due to freer movements of capital and improved financial systems;
- Efficiency gains from freer movement of skilled labor, with big effects on GDP as well;
- Benefits flowing from "ASEAN One Voice"; and
- Greater macroeconomic stability due to the conservative macroeconomic policies necessary to support the AEC.

On the basis of quantitative and qualitative analysis alike, we believe that the AEC process should generate substantial economic benefits, benefits that will be well worth the exertion of political will necessary to create a single market and production base and attain other AEC goals.

The AEC is a work in progress. New opportunities for cooperation will arise and an endogenous cooperative process could arise, in which the increasing ease of doing business in ASEAN begets demand for new integration measures.

NOTES

1. This misconception is pervasive in the literature and in the media. See, for example, the Economist Intelligence- Unit's recent report, "Trading Up: A New Export Landscape for ASEAN and Asia," in which ASEAN is criticized on the basis of such misguided indicators.

2. A few sectors are excluded for reasons of national security, public heath, and social stability. Such exclusions exist in all types of economic integration, including, for example, the EU.

3. The term NTB pertains to a wide range of measures, from import quotas and licensing to sanitary and phytosanitary standards (SPS). The ASEAN NTM Database, housed at the ASEAN Secretariat, provides comprehensive documentation of 24 different categories of NTBs in the region.

4. ASEAN-6 and Vietnam.

5. See, for example, Clemes, et al. (2003), who, focusing on the original ASEAN countries, Brunei, and Vietnam, use an applied econometric model to verify the strong spillover effects of services on manufacturing, and vice-versa.

6. Services liberalization can be complicated. Services can be high tech or low tech, inputs or final goods, privately provided or publicly provided, and are closely related to other areas of commercial policy (e.g., about three quarters of all services trade is delivered through the mode of a "commercial presence").

7. See, for example, Jacquemin and Sapir (1990).

8. See, for example, Plummer (2007).

9. Barro (2008) estimates the effects of income inequality on economic growth using a database with up to 120 countries and spanning the past four decades. He finds that any given increase in inequality yields a statistically significant and relatively large negative effect on GDP growth. Moreover, he finds that the effect is strongest for the poorest countries in the sample. De Gregorio and Lee (2004) argue that, in addition to direct effects, income inequality affects economic growth indirectly by influencing other determinants of growth.

10. Sensibilities regarding the control of foot-loose capital movements, particularly in times of crisis, however, must be respected.

11. Asian Development Bank (2008).

12. The Joint Media Statement of the Fortieth ASEAN Economic Ministers Meeting in Singapore, August 25–26, 2008, said that "completing the roadmap to become an ASEAN Economic Community (AEC) will require commitment and tough political decisions. Although the respective governments face pressing domestic economic and political pressures from time-to-time, [the meeting's host] Prime Minister Lee called on ASEAN to muster the political will to implement the AEC Blueprint."

13. Details are in Chapter 3. We allow for a convergence of existing policies to the most efficient economy in the region, which we proxy as "best practices."

References

AADCP-REPSF. 2005. Research Project 04/011. ASEAN and AusAID. Jakarta.

Abella, M. 2004. Labor migration in East Asian economies, conference paper, Annual Bank Conference on Development Economics, World Bank.

Adams, Philip and J. Horridge. 2000. Long-run effect of AFTA Trade liberalization, with special reference to the Thai economy. Monash University, Center of Policy Studies. October.

ADB. 2007. Beyond the crisis: Emerging trends and challenges. Philippines: ADB.

ADB. 2007. Workers in Asia, Part III. In *Asian Development Outlook*. Manila: ADB.

ADB. 2008. Emerging Asian regionalism: A partnership for shared prosperity. Manila: ADB.

ADB. 2008. Key indicators for Asia and the Pacific 2008. Manila: ADB.

ALMEC Corporation. 2002. ASEAN maritime transport development study.

Amri, P. D. 2007. ASEAN Roadmap integration for healthcare sector — an assessment: final report. Centre for Strategic and International Studies.

Ando, M. and S. Urata. 2006. The impact of East Asia FTA: A CGE model simulation study. Paper presented at JSPS (Kyoto University) — NSRT (Thamassat University) Core University Program Conference 2006 "Emerging Development in East Asia FTA/PTAs," Doshisha University.

Ando, Mitsuyo and Fukunari Kimura. 2008. Production fragmentation and trade patterns in East Asia: Further evidence. Paper presented at the Ninth Global Development Network Conference, Emerging Trends and Patterns of Trade and Investment in Asia workshop, Brisbane, Australia. February 1–2.

Ando, Mitsuyo and Fukunari Kimura. 2005. Formation of international production and distribution networks in East Asia. In *International Trade in East Asia NBER-East Asia Seminar on Economics*, vol. 14, edited by Takatoshi Ito and Andrew K. Rose. Chicago: University of Chicago Press.

Antara News. 2007. Minister lets toll road users go ahead with class action. 9 April.

Ariff, Mohamed. 2008. Competition Policy for ASEAN. In *ERIA Research Project Report 2007 no. 1-2 on Deepening Economic Integration in East Asia — the ASEAN Economic Community and Beyond*. Edited by Hadi Soesastro. 135–146.

Arkell, J. 2001. Services: trends, consequences and the effects of a new WTO round. 2001 Roundtable of the Committee for Trade, Industry and Enterprise Development, UN Economic Commission for Europe.

Arndt, Sven. 2003. Global Production Networks and Regional Integration, WP 2003-12. Claremont McKenna College, Lowe Institute of Political Economy.

Arnold, J. 2003. Logistics development and trade facilitation in Lao PDR, World Bank, Working Paper no. 3, Report no. 27840, Vol. 2 of 6, Washington, D.C.

Arnold, J. and Villareal, T. 2002. Philippines logistics study, World Bank, Report no. 27840, Vol. 3 of 6, Washington, D.C.

Arnold, J., B.S. Javarick, and A. Mattoo. 2007. Does services liberalization benefit manufacturing firms? Evidence from the Czech Republic, World Bank, Working Paper Series 4109.

Asasen, A. 2003. Proposed ASEAN blueprint for SME development 2004–2014. Research report. REPSF project no. 02/005, ASEAN and AusAID, Jakarta.

ASEAN Cooperation on Standards and Conformance to Facilitate Trade in the Region. http://www.aseansec.org/6667.htm.

ASEAN-ANU. 2005. Movement of workers in ASEAN health care and IT sectors. Final main report. REPSF project no. 04/007.

Association of Southeast Asian Nations. 2008. ASEAN Economic Community Blueprint. Jakarta: ASEAN Secretariat.

Athukorala, P. 2006. Product fragmentation and trade patterns in East Asia. Asian Economic Papers, 4(3): 1–28.

Atje, R. 2008. ASEAN Economic Community: In search of a coherent external policy. In *Deepening Economic Integration in East Asia — the ASEAN Economic Community and Beyond*. Edited by H. Soesastro. ERIA research project report no. 1-2. Tokyo: Japan External Trade Organization (JETRO).

Augier, P., M. Gasiorek, and C. Lai-Tong. 2005. Impact of rules of origin on trade flows, *Economic Policy*, vol. 20, no. 43 (July): 567–624.

Authokorala, P. 2007. The rise of China and East Asian export performance: Is the crowding-out fear warranted? Working Paper. Australian National University.

Balisacan, Arsenio M. 2007. Why does poverty persist in the Philippines? Agriculture and Development Discussion Paper no. 2007-1. Southeast Asian Regional Center for Graduate Study and Research in Agriculture (SEARCA).

Bano S. and P. Lane. 1995. The significance and determinants of trade in services: Canada and the world economy. In *International Trade and the New Economic Order*. Edited by Raul Moncarz. Amsterdam: Elsevier Science Ltd.

Banomyong, R. 2000. Multimodal corridors in ASEAN. Unpublished Ph.D. thesis. University of Wales.

Banomyong, R. 2004. Assessing import channels for a land-locked country. *Asia Pacific Journal of Marketing and Logistics*. vol. 16, no. 2: 62–81.

Barrell, Ray and Amanda Choy. 2003. Economic integration and openness in Europe and East Asia. Presented at the ASEM Symposium on Multilateral and Regional Economic Relations. Tokyo. March.

Barro, Robert. 2008. Inequality and growth revisited. ADB Working Paper Series on Regional Economic Integration no. 11 (January).

Bchir, Mohamed Hedi and Michel Fouquin. 2006. Economic integration in Asia: Bilateral free trade agreements versus Asian Single market. CEPII Discussion Papers no. 15 (October). Paris: Etudes prospectives et d'informations internationales.

Bhagwati, Jagdish N. 1984. Splintering and disembodiment of services and developing nations. *The World Economy*, 7 (2): 133–143.

Bilas, Vlatka. 2007. Regional economic integrations and capital movement: Measuring the level of capital mobility, *Proceedings of Rijeka Faculty of Economics — Journal of Economics and Business*, 2007, vol. 25, no. 2, 269–290, Croatia.

Bl^mstrom, Magnus and Ari Kokko. 1997. Regional integration and foreign direct investment, Working Paper 6019. National Bureau of Economic Research (Also appeared as Policy Research Working Paper 1750, World Bank).

Bonapace, Tiziana. 2005. Free trade areas in the ESCAP region: Progress, challenges and prospects. In *Asian economic cooperation and integration: Progress, prospects, and challenges*: 95–122. Manila: ADB.

Bourguignon, F. 2002. Growth elasticity of poverty reduction: Explaining heterogeneity across countries and time periods. In *Growth and Inequality*, ed. T. Eichler and S. Turnovsky. MIT Press.

Brenton, Paul and Hiroshi Imagawa. 2005. Rules of origin, trade and customs. In *Customs modernization handbook*, ed. Luc De Wulf and José B. Sokol. Washington, D.C.: World Bank.

Brooks, Douglas H., David Roland-Holst, and Fan Zhai. 2005. Asia's long-term growth and integration: Reaching beyond Trade policy barriers. ADB ERD Policy Brief no. 38 (September).

Brussick, P., A. Alvarez, and L. Cernat (eds.). 2005. Competition provisions in regional trade agreements: How to assure development gains. United Nations.

Busakorn, C. K., C. Fung, H. Iizaka, and A. Siu. 2005. The giant sucking sound: Is China diverting foreign direct investment from other Asian countries? *Asian Economic Papers*, vol. 3, issue 3 (Fall): 122–140.

Calvo, G., A. L. Leiderman, and C. M. Reinhart. 1994. The capital inflows problem: Concepts and issues. *Contemporary Economic Policy*. XII (July).

CAPA Consulting 2004. 2008. Developing ASEAN's single aviation market and regional air services arrangements with dialogue partners draft final report, REPSF project no. 07/003 (12 May).

Carana Corporation. 2004. Impact of transport and logistics on Indonesia's trade competitiveness.

Carana Corporation. 2005. Improving transport and logistics for trade: Final report for the special study on the impact of transport and logistics on trade competitiveness.

Carkovic, Maria and Ross Levine. 2002. Does foreign direct investment accelerate economic growth? Working Paper. University of Minnesota Department of Finance (June).

Cecchini, Paolo. 1998. The costs of Non-Europe. Brussels: EC Commission.

Chaisakul, S. 2004. Production Networks, trade and investment policies, and regional cooperation in Asia: a case study of automotive industry in Thailand. Presented at 6th Asian Development Research Forum General Meeting. Bangkok.

Chanda, R. 2002. GATS and its implications for developing countries: Key issues and concerns. DESA Discussion Paper no. 25. United Nations.

Cheong, Inkyo. 2005. Estimation of economic effects of FTAs in East Asia — A CGE approach. In East Asian economic regionalism: Feasibilities and challenges, ed. Choong Yong Ahn, Richard Baldwin, and Inkyo Cheong. Netherlands: Springer.

Chia Siow Yue. 2008. Demographic change and international labour mobility in Southeast Asia: issues, policies and implications for cooperation. In Labor mobility in the Asia Pacific region: Dynamics, issues and a new APEC agenda, ed. Graeme Hugo and Soogil Young. APECC and ABAC Study. Singapore: Institute of Southeast Asian Studies.

Chia, Siow Yue. 2007. ASEAN and narrowing the development gap. In *The inclusive regionalist: A festschrift dedicated to Jusuf Wanandi*, ed. Hadi Soesastro and Clara Joewono: 319–335. Jakarta: CSIS.

Chia, Siow Yue. 2005. Integrating East Asia's low-income countries into the regional and global markets. In *Policy coherence towards East Asia: Development challenges for OECD countries*, ed. K. Fukasaku, M. Kawai, M. Plummer, and A. Treciak-Duval: 527–574. Paris: OECD.

Chow, H. K., P. N. Kriz, R. S. Mariano, and A. H. H. Tan. 2007. Regional coordination of policy measures forward: Financial market liberalization and capital market development, final draft prepared for the ASEAN+3 Secretariat, ASEAN, Jakarta.

Ciravegna, Luciano. 2003. Global and regional integration of production in the Mercosur automotive value chains: the case of Fiat. London School of Economics, Development Studies Institute.

Clemes, M., A. Arifa, and A. Gani. 2003. An empirical investigation of the spillover effects of services and manufacturing sectors in ASEAN countries. *Asia-Pacific Development Journal*, vol. 10, no. 2: 29–40 (December).

Coakley, J., F. Kulasi, and R. Smith. 1998. The Feldstein — Horioka Puzzle and capital mobility: A review. *International Journal of Finance and Economics*, 3: 169–188.

Competition Commission of Singapore. 2007. CCS guidelines on the Section 34 prohibition (June).

Consumer Protection Act, B.E. 2522 (1979), Thailand.

Cuadrado-Roura, J. R., L. Rubalcaba-Bermejo, and J.R. Bryson (eds.). 2002. *Trading services in the global economy*. Northampton, Massachusetts: Edward Elgar.

Curtotti, R., A. Austin, A. Dickson, H. Lindsay, and P. Drysdale. 2006. Background paper on energy issues for the 2nd East Asia Summit, final report. REPSF project no. 06/003 (November).

Dang, Nguyen Anh. 2007. Labor export from Vietnam: issues of policy and practice. Paper presented at the Asia Pacific Migration Research Network Conference, Fujian Normal University, Fuzhou, China (26–29 May).

De Dios, L. C. 2006. An investigation into the measures affecting the integration of ASEAN's priority sectors (Phase 2) — Overview: Non-Tariff barriers to trade in the ASEAN priority goods sectors, REPSF project no. 06/001a (October).

De Gregorio, José and Jong-Wha Lee. 2002. Education and income inequality: New evidence from cross-country data. *Review of Income and Wealth*, vol. 48, no. 3: 395–416.

De Gregorio, José and Jong-Wha Lee. 2004. Growth and Adjustment in East Asia and Latin America, *Economia*, 5, Fall, 69–134.

De Guzman, O. 2003. Overseas Filipino workers, labor circulation in Southeast Asia, and the (Mis)management of overseas migration programs, *Kyoto Review of Southeast Asia*, Issue 4, October 2003.

de Souza, R., M. Goh, S. Gupta, and L. Lei. 2007. An investigation into the measures affecting the integration of ASEAN's priority sectors (Phase 2): The case of logistics, final report. REPSF project no. 06/001d (April).

Dean, Judith M., Robert Feinberg, Jose E. Signoret, Michael Ferrantino, and Rodney Ludema. 2006. Estimating the price effects of non-tariff measures. United States International Trade Commission. Preliminary, as cited in de Dios.

Delaunay, Jean-Claude and J. Gadrey. 1992. *Services in economic thought: Three centuries of debate*. Boston: Kluwer Academic Publishers.

Deunden Nikomborirak. 2005. Transport liberalization and competition concerns in ASEAN. *TDRI Quarterly Review*: 3–11 (December).

Dicken, P. 2003. Global production networks in Europe and East Asia: The automobile components industries, GPN Working Paper 7, Economic and Social Research Council Research Project R000238535: Making the Connections: Global Production Networks in Europe and East Asia.

Dieter, H. 2007. Transnational production networks in the automobile industry. Studies and Research no. 58/ 2007. Paris: Notre Europe.

Doner, R.F., G.W. Noble, and J. Ravenhill. 2004. Production networks in East Asia's auto parts industry. In *Global Production Networking and Technological Change in East Asia*, ed. S. Yusuf, M.A. Altaf, and K. Nabeshima: 159–208. Washington, D.C.: World Bank.

Drake-Brockman, J. 2003. Regional approaches to services trade and investment liberalisation. *Pacific Economic Papers*, no. 337. Australian National University.

Dutz, Mark A. and Aydin Hayri. 2000. Does more intense competition lead to higher growth? World Bank Policy Research Working Paper no. 2320.

Egger, P. and Michael Pfaffermayr. 2005. Determinants of intra-trade: In search for export-import magnification effects. DP Series 1, Economic Studies 12. Deutsche Bundesbank Research Center.

Eichengreen, B. 1998. Capital controls: capital idea or capital folly? Manuscript.

Eichengreen, B. 2007. The cautious case for capital flows. Speech delivered at the Rating Agency Malaysia conference, Free capital mobility: What's in store for Asia? Singapore (1 August).

Eichengreen, B. and Y. C. Park. 2004. Why has there been less financial integration in Asia than in Europe? Monetary Authority of Singapore (February).

Economic Research Institute for ASEAN and East Asia. 2008. *International infrastructure development in East Asia: Towards balanced regional development and integration*. Jakarta: Economic Research Institute for ASEAN and East Asia.

Ernst, Dieter. 2004. Global production networks in East Asia's electronics industry and upgrading prospects in Malaysia. In *Global production networking and technological change in East Asia*, ed. S. Yusuf, M.A. Altaf, and K. Nabeshima: 89–157. Washington, D.C.: World Bank.

Erskine, A. 2003. Liberalizing capital movements in the ASEAN region, abstract of main report. ASEAN-Australia Development Cooperation Program, Regional Economic Support Facility (July 6).

Estevadeordal, A. and K. Suominen. 2003. Rules of origin: A world map. Paper presented at PECC/LAEBA symposium on Regional Trading Agreements in Comparative Perspective: Latin America and the Caribbean and the Asia-Pacific. Inter-American Development Bank, Washington, D.C. (April 23).

Ezaki, M. and T.D. Nguyen. 2008. Regional economic integration and its impact on growth, income distribution, and poverty in East Asia: A CGE analysis. Graduate School of International Development Discussion Paper no. 167. Nagoya.

Feils, Dorothee J. and Mansur Rahman. 2008. Regional Economic Integration and Foreign Direct Investment: The Case of NAFTA.

Findlay, Christopher. 2007. An Investigation into the Measures Affecting the Integration of ASEAN's Priority Sectors (Phase 2): Overview: Summary, REPSF Project no. 06/001a (April).

Forsyth, P., J. King, C. Rodolfo, and K. Trace. 2004. Preparing ASEAN for Open Sky, final report. REPSF Project no. 02/008 , February.

Francois, F.F. and K.A. Reinert. 1996. The role of services in the structure of production and trade: Stylized facts from a cross-country analysis. *Asia-Pacific Economic Review*, 2(1): 35–43.

Francois, Joseph F. and Gamesman Wignaraja. 2008. Economic implications of Asian integration, *Global Economy Journal*, vol. 8, issue 3, article 1.

Francois, Joseph F. and Gamesman Wignaraja. 2008. Pan-Asian integration: Economic implications of integration scenarios. *World Development*. forthcoming.

Freund, C. and J. McLaren. 1999. On the dynamics of trade diversion: Evidence from four trade blocs. Federal Reserve Board, International Finance Discussion Papers no. 637 (June).

Fukao, Koki, Hikari Ishido, and Keiko Ito. 2003. Vertical intra-industry trade and foreign direct investment in East Asia. *Journal of the Japanese and International Economies*, 17, 4: 468–506 (December).

Garcia-Herrero, A. and P. Wooldridge. 2007. Global and regional financial integration: Progress in emerging markets. *BIS Quarterly Review* (September).

Gera, S., S.A. Laree, and T. Songsakul. 2004. International mobility of skilled labour: Analytical and empirical issues and research priorities. Working Paper Series/Collection Documents. Government of Canada.

Ghani, Azmat and Michael D. Clemes. 2002. Services and economic growth in ASEAN economies. *ASEAN Economic Bulletin*, vol. 19, no. 2 (August).

Gilbert, John, Robert Scollay, and Bajit Bora. 2004. New Regional trading developments in the Asia-Pacific Region. In *Global Change and East Asian Policy Initiatives*, ed. S. Yusuf, N. Altaf and K. Nabeshima (eds.): 121–190. Washington, D.C.: World Bank.

Goetz, Perl, Sherry and Szyliowicz. 2002. A case study of the intermodal issues facing the Puget Sound region and the port of Seattle. For APEC Transportation Working Group, Intermodal Task Force.

Goh, M. and A. Ang. 2000. Some logistics realities in Indochina. *International Journal of Physical Distribution and Logistics Management*, vol. 30 (9-10): 887–911.

Goldman Sachs. 2005. How solid are the BRICs? Global Economics Paper no. 134. New York: Goldman Sachs.

Green, David J. 2007. Bridging the ASEAN Development Divide: A Regional Overview. *ASEAN Economic Bulletin*, vol. 24: 15–34 (April).

Grenville, S. 2007. Globalization and capital flows: Unfinished business in the international financial architecture. Lowry Institute for International Policy Perspectives (February).

Grubel, H.G. and M.A. Walker. 1989. Service industry growth: causes and effects. In *The Economics of the Service Sector in Canada*. Fraser Institute.

Haddad, M. 2007. Trade integration in East Asia: The role of China and production networks. World Bank Policy Research Working Paper 4160. Washington, D.C.: World Bank.

Harrison, Ann. 1996. Openness and growth: A time-series, cross-country analysis for developing countries. *Journal of Development Economics*, vol. 48, no. 2: 419–447.

Hausman, Jerry A. 1978. Specification Tests in Econometrics, *Econometrica*, vol. 46: 1251–1271.

Hayashi, M. 2002. The role of subcontracting in SME development in Indonesia: Micro-level evidence from the metalworking and machinery industry. *Journal of Asian Economies* 13: 1–26.

Heston, A., Robert Summers, and Bettina Aten. 2006. Penn-World Table Version 6.2. University of Pennsylvania, Center for International Comparisons of Production, Income and Prices (September).

Hew, Denis (ed.). 2007. *Brick by Brick: The Building of an ASEAN Economic Community*. Singapore: ISEAS.

Hibbert, E. 2003. The new framework for global trade in services: All about GATS. *Service Industries Journal*, 23 (2): 67–78.

Hill, T.P. 1977. On Goods and Services. *Review of Income and Wealth*, 23 (4): 315–338.

Hirschman, A.O. 1958. *Strategy of Economic Development*. New Haven, Connecticut: Yale University Press.

Hodgkinson, A. 2000. Internalisation Process of Asian Small and Medium Firms. Working Paper Series (31). University of Wollongong.

Hoekman, B. and Carlos A. Braga. 1997. Protection and trade in services: A Survey, World Bank Policy Research Working Paper no. 1747.

Hufbauer, G. and T. Warren, T. 1999. The globalization of services: what has happened? What are the implications?, Peterson Institute for International Economics, Working Paper 99-12, Washington, D.C.

ILM. 2006. Migration Survey Report. International Labour Migration Database.

Institute of Health Policy and Development Studies. 2005. Migration of health workers: Country case study Philippines. Working Paper no. 236, Sectoral Activities Program. Geneva: International Labor Office.

Jacquemin, A. and A. Sapir. 1990. Competition and imports in the European market. In *European integration: Trade and industry*, A.L. Winters and A. Venables, eds.

Jakarta Post. 2008. New Electricity Tariff to Start in April (March 15).

James, William E. 2006. Rules of origin in emerging Asia-Pacific preferential trade agreements: Will PTAs promote trade and development? ARTNeT Working Paper Series, no. 19 (August). Bangkok: UNESCAP, Asia-Pacific Research and Training Network on Trade.

Jomo, K. S. 2006. Growth with Equity in East Asia? Working Paper No 33. DESA.

Jones, R. W. and H. Kierzkowski. 1990. The role of services in production and international trade: A theoretical framework. In *The Political Economy of International Trade*, ed. R.W. Jones and A.O. Krueger. Oxford: Blackwell.

Jones, R. W. and H. Kierzkowski. 2001. A Framework for Fragmentation. In *Fragmentation: New Production Patterns in the World Economy*, ed. S. Arndt and H. Kierzkowski: 17–34. Oxford University Press.

Jones, R. W. and H. Kierzkowski. 2004. What does the evidence tell us about fragmentation and outsourcing? HEI Working Paper no. 09/ 2004. Graduate Institute of International Studies.

Jones, Ronald W. 2006. Production fragmentation and outsourcing: General concerns. Presented at the SCAPE workshop, National University of Singapore.

Kanapathy, Vijayakumari. 2003. Services sector development in Malaysia: Education and health as alternative sources of growth, AT120 Research Conference.

Kanapathy, V. 2004. Country report Malaysia: International migration and labor market developments in Asia: Economic recovery, the labor market and migrant workers in Malaysia. Paper prepared for the workshop on international migration and labor markets in Asia. Japan Institute for Labor Policy and Training.

Kartadjoemena, H.S. 2003. Reforming trade in services negotiations in AFAS. REPSF project. ASEAN Secretariat.

Karthikeyan, K. 2007. Trade and FDI in services in Asia. Mimeo for Expert Meeting on Regional Integration in Asia, International Trade Centre-Indian Council for Research on International Economic Relations, Delhi, India.

Katouzian, M.A. 1970. Development of the service sector: A new approach. Oxford Economic Papers, 22: 362–382 (November).

Kawai, M. and Wignaraja, G. 2007. ASEAN+3 or ASEAN+6: Which Way Forward? Paper presented at the

Conference on Multilateralising Regionalism. Sponsored and organized by WTO HEI, co-organized by the Centre for Economic Policy Research. Geneva.

Kawai, Masahiro and Ganesh Wignaraja. 2008. Regionalism as an engine of multilateralism: A case for a single East Asian FTA. Working paper series on regional economic integration (14 February). Manila: ADB.

Kawai, Masahiro and Shujiro Urata. 2004. Trade and foreign direct investment in East Asia. In *Economic Linkages and Implications for Exchange Rate Regimes in East Asia*, ed. Gordon de Brouwer and Masahiro Kawai: 15–102. London and New York: Rutledge Curzon.

Kawai, Masahiro. 2004. Trade and investment integration for development in East Asia: A case for the trade-FDI nexus. University of Tokyo, Institute of Social Science.

Kawai, Masahiro. 2005. Trade and investment integration and cooperation in East Asia: Empirical evidence and issues. In *Asian Economic Cooperation and Integration Progress Prospects Challenges*. Manila: ADB.

Kim, S., J. Lee, and K. Shin. 2007. Regional and Global Financial Integration in East Asia. In *China, Asia, and the New World Economy*, ed. B. Eichengreen, C. Wyplosz, and Y. C. Park. London: Oxford University Press.

Kimura, F. 2006. International production and distribution networks in East Asia: Eighteen facts, mechanics, and policy implications. *Asian Policy Review* 1 (2): 326–344.

Kimura, F. 2008. The Strategic Framework for Deepening Integration. In *Deepening economic integration in East Asia: The ASEAN Economic Community and beyond*, ed. H. Soesastro, ERIA Research Project Report 2007 no. 1-2. Tokyo: JETRO.

Knudsen, Jette S. 2002. Germany's service sector reforms: Lessons for policy-makers. *Journal of Public Policy*, vol. 22, no. 1: 77–100.

Kovindha, O. 2005. Impact of trade liberalization on health services in ASEAN countries. Presented at 12th Canadian Conference on International Health. Ottawa (6-9 November).

Kubney, Julia, Florian M^lders, and Peter Nunnenkamp. 2008. Regional integration and FDI in emerging markets, Kiel Working Paper no. 1418, Kiel Institute for World Economics.

Kuchiki, A. 2005. A Flowchart Approach. In *Industrial Cluster in Asia: Analyses of Their Competition and Cooperation*, ed. A. Kuchiki and M. Tsuji: 169–199. New York: Palgrave MacMillan.

Kumar, N. 2008. Investment cooperation and liberalization in ASEAN+6. In *Deepening Economic Integration in East Asia: The ASEAN Economic Community and Beyond*, ed. H. Soesastro. ERIA Research Project Report 2007 no. 1-2. Tokyo: JETRO.

Kuroiwa, I. and Toh Mun Heng. 2008. Production networks and industrial clusters: Integrating economies in Southeast Asia. Singapore: Institute of Southeast Asian Studies.

Kyrkilis, D. and Pantelis Pantelidis. 2004. Economic convergence and intra regional foreign direct investment in the European Union. University of Macedonia and University of Piraeus, Greece.

Lao People's Democratic Republic. 2004. Prime Minister's Decree on Trade Competition. no. 15. Prime Minister's Office, Vientiane (4 February).

Republic of Indonesia. 1999. Law Concerning Consumer Protection Upon the Mercy of God the Almighty. no. 8.

Lay Hong, Tan and Samtani Anil. 2002. The Shifting Paradigm in Regional Economic Integration: The ASEAN Perspective, mimeo, Working Paper Series, Nanyang Technological University, Singapore.

Leamer, Edward E. 1983. Let's Take the Con Out of Econometrics. *American Economic Review*, vol. 73: 31–43.

Lejour, Arjan, Hugo Rojas-Romagosa, and Gerard Verweij. 2007. Opening services markets within Europe: Modeling foreign establishments in a CGE Framework. CPB Discussion Paper no. 80. CPB Netherlands Bureau for Economic Policy Analysis.

Levine, Ross and David Renelt. 1992. A Sensitivity analysis of cross-country growth regressions. *American Economic Review*, vol. 82: 942–963.

Licandro, Omar. 2004. The impact of regional integration on economic growth and convergence. Working Paper no. 26. European University Institute.

Lim, H. 2008. Policy recommendations to facilitate implementation. In *Deepening Economic Integration in East Asia: The ASEAN Economic Community and Beyond*, ed. H. Soesastro. ERIA Research Project Report 2007 no. 1-2. Tokyo: JETRO.

London Economics. 2002. Quantification of the macro-economic impact of integration of EU financial markets, executive summary, final report. European Commission, — Directorate-General for the Internal Market.

Lopez, AndrÈs and Eugenia Orlicki. 2005. Regional integration and foreign direct investment: The potential impact of the FTAA and the EU-Mercosur Agreement on FDI Flows into Mercosur Countries. Centro de Investigaciones para la Transformación.

Low, Linda. 2004. *The impact of regional economic integration on local and foreign investment in enterprises in ASEAN*. Singapore: Institute of South East Asian Studies.

Malaysia Ministry of Finance. 2007. Economic report (various issues). Kuala Lumpur: Ministry of Finance.

Malaysian Institute of Economic Research. Study on infrastructure development in Malaysia. ERIA Related Joint Research Project Series no. 12. Jakarta: Malaysian Institute of Economic Research.

Manchin, Miriam and Annette O. Pelkmans-Balaoing. 2007. Rules of origin and the web of East Asian free trade agreements. World Bank Policy Research Working Paper 4273 (July). Washington, D.C.: World Bank.

Manning, C. and A. Sidorenko. 2007. The regulation of professional migration in ASEAN: Insights from the health and IT sectors, *World Economy*, 30(7): 1084–1113.

Manning, C. and P. Bhatnagar. 2003. Movement of natural persons in Southeast Asia: How natural? Working Paper 2004-02. Australian National University.

Martin, W. 2006. Trade in services and Doha development agenda.

Maskus, K., T. Otsuki, and J. Wilson. 2001. *Quantifying the impact of technical barriers to trade*. Ann Arbor: University of Michigan Press.

Mattoo, A. 1999. Developing countries in the new round of GATS negotiations: from a defensive to a pro-active role., mimeo, WTO/World Bank Conference on Developing Countries in a Millennium Round, Geneva, September 20–21.

Mattoo, A. and C. Fink. 2004. Regional agreements and trade in services: Policy issues. *Journal of Economic Integration*, vol. 19, no. 4: 742–779.

Mattoo, A., R. Rathindran, and A. Subramaniam. 2001. Measuring services trade liberalization and its impacts on economic growth: An illustration. Policy Research Working Paper no. 2655. World Bank.

Maurer, Maria Clara Rueda. 2003. Regional integration and financial foreign direct investment, background paper to the Committee on Global Financial Systems, publication no. 22, *Foreign direct investment in the financial sector of emerging market economies*, Basel: Bank for International Settlement.

McCulloch, R. 1990. Services and the Uruguay Round. *World Economy*, vol. 13, no. 3: 329–348.

McKinnon, Ronald. 1993. *The order of economic liberalization: Financial control in the transition to market economy*. Baltimore, Maryland: Johns Hopkins University Press.

McLachlan, R., C. Clark, and I. Monday. 2002. Australia's service sector: A study in diversity. Staff Research Paper no. 1701. Productivity Commission, Australia.

Medvedev, Denis. 2006. Beyond trade: The impact of preferential agreements on foreign direct investment inflows. Working Paper Series 4065. World Bank.

Miles, Ian and Mark Boden, eds. 2000. Services and the knowledge-based economy. Science, Technology and International Political Economy Series. London and New York: Continuum Books.

Mirza, H. and A. Giroud. 2004 a. Regionalization, foreign direct investment and poverty reduction: Lessons from Vietnam in ASEAN. *Journal of the Asia Pacific Economy* 9 (2).

Mirza, H. and A. Giroud. 2004 b. Regional integration and benefits from foreign direct investment in ASEAN economies: The case of Vietnam. *Asian Development Review* 21, 1.

Mitaritonna, C. 2007. Service sectors, their importance and potential impacts of their liberalization: Lessons learned from multilateral and RTAs CGE simulations, OECD.

Mohanty, S.K., Sanjib Pohit, and Saikat Sinha Roy. 2004. Towards formation of close economic cooperation among Asian countries. RIS Discussion Papers 78 (September). Delhi: Research and Information Systems for the Non-Allied and Other Developing Countries.

Monge-Naranjo, Alexander. 2002. The impact of NAFTA on foreign direct investment flows in Mexico and the excluded countries. Northwestern University Department of Economics.

Neven, D. and P. Seabright. 1997. Trade liberalization and the coordination of competition policy. In *Competition Policy in the Global Economy*, ed. L. Waverman, W.S. Comanor and A. Goto. London: Routledge.

Obstfeld, M. 2007. International finance and growth in developing countries: What have we learned? Working Paper no. 34, Commission on Growth and Development, World Bank, Washington, D.C.

Ochiai, Ryo. 2006. An Investigation into the measures affecting the integration of ASEAN's priority sectors (Phase 2): Overview: Impediments to Trade in the Priority Services Sectors (December). REPSF Project 06/001a.

OECD. 1999. An assessment of the costs for international trade in meeting regulatory requirements. TD/TC/WP(99)8/FINAL. Paris: OECD.

OECD. 2002. GATS: The case for open services markets.

Park, Innwon and Soonchan Park. 2007. Reform-creating regional trade agreements and foreign direct investment: Applications for East Asia., Working Paper Series, Vol. 2007-01, International Centre for the Study of East Asian Development, Kitakyushu, Japan.

Pelkmans, J. 2007.Mutual recognition in goods: On promises and disillusions. *Journal of European Public Policy* 14 (5): 699–716.

Petri, Peter A. 2008. Multitrack integration in East Asian Trade: Noodle bowl or matrix? Asia Pacific issues No. 86. Honolulu: East-West Center.

Petri, Peter A.1997. AFTA and the global track. *ASEAN Economic Bulletin*, vol. 14, no. 2 (November): 192–204.

Plummer, M. 2007. Completing the AIA Road Traveled, Road Ahead, project for the ASEAN Secretariat. East-West Center.

Plummer, M. and G. Wignaraja, 2007. Integration strategies for ASEAN: Alone, together, or together with neighbors? Working Paper no. 92. Honolulu: East West Center.

Plummer, M.G. and G. Wignaraja 2007. The post-crisis sequencing of economic integration in East Asia: Trade as a complement to a monetary future. Working Paper Series on Regional Economic Integration no. 9 (May). ADB.

Plummer, Michael and David Cheong. 2007. FDI effects of ASEAN integration. Paper presented at conference Is Free Trade Optimal in the 21st Century? Brandeis University.

Plummer, Michael G. 2007. FDI Effects of ASEAN Integration. Paper presented at the Festschrift for Rachel McCulloch, International Business School, Brandeis University.

Plummer, Michael. 2007. Draft chapter for Emerging Asian Regionalism. Processed. Manila: ADB.

Prasad, E. S. and R. Rajan. 2008. A Pragmatic approach to capital account liberalization. Working Paper 14051 (June). National Bureau of Economic Research.

Pupphavesa, W. 2008. Investment liberalization and facilitation: Contribution to the ASEAN economic community blueprint. In *Deepening Economic Integration in East Asia — the ASEAN Economic Community and Beyond*, ed. H. Soesastro. ERIA Research Project Report 2007 no. 1-2, Tokyo: JETRO.

Quibria, M.G. 2002. Growth and poverty: Lesson from the East Asian miracle revisited. Research Paper No. 33. ADB Institute.

Rajan, R. S. 2008. Intra-Developing Asia FDI flows: Magnitudes, trends, and determinants. In Deepening economic integration in East Asia: The ASEAN Economic Community and beyond, ed. H. Soesastro. ERIA Research Project Report 2007 no. 1-2. Tokyo: JETRO.

Rajan, Ramkishen and Rahul Sen. 2002. International trade in services in selected ASEAN countries: Telecommunications and finance. *Economics and Finance*, no. 3.

Rana, Pradumna B. 2006. Economic integration in East Asia: Trends, prospects, and a possible roadmap. Working Paper Series on Regional Economic Integration, no. 2. ADB.

Reisen, H. 1998. Net capital inflows: How much to accept, how much to resist? In *Managing capital flows and exchange rates: Perspectives from the Pacific Basin*, ed. R. Glick. Cambridge University Press.

REPSF Project. 2005. Strategic directions for ASEAN airlines in a globalizing world: Ownership rules and investment issues. 04/008.

Rodrik, Dani, 1998. Who needs capital-account convertibility? In *Should the IMF Pursue Capital-Account Convertibility?* Essays in International Finance no. 207 (May). Princeton University, International Finance Section.

Rodrik, Dani. 1999. The new global economy and developing countries: Making openness work. Policy Essay 24. Washington, D.C.: Overseas Development Council.

Romero, I. and F.J. Santos. 2007. Firm size and regional linkages: A typology of manufacturing establishments in Southern Spain, *Regional Studies*, Vol. 41 (5): 571–584.

Royo, Sebastian, 2007. Financial integration and economic reforms: What can emerging markets learn from the case of Spain? Paper presented at the annual meeting of the American Political Science Association, Chicago, Illinois (30 August).

Ruffing, L. and J. Ferriere. 2007. Promoting sustainable TNC-SME linkages. Geneva: United Nations Centre for Trade and Development.

Rugman, A.M. 1997. Canada. In *Governments, Globalization, and International Business*, ed. John H. Dunning. London: Oxford University Press.

Sala-I Martin, Xavier. 2006. World distribution of income: Falling poverty and convergence period. *Quarterly Journal of Economics*, vol. 121, no. 2: 351–397.

Sampson, Gary P. and Richard H. Snape. 1985. Identifying the issues in trade in services. *World Economy*, 8 (2): 171–181.

Sauve, P. and R. M. Stern. 2000. GATS 2000: New directions in services trade liberalization, Brookings Institution Press, Washington, D.C.

Schiavo, Stefano. 2005. Financial integration, GDP correlation and the endogeneity of optimum currency areas, *Economica*, London School of Economics and Political Science, Vol. 75 (297), pp. 168–189.

Sekkat, Khalid and Olivia Galgau. 2001. The impact of the single market on foreign direct investment in the European Union, manuscript.

Shatz, H. and Anthony Venables. 2000. The geography of international investment policy research. Working Paper 2338. World Bank.

Sieh, L. M. L. and L.S. Yap. 1989. Role of the services sector in economic development — lead or lag. Unpublished paper. Kuala Lumpur: University Malaya.

Sieh L. M. L., Z. A. Mahani, and W. L. Loke. 2000. Liberalization and deregulation of Malaysia's service sector. Kuala Lumpur: University Malaya Press.

Soesastro, H. 2008. Executive Summary. In *Deepening Economic Integration in East Asia: The ASEAN economic community and beyond*, ed. H. Soesastro. ERIA Research Project Report 2007 no. 1-2. Tokyo: JETRO.

Subrahmanya, B. 2007. Development strategies for Indian SMEs: Promoting linkages with global transnational corporations. *Management Research News* 30 (10): 762–774.

Sudsawasd, S. 2008. Taxation, business regulation, and FDI in East Asia. In *Deepening economic integration in East Asia: The ASEAN Economic Community and beyond*, ed. H. Soesastro. ERIA Research Project Report 2007 no. 1-2. Tokyo: JETRO.

Sudsawasd, Sasatra and Robert E. Moore. 2006. Investment under trade policy uncertainty: An empirical investigation. *Review of International Economics*, vol. 14: 316–329.

Tambunan, T. 2007. Development of SMEs in ASEAN with reference to Indonesia and Vietnam. Research report. IDE-Jetro.

Te Velde, Dirk Willem and Dirk Bezemer. 2004. Regional Integration and foreign direct investment in developing countries. Department for International Development (U.K.).

Tucker, K. and M. Sundberg. 1988. *International trade in services*. London and New York: Routledge.

Tullao, T and M. Cortez. 2006. Enhancing the movement of natural persons in the ASEAN region: Opportunities and constraints. Working Paper Series no. 23/2006. Asia-Pacific Research and Training Network on Trade.

UFJ Institute. 2003. Final report on cross-border capital flows in the East Asian region (March).

UNCTAD. 1999. *World Investment Report*.

UNCTAD. 2004. *Promoting the export competitiveness in SMEs*. Geneva: United Nations Centre for Trade and Development.

UNCTAD. 2005. *Handbook of statistics: International trade in services*. New York: United Nations.

UNDP. 2008. *Human development report for Asia-Pacific 2008: Tackling corruption transforming lives*. Macmillan India.

UNIDO. 2004. Inserting local industries into global value chains and global production networks: Opportunities and challenges for upgrading with a focus of Asia. UNIDO Working Papers. Vienna: UNIDO.

Urata, Shujiro and Kozo Kiyota. 2003. Impacts of an East Asian FTA on foreign trade in East Asia. NBER Working Paper Series 10173 (December). Cambridge, Massachusetts: National Bureau of Economic Research.

Urata, Shujiro. 2001. Emergence of an FDI-trade nexus and economic growth in East Asia. In *Rethinking the East Asian Miracle*, ed. Joseph Stiglitz and Shahid Yusuf: 407–459. New York: Oxford Press.

Utton, M.A. 2006. *International competition policy: Maintaining open markets in the global economy*. Cheltenham, U.K. and Northampton, Massachusetts: Edward Elgar.

Valautham, A. 2007. The development of container landbridge train services between Malaysia and Thailand. *Transport and Communications Bulletin for Asia and the Pacific*, no. 77: 99–115.

Waelbroeck J. et al. 1985. ASEAN-EEC trade in services (June). Institute of Southeast Asian Affairs, ASEAN Economic Research Unit.

Wahba, J. and Mohieldin, M. 1998. Liberalizing trade in financial services: The Uruguay Round and the Arab countries. *World Development*, vol. 26, no. 7: 1331–1348.

Waldkirch, Andreas. 2008. The effects of foreign direct investment in Mexico since NAFTA. Colby College, Department of Economics.

Warr, P. 2006. Poverty and growth in Southeast Asia. *ASEAN Economic Bulletin*, vol. 23, no. 3: 279–3002.

Williamson, John and Molly Mahar. 1998. A Survey of Financial Liberalization. *Princeton Essays in International Finance*, no. 211 (November).

Wilson, John and B. Shepherd. 2008. Trade facilitation in ASEAN: Measuring progress and assessing priorities. Policy Research Working Paper. World Bank.

Wong, C. Y.P., J Wu, and A. Zhang. 2006. A model of trade liberalization in services. *Review of International Economics*, 14 (1): 148–168.

World Bank and OECD. 1999. *A Framework for the design and implementation of competition law and policy*.

World Bank. 2008. *Doing Business 2009*. Washington, D.C.: World Bank.

World Bank. 1993. *East Asian Miracle*. Washington, D.C.: World Bank.

World Bank. 2007. *World Development Indicators*. Washington, D.C.: World Bank.

WTO. 2005. Guide to the GATS: An overview of issues for further liberalization of trade in services. Kluwer Law International.

Ye, T. (ed.). 1993. *Trade in services in the SEACEN countries*. Kuala Lumpur: South East Asian Central Banks Research and Training Centre.

Yeyati, Eduardo Levy, Ernesto Stein, and Christian Daude. 2003. Regional integration and the location of FDI. Inter-American Development Bank.

Yi, Kei-Mu. 2003. Can vertical specialization explain the growth of world trade? *Journal of Political Economy*, 111 (1): 53–102.

Yusuf, S. 2004. Competitiveness through technological advances under global production networking. In *Global Production Networking and Technological Change in East Asia*, ed. S. Yusuf, M.A. Altaf, and K. Nabeshima (1–34). Washington, D.C.: World Bank.

Zhang, Y. et al. 2006. Towards an East Asia FTA: Modality and road map. Joint Expert Group for Feasibility Study on EAFTA. Jakarta: ASEAN.

Appendix A
AEC Components

In November 2002, the ASEAN Heads of Government meeting in Phnom Penh proposed that the region consider establishing an ASEAN Economic Community (AEC) by 2020. The ASEAN leaders agreed at the Bali ASEAN Summit in October 2003 to create a region in which goods, services, and skilled labor would flow freely, and capital would enjoy freer movement. In the 2007 Cebu Declaration the ASEAN leaders pushed the AEC deadline forward to 2015. In November 2007, the region approved the AEC Blueprint, which puts flesh to the bones of the commitment to create a unified market. The Blueprint was accompanied by a strategic schedule for implementing various measures. As part of this process, ASEAN developed the ASEAN Charter, which will significantly enhance the formal nature of ASEAN integration by making it an international legal entity. The Charter was signed on November 20, 2007 and went into effect after being ratified by all ASEAN Member States on December 15, 2008.

The AEC Blueprint has four parts:

1. **Single Market and Production Base**
   - *Free flow of goods*, including the elimination of tariffs and nontariff barriers (NTBs), rules of origin harmonization and rationalization, trade facilitation, customs integration (including the ASEAN Single Window), and standards and technical barriers to trade (including mutual-recognition arrangements, or MRAs). Trade in goods receives the most attention, in part because it includes areas relevant to the entire AEC project (such as customs and other areas of trade facilitation).
   - *Free flow of services* through a progressive increase in sectoral coverage, a commitment to advance mutual recognition of professional qualifications and services, and financial services liberalization through an ASEAN-X formula (i.e., an allowance for more advanced countries to proceed first).
   - *Free flow of investment*, particularly FDI, building on the process initiated by the ASEAN Investment Area (AIA). The AEC will integrate several agreements pertinent to FDI, such as

investment protection, and emphasize the cornerstones of the AIA (i.e., national treatment, investment facilitation and cooperation, and promotion). This will be done under the ASEAN Comprehensive Agreement on Investment (ACIA), which was approved by the ASEAN Economic Ministers in August 2008.

- *Freer flow of capital*, as a means to strengthen ASEAN capital-market development and harmonize capital market standards and practices in order to facilitate cross-border transactions. It also envisions greater capital mobility and liberalization, though with an emphasis on orderly processes and guarantees of safeguards to maintain stability.
- *Free flow of skilled labor*, especially to facilitate FDI and trade in services, through MRAs and concordance of skills and qualifications.
- *More rapid liberalization of the 12 priority integration sectors*, namely, wood-based products, automotives, rubber-based products, textiles and apparels, electronics, agro-based products, fisheries, e-ASEAN, healthcare, air travel, tourism and logistics.

2. **Competitive Economic Region**
   - Establishment of a *clear competition policy*, to ensure a level playing field in the integrated ASEAN market.
   - *Consumer protection*, including the creation of an ASEAN Coordinating Committee on Consumer Protection.
   - Regional commitments in *intellectual property rights protection*, based on the ASEAN IPR Action Plan (2004–2010) and accession to the Madrid Protocol.
   - *Infrastructure development* to improve transport links, narrow development gaps, and enhance regional information infrastructure.
   - *Sectoral cooperation in energy and mining*, to create stable supplies and enhance efficiency.
   - *Taxation rationalization*, featuring a bilateral network that would avoid double taxation.
   - Approaches to *e-commerce*, to be implemented through the e-ASEAN Framework Agreement.

3. **Equitable Economic Development**
   - *Fostering SME development* in ASEAN, with an emphasis on taking advantage of ASEAN's diversity.
   - *Enhancing the goals of the Initiative for ASEAN Integration* launched in 2000, to narrow development gaps between the older ASEAN-6 members and the newer ASEAN members (CLMV countries).

4. **Integration into the Global Economy**
   - ASEAN is to work toward "*ASEAN Centrality*" in external foreign economic relations (including in the area of free-trade areas and other preferential arrangements with non-partners).
   - *Enhanced participation in global supply networks*, with a strong dedication to the adoption of best international practices and standards.

The AEC embraces a wide range of deep integration policies and measures, many of which overlap or are mutually reinforcing. The specifics of many of the proposals will be developed over time, but the AEC Blueprint outlines an ambitious project. We argue that the framework bodes well for the establishment of a substantially unified and competitive marketplace.

Figure A-1
Applied Tariffs in Selected Product Categories

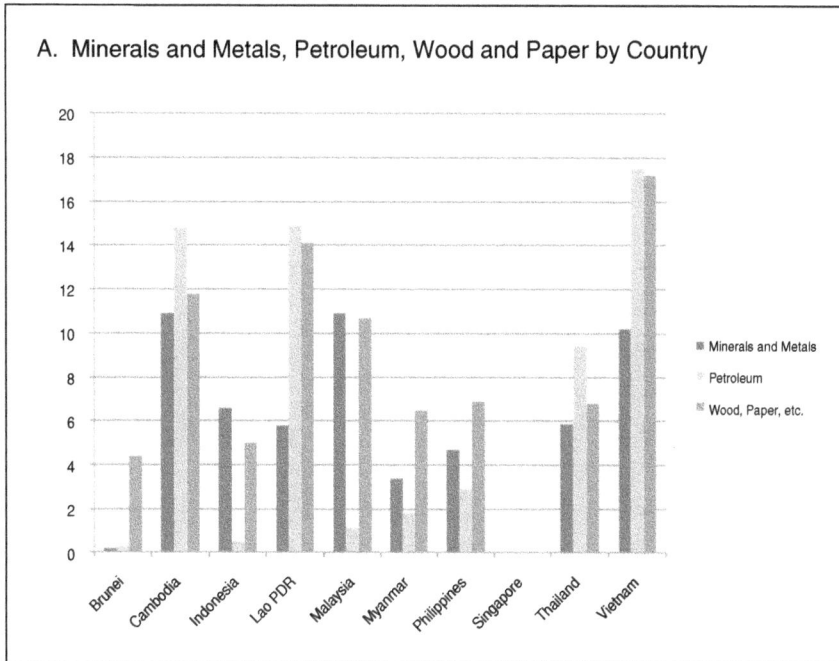

A. Minerals and Metals, Petroleum, Wood and Paper by Country

Note: Tariffs are average applied MFN rates, 2007.
Source: WTO Tariff Profiles 2008.

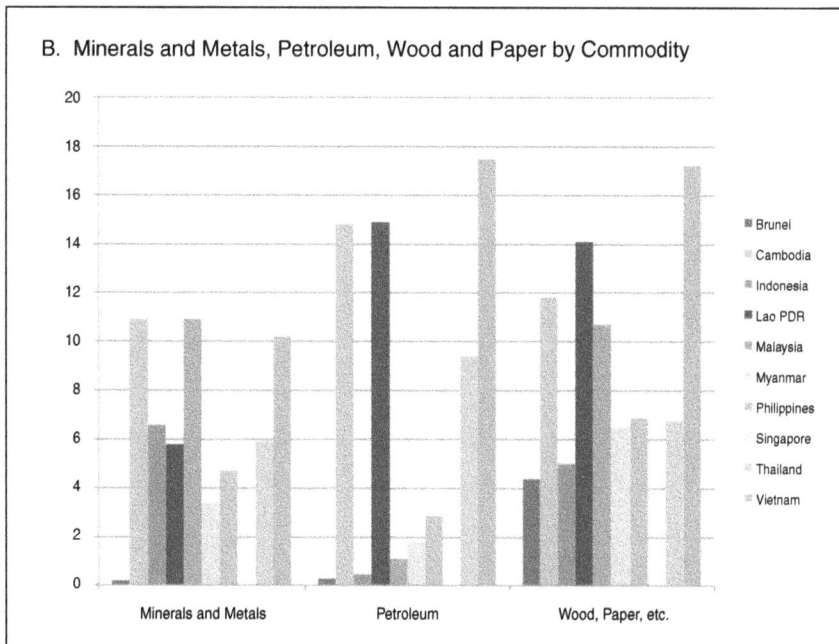

B. Minerals and Metals, Petroleum, Wood and Paper by Commodity

C. Manufactures, by Country

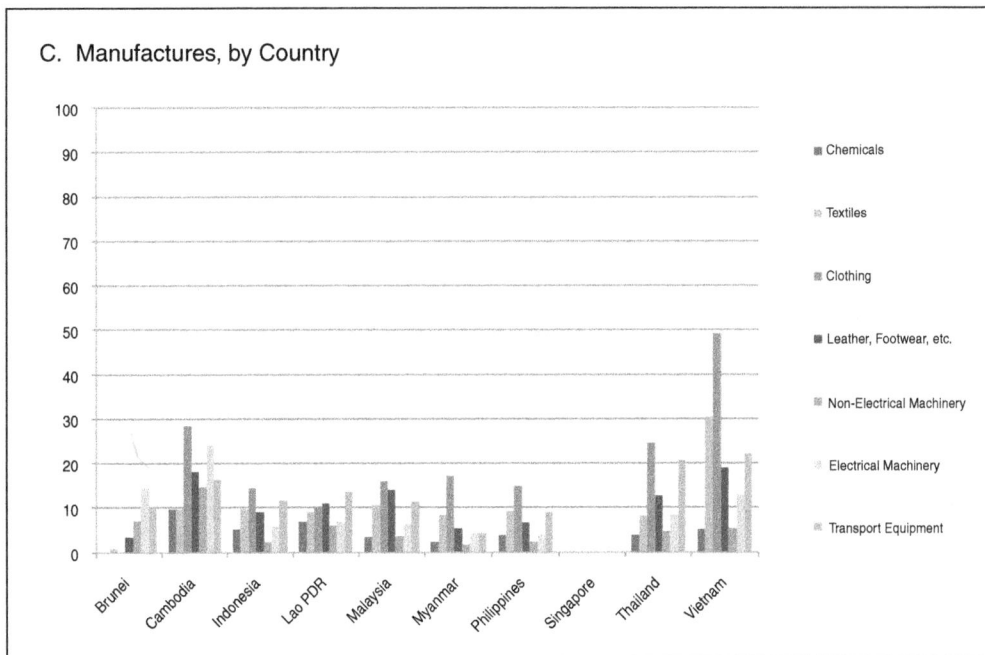

Legend:
- Chemicals
- Textiles
- Clothing
- Leather, Footwear, etc.
- Non-Electrical Machinery
- Electrical Machinery
- Transport Equipment

Countries: Brunei, Cambodia, Indonesia, Lao PDR, Malaysia, Myanmar, Philippines, Singapore, Thailand, Vietnam

Note: Tariffs are average applied MFN rates, 2007.
Source: WTO Tariff Profiles 2008.

Table A-1
Comparative Trade Regimes (2007/2008)

Applied Duties	Brunei	Cambodia	Indonesia	Lao PDR	Malaysia	Myanmar	Philippines	Singapore	Thailand	Vietnam
AVERAGE MFN APPLIED DUTIES										
Animal Products	0	27.8	4.4	24.9	0.5	10.7	21.3	0	28.1	20.1
Dairy Products	0	25.8	5.5	8.5	3.4	3.4	3.9	0	15.8	21.9
Fruit, Vegetables, Plants	0	14	5.9	30.3	4.2	11.5	9.4	0	27.6	30.6
Coffee, Tea	1.5	26.7	8.3	24.2	9	14.0	15.8	0	23.1	37.9
Cereals & Preparations	0.1	19.8	6.3	9.2	5.1	8.7	10.9	0	19.4	27.4
Oilseeds, fats & oils	0	9.1	4	12	1.7	1.7	5.6	0	19.1	13.4
Sugars & Confectionery	0	7	10.4	12.5	2.8	5.4	16	0	32.2	17.7
Beverages & Tobacco	138.1	33.1	51.8	31.3	136.6	23.2	8.2	2.1	33.4	66.6
Cotton	0	7	4	8	0	0.8	2.6	0	0	6
Other Agricultural Products	0	15.5	4.3	9.8	0.6	3.1	3.4	0	10.3	7.8
Fish & Fish Products	0	18.9	5.8	12.7	2.2	8.2	8.0	0	14.5	31.3
Minerals & Metals	0.2	10.9	6.6	5.8	10.9	3.4	4.7	0	5.9	10.2
Petroleum	0.3	14.8	0.5	14.9	1.1	1.8	2.9	0	9.4	17.5
Chemicals	0.4	9.6	5.2	6.8	3.3	2.3	3.8	0	3.8	5.2
Wood, Paper, etc.	4.4	11.8	5	14.1	10.7	6.5	6.9	0	6.8	17.2
Textiles	0.9	9.6	9.3	8.9	10.5	8.4	9.3	0	8.1	30.4
Clothing	0	28.5	14.4	10	16	17.2	14.9	0	24.5	49.3
Leather, Footwear, etc.	3.4	18	9	11	13.9	5.3	6.7	0	12.7	19
Non-Electrical Machinery	7	14.6	2.3	6	3.6	1.7	2.3	0	4.7	5.4
Electrical Machinery	14.4	24.2	5.8	6.8	6.5	4.3	3.8	0	8.3	12.8
Transport Equipment	10	16.3	11.6	13.5	11.4	4.2	9.0	0	20.7	22.2
Manufactures	5	14.6	6.9	10.3	4.9	6.5	4.8	0	11	15.2
MAXIMUM MFN APPLIED DUTIES										
Animal Products	0	35	25	30	20	15.0	45.0	0	50	50
Dairy Products	0	35	10	20	24	5.0	7.0	0	30	30
Fruit, Vegetables, Plants	0	35	25	40	82	15.0	40.0	0	123	50
Coffee, Tea	6	35	15	40	25	20.0	45.0	0	40	50
Cereals & Preparations	20	35	150	30	40	15.0	50.0	0	62	50
Oilseeds, fats & oils	0	35	15	30	20	15.0	15.0	0	40	50
Sugars & Confectionery	0	7	31	30	15	20.0	65.0	0	65	50
Beverages & Tobacco	>1000	35	150	40	>1000	40.0	15.0	112	215	100
Cotton	0	7	5	20	0	1.0	3.0	0	0	10
Other Agricultural Products	0	35	15	30	25	15.0	35.0	0	30	40
Fish & Fish Products	0	35	15	30	20	15.0	15.0	0	154	50
Minerals & Metals	20	35	30	20	60	30.0	20.0	0	30	60

continued on next page

Table A-1 — *cont'd*

Applied Duties	Brunei	Cambodia	Indonesia	Lao PDR	Malaysia	Myanmar	Philippines	Singapore	Thailand	Vietnam
MAXIMUM MFN APPLIED DUTIES										
Petroleum	4	35	10	20	5	3.0	3.0	0	20	30
Chemicals	30	35	30	40	50	20.0	30.0	0	30	50
Wood, Paper, etc.	20	35	15	40	40	15.0	30.0	0	138	50
Textiles	10	35	25	30	30	20.0	30.0	0	30	100
Clothing	0	35	15	10	20	20.0	15.0	0	60	50
Leather, Footwear, etc.	20	35	25	30	40	20.0	20.0	0	30	50
Non-Electrical Machinery	20	35	15	40	35	10.0	30.0	0	30	100
Electrical Machinery	20	35	15	20	50	20.0	30.0	0	30	50
Transport Equipment	20	35	60	40	60	40.0	30.0	0	80	150
Manufactures	20	35	20	40	50	30.0	15.0	0	141	60
DUTY-FREE MFN APPLIED RATES (%)										
Animal Products	100	9.3	16.2	0	97.2	24.7	0.0	100	13.8	7.2
Dairy Products	100	0	0	0	52.6	0.0	0.0	100	0	0
Fruit, Vegetables, Plants	100	4.5	6.2	0	63.9	7.8	0.0	100	1.1	8.8
Coffee, Tea	54.2	0	4.2	0	29.2	0.0	0.0	100	0	0
Cereals & Preparations	99.7	3.8	6.8	0	58.6	16.5	0.6	100	0.6	3.2
Oilseeds, fats & oils	100	1.9	38.2	0	69.2	0.6	0.0	100	0	15.6
Sugars & Confectionery	100	0	0	0	81.3	0.0	0.0	100	0	12.5
Beverages & Tobacco	48.6	0	1.1	0	10.9	0.0	0.0	96.9	2.2	0
Cotton	100	0	20	0	100	20.0	0.0	100	100	40
Other Agricultural Products	100	9.7	22.3	0	93.3	0.4	0.0	100	3.2	33.9
Fish & Fish Products	100	0.9	4.9	0	77.6	8.6	0.0	100	0	1.3
Minerals & Metals	96.3	6.1	19.7	0	49.9	6.0	0.9	100	28.9	38.1
Petroleum	81.9	0	95	0	77.9	0.0	0.0	100	24	0
Chemicals	94.4	11.6	21.6	0	82.4	1.2	0.8	100	43.4	62.4
Wood, Paper, etc.	71.1	1.5	27.6	0	42.7	4.9	2.8	100	23.4	12.4
Textiles	85.8	0.3	1	0	23.8	0.2	0.3	100	0	8
Clothing	100	0	0	0	17.3	0.0	0.0	100	0	0
Leather, Footwear, etc.	67.2	1.2	13	0	40.2	0.0	1.2	100	9.7	3.6
Non-Electrical Machinery	57.1	3.6	70.7	0	74.5	6.5	5.6	100	15.5	65.7
Electrical Machinery	10.2	0	32.6	0	56.4	0.0	21.0	100	23.2	33.1
Transport Equipment	49.9	8.6	39.2	0	41.4	3.0	0.6	100	5.7	38.5
Manufactures	54.2	12.9	18.5	0	66.7	0.2	7.8	100	14.2	35.2

Appendix B
The CGE Model

In this appendix, we provide details regarding the CGE model used in Chapter 2.

PRODUCTION AND TRADE

Agriculture, mining, and government services sectors are assumed to exhibit perfect competition. In each of these sectors, there is a representative firm operated under constant returns to scale technology. Trade is modeled using the Armington assumption for import demand. The manufacturing and private services sectors are characterized by monopolistic competition, and their structure of production and trade follows Melitz (2003). Each sector with monopolistic competition consists of a continuum of firms that are differentiated by the varieties they produce and their productivity. Firms face fixed production costs, resulting in increasing returns to scale. There is also a fixed cost and a variable cost associated with the exporting activities. On the demand side, the agents are assumed to have Dixit-Stiglitz preference over the continuum of varieties. As each firm is a monopolist for the variety it produces, it sets the price of its product at a constant markup over its marginal cost. A firm enters domestic or export markets if and only if the net profit generated from its domestic sales or exports in a given country is sufficient to cover the fixed cost. This zero cutoff profit condition defines the productivity thresholds for firms entering domestic and exports markets, and in turn determines the equilibrium distribution of non-exporting firms and exporting firms, as well as their average productivities. Usually, the combination of a fixed export cost and a variable (iceberg) export cost ensures that the exporting productivity threshold is higher than that for production for domestic market (i.e., only a small fraction of firms with high productivity are in export markets). These firms supply both domestic and export markets. We assume there is no entry or exit of firms in these monopolistic sectors (i.e., the number of firms is fixed).

Production technology in each sector is modeled using nested constant elasticity of substitution (CES) functions. At the top level, the output is produced as a combination of aggregate intermediate demand and value added. At the second level, aggregate intermediate demand is split into each commodity according to Leontief technology. Value added is produced by a capital-land bundle and aggregate labor. Finally, at the bottom level, aggregate labor is decomposed into unskilled and skilled labor, and the capital-land bundle is decomposed into capital and land (for the agriculture sector) or natural resources (for the mining sector). At each level of production is a unit cost function that is dual to the CES aggregator function and demand functions for corresponding inputs. The top-level unit cost function defines the marginal cost of sectoral output.

INCOME DISTRIBUTION, DEMAND AND FACTOR MARKETS

Incomes generated from production accrue to a single representative household in each region. A household maximizes utility using Extended Linear Expenditure System (ELES), which is derived from maximizing the Stone-Geary utility function. The consumption/savings decision is completely static. Savings enter the utility function as a "good" and its price is set as equal to the average price of consumer goods. Investment demand and government consumption are specified as a Leontief function. In each sector a composite good defined by the Dixit-Stiglitz aggregator over domestic and imported varieties is used for final and intermediate demand.

All commodity and factor markets are assumed to clear through price adjustment. There are five primary factors of production. Capital, agricultural land, and two types of labor (skilled and unskilled) are fully mobile across sectors within a region. In natural resource sectors of forestry, fishing, and mining, a sector-specific factor is introduced into the production function to reflect resource constraints. For all primary factors, their stocks are fixed.

MACRO CLOSURE

There are three macro closures in the model: the net government balance, the trade balance, and the investment and savings balance. We assume that government consumption and saving are exogenous in real terms. Any changes in the government budget are automatically compensated for by changes in income tax rates on households.

The second closure concerns the current account balance. In each region, the foreign savings are set exogenously. With the price index of OECD manufacturing exports being chosen as the numéraire of the model, the equilibrium of the foreign account is achieved by changing the relative price across regions (i.e., the real exchange rate).

Domestic investment is the endogenous sum of household savings, government savings, and foreign savings. As government and foreign savings are exogenous, changes in investment are determined by changes in the levels of household saving. This closure rule corresponds to the "neoclassical" macroeconomic closure in the CGE literature.

Appendix C
Developments in Logistics and Aviation

LOGISTICS SECTOR DEVELOPMENT IN ASEAN

Logistics is an important aspect of economic integration. An effective logistics system results from efficient coordination of infrastructure development across a region. A key issue is multimodal transportation. De Souza et al. (2007) note that the literature on this topic outlines the need for intermodal transport networks, benchmarking of intermodal freight transport, and evaluation of the cost and time benefits of using intermodal transport.

Several methods have been used to study multimodal transport. Case study research focusing on cost and time shows the cost and efficiency advantages of different combinations of routes and modes for freight transportation in ASEAN (Banomyong 2000, 2004). Studies on regional issues related to multimodal transport have been conducted in the EU (Lewis et al. 2001), APEC (Goetz et al. 2002), etc. The focus of these studies ranges from the benchmarking of costs and analysis of issues related to intermodal transport to theoretical studies of these transport networks (Stank and Roath 1998).

Furthermore, Arnold and Villareal (2002) examine the logistics of selected commodities produced in the Philippines for export. They assess the effects of logistics impediments on the total supply chain, market price, and household budgets. Arnold (2003) has also studied logistics development and trade facilitation in the Lao PDR. He identifies a number of problems in the transport network connected to the Lao PDR as well as in financial institutions, customs procedures and duties, and trade and transit agreements) and suggests improvements to facilitate trade. Related to this, Goh and Ang (2000) examine logistics development in the Greater Mekong Sub-region.

Carana (2004) examines the impact of transport and logistics on Indonesia's trade competitiveness. It investigates constraints on transport modes, intermodal networks, infrastructure, customs practices and procedures, trade-related banking and financial practices, transport intermediaries as well as the overall development of Indonesia's transport and logistics system. ALMEC (2002) analyzes the development of the maritime transport system in ASEAN, including the liberalization of shipping, port systems, and logistics development. It also employs a case study to investigate the access to maritime transport in the Lao PDR. REPSF (2005) identifies the measures of the efficiency and competitiveness of shipping services between ASEAN ports. It analyzes the status quo of intra-ASEAN shipping and proposes changes needed to improve system performance. None of these reports, however, quantify the benefits of regional cooperation. They suggest only that closer integration will bring about the full potential benefits of the maritime system.

De Sauza et al. (2007) identify barriers to service logistics development, including customs, foreign investment, and mode-specific constraints and show that "logistics friendliness" varies across member states: Singapore — very good; Brunei and Thailand — good; Philippines, Cambodia, Vietnam, Myanmar, Lao PDR and Malaysia — average; and Indonesia — weak.

AVIATION SECTOR

Policy and Policy Objectives

In their survey of ASEAN Member States' aviation policies, Forsyth et al. (2004) find that the more developed countries have clear policy objectives and well-developed policies for the sector. For example, policy in Singapore focuses on promoting Singapore as an aviation hub. To become a hub, Singapore has to adopt liberal policies that attract airlines. Thus, it has been willing to grant market access liberally to foreign carriers. In a world of bilateral aviation agreements, Singapore has been able to obtain market access for its own carrier. Thailand also has several broad objectives for aviation: support Thailand's aviation network; promote Thailand as a regional aviation hub and national economic and tourism development center; expand and upgrade facilities at regional airports in support of regional economic expansion and tourism and encourage their optimum use; expedite construction of Bangkok's new airport (Surarnabhumi Airport); and implement intermodal linkages between the aviation, road, rail and maritime sectors.

Malaysia too has adopted a liberal approach to aviation development in order to support growth drivers such as tourism. Policy was liberalized starting in 1993: new entrants were then allowed to compete with Malaysia Airlines, liberal traffic rights were granted to carriers from countries willing to offer reciprocal rights, and the government aggressively developed physical infrastructure (notably KLIA) and supported human resource development.

In contrast, aviation policies in Myanmar, Lao PDR, and Cambodia are just now being developed. Myanmar in fact does not have a clearly enunciated aviation policy, preferring to deal with each situation as it arises. In general, these countries are more concerned with subregional agreements than with the development of policies across ASEAN or between ASEAN and the wider world.

Liberalization Benefits

However, the benefits of a liberalized aviation sector are significant. In 1993, the EU formed a single aviation market. CAPA Consulting (2004) finds that the number of airline routes in the EU increased by 170 percent since then and the number of airlines operating in the EU-15 rose by 20 percent (as compared to 1990). More cities and remote regions are now being served by air transport, with passengers enjoying greater choice of destinations and more direct flights. CAPA Consulting also suggests that carrier competition has increased. Between 1992 and 2006, the number of routes with more than two competitors rose by 300 percent, with a corresponding drop in ticket prices. In countries that acceded to the EU in 2004[1] air traffic more than doubled in just two years (to 2006).

Overall, much of the growth is due to low-cost carriers, whose share of seat capacity grew from 1 percent in 1993 to 28 percent in 2006. In response, traditional network carriers have developed more consumer-friendly pricing and services. Apart from liberalizing the air transport industry, the European single aviation market has established common rules to secure a level playing field for market players.

Market integration has not compromised competition or standards for safety, security, or the environment. The EU now has plans to streamline regulations and rules into a single regulation on the internal aviation market, with a view to creating a full-fledged European Civil Aviation Code. The key principle here would be further regulatory convergence for the European aviation industry. In addition, the EU is increasingly behaving as a unified entity in negotiating aviation agreements with third states. This gives it more clout on the aero-political stage. It has strongly influenced the reform of the international framework for aviation, particularly in relation to rules on market access, cross-border mergers, and international competition.

EU carriers now stand to benefit from liberalized access to third states, as well as the ability to consolidate and merge and to draw greater equity injections across boundaries. Without doubt the single aviation market made possible the Air France–KLM and Lufthansa–Swiss mergers, when such consolidation would have been unthinkable two decades ago. With other EU carriers such as Alitalia and Iberia being potential merger candidates as well, the stage is set for a massive consolidation of the European aviation industry into several well-defined and highly competitive mega-carriers or groups of carriers, even if some nationalist tendencies persist (e.g., in the case of Alitalia in 2008). Overall, the lessons from the European single aviation market are clear: carriers benefit from increased market access and consolidation opportunities, while consumers get more choices and lower prices.

CAPA consulting (2004) also assessed the benefit of the single aviation market in Australia and New Zealand. As neighbors, Australia and New Zealand are very significant trading partners, aided by the "Closer Economic Relations" (CER) pact; a common labor market; and travel between the two countries has assumed domestic characteristics, though each has firm quarantine and related restrictions. They are also both far from their other trading partners and tourists and travelers tend to visit both countries. All these factors stoked the desire to form a single aviation market, though it took a decade to achieve one. CAPA Consulting (2007) suggests that the single aviation market opened up opportunities for airlines and related industries on both sides of the Tasman Sea. Although not all opportunities have been fully or successfully taken up, trade and travel have undoubtedly benefited, each contributing to the economic and social well-being of both countries.

Australia and New Zealand still maintain sovereignty over their bilateral rights, operate their own aviation safety systems and procedures, and have independent air navigation system providers. Rather than seeking full regulatory harmonization, the two countries have settled, at least for the time being, on mutual recognition. The differences in the areas to which their respective competition laws applied, together with the market prominence of the two major national carriers, Qantas and Air New Zealand, have precluded regulatory approval for their consolidation.

Aviation Infrastructure

Forsyth et al. (2004) note that lack of or inadequate airport infrastructure constrains the development of air transport, especially where air traffic is growing rapidly, as it is in several of the ASEAN Member States. The use of preferred airports may have to be rationed, and air transport policies often seek to divert traffic to less busy airports.

Some countries in ASEAN have good aviation infrastructure. For instance, Singapore is noted for the quality of its infrastructure. While Changi Airport has adequate capacity at the moment, further expansion is planned. A new terminal is being built and there are plans to build a new runway within the next decade. Similarly, there are no significant physical or economic infrastructure constraints in Malaysia, although the government aims to improve the efficiency of Kuala Lumpur International Airport (KLIA) in a bid to enhance its claims for hub status.

In other ASEAN Member States, inadequate infrastructure constrains the development of air services. For example, some Indonesian regional airports are unable to accommodate aircraft types operated by foreign airlines (e.g. Pontianak) while others have inadequate terminal facilities (e.g. Medan). Similarly, the Ninoy Aquino International Airport in Manila lacks facilities for transit and transfer passengers, in part due to delays in opening the recently constructed Terminal 3. Investment is required at secondary gateways such as Clark and Laoag. Inadequate runway length and/or width may also constrain air services. Yangon's international airport is limited to B763/AB6 short haul operations. While this is not a serious constraint at present, were the Myanmar economy to be opened up to tourism, runway limitations could pose a serious constraint on growth. Runway width limitations at Phnom Penh prevent landings by B777 and A320 aircraft.

Airline growth may be constrained by a scarcity of risk finance (Forsyth et al. 2004). Privately owned airlines need finance, and given the profit records of many airlines lenders may not be willing to lend or, when they do, demand a high risk premium. Airlines that have experienced low profitability recently or that are relatively new and have not had an opportunity to establish a sound record, may find it difficult to obtain risk finance for expansion.

Airline viability may be an issue: it is normally handled by the designating state. It is difficult for a state to refuse a designation by another state on the grounds of lack of financial viability. Many countries have imposed bonding requirements on charter operators, but in a liberalized environment the distinction between scheduled and charter operators is blurred, as the issues are linked. It may be that ASEAN Member States could agree among themselves on a bonding scheme for new entrant carriers in order to provide the desired level of consumer protection if it is felt that there is an unacceptable level of risk of financial failure resulting in financial loss to consumers. There are of course other regulatory issues. Some, such as air safety and licensing, are specific to the aviation sector while others, such as environmental protection, have broad application.

Forsyth et al. (2004) suggest that liberalization of the aviation sector in ASEAN will bring about benefits through two channels. First, passengers will gain from lower fares and better services and airlines will gain from access to new markets and overall lower costs (even though fares are lower). Second, countries gain from tourism expenditure as lower fares and better services stimulate inbound tourism. Outbound tourism will also increase for some countries, and some countries may lose from this effect. Forsyth et al. also note other impacts, such as on government revenue, foreign exchange, employment, and business communications within ASEAN.

NOTE

1. That is, Cyprus, the Czech Republic, Estonia, Hungary, Latvia, Lithuania, Malta, Poland, Slovakia and Slovenia.

Table C-1
Sensitivity Analysis Results for All Countries (Dependent variable: in GDP per capita)

Variable	Coefficient			S.E.	Obs.	Groups	Z-variables	EBA test
		COMPETITION POLICY						
Openness	High:	0.0002		0.0004	220	38	GOV,INF,GDC	
	Base:	−0.0003		0.0004	287	46		Fragile
	Low:	−0.0002		0.0004	287	46	GOV	
Legal and regulatory	High:	0.0083		0.0077	177	34	INF,GDC	
	Base:	0.0015		0.0079	246	45		Fragile
	Low:	−0.0023		0.0099	177	34	GDC	
Protectionism	High:	0.0128	*	0.0066	247	45	GOV,INF	
	Base:	0.0127		0.0080	247	45		Fragile
	Low:	0.0022		0.0094	178	34	GOV,GDC	
Public sector contracts	High:	0.0243	**	0.0105	247	45	GOV	
	Base:	0.0244	**	0.0100	247	45		Fragile
	Low:	0.0158		0.0126	178	34	GOV,GDC	
International transactions	High:	0.0111		0.0102	247	45	GOV	
	Base:	0.0118		0.0105	247	45		Fragile
	Low:	0.0002		0.0080	178	34	GOV,INF,GDC	
Foreign investors	High:	0.0463	***	0.0095	247	45	GOV	
	Base:	0.0467	***	0.0096	247	45		Robust
	Low:	0.0385	***	0.0091	178	34	INF,GDC	
Subsidies	High:	0.0213		0.0180	73	30	GDC	
	Base:	0.0203		0.0148	103	42		Fragile
	Low:	0.0103		0.0171	73	30	GOV,INF,GDC	
Competition legislation	High:	0.0288	***	0.0075	247	45	GOV	
	Base:	0.0293	***	0.0078	247	45		Fragile
	Low:	0.0120		0.0074	178	34	INF,GDC	
Product legislation	High:	0.0197	**	0.0090	247	45	GOV	
	Base:	0.0196	**	0.0092	247	45		Fragile
	Low:	0.0084		0.0102	178	34	GOV,GDC	
Value system	High:	0.0182	**	0.0090	247	45	GOV	
	Base:	0.0174	**	0.0087	247	45		Fragile
	Low:	−0.0045		0.0093	178	34	GOV,INF,GDC	
Capital markets	High:	0.0294		0.0194	66	35	GOV	
	Base:	0.0311		0.0194	66	35		Fragile
	Low:	0.0193		0.0233	45	24	INF,GDC	
Immigration laws	High:	0.0155	*	0.0080	178	34	GOV,INF,GDC	
	Base:	0.0148	**	0.0066	247	45		Fragile
	Low:	0.0105		0.0089	178	34	GOV,GDC	
Bureaucracy	High:	0.0188	**	0.0086	247	45	GOV	
	Base:	0.0189	**	0.0086	247	45		Fragile
	Low:	0.0142	*	0.0077	247	45	GOV,INF	
Transparency	High:	0.0103	*	0.0053	247	45	GOV	
	Base:	0.0103	*	0.0053	247	45		Fragile
	Low:	0.0002		0.0064	178	34	GOV,INF,GDC	
Price controls	High:	0.0209	**	0.0091	178	34	GDC	
	Base:	0.0203	**	0.0083	247	45		Robust
	Low:	0.0151	**	0.0065	247	45	INF	

continued on next page

Table C-1 — *cont'd*

Variable	Coefficient			S.E.	Obs.	Groups	Z-variables	EBA test
		INTELLECTUAL PROPERTY RIGHTS						
Patents granted to	High:	6.69E-07		1.59E-06	240	44	GOV	
residents	Base:	6.79E-07		1.94E-06	240	44		Fragile
	Low:	1.62E-08		1.57E-06	183	36	GOV,INF,GDC	
Securing patents abroad	High:	4.50E-06	***	1.11E-06	58	33	GDC	
	Base:	3.53E-06	**	1.88E-06	79	39		Fragile
	Low:	1.17E-06		1.23E-06	79	39	INF	
Intellectual property	High:	0.0367	***	0.0088	247	45	GOV	
rights	Base:	0.0372	***	0.0090	247	45		Robust
	Low:	0.0239	***	0.0063	178	34	GOV,INF,GDC	
Number of patents	High:	1.33E-04	***	4.28E-05	157	38	INF	
in force	Base:	1.35E-04	***	4.20E-05	157	38		Fragile
	Low:	−3.26E-05		1.38E-04	122	30	GOV,GDC	
Patent productivity	High:	0.0007		0.0006	198	42	INF	
	Base:	0.0008		0.0006	198	42		Fragile
	Low:	−0.0001		0.0006	147	34	GOV,INF,GDC	
		INFRASTRUCTURES						
General								
Customs' authorities	High:	0.0255	***	0.0066	247	45	GOV	
	Base:	0.0257	***	0.0068	247	45		Robust
	Low:	0.0153	**	0.0063	178	34	INF,GDC	
Distribution	High:	0.0224	***	0.0069	247	45	GOV	
infrastructure	Base:	0.0224	***	0.0070	247	45		Robust
	Low:	0.0137	**	0.0064	178	34	INF,GDC	
Roads	High:	0.4045	***	0.0818	185	39	GDC	
	Base:	0.2137	***	0.0574	235	47		Robust
	Low:	0.1968	***	0.0556	235	47	GOV,INF	
Air transportation	High:	6.04E-07	*	3.28E-07	263	46	GOV	
	Base:	6.00E-07	*	3.29E-07	263	46		Fragile
	Low:	4.08E-07		3.25E-07	196	38	INF,GDC	
Technology								
Technological	High:	0.0167	**	0.0075	247	45	GOV	
cooperation	Base:	0.0166	**	0.0075	247	45		Fragile
	Low:	0.0031		0.0071	178	34	INF,GDC	
Energy								
Energy infrastructure	High:	0.0219	**	0.0100	101	31	GDC	
	Base:	0.0256	***	0.0094	142	43		Fragile
	Low:	0.0135		0.0091	101	31	GOV,INF,GDC	

Note: ***, **, * denote 1%, 5%, 10% significance levels respectively.

Table C-2
Sensitivity Analysis Results for Developing Countries (Dependent variable: in GDP per capita)

Variable	Coefficient			S.E.	Obs.	Groups	Z-variables	EBA test
		COMPETITION POLICY						
Openness	High:	0.0008	***	0.0002	103	17	GDC	
	Base:	0.0003		0.0002	170	25		Fragile
	Low:	0.0002		0.0002	170	25	GOV,INF	
Legal and regulatory	High:	0.0206	***	0.0067	79	14	GDC	
	Base:	0.0146	***	0.0039	148	25		Robust
	Low:	0.0108	***	0.0039	148	25	GOV,INF	
Protectionism	High:	0.0266	***	0.0090	80	14	GOV,GDC	
	Base:	0.0182	**	0.0079	149	25		Robust
	Low:	0.0166	**	0.0080	149	25	INF	
Public sector contracts	High:	0.0185	*	0.0104	149	25	GOV	
	Base:	0.0145		0.0106	149	25		Fragile
	Low:	0.0143		0.0135	80	14	GOV,INF,GDC	
International transactions	High:	0.0274	**	0.0124	149	25	GOV	
	Base:	0.0268	**	0.0133	149	25		Fragile
	Low:	0.0159		0.0151	80.00	14	GOV,INF,GDC	
Foreign investors	High:	0.0388	***	0.0141	80	14	INF,GDC	
	Base:	0.0332	***	0.0115	149	25		Robust
	Low:	0.0321	***	0.0111	149	25	GOV	
Subsidies	High:	−0.0067		0.0071	64	24	GOV,INF	
	Base:	−0.0075		0.0079	64	24		Fragile
	Low:	−0.0178	**	0.0085	34	12	INF,GDC	
Competition legislation	High:	0.0362	***	0.0096	80	14	GOV,INF,GDC	
	Base:	0.0271	***	0.0099	149	25		Fragile
	Low:	0.0222	*	0.0121	80	14	GDC	
Product legislation	High:	0.0223	**	0.0090	149	25	INF	
	Base:	0.0225	**	0.0091	149	25		Fragile
	Low:	0.0088		0.0117	80	14	GOV,GDC	
Value system	High:	0.0240	***	0.0071	149	25	INF	
	Base:	0.0251	***	0.0070	149	25		Fragile
	Low:	−0.0027		0.0103	80	14	GOV,GDC	
Capital markets	High:	0.0629	***	0.0206	22	11	INF,GDC	
	Base:	0.0168		0.0144	43	22		Fragile
	Low:	0.0163		0.0142	43	22	GOV	
Immigration laws	High:	0.0097	*	0.0055	149	25	INF	
	Base:	0.0098	*	0.0056	149	25		Fragile
	Low:	0.0069		0.0078	80	14	GOV,INF,GDC	
Bureaucracy	High:	0.0185	**	0.0085	80	14	GDC	
	Base:	0.0179	***	0.0069	149	25		Robust
	Low:	0.0151	**	0.0068	149	25	GOV,INF	
Transparency	High:	0.0027		0.0052	149	25	INF	
	Base:	0.0012		0.0052	149	25		Fragile
	Low:	−0.0055		0.0081	80	14	GOV,GDC	
Price controls	High:	0.0776	***	0.0099	80	14	INF,GDC	
	Base:	0.0248	**	0.0120	149	25		Fragile
	Low:	0.0198		0.0121	149	25	GOV,INF	

continued on next page

Table C-2 — *cont'd*

Variable	Coefficient			S.E.	Obs.	Groups	Z-variables	EBA test
		INTELLECTUAL PROPERTY RIGHTS						
Patents granted to	High:	−5.16E-08		6.75E-07	145	25	INF	
residents	Base:	8.77E-09		6.69E-07	145	25		Fragile
	Low:	−3.09E-07		6.77E-07	145	25	GOV	
Securing patents abroad	High:	2.07E-06	***	6.36E-07	31	17	GOV,GDC	
	Base:	3.59E-07		6.62E-07	52	23		Fragile
	Low:	−1.15E-09		7.94E-07	52	23	GOV,INF	
Intellectual property	High:	0.0328	***	0.0091	149	25	INF	
rights	Base:	0.0329	***	0.0088	149	25		Fragile
	Low:	0.0198		0.0129	80	14	GOV,GDC	
Number of patents	High:	7.32E-05		7.54E-05	57	14	GDC	
in force	Base:	2.38E-05		2.46E-05	92	22		Fragile
	Low:	2.43E-05		2.48E-05	92	22	INF	
Patent productivity	High:	0.0004		0.0004	122	24	INF	
	Base:	0.0003		0.0004	122	24		Fragile
	Low:	0.0001		0.0004	71	16	GOV,GDC	
		INFRASTRUCTURES						
General								
Customs' authorities	High:	0.0252	**	0.0120	80	14	GOV,GDC	
	Base:	0.0183	**	0.0080	149	25		Robust
	Low:	0.0178	**	0.0082	149	25	INF	
Distribution	High:	0.0180	***	0.0069	149	25	GOV,INF	
infrastructure	Base:	0.0135	**	0.0069	149	25		Robust
	Low:	0.0149	**	0.0069	149	25	GOV	
Roads	High:	0.0233		0.0220	87	17	GDC	
	Base:	0.0205		0.0134	137	25		Fragile
	Low:	−0.0020		0.0178	87	17	GOV,INF,GDC	
Air transportation	High:	1.33E-07		1.86E-07	90	17	GDC	
	Base:	1.61E-07		1.54E-07	157	25		Fragile
	Low:	9.81E-08		1.79E-07	90	17	GOV,INF,GDC	
Technology								
Technological	High:	0.0162	**	0.0079	149	25	GOV,INF	
cooperation	Base:	0.0145	*	0.0084	149	25		Fragile
	Low:	0.0021		0.0119	80	14	INF,GDC	
Energy								
Energy infrastructure	High:	0.0213	***	0.0066	86	24	INF	
	Base:	0.0216	***	0.0069	86	24		Fragile
	Low:	0.0107		0.0086	45	12	GOV,INF,GDC	

Note: ***, **, * denote 1%, 5%, 10% significant levels respectively.

Table C-3
Sensitivity Analysis Results for All Countries (Dependent variable: share of FDI in GDP)

Variable	Coefficient			S.E.	Obs.	Groups	Z-variables	EBA test
		COMPETITION POLICY						
Openness	High:	6.97E-11	***	1.79E-11	2936	145	INF,GDC	
	Base:	1.08E-11		6.73E-12	3183	147		Fragile
	Low:	1.12E-10	***	3.19E-11	2839	141	GOV,GDC	
Legal and regulatory	High:	1.8343	*	1.0755	346	47	INF	
	Base:	1.7602	*	1.0309	346	47		Fragile
	Low:	0.5641	***	0.2090	255	36	GDC	
Protectionism	High:	2.2012	*	1.2196	341	47	GOV,INF	
	Base:	2.0719	*	1.1731	347	47		Fragile
	Low:	0.7335	***	0.2691	256	36	INF,GDC	
Public sector contracts	High:	2.1130	*	1.1165	341	47	GOV,INF	
	Base:	1.7105	*	0.9894	347	47		Fragile
	Low:	0.7101	***	0.2713	256	36	INF,GDC	
International transactions	High:	1.9938		1.7446	341	47	GOV	
	Base:	1.7621		1.6689	347	47		Fragile
	Low:	0.3213		0.3293	256	36	INF,GDC	
Foreign investors	High:	2.8700	*	1.5642	341	47	GOV,INF	
	Base:	2.5661	*	1.4765	347	47		Fragile
	Low:	1.0064	***	0.2548	256	36	INF,GDC	
Subsidies	High:	0.6839		0.4546	131	35	INF,GDC	
	Base:	−0.4435		0.9724	182	47		Fragile
	Low:	−0.4849		0.9814	182	47	INF	
Competition legislation	High:	4.2099		3.1105	341	47	GOV,INF	
	Base:	3.8946		3.0102	347	27		Fragile
	Low:	0.0142		0.3189	256	36	INF,GDC	
Product legislation	High:	3.1267		1.9511	347	47	INF	
	Base:	3.1209		1.9463	347	47		Fragile
	Low:	0.7990	***	0.2741	256	36	INF,GDC	
Value system	High:	3.5419		2.5622	347	47	INF	
	Base:	3.5421		2.5610	347	47		Fragile
	Low:	0.5218	*	0.2958	256	36	INF,GDC	
Capital markets	High:	2.5217	**	1.0175	136	46	INF	
	Base:	2.4719	**	1.0075	136	46		Fragile
	Low:	0.5379		0.3920	92	33	GOV,GDC	
Immigration laws	High:	1.0433		0.9861	341	47	GOV,INF	
	Base:	0.8483		0.9487	347	36		Fragile
	Low:	0.2462		0.5010	251	36	GOV,GDC	
Bureaucracy	High:	5.6260		4.0421	347	47	GOV	
	Base:	5.6267		4.0419	347	47		Fragile
	Low:	0.5774		0.3650	256	36	INF,GDC	
Transparency	High:	1.0260		0.9673	347	47	INF	
	Base:	1.0230		0.9616	347	47		Fragile
	Low:	−0.1024		0.2422	251	36	GOV,INF,GDC	
Price controls	High:	1.4118	***	0.4014	341	47	GOV	
	Base:	1.2022	***	0.3697	347	47		Robust
	Low:	0.5623	**	0.2490	256	36	INF,GDC	

continued on next page

Table C-3 — *cont'd*

Variable	Coefficient			S.E.	Obs.	Groups	Z-variables	EBA test
			INTELLECTUAL PROPERTY RIGHTS					
Patents granted to	High:	−1.73E-05	***	5.13E-06	300	45	INF,GDC	
residents	Base:	−2.00E-05		2.05E-05	374	48		Fragile
	Low:	−2.36E-05		2.40E-05	369	48	GOV,INF	
Securing patents abroad	High:	−1.59E-05		1.29E-05	133	48	INF	
	Base:	−2.15E-05		1.36E-05	133	48		Fragile
	Low:	−3.42E-05	**	1.39E-05	107	46	GDC	
Intellectual property	High:	2.0559		1.3166	341	47	GOV,INF	
rights	Base:	1.8039		1.2299	347	47		Fragile
	Low:	0.2230		0.2408	256	36	INF,GDC	
Number of patents	High:	0.0232	**	0.0092	240	42	GOV,INF	
in force	Base:	0.0162	*	0.0085	244	42		Fragile
	Low:	0.0003		0.0012	194	39	INF,GDC	
Patent productivity	High:	0.0091		0.0101	291	43	GOV,INF	
	Base:	0.0034		0.0082	291	43		Fragile
	Low:	−0.0017		0.0036	226	39	GDC	
			INFRASTRUCTURES					
General								
Customs' authorities	High:	1.5761		1.5426	341	47	GOV	
	Base:	1.4460		1.5107	347	47		Fragile
	Low:	0.1886		0.2417	246	36	INF,GDC	
Distribution	High:	0.1636		0.2422	251	36	GOV,GDC	
infrastructure	Base:	−0.6903		0.4923	347	47		Fragile
	Low:	−0.7468		0.5333	341	47	GOV,INF	
Roads	High:	3.2220		3.8934	356	49	INF	
	Base:	3.1595		3.8126	356	49		Fragile
	Low:	0.6669		0.4300	300	46	INF,GDC	
Air transportation	High:	−1.95E-06		1.48E-06	308	46	GDC	
	Base:	−2.86E-05		2.31E-05	389	48		Fragile
	Low:	−2.84E-05		2.31E-05	389	48	INF	
Technology								
Technological	High:	−0.4244		0.8215	341	47	GOV	
cooperation	Base:	−0.5413		0.7952	347	47		Fragile
	Low:	−1.0354	***	0.3674	251	36	GOV,INF,GDC	
Energy								
Energy infrastructure	High:	1.8028		1.8834	219	47	GOV	
	Base:	1.5271		1.7065	225	47		Fragile
	Low:	−0.1765		0.2453	157	35	GOV,GDC	

Note: ***, **, * denote 1%, 5%, 10% significant levels respectively.

Table C-4
Sensitivity Analysis Results for Developing Countries (Dependent variable: share of FDI in GDP)

Variable	Coefficient			S.E.	Obs.	Groups	Z-variables	EBA test
		COMPETITION POLICY						
Openness	High:	0.0008		0.0061	740	33	INF	
	Base:	0.0015		0.0062	743	33		Fragile
	Low:	−0.0266	**	0.0110	590	30	GOV,INF,GDC	
Legal and regulatory	High:	2.3100		1.4105	193	25	INF	
	Base:	2.3800	*	1.3142	193	25		Fragile
	Low:	0.9772	***	0.2824	102	14	INF,GDC	
Protectionism	High:	4.8953	*	2.9262	194	25	INF	
	Base:	4.9879	*	2.7850	194	25		Fragile
	Low:	1.4866	***	0.4123	103	14	INF,GDC	
Public sector contracts	High:	4.1317		3.0606	194	25	INF	
	Base:	4.3321		2.9195	194	25		Fragile
	Low:	0.8638	***	0.3253	103	14	GDC	
International transactions	High:	8.0400		6.3255	194	25	INF	
	Base:	8.0084		6.3472	194	25		Fragile
	Low:	1.3853	**	0.6062	103	24	INF,GDC	
Foreign investors	High:	7.0126	*	4.0507	194	25	INF	
	Base:	6.9045	*	4.0754	194	25		Fragile
	Low:	1.6598	***	0.3282	103	14	INF,GDC	
Subsidies	High:	0.3656		1.2075	44	13	GOV,GDC	
	Base:	−1.5346		1.7941	100	25		Fragile
	Low:	−2.9479		1.9848	94	25	GOV,INF	
Competition legislation	High:	6.5419		5.5302	188	25	GOV	
	Base:	6.6393		5.6005	194	25		Fragile
	Low:	−0.0810		0.5869	103	14	GDC	
Product legislation	High:	7.1052		4.9956	194	25	INF	
	Base:	7.1540		4.9741	194	25		Fragile
	Low:	0.8103		0.5641	103	14	INF,GDC	
Value system	High:	6.2015		4.8324	194	25	INF	
	Base:	6.1654		4.3665	194	25		Fragile
	Low:	0.8725	*	0.4795	103	14	INF,GDC	
Capital markets	High:	2.2166	***	0.7268	36	12	GDC	
	Base:	3.6439		2.4919	75	25		Fragile
	Low:	0.6678		2.5903	69	25	GOV,INF	
Immigration laws	High:	1.4791		1.3533	188	25	GOV	
	Base:	1.2788		1.3395	194	25		Fragile
	Low:	0.5386		0.6955	103	14	GDC	
Bureaucracy	High:	8.5446		6.2176	194	25	INF	
	Base:	8.5762		6.0654	194	25		Fragile
	Low:	0.6516	*	0.3508	103	14	INF,GDC	
Transparency	High:	1.9619		1.8252	194	25	INF	
	Base:	1.8453		1.8453	194	25		Fragile
	Low:	−0.4604		0.4620	98	14	GOV,GDC	
Price controls	High:	4.4613	***	1.2921	194	25	INF	
	Base:	4.4757	***	1.3205	194	25		Robust
	Low:	2.2416	***	0.5777	103	14	INF,GDC	

continued on next page

Table C-4 — *cont'd*

Variable	Coefficient			S.E.	Obs.	Groups	Z-variables	EBA test
			INTELLECTUAL PROPERTY RIGHTS					
Patents granted to	High:	−1.26E-05		7.69E-06	134	22	INF,GDC	
residents	Base:	−2.08E-05		2.38E-05	208	25		Fragile
	Low:	−7.68E-05		5.89E-05	203	25	GOV,INF	
Securing patents abroad	High:	7.44E-06		1.35E-05	44	23	GOV,GDC	
	Base:	−5.75E-06		2.21E-05	70	25		Fragile
	Low:	−7.30E-06		2.60E-05	70	25	GOV	
Intellectual property	High:	3.8148		2.3841	194	25	INF	
rights	Base:	3.9604	*	2.2918	194	25		Fragile
	Low:	0.2220		0.5354	103	24	INF,GDC	
Number of patents	High:	0.0284	***	0.0103	139	23	GOV,INF	
in force	Base:	0.0220	**	0.0103	143	23		Fragile
	Low:	0.0004		0.0026	89	20	GOV,INF,GDC	
Patent productivity	High:	0.0123		0.0409	169	24	INF	
	Base:	0.0105		0.0403	169	24		Fragile
	Low:	−0.0160	**	0.0067	104	24	GOV,INF,GDC	
			INFRASTRUCTURES					
General								
Customs' authorities	High:	3.5582		3.2422	188	25	GOV	
	Base:	2.4543		2.8379	194	25		Fragile
	Low:	0.7004		0.5444	103	14	INF,GDC	
Distribution	High:	0.6072	*	0.3563	98	14	GOV,GDC	
infrastructure	Base:	−2.0970		1.9211	194	25		Fragile
	Low:	−1.9087		2.0917	194	25	INF	
Roads	High:	2.1496		3.3155	175	25	GOV	
	Base:	1.8433		3.3179	175	25		Fragile
	Low:	−0.3300		0.5126	119	22	GOV,INF,GDC	
Air transportation	High:	1.63E-06		1.17E-06	125	23	GOV,INF,GDC	
	Base:	−4.41E-05		3.61E-05	206	25		Fragile
	Low:	−4.52E-05		3.58E-05	206	25	INF	
Technology								
Technological	High:	0.6713		2.3816	188	25	GOV	
cooperation	Base:	−0.8853		1.6540	194	25		Fragile
	Low:	−1.1632		0.7124	98	14	GOV,GDC	
Energy								
Energy infrastructure	High:	3.0215		3.1691	124	25	INF	
	Base:	2.9103		3.2013	124	25		Fragile
	Low:	−0.1120		0.5438	61	13	GDC	

Note: ***, **, * denote 1%, 5%, 10% significant levels respectively.

Appendix D
AEC Blueprint Excerpt

D. INTEGRATION INTO THE GLOBAL ECONOMY

64. ASEAN operates in an increasingly global environment, with interdependent markets and globalised industries. In order to enable ASEAN businesses to compete internationally, to make ASEAN a more dynamic and stronger segment of the global supply chain and to ensure that the internal market remains attractive for foreign investment, it is crucial for ASEAN to look beyond the borders of AEC. External rules and regulations must increasingly be taken into account when developing policies related to AEC.

D1. COHERENT APPROACH TOWARDS EXTERNAL ECONOMIC RELATIONS

65. ASEAN shall work towards maintaining "ASEAN Centrality" in its external economic relations, including, but not limited to, its negotiations for free trade (FTAs) and comprehensive economic partnership (CEPs) agreements. This shall be done by:

Actions:
i.   Review FTA/CEP commitments *vis-à-vis* ASEAN's internal integration commitments; and
ii. Establish a system for enhanced coordination, and possibly arriving at common approaches and/ or positions in ASEAN's external economic relations and in regional and multilateral fora.

D2. ENHANCED PARTICIPATION IN GLOBAL SUPPLY NETWORKS

66. ASEAN shall also enhance participation in global supply networks by:

Actions:
i.   Continuing the adoption of international best practices and standards in production and distribution, where possible; and
ii. Developing a comprehensive package of technical assistance for the less developed ASEAN Member States to upgrade their industrial capability and productivity to enhance their participation in regional and global integration initiatives.

Appendix E
ASEAN Free Trade Agreements

As of September 2008

Partner	Status	Description
China	Framework established in 2002, goods, services, dispute resolution now complete; no agreement yet on investment	ASEAN-China Comprehensive Economic Cooperation Agreement A framework agreement for the FTA plan was signed in 2002. The FTA is targeted to take full effect in 2010 for the six original ASEAN members and in 2015 for the other four. An early harvest program covering trade in goods came into force in July 2005. Negotiations on a dispute settlement were finalized in 2004 and in services in January 2007. The investment agreement is under development.
Japan	Signed 04/2008; implementation planned for 2008	ASEAN-Japan Comprehensive Economic Partnership Japan and ASEAN signed a general framework for a bilateral free trade agreement in October 2003 and agreed to initiate negotiations in November 2004. The Japan-ASEAN FTA Economic Partnership was signed in April 2008 and will have wide coverage, including goods, services, investments, rules of origin, dispute settlement, sanitary and phyto-sanitary regulations, technical barriers to trade, economic cooperation and, on Japan's request, intellectual property rights.
Korea	Implemented (ex. Thailand) 06/2007; agreement reached with Thailand 01/2008	ASEAN-Korea Comprehensive Economic Cooperation Agreement The initial agreement, except for Thailand (due to concerns about agriculture), took effect in June 2007. Thailand

		concluded its agreement in January 2008, receiving more flexibility in cutting and/or waiving tariffs in areas such as steel, cosmetics, and leather.
Australia, New Zealand	Agreement on an FTA reached in 08/2008	ASEAN-Australia and New Zealand Free Trade Agreement Negotiation on a comprehensive FTA in started in 2004 and was agreed on 8 August 2008 and is expected to be signed later in the year.
India	Framework signed, 07/2004, agreement on FTA reached in 08/2008	ASEAN-India Regional Trade and Investment Area FTA agreement was concluded in August 2008 and is expected to be signed later in the year.
United States	N/A	The US is focusing on FTAs with individual ASEAN countries rather than ASEAN as a group. Several negotiations have been launched.
European Union	Under negotiation	ASEAN-European Union Free Trade Agreement The negotiations started on 4 May 2007. The FTA is expected to deepen privatization and deregulation, with the goal of improving business opportunities for European TNCs in the region. The EU will likely push reforms in investment, services and intellectual property. ASEAN will be looking for improved market access to the EU.

Source: ADB Asian Regional Integration Center online data.

Appendix F
ASEAN Member States' Free Trade Agreements

As of July 2008

	Signed	Negotiation	Study	Name of Agreement
Brunei				
Japan	x			Brunei Darussalam-Japan Free Trade Agreement
Pakistan			x	Pakistan-Brunei Darussalam Free Trade Agreement
US			x	Brunei Darussalam-United States Free Trade Agreement
Cambodia				No bilateral FTAs
Indonesia				
Australia			x	Indonesia-Australia Free Trade Agreement
EU			x	Indonesia-European Free Trade Association Free Trade Agreement
India			x	India-Indonesia Comprehensive Economic Cooperation and Partnership Agreement
Japan	x			Indonesia-Japan Economic Partnership Agreement
Pakistan	FA	x		Pakistan-Indonesia Free Trade Agreement
US			x	Indonesia-United States Free Trade Agreement
Lao PDR				
Thailand	x			Lao PDR-Thailand Preferential Trading Arrangement
Malaysia				
Australia		x		Malaysia-Australia Free Trade Agreement
Chile		x		Malaysia-Chile Free Trade Agreement
India			x	India-Malaysia Comprehensive Economic Cooperation Agreement
Japan	x			Japan-Malaysia Economic Partnership Agreement
Korea			x	Korea-Malaysia Free Trade Agreement
NZ		x		Malaysia-New Zealand Free Trade Agreement
Pakistan	x			Malaysia-Pakistan Closer Economic Partnership Agreement
US		x		United States-Malaysia Free Trade Agreement

Country / Partner			Agreement
Myanmar			No bilateral FTAs
Philippines			
Japan	x		Japan-Philippines Economic Partnership Agreement
Pakistan		x	Pakistan-Philippines Free Trade Agreement
US		x	Philippines-United States Free Trade Agreement
Singapore			
Australia	x		Singapore-Australia Free Trade Agreement
Bahrain		x	Singapore-Bahrain Free Trade Agreement
Egypt		x	Singapore-Egypt Comprehensive Economic Cooperation Agreement
EU	x		Singapore-European Free Trade Association
India	x		India-Singapore Comprehensive Economic Cooperation Agreement
Japan	x		Japan-Singapore Economic Agreement for a New-Age Partnership
Jordan	x		Singapore-Jordan Free Trade Agreement
Korea	x		Korea-Singapore Free Trade Agreement
Kuwait		x	Singapore-Kuwait Free Trade Agreement
Mexico		x	Singapore-Mexico Free Trade Agreement
NZ	x		Singapore-New Zealand Closer Economic Partnership
Pakistan		x	Pakistan-Singapore Free Trade Agreement
Panama	x		Singapore-Panama Free Trade Agreement
PRC		x	People's Republic of China-Singapore Free Trade Agreement
Peru	x		Singapore-Peru Free Trade Agreement
Qatar		x	Singapore-Qatar Free Trade Agreement
Ukraine		x	Singapore-Ukraine Free Trade Agreement
UAE		x	Singapore-United Arab Emirates Free Trade Agreement
US	x		Singapore-United States Free Trade Agreement
Thailand			
Australia	x		Thailand-Australia Free Trade Agreement
Bahrain	FA	x	Thailand-Bahrain Free Trade Agreement
Chile		x	Thailand-Chile Free Trade Agreement
EU		x	Thailand-European Free Trade Association Free Trade Agreement
India		x	India-Thailand Free Trade Area
Japan	x		Japan-Thailand Economic Partnership Agreement
Korea		x	Korea-Thailand Free Trade Agreement
Lao PDR	x		Lao PDR-Thailand Preferential Trading Arrangement
Pakistan		x	Pakistan-Thailand Free Trade Agreement
PRC	x		People's Republic of China-Thailand Free Trade Agreement
Peru	FA	x	Thailand-Peru Free Trade Agreement
NZ	x		Thailand-New Zealand Closer Economic Partnership Agreement
US		x	Thailand-United States Free Trade Agreement
Vietnam			
Chile		x	Chile-Vietnam Free Trade Agreement
Japan		x	Japan-Vietnam Economic Partnership Agreement

Note: FA = Framework Agreement.
Source: Asian Development Bank, Asian Regional Integration Center database.

Appendix G
ASEAN Imports and Exports, 2000 and 2006

Imports (US$ million)

	ASEAN	CER	China	Japan	Korea	HK+TWN	India	US	EU	World
2000										
ASEAN	82,930	9,067	18,653	70,409	17,657	27,742	3,362	51,609	40,896	368,983
Brunei	823	31	17	67	16	75	4	154	225	1,427
Cambodia	554	7	113	58	77	451	9	33	94	1,424
Indonesia	6,487	1,922	2,022	5,397	2,083	2,076	525	3,393	4,216	33,515
Lao PDR	536	6	38	24	5	11	6	5	45	690
Malaysia	19,744	1,893	3,237	17,331	3,663	5,875	725	13,668	9,071	82,204
Myanmar	1,377	19	546	216	318	297	53	19	120	3,039
Philippines	5,364	989	786	6,511	2,754	4,278	167	6,413	3,161	34,491
Singapore	33,278	2,490	7,116	23,189	4,822	8,971	1,076	20,270	16,102	134,633
Thailand	10,319	1,356	3,377	15,315	2,165	3,446	620	7,291	6,489	61,924
Vietnam	4,449	355	1,401	2,301	1,754	2,262	178	364	1,373	15,637
China	22,181	5,737	—	41,520	23,208	13,649	1,350	22,376	30,847	225,175
India	4,382	1,151	1,449	2,016	989	1,561	—	3,152	10,731	50,336
World	435,093	82,702	397,311	512,406	175,382	211,124	47,319	847,988	2,333,280	6,591,170
2006										
ASEAN	187,719	17,392	83,828	85,252	33,408	47,003	10,454	68,405	69,247	705,806
Brunei	1,170	97	110	107	79	46	43	53	291	2,047
Cambodia	2,164	31	767	83	112	1,071	10	82	188	4,235
Indonesia	37,994	4,058	10,403	7,971	3,542	4,073	1,299	3,386	6,928	89,697

Lao PDR	1,269	21	186	23	18	18	6	7	39	1,633
Malaysia	32,035	2,764	15,887	17,338	7,068	8,394	1,333	16,424	14,946	130,477
Myanmar	1,776	31	1,328	106	155	112	143	8	112	3,910
Philippines	12,494	1,156	6,050	9,372	2,662	7,247	408	8,209	4,971	59,221
Singapore	62,343	4,091	27,242	19,927	10,477	13,382	4,884	30,352	27,253	238,790
Thailand	23,713	3,759	13,641	25,845	5,071	6,132	1,625	8,673	11,241	128,634
Vietnam	12,762	1,385	8,215	4,481	4,224	6,531	703	1,210	3,278	47,162
China	89,549	20,509	—	115,811	89,819	62,603	10,469	59,326	90,677	791,793
India	20,601	7,373	16,047	4,747	4,851	4,724	—	11,100	33,605	184,290
World	812,774	154,172	1,206,450	705,742	353,031	323,286	130,444	1,084,790	4,426,750	12,426,300

Source: ADB, based on UN data.

Exports (US$ million)

	ASEAN	CER	China	Japan	Korea	HK+TAI	India	US	EU	World
2000										
ASEAN	98,060	11,593	16,377	57,364	15,687	42,801	6,787	80,955	63,952	426,633
Brunei	732	165	56	1,286	407	1	0	378	115	3,161
Cambodia	76	2	24	11	0	15	0	740	232	1,123
Indonesia	10,884	1,626	2,768	14,415	4,318	4,569	1,151	8,489	8,950	62,118
Lao PDR	167	1	6	11	1	3	0	9	103	391
Malaysia	26,068	2,782	3,028	12,780	3,235	9,765	1,925	20,162	13,751	98,154
Myanmar	422	10	113	108	21	64	163	443	331	1,979
Philippines	5,983	328	663	5,609	1,173	5,501	64	11,406	6,919	38,216
Singapore	37,769	3,591	5,377	10,404	4,916	15,855	2,871	23,891	19,325	138,046
Thailand	13,340	1,797	2,806	10,164	1,265	6,242	566	14,706	11,241	68,963
Vietnam	2,619	1,291	1,536	2,575	353	785	47	733	2,986	14,483
China	17,341	3,845	—	41,654	11,293	50,743	1,561	52,162	41,056	249,208
India	2,749	469	758	1,767	457	3,122	—	9,083	10,393	42,626
World	367,458	78,182	211,844	340,085	145,509	323,010	45,056	1,181,050	2,454,500	6,386,460
2006										
ASEAN	197,919	30,633	76,093	82,292	29,363	73,053	18,978	110,662	99,515	791,733
Brunei	1,731	949	196	2,070	839	3	1	523	199	6,555
Cambodia	175	6	32	103	1	15	0	2,117	743	3,345
Indonesia	23,853	3,559	8,746	21,972	8,908	6,956	3,619	13,038	13,833	113,209
Lao PDR	602	27	45	11	2	40	0	8	116	1,055
Malaysia	41,876	5,227	11,646	14,241	5,806	13,999	5,129	30,191	20,539	160,664
Myanmar	2,378	16	230	223	60	98	527	0	325	4,361
Philippines	10,255	613	14,620	7,318	1,619	7,314	97	9,067	7,259	59,510
Singapore	83,925	11,579	26,513	14,854	8,736	32,675	7,673	27,621	30,638	272,049
Thailand	27,256	4,915	11,806	16,571	2,652	10,536	1,818	19,674	18,099	130,783
Vietnam	5,869	3,744	2,260	4,927	740	1,416	115	8,423	7,766	40,203
China	71,328	15,246	—	91,773	44,558	180,218	14,588	203,898	189,926	969,284
India	10,312	1,094	9,518	3,660	1,906	5,557	—	20,903	25,802	118,995
World	662,780	152,240	769,310	529,306	281,776	547,054	123,794	1,776,390	4,654,940	11,967,300

Source: ADB, based on UN data.

Index

www.ingramcontent.com/pod-product-compliance
Lightning Source LLC
Chambersburg PA
CBHW080247030426
42334CB00023BA/2727